THE Artist
AS Critic

THE Artist AS Critic

Critical Writings of OSCAR WILDE

Edited by Richard Ellmann

Vintage Books
A Division of Random House / New York

Contents

Contents

Contents

Introduction:
The Critic as Artist
as Wilde

Wilde is the one writer of the Nineties whom everyone still reads, or more precisely, has read. The mixture of frivolity and pathos in his career continues to arrest us. That career displays its self-conjugation in Wilde's own terms of "The Critic as Artist."

In 1914 Henry James could complain that there was not enough criticism about to give novelists their bearings, while T. S. Eliot and Saul Bellow have since regretted, for different reasons and in different tones of voice, that there is now too much. The obtrusive place of the critic today can be related to a methodological emphasis which is conspicuous in other disciplines as well. But Wilde was one of the first to see that the exaltation of the artist required a concomitant exaltation of the critic. If art was to have a special train, the critic must keep some seats reserved on it.

Wilde reached this conclusion by way of two others. The first is that criticism plays a vital role in the creative process. If this sounds like T. S. Eliot admonishing Matthew Arnold, Wilde had expressed it, also as an admonition to Arnold, almost thirty years before. The second is that criticism is an independent branch of literature with its own procedures. "I am always amused," says Wilde, "by the silly vanity of those writers and artists of our day who seem to imagine that the primary function of the critic is to chatter about their second-rate work." And he complains that "The poor reviewers are apparently reduced to be the reporters of the police-court of literature, the chroniclers of the doings of the habitual criminals of art." In protesting the independence of criticism, Wilde sounds like an ancestral Northrop Frye or Roland Barthes. These portentous comparisons do indeed claim virtue by association, and such claims may be broadened. André Gide found Nietzsche less exciting because he had read Wilde, and Thomas Mann in one of his last essays remarks almost with chagrin on how many of Nietzsche's aphorisms might have been expressed by Wilde, and how many of Wilde's by Nietzsche. What I think can be urged for Wilde then, is that for his own reasons and in his own way he laid the basis for many critical positions which are still debated in much the same terms, and which we like to attribute to more ponderous names.

When Wilde formulated his theories the public was more hostile to criticism than it is now, and Wilde was flaunting his iconoclasm, his contempt for the unconsidered and so uncritical pieties of his age. This in fact was his mode: not to speak for the Victorians, or for the prematurely old writers who dithered that they were the end of an era, as if they must expire with the 1800s. Wilde proposed to speak for the young, with even excessive eagerness. His own age was always a little embarrassing for him, because he had already spent three years at Trinity College, Dublin, when he went up to Oxford. He was not above a little deception on this score. In 1877, when he was twenty-three, he sent a poem to Gladstone with a letter saying, "I am little more than a boy." And in a poem written that year he spoke of his "boyish passion" and described himself as "one who scarce has seen some twenty summers." This line, in turn, he repeated in his poem "The Sphinx," finished when he was forty. Even in court he injudiciously testified he was two years younger than he was, so that he sounds a little like Falstaff shouting to Bardolph during the robbery, "They hate us youth." Wilde's mode was calculated juvenescence, and the characters in his books are always being warned by shrewder characters of the danger of listening to people older than themselves. To help reduce that danger, Wilde's characters are invariably parentless. The closest kin allowed is an aunt.

The Critic as Artist as Wilde

Like Stendhal, Wilde thought of himself as a voice of the age to be, rather than of the one that was fading. Yet like anyone else writing criticism in the nineteenth century, he had to come to terms with the age that had been, and especially with everybody's parent, Matthew Arnold. Wilde sought Arnold's approbation for his first book, *Poems*, 1881, which he sent with a letter stressing their shared Oxonian connections. These extended, though he wisely did not enforce the claim, to their both having won the Newdigate. Actually their prize-winning poems offer a contrast of manners, Arnold's being just as determined to appear older as Wilde's younger than his years. Arnold replied politely.

But by 1881 Arnold was genuinely old, and seven years later, in 1888, he was dead. Wilde's only book of criticism, *Intentions*, was written during the three years following Arnold's death and published in 1891, as if to take over that critical burden and express what Arnold had failed to say. Yeats thought the book "wonderful" and Walter Pater handsomely praised it for carrying on, "more perhaps than any other writer, the brilliant critical work of Matthew Arnold." Pater's encomium is a reminder, however, not to ignore *him*. There are not two but three critical phases in the late nineteenth century, with Pater transitional between Arnold and Wilde.

In 1864, lecturing from the Oxford Chair of Poetry on "The Function of Criticism at the Present Time," Arnold declared —to everyone's lasting memory—that the "aim of criticism is to see the object as in itself it really is." This statement went with his demand for "disinterested curiosity" as the mark of the critic; its inadvertent effect was to put the critic on his knees before the work he was discussing. Not everyone enjoyed this position. Nine years later Walter Pater wrote his preface to *Studies in the History of the Renaissance*. Pretending to agree with Arnold's definition of the aim of criticism, he quoted it, then added, "the first step towards seeing one's object as it really is, is to know one's impression as it really is, to discriminate it, to realise it distinctly." But Pater's corollary subtly altered the original proposition; it shifted the center of attention from the rock of the object to the winds of the perceiver's sensations. It made the critic's own work more important as well as more subjective. If observation is still the word, the critic looks within himself as often as out upon the object.

Wilde had been Pater's disciple, and in *Intentions* eighteen years later he tweaks Arnold's nose with the essay which in its first published form was entitled, "The True Function and Value of Criticism: with Some Remarks on the Importance of Doing Nothing." Here Wilde rounded on Arnold by asserting that the aim of criticism is to see the object as it really is not. This aim might seem to justify the highly personal criticism of Ruskin and Pater, and Wilde uses them as examples; his contention goes beyond their practice, however; he wishes to free critics from subordination, to grant them a larger share in the production of literature. While he does not forbid them to explain a book, they might prefer, he said, to deepen a book's mystery. (This purpose is amusing but out of date now; who could deepen the mystery of *Finnegans Wake?*) At any rate, their context would be different from that of the creative artist. For just as the artist claimed independence of received experience (Picasso tells us that art is "what nature is not"), so the critic claimed independence of received books. "The highest criticism," according to Wilde, "is the record of one's own soul." More closely he explained that the critic must have all literature in his mind and see particular works in that perspective rather than in isolation. Thus he, and we as well,

shall be able to realise, not merely our own lives, but the collective spirit of the race, and so to make ourselves absolutely modern, in the true meaning of the word modernity. For he to whom the present is the only thing that is present, knows nothing of the age in which he lives. To realise the nineteenth century, one must realise every century that has preceded it and that has contributed to its making.

Through knowledge the critic might become more creative than the creative artist, a paradox which has been expressed with more solemnity by Norman Podhoretz about literature of the present day.

Wilde reached these formulations of his aesthetic ideas late in his short life. They were latent, however, in his earliest known essay, "The Rise of Historical Criticism," which he wrote as a university exercise. While praising historians for their scrupulousness, Wilde finds the core of history to be the wish not merely to paint a picture, but to investigate laws and tendencies. He celebrates those historians who impose dominion upon fact instead of surrendering to it. Later he was to say much more boldly, "The one duty we owe to history is to rewrite it," and to praise Herodotus as father not of history but of lies. It is part of his larger conception that the one duty (or better, whim) we owe nature, reality, or the world, is to reconstruct it.

When Wilde turned to literary as distinguished from historical criticism, he at first was content to follow Pater. Wilde was won by Pater's espousal of gemlike flames and of high temperatures both in words and in life. Next to him Arnold sounded chilly, never so Victorian as when he was cogently criticizing Victorianism. That word "impression," with which Pater sought to unlock everything, became a favorite word in both Wilde and later in Arthur Symons, and was only arrested by Yeats in the late 1890s because he could not bear so much impermanence and insisted on a metaphysical basis—the *Anima Mundi*—for transitory moods. Like the word "absurd" today, though without a systematic philosophy behind it, the word "impression" agitated against pat assumptions and preconceptions.

Pater's vocabulary shapes the initial poem of Wilde's book of verse, published when he was twenty-five. This poem "Hélas!" encapsulates much of Wilde's temperament, but with Pater's coloring:

> To drift with every passion till my soul
> Is a stringed lute on which all winds can play,
> Is it for this that I have given away
> Mine ancient wisdom, and austere control?
> Methinks my life is a twice-written scroll
> Scrawled over on some boyish holiday
> With idle songs for pipe and virelay
> Which do but mar the secret of the whole.
> Surely there was a time I might have trod

> The sunlit heights, and from life's dissonance
> Struck one clear chord to reach the ears of God:
> Is that time dead? lo! with a little rod
> I did but touch the honey of romance—
> And must I lose a soul's inheritance?

To call the poem "Hélas!," to sigh in a foreign language, alerts us that the confession to follow will luxuriate in its penitence. The Biblical archaisms which occur later offer compunction suitably perfumed. "To drift" may well put us off as weak; on the other hand, "to drift with every passion" is not so bad. As its image of passivity, the poem offers "a stringed lute on which all winds can play." For the romantics the Aeolian harp was a favorable image because it harmonized man and nature. Here the winds are winds of temptation, rather than gusts of Lake Country air. The rhetorical question which begins, "Is it for this?" sounds reproachful enough, yet the phrases "ancient wisdom" and "austere control"—self-congratulatory since Wilde never had either—are so vague as to constitute a stately but equally unenergetic alternative to drifting.

The word "drift" comes down from Oxford in the 1870s. It occupies a prominent position in Pater's *Studies in the History of the Renaissance*, and specifically in the notorious conclusion to that book. This "Conclusion" was included in the edition of 1873, but omitted in 1877, when Wilde was at Oxford, on the ground that it "might possibly mislead" the young, who accordingly thronged to be misled by the first edition. It was the boldest thing Pater ever wrote; he drew upon the scientific work of his day to deny the integrity of objects. Physical life is now recognized, he says, to be a concurrence of forces rather than a group of things; the mind has no fixities either. He hits upon a metaphor of liquidity such as William James and Bergson were to adopt a little later in characterizing consciousness as a river or stream; Pater says more balefully that consciousness is a whirlpool, an image which later both Yeats and Pound relished. In our physical life, Pater grants, we sometimes feel momentarily at rest; in our consciousness, however, altering the whirlpool image, he finds "nothing but the race of the mid-stream,

a drift of momentary acts of sight and passion and thought."
To drift is not so wanton, then, as inevitable. To guide our
drifting we should rely not on sights or thoughts, in Pater's view,
but on "great passions." "Only be sure it is passion," he puts in
as a caveat. He urges his readers to recognize that "not the fruit
of experience, but experience itself, is the goal." "Our one hope
lies in getting as many pulsations as possible into the given
time." This attempt to render experience in terms of quantita-
tively measurable pulsations sounds a little like *Principles of
Literary Criticism*, but Pater's tone is not like Richards'; he
plays on the flute for the young to follow him.

When Pater at last decided to reprint this "Conclusion" (in
1888), he toned it down a little. In *Marius the Epicurean*
(1885), also later, the word "drift" is again prominent, but this
time is pejorative instead of merely descriptive. To suit his later
and more decorous manner, Pater, in reviewing *Dorian Gray*,
complained of the book's "dainty Epicurean theory" because,
he said:

A true Epicureanism aims at a complete though harmonious development of man's entire organism. To lose the moral sense
therefore, for instance, the sense of sin and righteousness . . . is
to lose, or lower, organisation, to become less complex, to pass from
a higher to a lower degree of development.

The letting-go, as well as the drawing-back, of Pater are both
evident in Wilde; his work celebrates both impulses, balancing
or disporting with them. In a letter of March 1887, written
four years before "Hélas!," he informs an Oxford friend:

I have got rather keen on Masonry lately and believe in it awfully
—in fact would be awfully sorry to have to give it up in case I
secede from the Protestant Heresy. I now breakfast with Father
Parkinson, go to St Aloysius, talk sentimental religion to Dunlop
and altogether am caught in the fowler's snare, in the wiles of the
Scarlet Woman—I may go over in the vac. I have dreams of a
visit to Newman, of the holy sacrament in a new Church, and of a
quiet and peace afterwards in my soul. I need not say, though, that

I shift with every breath of thought and am weaker and more self-deceiving than ever.

If I *could hope* that the Church would wake in me some earnestness and purity I would go over *as a luxury*, if for no better reasons. But I can hardly hope it would, and to go over to Rome would be to sacrifice and give up my two great gods "Money and Ambition."

In this letter Wilde testifies playfully to the same yearning to be earnest that he shows in "Hélas!" and then mocks in his later comedy. He is half-converted to Catholicism, half to Masonry—that these two groups cannot bear each other does not prevent their being equally attractive to him; they have parity as new areas of sensation, to be enjoyed willfully and passingly. If, as Wilde announced later, "the best way to resist temptation is to yield to it," the reason is that having done so, one may pass on to the next and the next, and in this concourse one may keep a residual freedom by not lingering with any single temptation long.

During the four years between writing this letter and writing "Hélas!," Wilde had put aside both Catholicism and Masonry. In his sonnet he has in mind chiefly his formal education as contrasted with his romantic self-indulgence. A classicist by training, Wilde considered Hellenism to be the more basic side of his nature, overlaid, but only as a palimpsest conceals the original, by a more modern mode. He berates himself, gently. His new life is made up of "idle songs for pipe and virelay," a self-accusation which only concedes frivolity, not depravity. Moreover, it is artistic frivolity, a further mitigation. Wilde remembered Pater's comment in the same "Conclusion" that "the wisest" instead of living spend their lives in "art and song." If it is wrong to drift, and Wilde hedges a little, then it is less wrong to drift gracefully. A "boyish holiday" is also not the most offensive way to spend one's time, especially if one likes boys.

The sestet of the poem restates the issue, with new dashes of metaphor. The poet then asks histrionically, "Is that time dead?" He won't say for sure, but again he sweetens his offense: he has but touched with Jonathan's rod the honey of romance.

The last question is not so much despairing as hopeful. Wilde felt he was superior to both classical and romantic modes, because he could manipulate both: he said in his essay on the English renaissance that this variability was the strength of the new movement in letters to which he belonged. He thought he had physiological as well as artistic support for his method, because "the desire of any very intensified emotion [is] to be relieved by some emotion that is its opposite." He shifts therefore from foot to foot in other poems besides "Hélas!" "The Sphinx" begins with a fascinated invocation of the sphinx and ends with a strident rejection of her. Wilde summarizes his state or rather his flow of mind in a letter:

Sometime you will find, even as I have found, that there is no such thing as a romantic experience; there are romantic memories, and there is the desire of romance—that is all. Our most fiery moments of ecstasy are merely shadows of what somewhere else we have felt, or of what we long some day to feel. So at least it seems to me. And, strangely enough, what comes of all this is a curious mixture of ardour and of indifference. I myself would sacrifice everything for a new experience, and I know there is no such thing as a new experience at all. I think I would more readily die for what I do not believe in than for what I hold to be true. I would go to the stake for a sensation and be a sceptic to the last! Only one thing remains infinitely fascinating to me, the mystery of moods. To be master of these moods is exquisite, to be mastered by them more exquisite still. Sometimes I think that the artistic life is a long and lovely suicide, and am not sorry that it is so.

Life then is a willed deliquescence, or more exactly, a progressive surrender of the self to all the temptations appropriate to it.

What Wilde needed was not to avoid the precious occasions of evil in "Hélas!" but to approach more enterprising ones. Yet after his *Poems* appeared in 1881 he was at check for almost six years. He kept busy; he went on a lecture tour for a whole year to America; he returned to England and went lecturing on; he tried unsuccessfully for a post as school inspector such as Matthew Arnold had; erratically still, he married in 1884 and took up husbanding, begetting two children born in 1885 and 1886. Then in 1887 Wilde began the publications by which he is known. He wrote a volume of stories, and one of fairy tales, then one of criticism, then five plays, besides editing from 1887 to 1889 a magazine, *Woman's World*—a patrician equivalent of the A & P *Woman's Day*. It would seem that something roused him from the pseudo-consolidation of marriage and lectures, which were dilettantism for him, to genuine consolidation which seemed dilettantism to others.

This something appears in the original version of *The Picture of Dorian Gray*, published in *Lippincott's Magazine*. Wilde emphasizes more there than in the final version the murder of the painter Basil Hallward by Dorian; it is the turning-point in Dorian's experience, a plunge from insinuations of criminal tendency to crime itself. The murder at once protects the secret of his double life and vents his revulsion against the man who wants him innocent still. In *Lippincott's* Wilde specifies: "It was on the 7th of November, the eve of his own thirty-second birthday, as he often remembered afterwards. . . ." Then when the novel was published as a book, Wilde altered this date: "It was on the ninth of November, the eve of his own thirty-eighth birthday, as he often remembered afterwards."

Altering Dorian's age would be gratuitous if Wilde had not attached significance to his own thirty-second year which began in 1886. The passage must have been autobiographical, and such a conjecture receives support from Robert Ross, who boasted that it was he, at the age of seventeen, who in 1886 first seduced Wilde to homosexual practices. (Dorian's Sibyl Vane was also seventeen.) Wilde evidently considered this sudden alteration of his life a pivotal matter, to be recast as Dorian's murder of Hallward. He himself moved from pasteboard marriage to the expression of long latent proclivities, at some remove from the "ancient wisdom" and "austere control" to which he had earlier laid claim as his basic nature. Respectability, always an enemy, was destroyed in his own house. The first work which came out of the new Wilde was, appropriately, "Lord Arthur Savile's Crime," in which murder is comically enacted and successfully concealed.

From late in the year 1886 then, Wilde was able to think of

himself, if he wanted to, as criminal. Up to that time he could
always consider himself an innocent misunderstood; now he
lived in such a way as to confirm suspicions. Instead of chal-
lenging Victorian society only by words, he acted in such a way
as to create scandal. Indiscreet by nature, he was indiscreet also
by conviction, and he waged his war somewhat openly. He
sensed that his new life was a source of literary effect. As he
wrote later of Thomas Wainewright: "His crimes seem to have
had an important effect upon his art. They gave a strong personality to his style, a quality that his early work certainly
lacked." He returned to this idea: "One can fancy an intense
personality being created out of sin," and in "The Soul of Man
Under Socialism," he thought that "Crime . . . under certain
conditions, may be said to have created individualism." In "The
Portrait of Mr W. H." (1889), he made Shakespeare's sonnets
depend upon a similarly forbidden love affair, with an actor
the same age as Ross. Thomas Mann's Mario Kröger speaks of
a banker who discovers his literary talent by committing a serious crime for which he is put in prison. The artist-criminal is
implicit in romantic and symbolistic theories of art, but Wilde
anticipates the explicitness on this subject of both Mann and
Gide, as he does that of Cavafy in "Their Beginning" or of
Auden in *About the House*:

> Time has taught you
>   how much inspiration
> your vices brought you. . . .

Wilde might have discounted the sinfulness of his conduct
and applied to himself his own epigram: "Wickedness is a
myth invented by good people to account for the curious attractiveness of others." But he was quite content to think of
himself as sinful.

He now succeeded in relating his new discoveries about himself to aesthetic theory. His only formal book of criticism, *Intentions*, has the same secret spring as his later plays and stories.
Ostensibly he generally says that the spheres of art and of ethics

are absolutely distinct and separate. But occasionally, overtly or covertly, he states that for the artist crime does pay, by instilling itself in his content and affecting his form. Each of the four essays that make up *Intentions* is to some degree subversive, as if to demonstrate that the intentions of the artist are not strictly honorable. The first and the last, "The Decay of Lying" and "The Truth of Masks," celebrate art for rejecting truths, faces, and all that paraphernalia in favor of lies and masks. Wilde doesn't do this in the romantic way of extolling the imagination, for while he uses that word he is a little chary of it; the imagination is itself too natural, too involuntary, for his view of art. He prefers lying because it sounds more willful, because it is no outpouring of the self, but a conscious effort to mislead. "All fine imaginative work," Wilde affirms, "is self-conscious and deliberate. A great poet sings because he chooses to sing." On the other hand, "if one tells the truth, one is sure, sooner or later, to be found out!" "All bad poetry springs from genuine feeling." Wilde celebrates art not in the name of Ariel, as the romantics would, but in the name of Ananias.

He finds art to have two basic energies, both of them subversive. One asserts its magnificent isolation from experience, its unreality, its sterility. He would concur with Nabokov that art is a kind of trick played on nature, an *illicit* creation by man. "All art is entirely useless," Wilde declares. "Art never expresses anything but itself." "Nothing that actually occurs is of the smallest importance." Form determines content, not content form, a point which Auden also sometimes affirms and which is often assumed by symbolists. With this theory Wilde turns Taine upon his head; the age does not determine what its art should be, rather it is art which gives the age its character. So far from responding to questions posed by the epoch, art offers answers before questions have been asked. "It is the ages that are her symbols." Life, straggling after art, seizes upon forms in art to express itself, so that life imitates art rather than art life. ". . . This unfortunate aphorism about Art holding the mirror up to Nature, is," according to Wilde, "deliberately said by Hamlet in order to convince the bystanders of his absolute insanity in all art-matters." If art be a mirror, we look into it to see—a mask. But more precisely, art is no mirror; it is a "mist of words," "a veil."

Sometimes the veil is pierced. This indifferent conferral of forms upon life by art may have unexpected consequences which implicate art instead of isolating it. In "The Decay of Lying" Wilde speaks of "silly boys who, after reading the adventures of Jack Sheppard or Dick Turpin, pillage the stalls of unfortunate applewomen, break into sweetshops at night, and alarm old gentlemen who are returning home from the city by leaping out on them in suburban lanes, with black masks and unloaded revolvers." In *Dorian Gray* the effect is more sinister; Dorian declares he has been poisoned by a book, and while Lord Henry assures him that art is too aloof to influence anybody, Dorian is felt to be right. Art may then transmit criminal impulses to its audience. Like Whitman, Wilde could and did say, "Nor will my poems do good only, they will do just as much evil, perhaps more."

The artist may be criminal and instill his work with criminality. Wilde's second essay in *Intentions* is "Pen Pencil and Poison." He uses Thomas Wainewright as the type of the artist. We need not expect to find a beautiful soul; Wainewright was instead "a forger of no mean or ordinary capabilities, and . . . a subtle and secret poisoner almost without rival in this or any age." Among his interesting tastes, Wainewright had "that curious love of green, which in individuals is always the sign of a subtle artistic temperament, and in nations is said to denote a laxity, if not a decadence of morals." When a friend reproached him with a murder, he shrugged his shoulders and gave an answer that Susan Sontag would call camp: "Yes; it was a dreadful thing to do, but she had very thick ankles." Wilde concludes that "the fact of a man being a poisoner is nothing against his prose," and "there is no essential incongruity between crime and culture." Wainewright's criminal career turns out to be strictly relevant to his art, fortifying it and giving it character. The quality of that art it is too early to judge, Wilde says, but he clearly believes that Wainewright's personality achieves sufficient criminality to have great artistic promise.

"The Critic as Artist" is the most ambitious of the essays in

Introduction

Intentions. It too conveys the notion that art undermines things as they are. The critic is the artist's accomplice in crime, or even masterminds the plot in which they are mutually engaged. Criticism overcomes the tendency of creation to repeat itself; it helps the artist discover unused possibilities. For at bottom, Wilde says, criticism is self-consciousness; it enables us to put our most recent phase at a distance and so go on to another. It disengages us so we may reengage ourselves in a new way.

From this argument Wilde proceeds to find criticism and self-consciousness to be as necessary as sin. "What is termed Sin is an essential element of progress"; without it, he holds, the world would stagnate or grow old or become colorless.

By its curiosity [there is Arnold's word with Wilde's meaning] Sin increases the experience of the race. Through its intensified assertion of individualism it saves us from monotony of type. In its rejection of the current notions about morality, it is one with the highest ethics.

By a dexterous transvaluation of words, Wilde makes good and evil exchange places. Even socially sin is far more useful than martyrdom, he says, since it is self-expressive rather than self-repressive. The goal of man is the liberation of personality; when the day of true culture comes, sin will be impossible because the soul will be able to transform

into elements of a richer experience, or a finer susceptibility, or a newer mode of thought, acts or passions that with the common would be commonplace, or with the uneducated ignoble, or with the shameful vile. Is this dangerous? Yes; it is dangerous—all ideas, as I told you, are so.

What muddies this point of view in Wilde is his looking back to conventional meanings of words like sin, ignoble, and shameful. He is not so ready as Nietzsche to transvaluate these, though he does reshuffle them. His private equation is that sin is the perception of new and dangerous possibilities in action as self-consciousness is in thought and criticism is in art. He espouses individualism, and he encourages society to make individualism more complete than it can be now, and for this reason he sponsors socialism as a communal egotism, like the society made up of separate but equal works of art.

Meantime, before socialism, what should be thought of the criminal impulses of the artist? Increasingly in his later writings, Wilde spreads the guilt from the artist to all men. If we are all insincere, masked, and lying, then the artist is prototype rather than exception. If all the sheep are black, then the artist cannot be blamed for not being white. Such an exculpation is implied in three of Wilde's plays after *Salome*—*Lady Windermere's Fan, A Woman of No Importance, An Ideal Husband*. Wilde allows his characters to be found guilty, but no guiltier than others, and more courageous in their wrongdoing.

Even as he defends them, he allows them to be mildly punished. Half-consciously, Wilde was preparing himself for another abrupt shift in his experience, such as he had made in 1886. It would be false to say that Wilde wanted to go to prison, yet the notion had frequently crossed his mind. He had always associated himself with the *poètes maudits*, always considered obloquy a certificate of literary merit. In "The Soul of Man under Socialism" he had opposed suffering, yet acknowledged that the Russian novelists had rediscovered a great medieval theme, the realization of man through suffering. More particularly, in a review of a new book of poems by Wilfrid Scawen Blunt in 1889, he began: "Prison has had an admirable effect on Mr. Wilfrid Blunt as a poet." It was like the effect of crime on Wainewright. Blunt had been merely witty and affected earlier, now his work had more depth. "Mr. Balfour must be praised," Wilde says jestingly, since "by sending Mr. Blunt to gaol . . . [he] has converted a clever rhymer into an earnest and deep-thinking poet." Six years later, just before his own disgrace, Wilde wrote in "The Soul of Man under Socialism," "After all, even in prison a man can be quite free." These hints indicate that Wilde was prepared, or thought he was, for trial and prison, and expected he would derive artistic profit from them. He had no idea of running away, even on a boyish holiday, whatever his friends might say. Instead he accepted imperial authority as readily as Christ had done—a precedent he discovered for himself, though hardly the first or last in hot water to do so. Blunt's poems written in prison were called *In Vinculis,* and Wilde's letter to Douglas from prison, which we know by Ross's title as *De Profundis,* was originally entitled by Wilde *Epistola: In Carcere et Vinculis.*

Hélas! Wilde's literary career was not transmogrified by prison as he hoped, but his experiences there, which were so much worse than he anticipated, gave him his final theme. "*La prison m'a complètement changé,*" he said to Gide at Berneval; "*je comptais sur elle pour cela.*" As before, he made no effort to exonerate himself by saying that his sins were venial or not sins at all. Defenses of homosexual or "Uranian" love were common enough at this period; except once at his trial, he did not make them. But he reached for the main implication of his disgrace through a double negative; though men thought he was unlike them, he was *not.* He was a genuine scapegoat.

This ultimate conception of himself was never put into an essay, but it is involved in his *De Profundis* letter to Douglas, and in *The Ballad of Reading Gaol.* Both are predictably full of imagery of Christ. Before this Wilde had depreciated pity as a motive in art; now he embraced it. The hero of his poem is a man who has murdered his mistress and is about to be hanged for his crime. Wilde identifies himself closely with this prisoner. The poem's tenor is that the prisoners are humanity, all of whom are felons:

> Yet each man kills the thing he loves,
>   By each let this be heard,
> Some do it with a bitter look,
>   Some with a flattering word,
> The coward does it with a kiss,
>   The brave man with a sword! . . .
>
> Some love too little, some too long,
>   Some sell, and others buy;
> Some do the deed with many tears,
>   And some without a sigh:

> For each man kills the thing he loves,
> Yet each man does not die.

This poem was chosen for the *Oxford Book of Modern Verse* by Yeats, but he removed what he regarded as the commentary, including these stanzas. His effort to improve the poem evokes sympathy; it must be said, however, that whatever the quality of the bare narrative that Yeats prints, for Wilde—as for D. H. Lawrence and most readers—the commentary was the excessive and yet determining part of the poem. During the six years before his imprisonment he had demonstrated first that the artist was basically and usefully criminal, and second that criminality was not confined to artists, but was to be found as commonly among members of the Cabinet. Where most men pretend to a virtue they don't have, the artist, fully aware of his own sins, takes on those they don't acknowledge. The purpose of sin has subtly shifted in Wilde's mind—it is no longer a means for the artist of extending the boundaries of action, it is a means for him to focus and enshrine guilt. He has the courage, exceptional among men, of looking into the heart of things and finding there not brotherly love so much as murder, not self-love so much as suicide. In recognizing the universality of guilt he is like Christ; in revealing his own culpability he plays the role of his own Judas. Wilde, who had written in one of his poems that we are ourselves "the lips betraying and the life betrayed," had in fact brought about his own conviction. The result was that he was remarried to the society from which he had divorced himself; he was no outcast, for he accepted and even sought the punishment which other men, equally guilty, would only submit to vicariously through him, just as all the prisoners suffer with the doomed murderer. By means of submission and suffering he gives his life a new purpose, and writes over the palimpsest once again.

In this concern with social role Wilde has clearly moved away from Pater, and perhaps we can conceive of him as moving toward another writer, Jean Genet. Genet is of course ferocious and remorseless in a way that Wilde was not, and makes much less concession to the world. But the two men share an insistence on their own criminality and on a possible sanction for it. The comparison with Christ has been irresistible for both. As Genet says in *Thief's Journal*:

Let us ignore the theologians. "Taking upon Himself the sins of the world" means exactly this: experiencing potentially and in their effects all sins; it means having subscribed to evil. Every creator must thus shoulder—the expression seems feeble—must make his own, to the point of knowing it to be his substance, circulating in his arteries, the evil given by him, which his heroes choose freely.

Wilde in *De Profundis* remembered having remarked to Gide that "there was nothing that . . . Christ had said that could not be transferred immediately into the sphere of Art, and there find its complete fulfilment." And again, Genet speaks like Wilde of the courage required to do wrong, saying: "If he has courage, the guilty man decides to be what crime has made him." He wishes to obtain "the recognition of evil." Both writers envisage a regeneration which can come only from total assumption of their proclivities and their lot; as Genet puts it:

I shall destroy appearances, the casings will burn away and one evening I shall appear there, in the palm of your hand, quiet and pure, like a glass statuette. You will see me. Round about me there will be nothing left.

Wilde summons for this sacred moment a red rose growing from the hanged man's mouth, a white one from his heart. He had terrified André Gide by trying to persuade that strictly reared young man to authorize evil, as to some extent in the *acte gratuit* Gide did, and it is just such authorization that Genet asserts with more fierceness than Wilde.

In his criticism and in his work generally, Wilde balanced two ideas which, we have observed, look contradictory. One is that art is disengaged from actual life, the other that it is deeply incriminated with it. The first point of view is sometimes taken by Yeats, though only to qualify it, the second without qualification by Genet. That art is sterile, and that it is infectious, are attitudes not beyond reconciliation. Wilde never formulated their union, but he implied something like this: by its creation of beauty art reproaches the world, calling attention to the world's faults through their very omission; so the sterility of art is an affront or a parable. Art may also outrage the world by flouting its laws or by picturing indulgently their violation. Or art may seduce the world by making it follow an example which seems bad but is discovered to be better than it seems. In these various ways the artist forces the world toward self-recognition, with at least a tinge of self-redemption.

Yet this ethical or almost ethical view of art coexists in Wilde with its own cancelation. He could write *Salome* with one hand, dwelling upon incest and necrophilia, and show them as self-defeated, punished by execution and remorse. With the other hand, he could dissolve by the critical intellect all notions of sin and guilt. He does so in *The Importance of Being Earnest*, which is all insouciance where *Salome* is all incrimination. In *The Importance of Being Earnest* sins which are presented as accursed in *Salome* and unnameable in *Dorian Gray* are translated into a different key, and appear as Algernon's inordinate and selfish craving for—cucumber sandwiches. The substitution of mild gluttony for fearsome lechery renders all vice harmless. There *is* a wicked brother, but he is just our old friend Algernon. The double life which is so serious a matter for Dorian or for The Ideal Husband, becomes a harmless Bunburying, or playing Jack in the country and Ernest in town. In the earlier, four-act version of the play, Wilde even parodied punishment, by having a bailiff come to take Jack to Holloway Prison (as Wilde himself was soon to be taken) not for homosexuality, but for running up food bills at the Savoy. Jack is disinclined, he says, to be imprisoned in the suburbs for dining in town, and makes out a check. The notion of expiation is also mocked; as Cecily observes: "They have been eating muffins. That looks like repentance." Finally, the theme of regeneration is parodied in the efforts of Ernest and Jack to be baptized. (By the way, in the earlier version Prism is also about to be baptized, and someone comments, "To be born again would be of considerable advantage to her.") The ceremonial unmasking at the play's end, which had meant death for Dorian Gray, leaves everyone bare-faced for a new puppet show, that of matrimony. Yet amusing as it all is, much of the comedy derives from Wilde's own sense of the realities of what are being mocked. He was in only momentary refuge from his more usual cycle which ran from scapegrace to scapegoat.

During his stay in prison Wilde took up the regeneration theme in *De Profundis* and after being freed he resumed it in *The Ballad of Reading Gaol.* But he was too self-critical not to find the notion of rebirth a little preposterous. When his friends complained of his resuming old habits, he said, "A patriot put in prison for loving his country, loves his country, and a poet in prison for loving boys, loves boys." But to write about himself as unredeemed, unpunished, unreborn, to claim that his sins were nothing, that his form of love was more noble than most other people's, that what had happened to him was the result merely of legal obtuseness, was impossible for Wilde. So long as he had been a scapegrace the door to comedy was still open; once having accepted the role of scapegoat the door was closed. He conceived of a new play, but it was in his earlier mode and he could not write it. Cramped to one myth, and that somber and depleted, Wilde could not extricate himself. There was nothing to do but die, which accordingly he did. But not without one final assertion of a past enthusiasm: he was converted to Catholicism the night before his death.

RICHARD ELLMANN

A NOTE ON THE TEXT

As indicated in footnotes, the text (including spelling and punctuation) of the essays in this book follows that of the original magazine publication or Wilde's own revision of it.

THE Artist
AS Critic

The Tomb
of Keats*

As one enters Rome from the Via Ostiensis by the Porta San
Paolo, the first object that meets the eye is a marble pyramid
which stands close at hand on the left.

There are many Egyptian obelisks in Rome, tall, snake-like
spires of red sandstone, mottled with strange writings, which
remind us of the pillars of flame which led the children of Is-
rael through the desert away from the land of the Pharaohs; but
more wonderful than these to look upon is this gaunt, wedge-
shaped pyramid standing here in this Italian city, unshattered
amid the ruins and wrecks of time, looking older than the Eternal City itself, like terrible impassiveness turned to stone. And
so in the middle ages men supposed this to be the sepulchre of
Remus, who was slain by his own brother at the founding of
the city, so ancient and mysterious it appears; but we have now,
perhaps unfortunately, more accurate information about it, and
know that it is the tomb of one Caius Cestius, a Roman gentleman of small note, who died about 30, B.C.

Yet though we cannot care much for the dead man who lies
in lonely state beneath it, and who is only known to the world
through his sepulchre, still this pyramid will be ever dear to the
eyes of all English-speaking people, because at evening its
shadow falls on the tomb of one who walks with Spenser, and
Shakespeare, and Byron, and Shelley, and Elizabeth Barrett

* *Irish Monthly* V : 49 (July 1877) 476–78.

3

Browning, in the great procession of the sweet singers of England.

For at its foot there is a green sunny slope, known as the Old Protestant cemetery, and on this a common-looking grave, which bears the following inscription:—

"This grave contains all that was mortal of a young English poet, who, on his death-bed, in the bitterness of his heart, desired these words to be engraven on his tomb-stone: 'Here lies one whose name was writ in water.' February 24, 1821."

And the name of the young English poet is John Keats.

Lord Houghton calls this cemetery "one of the most beautiful spots on which the eye and heart of man can rest," and Shelley speaks of it as "making one in love with death, to think one should be buried in so sweet a place"; and indeed when I saw the violets, and the daisies, and the poppies that overgrow the tomb, I remembered how the dead poet had once told his friend that he thought the "intensest pleasures he had received in life was watching the growth of flowers," and how another time, after lying a while quite still, he murmured in some strange prescience of early death, "I feel the flowers growing over me."

But this time-worn stone and these wild flowers are but poor memorials[1] of one so great as Keats; most of all, too, in this city of Rome, which pays such honour to her dead; where popes, and emperors, and saints, and cardinals, lie hidden in "porphyry wombs," or couched in baths of jasper and chalcedony, and malachite, ablaze with precious stones and metals, and tended with continual service. For very noble is the site, and worthy

[1] Recently some well-meaning persons have placed a marble slab on the wall of the cemetery with a medallion-profile of Keats on it, and some mediocre lines of poetry. The face is ugly, and rather hatchet-shaped, with thick, sensual lips, and is utterly unlike the poet himself, who was very beautiful to look upon. "His countenance," says a lady, who saw him at one of Hazlitt's lectures, "lives in my mind as one of singular beauty and brightness; it had the expression as if he had been looking on some glorious sight." And this is the idea which Severn's picture of him gives. Even Haydon's rough pen and ink sketch of him is better than this "marble libel," which I hope will soon be taken down. I think the best representation of the poet would be a coloured bust, like that of the young Rajah of Koolapoor at Florence, which is a lovely and life-like work of art.

of a noble monument; behind looms the gray pyramid, symbol of the world's age, and filled with memories of the sphinx, and the lotus leaf, and the glories of old Nile; in front is the Monte Testaccio, built, it is said, with the broken fragments of the vessels in which all the nations of the East and the West brought their tribute to Rome; and a little distance off, along the slope of the hill under the Aurelian wall, some tall gaunt cypresses rise, like burnt-out funeral torches, to mark the spot where Shelley's heart (that "heart of hearts!") lies in the earth; and above all, the soil on which we tread is very Rome!

As I stood beside the mean grave of this divine boy, I thought of him as of a Priest of Beauty slain before his time; and the vision of Guido's St. Sebastian came before my eyes as I saw him at Genoa, a lovely brown boy, with crisp, clustering hair and red lips, bound by his evil enemies to a tree, and, though pierced by arrows, raising his eyes with divine, impassioned gaze towards the Eternal Beauty of the opening heavens. And thus my thoughts shaped themselves to rhyme:—

HEU MISERANDE PUER

Rid of the world's injustice and its pain,
  He rests at last beneath God's veil of blue;
  Taken from life while life and love were new
The youngest of the martyrs here is lain,
Fair as Sebastian and as foully slain.
  No cypress shades his grave, nor funeral yew,
  But red-lipped daisies, violets drenched with dew,
And sleepy poppies, catch the evening rain.

O proudest heart that broke for misery!
  O saddest poet that the world hath seen!
    O sweetest singer of the English land!
    Thy name was writ in water on the sand,
  But our tears shall keep thy memory green,
And make it flourish like a Basil-tree.

Impressions of America[*]

I fear I cannot picture America as altogether an Elysium—perhaps, from the ordinary standpoint I know but little about the country. I cannot give its latitude or longitude; I cannot compute the value of its dry goods, and I have no very close acquaintance with its politics. These are matters which may not interest you, and they certainly are not interesting to me.

The first thing that struck me on landing in America was that if the Americans are not the most well-dressed people in the world, they are the most comfortably dressed. Men are seen there with the dreadful chimney-pot hat, but there are very few hatless men; men wear the shocking swallow-tail coat, but few are to be seen with no coat at all. There is an air of comfort in the appearance of the people which is a marked contrast to that seen in this country, where, too often, people are seen in close contact with rags.

The next thing particularly noticeable is that everybody seems in a hurry to catch a train. This is a state of things which is not favourable to poetry or romance. Had Romeo or Juliet been in a constant state of anxiety about trains, or had their minds been agitated by the question of return-tickets, Shakespeare could not have given us those lovely balcony scenes which are so full of poetry and pathos.

[*] A lecture given by Wilde after his return from the United States in 1882. Text from *Impressions of America*, ed. Stuart Mason (London, 1912).

America is the noisiest country that ever existed. One is waked up in the morning, not by the singing of the nightingale, but by the steam whistle. It is surprising that the sound practical sense of the Americans does not reduce this intolerable noise. All Art depends upon exquisite and delicate sensibility, and such continual turmoil must ultimately be destructive of the musical faculty.

There is not so much beauty to be found in American cities as in Oxford, Cambridge, Salisbury or Winchester, where are lovely relics of a beautiful age; but still there is a good deal of beauty to be seen in them now and then, but only where the American has not attempted to create it. Where the Americans have attempted to produce beauty they have signally failed. A remarkable characteristic of the Americans is the manner in which they have applied science to modern life.

This is apparent in the most cursory stroll through New York. In England an inventor is regarded almost as a crazy man, and in too many instances invention ends in disappointment and poverty. In America an inventor is honoured, help is forthcoming, and the exercise of ingenuity, the application of science to the work of man, is there the shortest road to wealth. There is no country in the world where machinery is so lovely as in America.

I have always wished to believe that the line of strength and the line of beauty are one. That wish was realised when I contemplated American machinery. It was not until I had seen the water-works at Chicago that I realised the wonders of machinery; the rise and fall of the steel rods, the symmetrical motion of the great wheels is the most beautifully rhythmic thing I have ever seen. One is impressed in America, but not favourably impressed, by the inordinate size of everything. The country seems to try to bully one into a belief in its power by its impressive bigness.

I was disappointed with Niagara—most people must be disappointed with Niagara. Every American bride is taken there, and the sight of the stupendous waterfall must be one of the earliest, if not the keenest, disappointments in American married life. One sees it under bad conditions, very far away, the point of view not showing the splendour of the water. To appreciate it really one has to see it from underneath the fall, and to do that it is necessary to be dressed in a yellow oil-skin, which is as ugly as a mackintosh—and I hope none of you ever wears one. It is a consolation to know, however, that such an artist as Madame Bernhardt has not only worn that yellow, ugly dress, but has been photographed in it.

Perhaps the most beautiful part of America is the West, to reach which, however, involves a journey by rail of six days, racing along tied to an ugly tin-kettle of a steam engine. I found but poor consolation for this journey in the fact that the boys who infest the cars and sell everything that one can eat—or should not eat—were selling editions of my poems vilely printed on a kind of grey blotting paper, for the low price of ten cents. Calling these boys on one side I told them that though poets like to be popular they desire to be paid, and selling editions of my poems without giving me a profit is dealing a blow at literature which must have a disastrous effect on poetical aspirants. The invariable reply that they made was that they themselves made a profit out of the transaction and that was all they cared about.

It is a popular superstition that in America a visitor is invariably addressed as "Stranger." I was never once addressed as "Stranger." When I went to Texas I was called "Captain"; when I got to the centre of the country I was addressed as "Colonel," and, on arriving at the borders of Mexico, as "General." On the whole, however, "Sir," the old English method of addressing people[,] is the most common.

It is, perhaps, worth while to note that what many people call Americanisms are really old English expressions which have lingered in our colonies while they have been lost in our own country. Many people imagine that the term "I guess," which is so common in America, is purely an American expression, but it was used by John Locke in his work on "The Understanding," just as we now use "I think."

It is in the colonies, and not in the mother country, that the old life of the country really exists. If one wants to realise what English Puritanism is—not at its worst (when it is very bad), but at its best, and then it is not very good—I do not think one can find much of it in England, but much can be found about

Boston and Massachusetts. We have got rid of it. America still preserves it, to be, I hope, a short-lived curiosity.

San Francisco is a really beautiful city. China Town, peopled by Chinese labourers, is the most artistic town I have ever come across. The people—strange, melancholy Orientals, whom many people would call common, and they are certainly very poor—have determined that they will have nothing about them that is not beautiful. In the Chinese restaurant, where these navvies meet to have supper in the evening, I found them drinking tea out of china cups as delicate as the petals of a rose-leaf, whereas at the gaudy hotels I was supplied with a delf cup an inch and a half thick. When the Chinese bill was presented it was made out on rice paper, the account being done in Indian ink as fantastically as if an artist had been etching little birds on a fan.

Salt Lake City contains only two buildings of note, the chief being the Tabernacle, which is in the shape of a soup-kettle. It is decorated by the only native artist, and he has treated religious subjects in the naive spirit of the early Florentine painters, representing people of our own day in the dress of the period side by side with people of Biblical history who are clothed in some romantic costume.

The building next in importance is called the Amelia Palace, in honour of one of Brigham Young's wives. When he died the present president of the Mormons stood up in the Tabernacle and said that it had been revealed to him that he was to have the Amelia Palace, and that on this subject there were to be no more revelations of any kind!

From Salt Lake City one travels over the great plains of Colorado and up the Rocky Mountains, on the top of which is Leadville, the richest city in the world. It has also got the reputation of being the roughest, and every man carries a revolver. I was told that if I went there they would be sure to shoot me or my travelling manager. I wrote and told them that nothing that they could do to my travelling manager would intimidate me. They are miners—men working in metals, so I lectured them on the Ethics of Art. I read them passages from the autobiography of Benvenuto Cellini and they seemed much delighted. I was reproved by my hearers for not having brought him with me. I explained that he had been dead for some little time which elicited the enquiry "Who shot him"? They afterwards took me to a dancing saloon where I saw the only rational method of art criticism I have ever come across. Over the piano was printed a notice:—

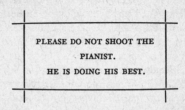

PLEASE DO NOT SHOOT THE
PIANIST.
HE IS DOING HIS BEST.

The mortality among pianists in that place is marvellous. Then they asked me to supper, and having accepted, I had to descend a mine in a rickety bucket in which it was impossible to be graceful. Having got into the heart of the mountain I had supper, the first course being whisky, the second whisky and the third whisky.

I went to the Theatre to lecture and I was informed that just before I went there two men had been seized for committing a murder, and in that theatre they had been brought on to the stage at eight o'clock in the evening, and then and there tried and executed before a crowded audience. But I found these miners very charming and not at all rough.

Among the more elderly inhabitants of the South I found a melancholy tendency to date every event of importance by the late war. "How beautiful the moon is to-night," I once remarked to a gentleman who was standing next to me. "Yes," was his reply, "but you should have seen it before the war."

So infinitesimal did I find the knowledge of Art, west of the Rocky Mountains, that an art patron—one who in his day had been a miner—actually sued the railroad company for damages because the plaster cast of Venus of Milo, which he had imported from Paris, had been delivered minus the arms. And, what is more surprising still, he gained his case and the damages.

Pennsylvania, with its rocky gorges and woodland scenery, reminded me of Switzerland. The prairie reminded me of a piece of blotting-paper.

The Spanish and French have left behind them memorials in the beauty of their names. All the cities that have beautiful names derive them from the Spanish or the French. The English people give intensely ugly names to places. One place had such an ugly name that I refused to lecture there. It was called Grigsville. Supposing I had founded a school of Art there—fancy "Early Grigsville." Imagine a School of Art teaching "Grigsville Renaissance."

As for slang I did not hear much of it, though a young lady who had changed her clothes after an afternoon dance did say that "after the heel kick she shifted her day goods."

American youths are pale and precocious, or sallow and supercilious, but American girls are pretty and charming—little oases of pretty unreasonableness in a vast desert of practical common-sense.

Every American girl is entitled to have twelve young men devoted to her. They remain her slaves and she rules them with charming nonchalance.

The men are entirely given to business; they have, as they say, their brains in front of their heads. They are also exceedingly acceptive of new ideas. Their education is practical. We base the education of children entirely on books, but we must give a child a mind before we can instruct the mind. Children have a natural antipathy to books—handicraft should be the basis of education. Boys and girls should be taught to use their hands to make something, and they would be less apt to destroy and be mischievous.

In going to America one learns that poverty is not a necessary accompaniment to civilisation. There at any rate is a country that has no trappings, no pageants and no gorgeous ceremonies. I saw only two processions—one was the Fire Brigade preceded by the Police, the other was the Police preceded by the Fire Brigade.

Every man when he gets to the age of twenty-one is allowed to vote, and thereby immediately acquires his political educa-

11

tion. The Americans are the best politically educated people in the world. It is well worth one's while to go to a country which can teach us the beauty of the word FREEDOM and the value of the thing LIBERTY.

Mr. Whistler's Ten O'Clock*

Last night, at Prince's Hall, Mr. Whistler made his first public appearance as a lecturer on art, and spoke for more than an hour with really marvellous eloquence on the absolute uselessness of all lectures of the kind. Mr. Whistler began his lecture with a very pretty *aria* on pre-historic history, describing how in earlier times hunter and warrior would go forth to chase and foray, while the artist sat at home making cup and bowl for their service. Rude imitations of nature they were first, like the gourd bottle, till the sense of beauty and form developed, and, in all its exquisite proportions, the first vase was fashioned. Then came a higher civilization of architecture and arm chairs, and with exquisite design, and dainty diaper, the useful things of life were made lovely; and the hunter and the warrior lay on the couch when they were tired, and, when they were thirsty, drank from the bowl, and never cared to lose the exquisite proportions of the one, or the delightful ornament of the other; and this attitude of the primitive anthropophagous Philistine formed the text of the lecture, and was the attitude which Mr. Whistler entreated his audience to adopt towards art. Remembering, no doubt, many charming invitations to wonderful private views, this fashionable assemblage seemed somewhat aghast, and not a little amused, at being told that the slightest appearance among a civilized people of any joy in beautiful things is a

* *Pall Mall Gazette* XLI : 6224 (21 February 1885) 1–2.

13

grave impertinence to all painters; but Mr. Whistler was relentless, and with charming ease, and much grace of manner, explained to the public that the only thing they should cultivate was ugliness, and that on their permanent stupidity rested all the hopes of art in the future.

The scene was in every way delightful; he stood there, a miniature Mephistopheles mocking the majority! he was like a brilliant surgeon lecturing to a class composed of subjects destined ultimately for dissection, and solemnly assuring them how valuable to science their maladies were, and how absolutely uninteresting the slightest symptoms of health on their part would be. In fairness to the audience, however, I must say that they seemed extremely gratified at being rid of the dreadful responsibility of admiring anything, and nothing could have exceeded their enthusiasm when they were told by Mr. Whistler that no matter how vulgar their dresses were, or how hideous their surroundings at home, still it was possible that a great painter, if there was such a thing, could, by contemplating them in the twilight, and half closing his eyes, see them under really picturesque conditions, and produce a picture which they were not to attempt to understand, much less dare to enjoy. Then there were some arrows, barbed and brilliant, shot off, with all the speed and splendour of fireworks, at the archaeologists, who spend their lives in verifying the birthplaces of nobodies, and estimate the value of a work of art by its date or its decay, at the art critics who always treat a picture as if it were a novel, and try and find out the plot; at dilettanti in general, and amateurs in particular, and (*O mea culpa!*) at dress reformers most of all. "Did not Velásquez paint crinolines? what more do you want?"

Having thus made a holocaust of humanity, Mr. Whistler turned to Nature, and in a few moments convicted her of the Crystal Palace, Bank holidays, and a general overcrowding of detail, both in omnibuses and in landscapes; and then, in a passage of singular beauty, not unlike one that occurs in Carot's [Corot's] letters, spoke of the artistic value of dim dawns and dusks, when the mean facts of life are lost in exquisite and evanescent effects, when common things are touched with mystery and transfigured with beauty; when the warehouses become as palaces, and the tall chimneys of the factory seem like campaniles in the silver air.

Finally, after making a strong protest against anybody but a painter judging of painting, and a pathetic appeal to the audience not to be lured by the aesthetic movement into having beautiful things about them, Mr. Whistler concluded his lecture with a pretty passage about Fusiyama on a fan, and made his bow to an audience which he had succeeded in completely fascinating by his wit, his brilliant paradoxes, and, at times, his real eloquence. Of course, with regard to the value of beautiful surroundings I differ entirely from Mr. Whistler. An artist is not an isolated fact, he is the resultant of a certain millieu [*sic*] and a certain entourage, and can no more be born of a nation that is devoid of any sense of beauty than a fig can grow from a thorn or a rose blossom from a thistle. That an artist will find beauty in ugliness, *le beau dans l'horrible*, is now a commonplace of the schools, the argot of the atelier, but I strongly deny that charming people should be condemned to live with magenta ottomans and Albert blue curtains in their rooms in order that some painter may observe the side lights on the one and the values of the other. Nor do I accept the dictum that only a painter is a judge of painting. I say that only an artist is a judge of art; there is a wide difference. As long as a painter is a painter merely, he should not be allowed to talk of anything but mediums and megilp, and on those subjects should be compelled to hold his tongue; it is only when he becomes an artist that the secret laws of artistic creation are revealed to him. For there are not many arts, but one art merely; poem, picture, and Parthenon, sonnet and statue—all are in their essence the same, and he who knows one, knows all. But the poet is the supreme artist, for he is the master of colour and of form, and the real musician besides, and is lord over all life and all arts; and so to the poet beyond all others are these mysteries known; to Edgar Allan Poe and to Baudelaire, not to Benjamin West and Paul Delaroche. However, I would not enjoy anybody else's lectures unless in a few points I disagreed with them, and Mr. Whistler's lecture last night was, like everything that he does, a masterpiece. Not merely for its clever satire and amusing jests will it be remembered, but for the pure and perfect beauty of many of its passages—passages delivered with an earnestness which seemed to amaze those who had looked on Mr. Whistler as a master of persiflage merely, and had not known him, as we do, as a master of painting also. For that he is indeed one of the very greatest masters of painting, is my opinion. And I may add that in this opinion Mr. Whistler himself entirely concurs.

The Relation of Dress to Art. A Note in Black and White on Mr. Whistler's Lecture*

"How can you possibly paint these ugly three-cornered hats?" asked a reckless art critic once of Sir Joshua Reynolds. "I see light and shade in them," answered the artist. *"Les grands coloristes,"* says Baudelaire, in a charming article on the artistic value of frock coats, *"les grands coloristes savent faire de la couleur avec un habit noir, une cravate blanche, et un fond gris."*

"Art seeks and finds the beautiful in all times, as did her high priest Rembrandt, when he saw the picturesque grandeur of the Jews' quarter of Amsterdam, and lamented not that its inhabitants were not Greeks," were the fine and simple words used by Mr. Whistler in one of the most valuable passages of his lecture. The most valuable, that is, to the painter; for there is nothing of which the ordinary English painter more needs to be reminded than that the true artist does not wait for life to be made picturesque for him, but sees life under picturesque conditions always—under conditions, that is to say, which are at once new and delightful. But between the attitude of a painter towards the public, and the attitude of a people towards art, there is a wide difference. That, under certain conditions

* *Pall Mall Gazette* XLI : 6230 (28 February 1885) 4.

of light and shade, what is ugly in fact may, in its effect, become beautiful, is true; and this, indeed, is the real *modernité* of art; but these conditions are exactly what we cannot be always sure of, as we stroll down Piccadilly in the glaring vulgarity of the noonday, or lounge in the park with a foolish sunset as a background. Were we able to carry our *chiaroscuro* about with us, as we do our umbrellas, all would be well; but, this being impossible, I hardly think that pretty and delightful people will continue to wear a style of dress, as ugly as it is useless, and as meaningless as it is monstrous, even on the chance of such a master as Mr. Whistler is spiritualizing them into a symphony, or refining them into a mist. For the arts are made for life, and not life for the arts.

Nor do I feel quite sure that Mr. Whistler has been himself always true to the dogma he seems to lay down, that a painter should only paint the dress of his age, and of his actual surroundings; far be it from me to burden a butterfly with the heavy responsibility of its past: I have always been of opinion that consistency is the last refuge of the unimaginative: but have we not all seen, and most of us admired, a picture from his hand of exquisite English girls strolling by an opal sea in the fantastic dresses of Japan? Has not Tite-street been thrilled with the tidings that the models of Chelsea were posing to the master, in peplums, for pastels?

Whatever comes from Mr. Whistler's brush is far too perfect in loveliness, to stand, or fall, by any intellectual dogmas on art, even his own: for Beauty is justified by all her children, and cares nothing for explanations; but it is impossible to look through any collection of modern pictures in London, from Burlington House to the Grosvenor Gallery, without feeling that the professional model is ruining painting, and reducing it to a condition of mere pose and *pastiche*.

Are we not all weary of him, that venerable impostor, fresh from the steps of the Piazza di Spagna, who, in the leisure moments that he can spare from his customary organ, makes the round of the studios, and is waited for in Holland Park? Do we not all recognize him, when, with the gay *insouciance* of his nation, he reappears on the walls of our summer exhibitions, as everything that he is not, and as nothing that he is, glaring at us here as a patriarch of Canaan, here beaming as a brigand from the Abruzzi? Popular is he, this poor peripatetic professor of posing, with those whose joy it is to paint the posthumous portrait of the last philanthropist who, in his lifetime, had neglected to be photographed,—yet, he is the sign of the decadence, the symbol of decay.

For all costumes are caricatures. The basis of Art is not the Fancy Ball. Where there is loveliness of dress, there is no dressing up. And so, were our national attire delightful in colour, and in construction simple and sincere; were dress the expression of the loveliness that it shields, and of the swiftness and motion that it does not impede; did its lines break from the shoulder, instead of bulging from the waist; did the inverted wineglass cease to be the ideal of form: were these things brought about, as brought about they will be, then would painting be no longer an artificial reaction against the ugliness of life, but become, as it should be, the natural expression of life's beauty. Nor would painting merely, but all the other arts also, be the gainers by a change such as that which I propose; the gainers, I mean, through the increased atmosphere of Beauty by which the artists would be surrounded, and in which they would grow up. For Art is not to be taught in Academies. It is what one looks at, not what one listens to, that makes the artist. The real schools should be the streets. There is not, for instance, a single delicate line, or delightful proportion in the dress of the Greeks, which is not echoed exquisitely in their architecture. A nation arrayed in stove-pipe hats, and dress improvers, might have built the Pantechnicon, possibly, but the Parthenon, never. And, finally, there is this to be said: art, it is true, can never have any other aim but her own perfection, and, it may be, that the artist, desiring merely to contemplate and to create, is wise in not busying himself about change in others: yet wisdom is not always the best; there are times when she sinks to the level of common sense; and from the passionate folly of those, and there are many, who desire that Beauty shall be confined no longer to the *bric-à-brac* of the collector, and the dust of the museum, but shall be, as it should be, the natural and national inheritance of all,—from this noble unwisdom, I say, who knows what new loveliness shall be given to life, and, under these more exquisite conditions, what perfect artist born? *Le milieu se renouvelant, l'art se renouvelle.*

Speaking however from his own passionless pedestal, Mr. Whistler in pointing out that the power of the painter is to be found in his powers of vision, not in his cleverness of hand, has expressed a truth which needed expression, and which, coming from the lord of form and colour, cannot fail to have its influence. His lecture, the Apocrypha though it be for the people, yet remains from this time as the Bible for the painter, the masterpiece of masterpieces, the song of songs. It is true he has pronounced the panegyric of the Philistine, but I can fancy Ariel praising Caliban for a jest: and, in that he has read the Commination Service over the critics, let all men thank him, the critics themselves indeed most of all, for he has now relieved them from the necessity of a tedious existence. Considered, again, merely as an orator, Mr. Whistler seems to me to stand almost alone. Indeed, among all our public speakers, I know but few who can combine, so felicitously as he does, the mirth and malice of Puck, with the style of the major prophets.

Dinners
and Dishes*

A man can live for three days without bread, but no man can
live for one day without poetry, was an aphorism of Baudelaire's:
you can live without pictures and music, but you can't live without eating, says the author of "Dinners and Dishes:" and this
latter view is no doubt the more popular. Who indeed, in these
degenerate days, would hesitate between an ode and an om-
elette, a sonnet and a salmi? Yet the position is not entirely
Philistine; cookery is an art; are not its principles the subject
of South Kensington lectures, and does not the Royal Academy
give a banquet once a year? Besides, as the coming democracy
will no doubt insist on feeding us all on penny dinners, it is
well that the laws of cookery should be explained; for were
the national meal burned, or badly seasoned, or served up with
the wrong sauce, a dreadful revolution might follow.

Under these circumstances we strongly recommend "Dinners and Dishes" to every one: it is brief, and concise, and
makes no attempts at eloquence, which is extremely fortunate.
For even on ortolans who could endure oratory? It also has
the advantage of not being illustrated. The subject of a work
of art has of course nothing to do with its beauty, but still
there is always something depressing about the coloured litho-
graph of a leg of mutton.

* An unsigned review of "Wanderer" [pseudonym], *Dinners and Dishes*.
Pall Mall Gazette XLI : 6236 (7 March 1885) 5.

As regards the author's particular views, we entirely agree with him on the important question of macaroni. "Never," he says, "ask me to back a bill for a man who has given me a macaroni pudding." Macaroni is essentially a savoury dish, and may be served with cheese, or tomatoes, but never with sugar and milk. There are also, a useful description of how to cook risotto, a delightful dish too rarely seen in England, an excellent chapter on the different kinds of salads, which should be carefully studied by those many hostesses whose imaginations never pass beyond lettuce and beetroot, and actually a recipe for making Brussels sprouts eatable. This last is of course a masterpiece.

The real difficulty, however, that we all have to face in life, is not so much the science of cookery, as the stupidity of cooks. And in this little handbook to practical Epicureanism, the tyrant of the English kitchen is shown in her proper light. Her entire ignorance of herbs, her passion for extracts and essences, her total inability to make a soup which is anything more than a combination of pepper and gravy, her inveterate habit of sending up bread-poultices with pheasants,—all these sins, and many others, are ruthlessly unmasked by the author. Ruthlessly and rightly. For the British cook is a foolish woman, who should be turned, for her iniquities, into a pillar of that salt which she never knows how to use.

But our author is not local merely. He has been in many lands; he has eaten back-hendl at Vienna, and kulibatsch at St. Petersburg; he has had the courage to face the buffalo veal of Roumania, and to dine with a German family at one o'clock; he has serious views on the right method of cooking those famous white truffles of Turin, of which Alexandre Dumas was so fond, and, in the face of the Oriental Club, declares that Bombay curry is better than the curry of Bengal. In fact he seems to have had experience of almost every kind of meal, except the "square meal" of the Americans. This he should study at once; there is a great field for the philosophic epicure in the United States. Boston beans may be dismissed at once as delusions, but soft shell crabs, terrapin, canvas-back ducks, blue fish, and the pompono of New Orleans, are all wonderful delicacies, particularly when one gets them at Delmonico's.

Indeed, the two most remarkable bits of scenery in the States are undoubtedly Delmonico's, and the Yosemité Valley, and the former place has done more to promote a good feeling between England and America than anything else has in this century.

We hope that "Wanderer" will go there soon, and add a chapter to "Dinners and Dishes," and that his book will have in England the influence it deserves. There are twenty ways of cooking a potato, and three hundred and sixty-five ways of cooking an egg, yet the British cook up to the present moment knows only three methods of sending up either one or the other.

[George Saintsbury:] "Half Hours with the Worst Authors"*

A well-known literary man, who signs himself "Oxoniensis," sends us the following energetic protest against certain "atrocities" recently perpetrated upon the English language:

I am very much pleased to see that you are beginning to call attention to the extremely slip-shod and careless style of our ordinary magazine-writers. Will you allow me to refer your readers to an article on Borrow, in the current number of *Macmillan*, which exemplifies very clearly the truth of your remarks? The author of the article is Mr. George Saintsbury, a gentleman who has recently written a book on Prose Style, and here are some specimens of the prose of the future, according to the *système Saintsbury*.

1. "He saw the rise, and, *in some instances, the death of Tennyson*, Thackeray, Macaulay, Carlyle, Dickens."

2. "*See a place* which Kingsley, *or Mr. Ruskin, or* some other master of our decorative school, *have* described—*much more* one which has fallen into the hands of the small fry of their imitators—and you are almost sure to find that *it has been overdone.*"

3. "The great mass of his translations, published and unpublished, and the smaller mass of his early hackwork, no doubt *deserves* judicious excerption."

* *Pall Mall Gazette* XLIII : 6501 (15 January 1886) 4.

4. "The Romany Rye *did not appear* for six years, *that is to say, in* 1857."

5. "The elaborate apparatus which most prose tellers of fantastic tales *use,* and generally *fail in using . . .*"

6. "The great writers, whether they try to be like other people or try not to be like them (*and sometimes in the first place most of all*), succeed *only* in being themselves."

7. "If he had a slight *overdose* of Celtic blood and Celtic peculiarity, it was *more than made up* by the readiness of literary expression which it gave him. He, if any one, bore an English heart, though, *as there often has been,* there was something perhaps more than English as well as less than it in his fashion of expression."

8. "His flashes of ethical reflection, though like *all* ethical reflections *often* one-sided."

9. "He certainly was an *unfriend* to Whiggery."

10. "*That it contains* a great deal of quaint and piquant writing *is only to say* that its writer wrote it."

11. "Wild Wales, too, because of *its* easy and direct *opportunity* of comparing its description with the originals."

12. "The capital *and* full-length portraits."

13. "His attraction is *one* neither mainly nor in any very great degree one of pure form."

14. "*Constantly* right *in general.*"

These are merely a few examples of the style of Mr. Saintsbury, a writer who seems quite ignorant of the commonest laws both of grammar and of literary expression, who has apparently no idea of the difference between the pronouns "this" and "that," and who has as little hesitation in ending the clause of a sentence with a preposition, as he has in inserting a parenthesis between a preposition and its object, a mistake of which the most ordinary school-boy would be ashamed. And why cannot our magazine-writers use plain, simple English? "*Unfriend,*" quoted above, is a quite unnecessary archaism, and so is such a phrase as "*with this Borrow could not away,*" in the sense of "this Borrow could not endure." "Borrow's *abstraction* from general society" may, I suppose, pass muster, Pope talks somewhere of a hermit's "abstraction," but what is the meaning of saying that the author of Lavengro "*quartered* Castile and Leon in the most interesting manner, riding everywhere with his servant"? And what defence can be made for such an expression as "Scott and other *black beasts* of Borrow's"? Black beast for *bête noire* is really abominable.

The object of my letter, however, is not to point out the deficiencies of Mr. Saintsbury's style, but to express my surprise that his article should have been admitted into the pages of a magazine like *Macmillan's*. Surely it does not require much experience to know that such an article as this is a disgrace to even magazine literature.

To Read, or Not To Read*

As we have published so many letters advising what to read, the following advice "what not to read" from so good an authority as Mr. Oscar Wilde may be of service:—

Books, I fancy, may be conveniently divided into three classes:—

1. Books to read, such as Cicero's Letters, Suetonius, Vasari's Lives of the Painters, the Autobiography of Benvenuto Cellini, Sir John Mandeville, Marco Polo, St. Simon's Memoirs, Mommsen, and (till we get a better one) Grote's History of Greece.

2. Books to re-read, such as Plato and Keats. In the sphere of poetry, the masters not the minstrels, in the sphere of philosophy, the seers not the *savants*.

3. Books not to read at all, such as Thomson's Seasons, Rogers' Italy, Paley's Evidences, all the Fathers, except St. Augustine, all John Stuart Mill, except the essay on Liberty, all Voltaire's plays without any exception, Butler's Analogy, Grant's Aristotle, Hume's England, Lewes' History of Philosophy, all argumentative books, and all books that try to prove anything. This third class is by far the most important. To tell people what to read is as a rule either useless or harmful, for the true appreciation of literature is a question of temperament not of teaching, to Parnassus there is no primer, and nothing that one

* *Pall Mall Gazette* XLIII : 6521 (8 February 1886) 11.

can learn is ever worth learning. But to tell people what not to read is a very different matter, and I venture to recommend it as a mission to the University Extension Scheme. Indeed, it is one that is eminently needed in this age of ours, an age which reads so much that it has no time to admire, and writes so much that it has no time to think. Whoever will select out of the chaos of our modern curricula "The Worst Hundred Books," and publish a list of them, will confer on the rising generation a real and lasting benefit.

After expressing these views I suppose that I should not offer any suggestions at all with regard to "The Best Hundred Books," but I hope that you will allow me the pleasure of being inconsistent, as I am anxious to put in a claim for a book that has been strangely omitted by most of the excellent judges who have contributed to your columns. I mean the Greek Anthology. The beautiful poems contained in this collection seem to me to hold the same position with regard to Greek Dramatic Literature, as do the delicate little figurines of Tanagra to the Pheidian marbles, and to be quite as necessary for the complete understanding of the Greek Spirit.

I am also amazed to find that Edgar Allan Poe has been passed over. Surely this marvellous lord of rhythmic expression deserves a place? If in order to make room for him, it be necessary to elbow out some one else, I should elbow out Southey, and I think that Baudelaire might be most advantageously substituted for Keble. No doubt, both in The Curse of Kehama and in the Christian Year there are poetical qualities of a certain kind, but absolute catholicity of taste is not without its dangers. It is only an auctioneer who should admire all schools of art.

Balzac in English*

Many years ago, in a number of *All the Year Round*, Charles Dickens complained that Balzac was very little read in England, and although since then the public have become more familiar with the great master-pieces of French fiction, still it may be doubted whether the "Comédie Humaine" is at all appreciated or understood by the general run of novel-readers. It is really the greatest monument that literature has produced in our century, and M. Taine hardly exaggerates when he says that, after Shakespeare, Balzac is our most important magazine of documents on human nature. Balzac's aim, in fact, was to do for humanity what Buffon had done for the animal creation. As the naturalist studied lions and tigers, so the novelist studied men and women. Yet he was no mere reporter. Photography and *proces-verbal* were not the essentials of his method. Observation gave him the facts of life, but his genius converted facts into truths, and truths into truth. He was, in a word, a marvellous combination of the artistic temperament with the scientific spirit. The latter he bequeathed to his disciples; the former was entirely his own. The distinction between such a book as M. Zola's "L'Assommoir" and such a book as Balzac's "Illusions Perdues" is the distinction between

* Unsigned review of Honoré de Balzac, *The Duchesse de Langeais, and Other Stories: César Birotteau* (Balzac's Novels in English), 2 vols. *Pall Mall Gazette* XLIV : 6706 (13 September 1886) 5.

unimaginative realism and imaginative reality. "All Balzac's characters," said Baudelaire, "are gifted with the same ardour of life that animated himself. All his fictions are as deeply coloured as dreams. Every mind is a weapon loaded to the muzzle with will. The very scullions have genius." He was of course accused of being immoral. Few writers who deal directly with life escape that charge. His answer to the accusation was characteristic and conclusive. "Whoever contributes his stone to the edifice of ideas," he wrote, "whoever proclaims an abuse, whoever sets his mark upon an evil to be abolished, always passes for immoral. If you are true in your portraits, if, by dint of daily and nightly toil, you succeed in writing the most difficult language in the world, the word immoral is thrown in your face." The morals of the personages of the "Comédie Humaine" are simply the morals of the world around us. They are part of the artist's subject-matter, they are not part of his method. If there be any need of censure it is to life not to literature that it should be given. Balzac, besides, is essentially universal. He sees life from every point of view. He has no preferences and no prejudices. He does not try to prove anything. He feels that the spectacle of life contains its own secret. "Il crée un monde et se tait."

And what a world it is! What a panorama of passions! What a pell-mell of men and women! It was said of Trollope that he increased the number of our acquaintances without adding to our visiting lists; but after reading the "Comédie Humaine" one begins to believe that the only real people are the people who have never existed. Lucien de Rubempré, le Père Goriot, Ursule Mirouët, Marguerite Claës, the Baron Hulot, Mdme. Marneffe, le Cousin Pons, De Marsay—all bring with them a kind of contagious illusion of life. They have a fierce vitality about them: their existence is fervent and fiery-coloured: we not merely feel for them, but we see them—they dominate our fancy and defy scepticism. A steady course of Balzac reduces our living friends to shadows, and our acquaintances to the shadows of shades. Who would care to go out to an evening party to meet Tomkins, the friend of one's boyhood, when one can sit at home with Lucien de Rubempré? It is pleasanter to have the entrée to Balzac's society than to receive cards from all the duchesses in Mayfair.

In spite of this there are many people who have declared the "Comédie Humaine" to be indigestible. Perhaps it is, but then what about truffles? Balzac's publisher refused to be disturbed by any such criticism as that. "Indigestible, is it?" he exclaimed, with what, for a publisher, was rare good sense. "Well, I should hope so; who ever thinks of a dinner that isn't?" And our English publisher Mr. Routledge clearly agrees with M. Poulet-Malassis, as he is occupied in producing a complete translation of the "Comédie Humaine." The two volumes that at present lie before us contain "César Birotteau," that terrible tragedy of finance, "L'Illustre Gaudissart," the apotheosis of the commercial traveller, the "Duchesse de Langeais," most marvellous of modern love stories, "Le Chef-d'oeuvre Inconnu," from which Mr. Henry James took his "Madonna of the Future," and that extraordinary romance "Une Passion dans le Désert." The choice of stories is quite excellent, but the translations are very unequal, and some of them are positively bad. "L'Illustre Gaudissart," for instance, is full of the most grotesque mistakes, mistakes that would disgrace a schoolboy. "Bon conseil vaut un oeil dans la main," is translated, "Good advice is an egg in the hand!" "Ecus rebelles" is rendered "rebellious lucre," and such common expressions as "faire la barbe," "attendre la vente," "n'entendre rien," "pâlir sur une affaire," are all mistranslated. "Des bois de quoi se faire un cure-dent" is not "a few trees to slice into toothpicks," but "as much timber as would make a toothpick;" "son horloge enfermée dans une grande armoire oblongue," is not "a clock which he kept shut up in a large oblong closet," but simply a clock in a tall clock case; "journal viager" is not "an annuity," "garce" is not the same as "farce," and "dessins des Indes" are not "drawings of the Indies." On the whole, nothing can be worse than this translation, and if Mr. Routledge wishes the public to read his version of the "Comédie Humaine" he should engage translators who have some slight knowledge of French. "César Birotteau" is better, though it is not by any means free from mistakes. "To suffer under the maximum" is an absurd rendering of "subir le maximum;"

31

"perse" is "chintz," not "Persian chintz;" "rendre le pain bénit" is not to "take the wafer;" "rivière" is hardly a "*fillet of diamonds;*" and to translate, "Son coeur avait un calus à l'endroit du loyer," by "His heart was a callus in the direction of a lease," is an insult to two languages. On the whole the best version is that of the "Duchesse de Langeais," though even this leaves much to be desired. Such a sentence as "to imitate the rough logician who marched before the Pyrrhonians *while denying his own movement*" entirely misses the point of Balzac's "imiter le rude logician qui marchait devant les pyrrhoniens, qui niaient le mouvement." We fear that Mr. Routledge's edition will not do. It is well printed, and nicely bound; but his translators do not understand French. It is a great pity, for "La Comédie Humaine" is one of the masterpieces of the age.

Ben Jonson[*]

In selecting Mr. John Addington Symonds to write the life of
Ben Jonson for his series of "English Worthies," Mr. Lang
no doubt exercised a wise judgment. Mr. Symonds, like the
author of "Volpone," is a scholar and a man of letters: his book
on "Shakespeare's Predecessors" showed a marvellous knowledge of the Elizabethan period, and he is a recognized authority on the Italian Renaissance. The last is not the least of
his qualifications. Without a full appreciation of the meaning
of the Humanistic movement it is impossible to understand
the great struggle between the Classical form and the Romantic
spirit which is the chief critical characteristic of the golden age
of the English drama, an age when Shakspeare found his chief
adversary, not among his contemporaries, but in Seneca, and
when Jonson armed himself with Aristotle to win the suffrages
of a London audience. Mr. Symonds's book consequently will
be opened with interest. It does not, of course, contain much
that is new about Jonson's life. But the facts of Jonson's life are
already well known, and in books of this kind what is true is of
more importance than what is new, appreciation more valuable
than discovery. Scotchmen, however, will no doubt be interested to find that Mr. Symonds has succeeded in identifying

* Unsigned review of John Addington Symonds, *Ben Jonson* in the series
English Worthies, ed. Andrew Lang. *Pall Mall Gazette* XLIV : 6712 (20
September 1886) 6.

The Artist as Critic

Jonson's crest with that of the Johnstones of Annandale, and the story of the way the literary Titan escaped from hanging, by proving that he could read, is graphically told. On the whole, we have a vivid picture of the man as he lived. Where picturesqueness is required, Mr. Symonds is always good. The usual comparison with Dr. Johnson is of course brought out. Few of "Rare Ben's" biographers spare us that, and the point is possibly a natural one to make. But when Mr. Symonds calls upon us to notice that both men made a journey to Scotland, and that each found in a Scotchman his biographer, the parallel loses all value. There is an M in Monmouth and an M in Macedon, and Drummond of Hawthornden and Boswell of Auchinleck were both born the other side of the Tweed, but from such analogies nothing is to be learned. There is no surer way of destroying a similarity than to strain it.

As for Mr. Symonds's estimate of Jonson's genius, it is in many points quite excellent. He ranks him with the giants rather than with the gods, with those who compel our admiration by their untiring energy and huge strength of intellectual muscle, not with those "who share the divine gifts of creative imagination and inevitable instinct." Here he is right. Pelion more than Parnassus was Jonson's home. His art has too much effort about it, too much definite intention. His style lacks the charm of chance. Mr. Symonds is right also in the stress he lays on the extraordinary combination in Jonson's work of the most concentrated realism with encyclopaedic erudition. In Jonson's comedies London slang and learned scholarship go hand in hand. Literature was as living a thing to him as life itself. He used his classical lore not merely to give form to his verse, but to give flesh and blood to the persons of his plays. He could build up a breathing creature out of quotations. He made the poets of Greece and Rome terribly modern, and introduced them to the oddest company. His very culture is an element in his coarseness. There are moments when one is tempted to liken him to a beast that has fed off books. We cannot, however, agree with Mr. Symonds when he says that Jonson "rarely touched more than the outside of character," that his men and women are "the incarnations of abstract properties rather than living human beings," that they are in fact

34

mere "masqueraders and mechanical puppets." Eloquence is a beautiful thing, but rhetoric ruins many a critic; and Mr. Symonds is essentially rhetorical. When, for instance, he tells us that "Jonson made masks, while Dekker and Heywood created souls," we feel that he is asking us to accept a crude judgment for the sake of a smart antithesis. It is of course true that we do not find in Jonson the same growth of character that we find in Shakspeare,[1] and we may admit that most of the characters in Jonson's plays are, so to speak, ready-made. But a ready-made character is not necessarily either mechanical or wooden, two epithets Mr. Symonds uses constantly in his criticism.

We cannot tell, and Shakespeare himself does not tell us, why Iago is evil, why Regan and Goneril have hard hearts, or why Sir Andrew Aguecheek is a fool. It is sufficient that they are what they are, and that nature gives warrant for their existence. If a character in a play is life-like, if we recognize it as true to nature, we have no right to insist on the author explaining its genesis to us. We must accept it as it is; and in the hands of a good dramatist mere presentation can take the place of analysis, and indeed is often a more dramatic method, because a more direct. And Jonson's characters are true to nature. They are in no sense abstractions; they are types. Captain Bobadil and Captain Tucca, Sir John Daw and Sir Amorous La Foole, Volpone and Mosca, Subtle and Sir Epicure Mammon, Mrs. Purecraft and the Rabbi Busy are all creatures of flesh and blood, none the less life-like because they are labelled. In this point Mr. Symonds seems to us unjust towards Jonson.

We think also that a special chapter might have been devoted to Jonson as a literary critic. The creative activity of the English Renaissance is so great that its achievements in the sphere of criticism are often overlooked by the student. Then for the first time was language treated as an art. The laws of expression and composition were investigated and formulated. The importance of words was recognized. Romanticism, Realism, and Classicism fought their first battles. The dramatists are full of literary and art criticisms, and amused the public

---

[1] Wilde's (or the printer's) spelling of this name varies.—Ed.

with slashing articles on one another in the form of plays. Mr. Symonds, of course, deals with Jonson in his capacity as a critic, and always with just appreciation, but the whole subject is one that deserves fuller and more special treatment. Some small inaccuracies, too, should be corrected in the second edition. Dryden, for instance, was not "Jonson's successor on the Laureate's throne," as Mr. Symonds eloquently puts it, for Sir William Davenant came between them, and when one remembers the predominance of rhyme in Shakespeare's early plays it is too much to say that "after the production of the first part of 'Tamburlaine' blank verse became the regular dramatic metre of the public stage." Shakespeare did not accept blank verse at once as a gift from Marlowe's hand, but himself arrived at it after a long course of experiments in rhyme. Indeed, some of Mr. Symonds's remarks on Marlowe are very curious. To say of his "Edward II," for instance, that "it is not at all inferior to the work of Shakspere's younger age," is very niggardly and inadequate praise, and comes strangely from one who has elsewhere written with such appreciation of Marlowe's great genius; while to call Marlowe Jonson's "master" is to make for him an impossible claim. In comedy Marlowe had nothing whatsoever to teach Jonson, in tragedy Jonson sought for the classical not the romantic form.

As for Mr. Symonds's style, it is, as usual, very fluent, very picturesque, and very full of colour. Here and there, however, it is really irritating. Such a sentence as "the tavern had the defects of its quality" is an awkward Gallicism; and when Mr. Symonds, after genially comparing Jonson's blank verse to the front of Whitehall, a comparison, by the way, that would have enraged the poet beyond measure, proceeds to play a fantastic aria on the same string, and tells us that "Massinger reminds us of the intricacies of Sansovino, Shakspere of Gothic aisles or heaven's cathedral, Ford of glittering Corinthian colonnades, Marlowe of masoned clouds, Webster of vaulted crypts, and Marston, in his better moments, of the fragmentary vigour of a Roman ruin," one begins to regret that any one ever thought of the unity of the arts. Similes such as these obscure, they do not illumine. To say that Ford is like a glittering Corinthian colonnade adds nothing to our knowledge of either Ford or

Greek architecture. Mr. Symonds has written some charming poetry, but his prose, unfortunately, is always poetical prose, never the prose of a poet. Still the volume is worth reading, though decidedly Mr. Symonds, to use one of his own phrases, has "the defects of his quality."

Two Biographies of Sir Philip Sidney*

In an article on Sir Philip Sidney in the *Contemporary Review* of last month Mr. Gosse told us of the pleasure with which he looked forward to a monograph on the same subject from the "genial and learned pen of Mr. J. A. Symonds." This monograph has now appeared in Mr. Morley's "English Men of Letters Series," and "learned" Mr. Symonds certainly shows himself to be, though "genial" seems to us hardly a felicitous term by which to describe his style. Still Mr. Gosse was more than justified in making use of this expression as it had been previously applied to himself by no less a person than Mr. Symonds, and in matters of this kind reciprocity is everything. It now only remains for Mr. Symonds to speak of the "learned" Mr. Gosse and the balance sheet will be fully made up.

In the account they give of Sidney there are many points of similarity between these two last biographers of the great Elizabethan hero. They both agree in rejecting Ben Jonson's description of him as "no pleasant man in countenance, his face being spoiled with pimples, and of high blood, and long," Mr. Gosse talking of his "girlish face of pink and white," and Mr. Symonds dwelling at length upon his beauty. They both protest against Shelley's fine panegyric,—

---

* Unsigned review of J. A. Symonds, *Sir Philip Sidney* (English Men of Letters Series), ed. John Morley, and Edmund Gosse, "Sir Philip Sidney," in *Contemporary Review* (November 1886). *Pall Mall Gazette* XLIV : 6783 (11 December 1886) 5.

Two Biographies of Sir Philip Sidney

Sidney as he fought,
And as he fell, and as he lived and loved,
Sublimely mild, a spirit without spot,—

Mr. Symonds suggesting that Astrophel was far from spotless in his relations to Stella, while Mr. Gosse, after telling us that the lines border upon "the namby-pamby," says very frankly, "I do not like 'sublimely mild,' " which of course settles the question, and goes on to warn us that we must drop this epithet "even in the *peculiar sense* in which Shelley may have used it as equivalent to *benignantly unperturbed*," a paraphrase which is at once luminous and pleasing. They both also concur in regarding Sidney as one whose renown transcends his actual achievement. Mr. Symonds however has this advantage over Mr. Gosse that he knows a good deal about the subject on which he is writing. He knows for instance that Sidney was of illustrious ancestry, notably by his mother's side, while Mr. Gosse remarks that he was "without the leverage of . . . rank." He knows that Sidney was an earnest and ardent politician, and one of the most remarkable statesmen of his day; that he foresaw the terrible consequences to the cause of liberty and civilization that would result from the conjunction of the material forces of Spain with the spiritual tyranny of Rome; and that, while championing the *Foedus Evangelicum* of the Teutonic races, he still recognized clearly that it was only through its colonies that the Spanish empire was really vulnerable, and that it was in the New World that the problems of the Old World were to find their solution. He knows that Sidney was fully conscious of the necessity of England maintaining her supremacy by means of her navy, and worked stoutly for that end; that from his seat in the House of Commons he rendered valuable assistance to Raleigh on the subject of the Virginia plantation; and that, in words which as we read them now seem almost instinct with the spirit of prophecy, he may be said to have traced the future of America, appealing to England to make of it, "not an asylum for fugitives, a *velum piraticum* for banditti, or any such base *ramas* of people, but an emporium for the confluence of all nations that love or profess any kind of virtue or commerce." Mr. Gosse, however, calmly informs us that *"it does not seem that he took any interest in politics,"* which is really the most astounding statement ever made about Sidney by any writer. Mr. Symonds also is never guilty of "the detestable vice of simulating familiarity" with authors whom he has not read, and works with which he is unacquainted. He has carefully studied Fulke Greville's personal recollections of Sidney, and quotes from them at length, while Mr. Gosse (who by the way always writes of *Fulk* Greville), has studied them with so little care that he entirely spoils the whole point of Lord Brooke's charming story about Don John of Austria by representing Sidney as being at the time the English Ambassador to the Spanish Viceroy, and shows elsewhere that his reading of the book has been of the most casual and cursory character. Mr. Symonds is a high authority on all Elizabethan literature, but who can recognize that English Aretine and reckless satirist, Thomas Nash, in Mr. Gosse's description of him as "a severe moralist," and who that has ever read Mathew Roydon's Elegy on Sidney can feel anything but amused contempt for Mr. Gosse's gross misrepresentation of the poem in question? And finally Mr. Symonds is quite aware of the reasons which led Spenser to celebrate Sidney in a pastoral elegy, and fully understands the significance of that form in literature, a subject which we fear Mr. Gosse has not sufficiently studied as he severely censures Spenser's verses on the ground that they "falsify history," Sidney never at any time of his life having been a merry shepherd, and concludes a most inaccurate and careless account of the poem by exclaiming "what could be more deplorably *Byzantine* in taste?" —an epithet which the Clark Professor of English Literature evidently imagines is equivalent to Alexandrian!

On the whole then we prefer Mr. Symonds' monograph to Mr. Gosse's article, though it is not by any means perfect, being both diffuse and incomplete. Within a volume of two hundred pages a full account of Sidney's life and work could be easily included, but so fatally facile and fluent is Mr. Symonds' pen that he often forgets the conditions under which he is working, and in his desire to emphasize the picturesqueness of the background omits many of the details of his central figure. A really great artist can always transform the limitations of his art into valuable qualities, but Mr. Symonds has not gained either condensation or directness of style from the limits imposed on him, and we would gladly surrender many of his pretty descriptions of Elizabethan society for the letter Sidney wrote to his brother on the study of history, or for more of the correspondence of Hubert Languet with his young friend, or for something like an adequate account of Sidney's attitude towards the Drama. Mr. Gosse gravely tells us that Sidney was elected by popular acclaim to point the way for "Marlowe and Shakespeare," but in all Sidney's philosophy of art there is nothing more interesting psychologically than his absolute unconsciousness of the possibilities of the Romantic form. He upheld the pseudo-classical school with brilliant eloquence and caustic wit, insisted on the unities, thought Seneca the model tragedian, objected to the blending of comedy with tragedy, and to kings and rustics figuring together, preferred narration to presentation and description to action, and sought to banish from the stage the marvel of Life itself, with all its vivid contrasts, its play of passion, and the fine freedom of its movement. Fortunately for our literature the romantic method of Marlowe and Shakespeare triumphed, and in spite of the Defence of Poesy and the school that it represented the true Elizabethan Drama was born. All this side of Sidney's aesthetic, however, so fertile in suggestion and so historically valuable, is dismissed by Mr. Symonds in less than a page, and we cannot think that in so doing he has shown any real sense of artistic proportion. Some clerical errors also should be corrected in a second edition, such as the misprint of "genius" for "genus" on page 160, the misquotation from Shelley on page 122, and the description of the Shakespearian sonnet as consisting of "*four* separate quatrains clinched with a final couplet;" nor can we agree with Mr. Symonds when he suggests, as he seems to do on page 90, that it is "humour" and "solid human realism" that confer immortality on a work of art, for it is not by qualities such as these that Milton still lives, or that Shelley has his place among the great poets.

In many respects, however, Mr. Symonds' book is a most useful contribution to modern literature. A good popular life of Sir Philip Sidney has long been wanted, and to a certain degree

Mr. Symonds supplies the deficiency. His style, though often open to criticism, is at least free from pretentiousness and affectation; he writes, as a rule, with the ease of a man of letters, and he always pleases even where he may fail to convince. And what a subject Sidney is to write on! England, as Mr. Symonds himself points out, had the good fortune to receive the Reformation and the Renaissance at the same epoch, and Sidney may be said to have summed up in himself all that in each movement was finest and most noble, taking from the one a certain gravity of mind and lofty independence of thought, and from the other culture, chivalry, statesmanship, and urbanity. Graceful writer though he was of sonnet and lyric, master of delicate and refined prose, yet "his end," as Fulke Greville tells us, "was not writing, even while he wrote." The whole tenor of his career shows his determination "to subordinate self-culture to useful public action," and the most perfect of all his poems was his own life. Three centuries have passed since he died at Arnheim, yet we can still feel the fascination of his gracious personality, and catch something of the charm that made all men love him. New ideals may have come before our eyes, and life has perhaps been made more complex and more difficult for us than it was for him, but it is well to keep him in our memory, the courtly Elizabethan hero, the writer of the sonnets to Stella, the Christian gentleman who gave the cup of water to the wounded soldier at Zutphen.

The Poets
and the People[*]

By One of the Latter

Never was there a time in our national history when there was
more need than there is now for the creation of a spirit of enthusiasm among all classes of society, inspiring men and women
with that social zeal and the spirit of self-sacrifice which alone
can save a great people in the throes of national misfortune.
Tirades of pessimism require but little intellectual effort, and
the world is not much the better for them; but to inspire a people with hope and courage, to fill them with a desire after righteousness and duty, this is work that requires the combination of
intelligence and feeling of the highest order. Who, in the midst
of all our poverty and distress, that threatens to become intensified, will step into the breach and rouse us to the almost super-
human effort that is necessary to alter the existing state of
things?

There is one class of men to whom we have a right to look
for assistance, to whom the task of stirring the national conscience should be accepted with delight. When the poor are
suffering from inherent faults of their own, and the greediness
of capitalists, and both are in danger of suffering still more from
causes over which they have but partial control, surely the hour

[*] Unsigned article. *Pall Mall Gazette* XLV : 6840 (17 February 1887) 4.

43

has come when the poets should exercise their influence for good, and set fairer ideals before all than the mere love of wealth and ostentatious display on one side and the desire to appropriate wealth on the other. But we listen in vain for any inspiring ode or ballad that shall reach the hearts of the people or touch the consciences of capitalists. What do those who are designated in the columns of our newspapers as great poets bring to us in this hour of national trial, when we are so much in need of the service of a truly great poet? One[1] gives us a string of melancholy pessimism that has achieved no higher results than increasing the poet's fortune and drawing a magazine article from Mr. Gladstone. Another[2] who has hitherto posed as the poet of freedom, and even licence—some would say licentiousness—when he does turn his attention to practical affairs does his best to abuse and dishearten a nation that is heroically struggling against the injustice of centuries and panting for national freedom. These things are bad enough, but what shall be said of the conduct of one who in the eyes of many is esteemed the greatest of living poets? He, at the hour when his country requires inspiration and encouragement, prostitutes his intelligence to the production of a number of unwieldy lines that to the vast majority of Englishmen are unintelligible jargon. What right has a man to the title of poet when he fails to produce music in his lines, who cannot express his thoughts in simple language that the people can understand; but, on the contrary, has so imperfect a command of his mother tongue that all the efforts of a society of intellectual pickaxes cannot discover what his words really mean? Above all, what right has a man to the title of poet who has so little sense of his duty to his fellow men as to indulge in composition of word puzzles and ear-torturing sentences when a whole people needs the assistance of every man and woman who is capable of thinking and acting? The Roman despot who played the fiddle while his city was burning might plead the ignorance of himself and his time, but Mr. Browning is living in the nineteenth century, and has no such excuses for banging his intellectual tin kettle

---

[1] Tennyson.—Ed.
[2] Swinburne.—Ed.

while a fourth part of his fellow-countrymen are struggling against poverty, and are weighed down by the gloomy outlook towards the future. We are assured by his admirers that he is a great thinker—yes, more, a philosopher as well as a poet. Now, England was never in greater need of such a man, and it is Mr. Browning's duty, if he has the ability, to write plain English and act the poet's true part. Let any sensible man outside the Browning Society dip into the mysterious volume of literary hocus-pocus that has recently been so solemnly reviewed, and see whether he can find a single passage likely to stir the pulses of any man or woman, create a desire to lead a higher, a holier, and a more useful life in the breast of the indifferent average citizen. The struggle to live in all parts of Western Europe, and perhaps especially England, is so fierce that we are in danger of having all that is idealistic and beautiful crushed out of us by the steam engine and the manipulations of the Stock Exchanges. We were never in greater need of good poets, and never better able than in this practical age to do without literary medicine men and mystery mongers. Is it possible that Mr. Browning can see nothing in the world around him to induce him to make an earnest endeavour to help the people out of their difficulties and to make their duty plain? He may be a man of genius so sublime that the language of the common people is inadequate to clothe his thoughts, but his right to the title of poet is not so clear as that of the humblest writer of doggerel lines in the poets' corner of a provincial newspaper, who is aiming in his own honest way to set his followers straight. The people are suffering, and are likely to suffer more; where is the poet who is the one man needful to rouse the nation to a sense of duty and inspire the people with hope?

A New Book
on Dickens*

Mr. Marzials' "Dickens" is a great improvement on the "Long-fellow" and "Coleridge" of his predecessors. It is certainly a little sad to find our old friend the manager of the Theatre Royal, Portsmouth, appearing as "Mr. Vincent Crumules" (*sic*), but such misprints are not by any means uncommon in Mr. Walter Scott's publications, and on the whole this is a very pleasant book indeed. It is brightly and cleverly written, admir-ably constructed, and gives a most vivid and graphic picture of that strange modern drama, the drama of Dicken's life. The earlier chapters are quite excellent, and though the story of the famous novelist's boyhood has been often told before, Mr. Marzials shows that it can be told once again without losing any of the charm of its interest, while the account of Dickens in the plenitude of his glory is most appreciative and genial. We are really brought close to the man, with his indomitable energy, his extraordinary capacity for work, his high spirits, his fascinating, tyrannous personality. The description of his method of reading is admirable, and the amazing stump-cam-paign in America attains, in Mr. Marzials' hands, to the dignity of a mock-heroic poem. One side of Dickens' character, how-ever, is left almost entirely untouched, and yet it is one in every

* Unsigned review of Frank T. Marzials, *Life of Charles Dickens* (Great Writers Series). *Pall Mall Gazette* XLV : 6876 (31 March 1887) 5.

way deserving of close study. That Dickens should have felt bitterly towards his father and mother is quite explicable, but that, while feeling so bitterly, he should have caricatured them for the amusement of the public, with an evident delight in his own humour, has always seemed to us a most curious psychological problem. We are far from complaining that he did so. Good novelists are much rarer than good sons, and none of us would part readily with Micawber and Mrs. Nickleby. Still the fact remains that a man who was affectionate and loving to his children, generous and warm-hearted to his friends, and whose books are the very bacchanalia of benevolence, pilloried his parents to make the groundlings laugh, and this fact every biographer of Dickens should face, and if possible explain.

As for Mr. Marzials' critical estimate of Dickens as a writer, he tells us quite frankly that he believes that Dickens at his best was "one of the greatest masters of pathos who ever lived," a remark that seems to us an excellent example of what novelists call "the fine courage of despair." Of course no biographer of Dickens could say anything else just at present. A popular series is bound to express popular views, and cheap criticism may be excused in cheap books. Besides, it is always open to every one to accept G. H. Lewes' unfortunate maxim that any author who makes one cry possesses the gift of pathos, and indeed there is something very flattering in being told that one's own emotions are the ultimate test of literature. When Mr. Marzials discusses Dickens' power of drawing human nature we are upon somewhat safer ground, and we cannot but admire the cleverness with which he passes over his hero's innumerable failures. For in some respects Dickens might be likened to those old sculptors of our Gothic cathedrals who could give form to the most fantastic fancy, and crowd with grotesque monsters a curious world of dreams, but who saw little of the grace and dignity and beauty of the men and women among whom they lived, and whose art lacking sanity was therefore incomplete. Yet they at least knew the limitations of their art, while Dickens never knew the limitations of his. When he tries to be serious, he only succeeds in being dull, when he aims at truth, he merely reaches platitude. Shakespeare could place Ferdinand and Miranda by the side of Caliban, and Life recognizes them all as her own, but Dickens' Mirandas are the young ladies out of a fashion-book, and his Ferdinands the walking-gentlemen of an unsuccessful company of third-rate players. So little sanity indeed had Dickens' art, that he was never able even to satirize, he could only caricature; and so little does Mr. Marzials realize where Dickens' true strength and weakness lie, that he actually complains that Cruikshank's illustrations are too exaggerated, and that he could never draw either a lady or a gentleman. The latter was hardly a disqualification for illustrating Dickens as few such characters occur in his books, unless we are to regard Lord Frederick Verisopht and Sir Mulberry Hawk as valuable studies of high life, and for our own part we have always considered that the greatest injustice ever done to Dickens has been done by those who have tried to illustrate him seriously. In conclusion Mr. Marzials expresses his belief that a century hence Dickens will be read as much as we now read Scott, and says rather prettily that as long as he is read "there will be one gentle and humanizing influence the more at work among men," which is always a useful tag to append to the life of any popular author. Remembering that of all forms of error prophecy is the most gratuitous, we will not take upon ourselves to decide the question of Dickens' immortality. If our descendants do not read him they will miss a great source of amusement, and if they do, we hope they will not model their style upon his. Of this however there is but little danger, for no age ever borrows the slang of its predecessor. As for "the gentle and humanizing influence," this is taking Dickens just a little too seriously.

A Cheap Edition
of a Great Man
[Rossetti]*

Formerly we used to canonize our great men, now-a-days we
vulgarize them. The vulgarization of Rossetti has been going
on for some time past with really remarkable success, and there
seems no probability at present of the process being discon-
tinued. The grass was hardly green upon the quiet grave in
Birchington churchyard when Mr. Hall Caine and Mr. William Sharp rushed into print with their Memoirs and recollections, then came the usual mob of magazine hacks with their
various views and attitudes, and now Mr. Joseph Knight has
produced for the edification of the British public a popular biography of the poet of the Blessed Damozel, the painter of
Dante's Dream. It is only fair to state that Mr. Knight's work
is much better than that of his predecessors in the same field.
His book is, on the whole, modestly and simply written; whatever its other faults may be, it is at least free from affectation
of any kind; and it makes no serious pretence at being either
exhaustive or definitive. Yet the best that we can say of it is that
it is just the sort of biography Guildenstern might have written
of Hamlet. Nor does its unsatisfactory character come merely
from the ludicrous inadequacy of the materials at Mr. Knight's
disposal, it is the whole scheme and method of the book that is

* Unsigned review of Joseph Knight, Life of *Dante Gabriel Rossetti*
(Great Writers Series). *Pall Mall Gazette* XLV : 6890 (18 April 1887)
5.

radically wrong. Rossetti's was a giant personality, and personalities such as his do not easily survive shilling primers. Sooner or later they have inevitably to come down to the level of their biographers, and in the present instance nothing could be more absolutely commonplace than the picture Mr. Knight gives us of the wonderful seer and singer whose life he has so recklessly essayed to write. No doubt there are many people who will be deeply interested to know that Rossetti was once chased round his garden by an infuriated zebu he was trying to exhibit to Mr. Whistler, or that he had a great affection for a dog called "Dizzy," or that "sloshy" was one of his favourite words of contempt, or that Mr. Gosse thought him very like Chaucer in appearance, or that he had "an absolute disqualification" for whist-playing, or that he was very fond of quoting the Bab Ballads, or that he once said that if he could live by writing poetry he would see painting d——d! For our own part, however, we cannot help expressing our regret that such a shallow and superficial biography as this should ever have been published. It is but a sorry task to rip the twisted ravel from the worn garment of a life, and to turn the grout in a drained cup. Better after all that we only knew a painter through his vision and a poet through his song, than that the image of a great man should be marred and made mean for us by the clumsy geniality of good intentions. A true artist, and such Rossetti undoubtedly was, reveals himself so perfectly in his work, that unless a biographer has something more valuable to give us than idle anecdotes and unmeaning tales, his labour is misspent and his industry misdirected.

Bad however as is Mr. Knight's treatment of Rossetti's life, his treatment of Rossetti's poetry is infinitely worse. Considering the small size of the volume, and the consequently limited number of extracts, the amount of misquotations is almost incredible, and puts all recent achievements in this sphere of modern literature completely into the shade. The fine line in the first canto of Rose Mary—

> What glints there like a lance that flees?

appears as

> What glints there *like a glance that flees?*

which is very painful nonsense; in the description of that graceful and fanciful sonnet "Autumn Idleness," the deer are represented as "*grazing* from hillock eaves," instead of gazing from hillock-eaves; the opening of "Dantis Tenebrae" is rendered quite incomprehensible by the substitution of "my" for "thy" in the second line; even such a well-known ballad as Sister Helen is misquoted, and indeed from the Burden of Nineveh, the Blessed Damozel, the King's Tragedy, and Guido Cavalcanti's lovely *ballata*, down to the Portrait and such sonnets as Love-Sweetness, Farewell to the Glen, and A Match with the Moon, there is not one single poem that does not display some careless error or some stupid misprint. As for Rossetti's elaborate system of punctuation, Mr. Knight pays no attention to it whatsoever. Indeed he shows quite a rollicking indifference to all the secrets and subtleties of style, and inserts or removes stops in a manner that is absolutely destructive to the logical beauty of the verse. The hyphen also, so constantly employed by Rossetti in the case of such expressions as "hillock-eaves," quoted above, "hill-fire," "birth-hour," and the like, is almost invariably disregarded, and by the brilliant omission of a semicolon Mr. Knight has succeeded in spoiling one of the best stanzas in "The Staff and Scrip," a poem, by the way, that he speaks of as "The Staff and the Scrip" (*sic*). After this tedious comedy of errors it seems almost unnecessary to point out that the earliest Italian poet is not called Ciullo *D'Alcano* (*sic*), or that "The Bothie of *Toper-na-Fuosich*" (*sic*) is not the title of Clough's boisterous epic, or that "Dante and his *Cycle*" (*sic*) is not the name Rossetti gave to his collection of translations, and why "Troy Town" should appear in the index as "*Tory Town*" is really quite inexplicable, unless it is intended as a compliment to Mr. Hall Caine who once dedicated, or rather tried to dedicate to Rossetti a lecture on the relations of poets to politics. We are sorry too to find an English dramatic critic misquoting Shakespeare, as we had always been of opinion that this was a privilege reserved specially for our English actors.

We sincerely hope that there will soon be an end to all biographies of this kind. They rob life of much of its dignity and its wonder, add to death itself a new terror, and make one wish that all art were anonymous. Cheap editions of great books are always welcome, but cheap editions of great men are detestable. Nor could there have been any more unfortunate choice of a subject for popular treatment than that to which we owe the memoir that now lies before us. A pillar of fire to the few who knew him, and of cloud to the many who knew him not, Dante Gabriel Rossetti lived apart from the gossip and tittle-tattle of a shallow age. He never trafficked with the merchants for his soul, nor brought his wares into the market-place for the idle to gape at. Passionate and romantic though he was, yet there was in his nature something of high austerity. He loved seclusion, and hated notoriety, and would have shuddered at the idea that within a few years after his death he was to make his appearance in a series of popular biographies, sandwiched between the author of Pickwick and the Great Lexicographer. One man alone, the friend his verse won for him, did he desire should write his life, and it is to Mr. Theodore Watts that we too must look to give us the real Rossetti. It may be admitted at once that Mr. Watts' subject has for the moment been a little spoiled for him. Rude hands have touched it, and unmusical voices have made it sound almost common in our ears. Yet none the less is it for him to tell us of the marvel of this man, whose art he has analysed with such exquisite insight, whose life he knows as no one else can know it, whom he so loyally loved and tended, and by whom he was so loyally beloved in turn. As for the other, the scribblers and nibblers of literature, if they indeed reverence Rossetti's memory, let them pay him the one homage he would most have valued, the gracious homage of silence. "Though you can fret me, you cannot play upon me," says Hamlet to his false friend, and even so might Rossetti speak to these well-intentioned mediocrities who would seem to know his stops, and would sound him to the top of his compass. True, they cannot fret him now, for he has passed beyond the possibility of pain, yet they cannot play upon him either, it is not for them to pluck out the heart of his mystery.

There is, however, one feature of this book that deserves unstinted praise. Mr. Anderson's Bibliography will be found of immense use by every student of Rossetti's work and influence. Perhaps Young's very powerful attack on Pre-Raphaelitism, as expounded by Mr. Ruskin (Longmans, 1857), might be included, but in all other respects it seems quite complete, and the chronological list of paintings and drawings is really admirable. When this unfortunate "Great Writers" series comes to an end, Mr. Anderson's Bibliographies should be collected together, and published in a separate volume. At present they are in very second-rate company indeed.

The American Invasion*

A terrible danger is hanging over the Americans in London.
Their future, and their reputation this season, depend entirely
on the success of Buffalo Bill and Mrs. Brown-Potter. The
former is certain to draw; for English people are far more interested in American barbarism than they are in American civilization. When they sight Sandy Hook, they look to their rifles
and ammunition; and after dining once at Delmonico's, start
off for Colorado or California, for Montana or the Yellow Stone
Park. Rocky Mountains charm them more than riotous millionaires; they have been known to prefer buffaloes to Boston.
Why should they not? The cities of America are inexpressibly
tedious. The Bostonians take their learning too sadly; culture
with them is an accomplishment rather than an atmosphere;
their 'Hub,' as they call it, is the paradise of prigs. Chicago is
a sort of monster-shop, full of bustle and bores. Political life at
Washington is like political life in a suburban vestry. Baltimore
is amusing for a week, but Philadelphia is dreadfully provincial;
and though one can dine in New York, one could not dwell
there. Better the Far West, with its grizzly bears and its un-
tamed cowboys, its free, open-air life and its free, open-air manners, its boundless prairie and its boundless mendacity! This is

* Unsigned article, *Court and Society Review* IV : 142 (23 March
1887) 270–71.

what Buffalo Bill is going to bring to London; and we have no
doubt that London will fully appreciate his show.

With regard to Mrs. Brown-Potter, as acting is no longer
considered absolutely essential for success on the English stage,
there is really no reason why the pretty, bright-eyed lady, who
charmed us all last June by her merry laugh and her *nonchalant*
ways, should not, to borrow an expression from her native language, make a big boom, and paint the town red. We sincerely
hope she will; for, on the whole, the American invasion has done
English society a great deal of good. American women are
bright, clever, and wonderfully cosmopolitan. Their patriotic
feelings are limited to an admiration for Niagara, and a regret
for the Elevated Railway, and, unlike the men, they never bore
us with Bunker's Hill. They take their dresses from Paris, and
their manners from Piccadilly, and wear both charmingly. They
have a quaint pertness, a delightful conceit, a naïve self-asser-
tion. They insist on being paid compliments, and have almost
succeeded in making Englishmen eloquent. For our aristocracy
they have an ardent admiration; they adore titles, and are a permanent blow to Republican principles. In the art of amusing
men they are adepts, both by nature and education, and can
actually tell a story without forgetting the point—an accomplishment that is extremely rare among the women of other
countries. It is true that they lack repose, and that their voices
are somewhat harsh and strident when they land first at Liver-
pool; but after a time one gets to love these pretty whirlwinds
in petticoats, that sweep so recklessly through society, and are
so agitating to all duchesses who have daughters. There is
something fascinating in their funny, exaggerated gestures, and
their petulant way of tossing the head. Their eyes have no magic
nor mystery in them, but they challenge us for combat; and
when we engage, we are always worsted. Their lips seem made
for laughter, and yet they never grimace. As for their voices,
they soon get them into tune. Some of them have been known
to acquire a fashionable drawl in two seasons; and after they
have been presented to Royalty they all roll their R's as vigorously as a young equerry or an old lady-in-waiting. Still, they
never really lose their accent, it keeps peeping out here and

there, and when they chatter together they are like a bevy of peacocks. Nothing is more amusing than to watch two American girls greeting each other in a drawing-room or in the Row. They are like children, with their shrill *staccato* cries of wonder, their odd little exclamations. Their conversation sounds like a series of exploding crackers; they are exquisitely incoherent, and use a sort of primitive, emotional language. After five minutes they are left beautifully breathless, and look at each other, half in amusement and half in affection. If a stolid young Englishman is fortunate enough to be introduced to them, he is amazed at their extraordinary vivacity; their electric quickness of repartee; their inexhaustible store of curious catchwords. He never really understands them, for their thoughts flutter about with the sweet irresponsibility of butterflies; but he is pleased and amused, and feels as if he were in an aviary. On the whole, American girls have a wonderful charm, and, perhaps, the chief secret of their charm is that they never talk seriously, except to their dressmaker, and never think seriously, except about amusements.

They have, however, one grave fault—their mothers.

Dreary as were those old Pilgrim Fathers, who left our shores more than two centuries ago to found a New England beyond seas, the Pilgrim Mothers, who have returned to us in the nineteenth century, are drearier still. Here and there, of course, there are exceptions, but as a class they are either dull, dowdy, or dyspeptic. It is only fair to the rising generation of America to state that they are not to blame for this. Indeed, they spare no pains at all to bring up their parents properly, and to give them a suitable, if somewhat late, education. From its earliest years, every American child spends most of its time in correcting the faults of its father and mother; and no one who has had the opportunity of watching an American family on the deck of an Atlantic steamer, or in the refined seclusion of a New York boarding-house, can fail to have been struck by this characteristic of their civilisation. In America, the young are always ready to give to those who are older than themselves the full benefits of their inexperience. A boy of only eleven or twelve years of age will firmly, but kindly, point out to his father his defects of manner or temper; will never weary of warning him against extravagance, idleness, late hours, unpunctuality, and the other temptations to which the aged are so particularly exposed; and sometimes, should he fancy that he is monopolising too much of the conversation at dinner, will remind him, across the table, of the new child's adage, "Parents should be seen, not heard." Nor does any mistaken idea of kindness prevent the little American girl from censuring her mother whenever it is necessary. Often, indeed, feeling that a rebuke conveyed in the presence of others is more truly efficacious than one merely whispered in the quiet of the nursery, she will call the attention of perfect strangers to her mother's general untidiness, her want of intellectual Boston conversation, immoderate love of iced-water and green corn, stinginess in the matter of candy, ignorance of the usages of the best Baltimore society, bodily ailments, and the like. In fact, it may be truly said that no American child is ever blind to the deficiencies of its parents, no matter how much it may love them.

Yet, somehow, this educational system has not been so successful as it deserved. In many cases, no doubt, the material with which the children had to deal was crude and incapable of real development; but the fact remains that the American mother is a tedious person. The American father is better, for he is never seen in London. He passes his life entirely in Wall Street, and communicates with his family once a month by means of a telegram in cipher. The mother, however, is always with us, and, lacking the quick imitative faculty of the younger generation, remains uninteresting and provincial to the last. In spite of her, however, the American girl is always welcome. She brightens our dull dinner parties for us, and makes life go pleasantly by for a season. In the race for coronets she often carries off the prize; but once that she has gained the victory, she is generous, and forgives her English rivals everything, even their beauty. Warned by the example of her mother that American women do not grow old gracefully, she tries not to grow old at all, and often succeeds. She has exquisite feet and hands, is always *bien chaussée et bien gantée*, and can talk brilliantly upon any subject, provided that she knows nothing about it. Her sense of humour keeps her from the tragedy of a *grande passion*, and, as there is neither romance nor humility in her love, she makes an excellent wife. What her ultimate influence on English life will be, it is difficult to estimate at present; but there can be no doubt that of all the factors that have contributed to the social revolution of London, there are few more important, and none more delightful, than the American invasion.

The American Man[*]

One of our prettiest Duchesses enquired the other day of a distinguished traveller whether there was really such a thing as an American man, explaining, as the reason for her question, that, though she knew many fascinating American women, she had never come across any fathers, grandfathers, uncles, brothers, husbands, cousins, or, indeed, male relatives of any kind whatsoever.

The exact answer the Duchess received is not worth recording, as it took the depressing form of useful and accurate information; but there can be no doubt that the subject is an extremely interesting one, pointing, as it does, to the curious fact that, as far as society is concerned, the American invasion has been purely female in character. With the exception of the United States Minister, always a welcome personage wherever he goes, and an occasional lion from Boston or the Far West, no American man has any social existence in London. His women-folk, with their wonderful dresses, and still more wonderful dialogue, shine in our *salons*, and delight our dinner-parties; our guardsmen are taken captive by their brilliant complexions, and our beauties made jealous by their clever wit; but the poor American man remains permanently in the background, and never rises beyond the level of the tourist. Now and then he makes an appearance

* Unsigned article, *Court and Society Review* IV : 145 (13 April 1887) 341–43.

in the Row, looking a somewhat strange figure in his long frock coat of glossy black cloth, and his sensible soft-felt hat; but his favourite haunt is the Strand, and the American Exchange his idea of Heaven. When he is not lounging in a rocking-chair with a cigar, he is loafing through the streets with a carpet bag, gravely taking stock of our products, and trying to understand Europe through the medium of the shop windows. He is M. Renan's *l'homme sensuel moyen*, Mr. Arnold's middle-class Philistine. The telephone is his test of civilisation, and his wildest dreams of Utopia do not rise beyond elevated railways and electric bells. His chief pleasure is to get hold of some unsuspecting stranger, or some sympathetic countryman, and then to indulge in the national game of 'matching.' With a *naivete* and a nonchalance that are absolutely charming, he will gravely compare St. James' Palace to the grand central depot at Chicago, or Westminster Abbey to the Falls of Niagara. Bulk is his canon of beauty, and size his standard of excellence. To him the greatness of a country consists in the number of square miles that it contains; and he is never tired of telling the waiters at his hotel that the State of Texas is larger than France and Germany put together.

Yet, on the whole, he is happier in London than anywhere else in Europe. Here he can always make a few acquaintances, and, as a rule, can speak the language. Abroad, he is terribly at sea. He knows no one, and understands nothing, and wanders about in a melancholy manner, treating the Old World as if it were a Broadway store, and each city a counter for the sampling of shoddy goods. For him Art has no marvel, and Beauty no meaning, and the Past no message. He thinks that civilisation began with the introduction of steam, and looks with contempt upon all centuries that had no hot-water apparatuses in their houses. The ruin and decay of Time has no pathos in his eyes. He turns away from Ravenna, because the grass grows in her streets, and can see no loveliness in Verona, because there is rust on her balconies. His one desire is to get the whole of Europe into thorough repair. He is severe on the modern Romans for not covering the Colosseum with a glass roof, and utilising the building as a warehouse for dry goods. In a word, he is the

Don Quixote of common sense, for he is so utilitarian that he is absolutely unpractical. As a *compagnon de voyage* he is not desirable, for he always looks *déplacé*, and feels depressed. Indeed, he would die of weariness if he were not in constant telegraphic communication with Wall Street; and the only thing that can console him for having wasted a day in a picture-gallery is a copy of the New York Herald or the Boston Times. Finally, having looked at everything, and seen nothing, he returns to his native land.

There he is delightful. For the strange thing about American civilisation is, that the women are most charming when they are away from their own country, the men most charming when they are at home.

At home, the American man is the best of companions, as he is the most hospitable of hosts. The young men are especially pleasant, with their bright, handsome eyes, their unwearying energy, their amusing shrewdness. They seem to get a hold on life much earlier than we do. At an age when we are still boys at Eton, or lads at Oxford, they are practising some important profession, making money in some intricate business. Real experience comes to them so much sooner than it does to us, that they are never awkward, never shy, and never say foolish things, except when they ask one how the Hudson River compares with the Rhine, or whether Brooklyn Bridge is not really more impressive than the dome of St. Paul's. Their education is quite different from ours. They know men much better than they know books, and life interests them more than literature. They have no time to study anything but the stock markets, no leisure to read anything but newspapers. Indeed, it is only the women in America who have any leisure at all; and, as a necessary result of this curious state of things, there is no doubt but that, within a century from now, the whole culture of the New World will be in petticoats. Yet, though these cute young speculators may not have culture, in the sense in which we use it, as the knowledge of the best that has been thought and said in the world, they are by no means dull. There is no such thing as a stupid American. Many Americans are horrid, vulgar, intrusive, and impertinent, just as many English people are also; but stupidity is not one of the national vices. Indeed, in America there is no opening for a fool. They expect brains even from a boot-black, and get them.

As for marriage, it is one of their most popular institutions. The American man marries early, and the American woman marries often; and they get on extremely well together. From childhood, the husband has been brought up on the most elaborate fetch-and-carry system, and his reverence for the sex has a touch of compulsory chivalry about it; while the wife exercises an absolute despotism, based upon female assertion, and tempered by womanly charm. On the whole, the great success of marriage in the States is due partly to the fact that no American man is ever idle, and partly to the fact that no American wife is considered responsible for the quality of her husband's dinners. In America, the horrors of domesticity are almost entirely unknown. There are no scenes over the soup, nor quarrels over the *entrées*, and as, by a clause inserted in every marriage settlement, the husband solemnly binds himself to use studs and not buttons for his shirts, one of the chief sources of disagreement in ordinary middle-class life is absolutely removed. The habit also of residing in hotels and boarding-houses does away with any necessity for those tedious *tête-à-têtes* that are the dream of engaged couples, and the despair of married men. Vulgarising though a *table-d'hôte* may be, it is at least better than that eternal duologue about bills and babies to which Benedict and Beatrice so often sink, when the one has lost his wit, and the other her beauty. Even the American freedom of divorce, questionable though it undoubtedly is on many grounds, has at least the merit of bringing into marriage a new element of romantic uncertainty. When people are tied together for life they too often regard manners as a mere superfluity, and courtesy as a thing of no moment; but where the bond can be easily broken, its very fragility makes its strength, and reminds the husband that he should always try to please, and the wife that she should never cease to be charming.

As a consequence of this liberty of action, or, it may be, in spite of it, scandals are extremely rare in America, and should one occur, so paramount in society is female influence, that it is the man who is never forgiven. America is the only country in the world where Don Juan is not appreciated, and where there is sympathy for Georges Dandin.

On the whole, then, the American man at home is a very worthy person. There is just one point in which he is disappointing. American humour is a mere travellers' tale. It has no real existence. Indeed, so far from being humorous, the male American is the most abnormally serious creature who ever existed. He talks of Europe as being old; but it is he himself who has never been young. He knows nothing of the irresponsible light-heartedness of boyhood, of the graceful *insouciance* of animal spirits. He has always been prudent, always practical, and pays a heavy penalty for having committed no mistakes. It is only fair to admit that he can exaggerate; but even his exaggeration has a rational basis. It is not founded on wit or fancy; it does not spring from any poetic imagination; it is simply an earnest attempt on the part of language to keep pace with the enormous size of the country. It is evident that where it takes one twenty-four hours to go across a single parish, and seven days' steady railway travelling to keep a dinner engagement in another State, the ordinary resources of human speech are quite inadequate to the strain put on them, and new linguistic forms have to be invented, new methods of description resorted to. But this is nothing more than the fatal influence of geography upon adjectives; for naturally humorous the American man certainly is not. It is true that when we meet him in Europe his conversation keeps us in fits of laughter; but this is merely because his ideas are so absolutely incongruous with European surroundings. Place him in his own environment, in the midst of the civilisation that he has made for himself, and the life that is the work of his own hands, and the very same observations will fail even to excite a smile. They have sunk to the level of the commonplace truism, or the sensible remark; and what seemed a paradox when we listened to it in London, becomes a platitude when we hear it in Milwaukee.

America has never quite forgiven Europe for having been discovered somewhat earlier in history than itself. Yet how immense are its obligations to us! How enormous its debt! To gain a reputation for humour, its men have to come to London; to be famous for their *toilettes*, its women have to shop in Paris.

Yet, though the American man may not be humorous, he is certainly humane. He is keenly conscious of the fact that there is a great deal of human nature in man, and tries to be pleasant to every stranger who lands on his shores. He has a healthy freedom from all antiquated prejudices, regards introductions as a foolish relic of mediæval etiquette, and makes every chance visitor feel that he is the favoured guest of a great nation. If the English girl ever met him, she would marry him; and if she married him, she would be happy. For, though he may be rough in manner, and deficient in the picturesque insincerity of romance, yet he is invariably kind and thoughtful, and has succeeded in making his own country the Paradise of Women.

This, however, is perhaps the reason why, like Eve, the women are always so anxious to get out of it.

The Butterfly's Boswell*

Every great man nowadays has his disciples, and it is usually Judas who writes the biography. Mr. Whistler, however, is more fortunate than most of his *confrères*, as he has found in Mr. Walter Dowdeswell the most ardent of admirers, indeed we might almost say the most sympathetic of secretaries.

In the current number of the *Art Journal*, Mr. Dowdeswell publishes a very valuable account of Mr. Whistler's life and work, and gives us an extremely graphic picture of this remarkable artist, from his tall hat and wand, of which an illustration is duly given, down to the sly smile that we have all heard echoing through the Suffolk Street Gallery on the occasion of a private view, and that used, in old days, to deafen the Royal Academicians at their annual *soirée*.

From Mr. Dowdeswell's interesting monograph we learn that Mr. Whistler is of most ancient English lineage. Indeed his family tree seems to go back perilously near to those old mediæval days that he himself has often so charmingly satirized, and always so cleverly misunderstood. The particular branch, however, from which the President of the British Artists is immediately descended is partly Irish and American, a fact that explains a great deal of the peculiar quality of his wonderful wit, just as to his early residence in Russia, where his father was a distin-

* Unsigned article, *Court and Society Review* IV : 146 (20 April 1887) 378.

guished engineer, we may attribute the origin of that winning
and fascinating manner that makes the disciples murmur to each
other after each exhibition, *"Grattez le maître, et vous trouverez
le Tartare!"*

On his father's death, Mr. Whistler seems to have returned
to America, where in a short time we find him a cadet at West
Point. Nature, however, seeing that he was destined to be a Ve-
lasquez, not a *Vilainton*, brought his military career to a premature and inglorious end, and we next come across him at Paris,
in the *atelier* of Gleyre. His Paris successes are well-known; but
like all true Americans, he gravitated towards England, and having thrilled France with the strange beauty of his 'White Girl,'
a picture exhibited at the *Salon des Refusés*, he crossed over to
London, where, according to Mr. Dowdeswell, he discovered the
Thames.

From this point on, the article becomes extremely interesting,
and Mr. Dowdeswell displays a really remarkable power, not
merely of writing, but of writing from dictation, especially in
his very generous and appreciative estimate of Mr. Whistler's
genius. We are glad, too, to notice Mr. Dowdeswell's distinct
recognition of the complete absence from Mr. Whistler's work
of any alien quality, and of the great service he has rendered to
Art by his absolute separation of painting from literature. Before the fortunate arrival of Mr. Whistler on these benighted
but expectant shores, our English painters, with but few exceptions, had spent their wicked and wasted lives in poaching upon
the domain of the poets, marring their motives by clumsy treatment, and striving to render, by visible form and colour, the
marvel of what is invisible, the splendour of what is not seen.
Now that the *cénacle* is well established in Suffolk Street, and
that the style of the master has produced the school of the mediocrity, we have every reason to hope that the old state of
things has passed away. For the domain of the painter is widely
different from the domain of the poet. To the latter belongs
Life in its full and absolute entirety; not only the world that
men look at, but the world that men listen to also; not merely
the momentary grace of form, or the transient gladness of colour, but the whole sphere of feeling, the perfect cycle of thought,
the growth and progress of passion, the spiritual development of

the soul. The painter is so far limited, that it is only through the mask of the body that he can show us the mystery of the soul; only through images that he can handle ideas; only through its physical equivalents that he can deal with psychology. And how inadequately does he do it then, asking us to accept a blackamoor with a frown for the noble rage of Othello, and an old gentleman in a storm for the wild madness of Lear!

Yet, in emphasising the painter's limitation of subject matter, Mr. Whistler has not, by any means, limited the painter's vision. It would be more just to say that he has pointed out possibilities of beauty hitherto undreamt of, and that by his keen critical faculty, no less than by the dominance of his assertive personality, he has given to Art itself a new creative impulse. Indeed, when the true history of Art comes to be written, a task that Mr. Whistler is eminently capable of doing himself, at least in the form of an autobiography, there can be no doubt but that his name will stand high among the highest on its record, for he has opened the eyes of the blind, and given great encouragement to the short-sighted.

The best answer, however, to those who would censure him for suffering the poet to sing in peace, and mock at him for leaving to literature its proper province, is the rare and exquisite wonder of his own work; and not its wonder merely, but its width also, its mastery over all chords, its possession of all secrets. There is nothing of the specialist in Mr. Whistler. As he can deal with every medium, so he can appeal to every mood. Some of his arrangements in colour, such as the 'Little Grey Note,' or the 'Note in Blue and Opal,' have all the delicate loveliness of lyrics. The silver silences of his nocturnes seem at times almost passing into music. He has done etchings with the brilliancy of epigrams, and pastels with the charm of paradoxes, and many of his portraits are pure works of fiction.

On the whole, then, the biography in the *Art Journal* is well worth reading. It is not, of course, complete, and some of the most distinguishing characteristics of Mr. Whistler's nature are hardly alluded to at all. Still, as Mr. Whistler once himself remarked, no man alive is life-size; and it would be ungracious to criticize with too much severity an article that shows such memory on the part of the writer, and such journalistic ability on the part of the subject. For one thing, however, we hope that Mr. Dowdeswell is not responsible. Previous to this article's publication, there appeared in the daily newspapers an extremely vulgar and blatant advertisement, which ultimately found its way into the pages of some of the catalogues at the Suffolk Street Private View. It would be sad to think that a disciple so devoted as Mr. Dowdeswell has shown himself to be could have thus desecrated the dignity of his master; for, while it is all very well to be the Butterfly's Boswell, to be the Butterfly's Barnum is immodest, and unnecessary.

The Rout of the R[oyal] A[cademy]*

The annual attacks upon the Royal Academy, with which we are all so familiar, and of which most of us are so tired, have, as a rule, been both futile and depressing. The dull have cried out upon dulness, and the mediocre have denounced mediocrity, and each side has taken itself very seriously indeed. It is always a sorry spectacle when the Philistines of Gath go out against the Philistines of Gaza; so we are delighted to find that there has risen up, at last, a young and ruddy David to slay this lumbering Goliath of middle-class art. Punch has sent forth this Paladin of the Beautiful, the Gainsborough Gallery in Bond Street has given him his vantage ground of attack, and before Mr. Harry Furniss' brilliant wit and clever satire the Royal Academicians are now in full retreat, and the opinion of the best military and artistic experts is, that they are rapidly retiring in the direction of Bayswater, a desolate tract of country lying to the north of the Park, where it would be almost impossible to find them, owing to the difficulty of obtaining guides. The final encounter, however, will not take place till the end of this week, when Goliath, who is now occupied in varnishing, the only artistic process with which he is thoroughly familiar, will display his forces in Burlington House, under the patronage of the

* Unsigned article, *Court and Society Review* IV : 147 (27 April 1887) 390.

British public, and under the protection of the British police-man.

Perhaps, however, it is somewhat fanciful to treat Mr. Furniss' Exhibition as an attack on the Royal Academy at all. It would be more just to regard it as an attempt on Mr. Furniss' part to show the Academician the possibilities of real beauty, and won-der, and pleasure that lie hidden in his work. Take, for instance, the Tadema (No. 31). Here is all the archæological detail so dear to this industrious painter; all the cups of polished metal, the strangely-embroidered robes, and the richly-veined marbles, that exemplify so clearly the 'rights of properties' in art; and the one thing that was wanting in Mr. Tadema's work has been added, the passionate interest in human life, and the power to portray it. The two central figures are absolutely fascinating, and where we yawned before, we now cannot help laughing. Charming, too, in its delicate feeling for purity is Mr. Horsley's 'Lady Godiva' (No. 27). Nothing could possibly be more chaste than this draped lay-figure, that rides through the empty streets of Coventry on a blindfolded horse. The legs of the quadruped are carefully encased in canvas bags, lest the modest should be offended; the heroine carries a large umbrella, for fear of acci-dents; while the introduction of Mr. Horsley himself in the character of Peeping Tom is a masterpiece of autobiographical art. As for Sir Frederick Leighton, he has rarely been seen to more advantage than in the specimen of his work that Mr. Furniss has so kindly provided for him. His 'Pygmalion and Galatea in the Lowther Arcadia' (No. 49) has all that wax-doll grace of treatment that is so characteristic of his best work, and is eminently suggestive of the President's earnest and continual struggles to discover the difference between chalk and colour. Indeed, every Academician is thoroughly well represented. Mr. Frith, who has done so much to elevate painting to the dignity of photography, sends a series of five pictures, exemplifying that difference between Virtue and Vice which moralists have never been able to discover, but which is the real basis of the great Drury Lane school of melo-drama. Owing to the exigencies of space, only one of these pictures has been hung, but the other four appear in the delightfully-illustrated catalogue, and never has the contrast between life, when it is 'penny plain,' and life, when it is 'twopence coloured,' been so forcibly put forward. The whole series is like the very finest platitude from the pulpit, and shows clearly the true value of didactic art. Mr. Macbeth, the variety of whose work is so well known, exhibits a group of peasant women at their customary occupation of 'Pot Boiling in the Fens'; Mr. Briton Riviere's 'Love me, Love my Dog' (No. 41), a careful study from life, in which the navvy and the bull pup have changed heads, has all the simple truth of that popular school that treats human beings as if they were animals, and animals as if they were human beings; Mr. Boughton's 'Newest England, Tarred with an American Brush,' is, as the catalogue remarks, somewhat low in tone, though high in price; but Mr. Goodall's 'Tracts in the Desert,' a spirited picture of a missionary distributing leaflets from the back of a camel, while the Sphinx looks on in amused wonder, is one of this painter's most noble productions, and will, no doubt, be highly appreciated by that refined patron of art who, as the daily papers have recently informed us, was so impressed by the worthy Academician's last sacred picture, that he at once gave him a commission to paint one of double the size! Elsewhere on the walls of this delightful exhibition we notice a masterly Frank Holl, with the usual lime-light effects; a fine 'Salvation Armitage' (No. 26), that combines the spirit of Exeter Hall with the close study of the plaster cast; an interesting example of Mr. Frank Dicksee, full of chocolate-box culture and school-girl sentimentality; and a really splendid Brett, of the billows as seen from a bathing box. Nor are there wanting specimens of the work of Mr. Seymour Lucas, Mr. Gow, and those other great historical painters of our day who rival the theatrical costumiers in their passion for fancy-dress balls, and collect armour that has borne the brunt of Wardour Street for so many years; there is a magnificent Orchardson (No. 72), with a delicate suggestion of that mustard-yellow atmosphere through which this Thackeray of painters loves to look out on life; the Leslies and the Marcus Stones have all that faint and fading prettiness that makes one long for the honest ugliness of naturalism; and there are some excellent examples of the work of that poetic school of artists, who imagine that the true way of idealising a sitter is to paint the portrait of somebody else.

On the whole, then, the Royal Academicians have never appeared under more favourable conditions than in this pleasant gallery. Mr. Furniss has shown that the one thing lacking in them is a sense of humour, and that, if they would not take themselves so seriously, they might produce work that would be a joy, and not a weariness, to the world. Whether or not they will profit by the lesson, it is difficult to say, for dulness has become the basis of respectability, and seriousness the only refuge of the shallow. Still, even for the Academician there is hope, and though it is too late now for any immediate reform, who knows but next year we may have an exhibition at Burlington House not merely to laugh at, but to laugh with, not merely for mockery, but also for kindly mirth? Should this desirable result be attained, Mr. Furniss will have done a great service to English art; and, in any case, his gallery will be remembered as the most brilliant criticism upon the British school that has been made in this century.

William Morris's Odyssey*

Of all our modern poets Mr. William Morris is the one best
qualified by nature and by art to translate for us the marvellous
epic of the wanderings of Odysseus. For he is our only true
story singer since Chaucer; if he is a Socialist, he is also a Saga-
man; and there was a time when he was never wearied of telling
us strange legends of gods and men, wonderful tales of chivalry
and romance. Master as he is of decorative and descriptive verse,
he has all the Greek's joy in the visible aspect of things, all the
Greek's sense of delicate and delightful detail, all the Greek's
pleasure in beautiful textures, and exquisite materials, and imaginative designs; nor can any one have a keener sympathy with
the Homeric admiration for the workers and craftsmen in the
various arts, from the stainers of white ivory and the embroider-
ers in purple and gold, to the weaver sitting by the loom and the
dyer dipping in the vat, the chaser of shield and helmet, the
carver of wood or stone. And to all this is added the true temper of high romance, the power to make the past as real to us
as the present, the subtle instinct to discern passion, the swift
impulse to portray life.

It is no wonder then the lovers of Greek literature have so
eagerly looked forward to Mr. Morris's version of the Odyssean

* Unsigned review, "Mr. Morris's Odyssey," of *The Odyssey of Homer*
done into English verse by William Morris, Vol. I. *Pall Mall Gazette*
XLV : 6897 (26 April 1887) 5.

73

epic, and now that the first volume has appeared it is not extravagant to say that of all our English translations this is the most perfect and the most satisfying. In spite of Coleridge's well known views on the subject, we have always held that Chapman's Odyssey is immeasurably inferior to his Iliad, the mere difference of metre alone being sufficient to set the former in a secondary place. Pope's Odyssey with its glittering rhetoric and smart antitheses has nothing of the grand manner of the original; Cowper is dull, and Bryant dreadful, and Worsley too full of Spenserian prettinesses, while excellent though Messrs. Butcher and Lang's version undoubtedly is in many respects, still, on the whole, it merely gives us the facts of the Odyssey without producing anything of its artistic effect. Avia's translation even, though better than almost all its predecessors in the same field, is not worthy of taking rank beside Mr. Morris's, for here we have a true work of art, a rendering, not merely of language into language, but of poetry into poetry, and though the new spirit added in the transfusion may seem to many rather more Norse than Greek, and perhaps at times more boisterous than beautiful, there is yet a vigour of life in every line, a splendid ardour through each canto, that stirs the blood while one reads like the sound of a trumpet, and that, producing a physical as well as a spiritual delight, exults the senses no less than it exalts the soul. It may be admitted at once that, here and there, Mr. Morris has missed something of the marvellous dignity of the Homeric verse, and that in his desire for rushing and ringing metre he has occasionally sacrificed majesty to movement, and made stateliness give place to speed, but it is really only in such blank verse as Milton's that this effect of calm and lofty music can be attained, and in all other respects blank verse is the most inadequate medium for reproducing the full flow and fervour of the Greek hexameter. One merit at any rate Mr. Morris's version entirely and absolutely possesses. It is, in no sense of the word, literary; it seems to deal immediately with life itself, and to take from the reality of things its own form and colour; it is always direct and simple, and at its best has something of the "large utterance of the early gods."

As for individual passages of beauty, nothing could be better than the wonderful description of the house of the Phaeacian King, or the whole telling of the lovely legend of Circe, or the manner in which the pageant of the pale phantoms in Hades is brought before our eyes. Perhaps the basic epic humour of the escape from the Cyclops is hardly realised, but there is always a linguistic difficulty about rendering this fascinating story into English, and where we are given so much poetry we should not complain about losing a pun, and the exquisite idyll of the meeting and parting with the daughter of Alcinoüs is really delightfully told. How good for instance is this passage taken at random from the Sixth book:—

But therewith unto the handmaids goodly Odysseus spake:
"Stand off I bid you, damsels, while the work in hand I take,
And wash the brine from my shoulders, and sleek them all around.
Since verily now this long while sweet oil they have not found.
But before you nought will I wash me, for shame I have indeed,
Amidst of fair-tressed damsels to be all bare of weed."
So he spake and aloof they gat them, and thereof they told the may,
But Odysseus with the river from his body washed away
The brine from his back and shoulders wrought broad and mightily,
And from his head he was wiping the foam of the untilled sea:
But when he had thoroughly washed him, and the oil about him had
    shed,
He did upon him the raiment the gift of the maid unwed.
But Athene, Zeus-begotten, dealt with him in such wise
That bigger was his seeming, and mightier to all eyes,
With the hair on his head crisp curling as the bloom of the daffodil.
And as when the silver with gold is o'erlaid by a man of skill,
Yea a craftsman whom Hephaestus and Pallas Athene have taught
To be master over masters, and lovely work he has wrought;
So she round his head and his shoulders shed grace abundantly.

It may be objected by some that the line

With the hair on his head crisp curling as the bloom of the daffodil,

is a rather fanciful version of—

οὔλας ἧκε κόμας, ὑακινθίνῳ ἄνθει ὁμοίας,

75

and it certainly seems probable that the allusion is to the dark colour of the hero's hair, still the point is not one of much importance, though it may be worth noticing that a similar expression occurs in Ogilby's superbly illustrated translation of the Odyssey, published in 1665, where Charles II's Master of the Revels in Ireland gives the passage thus,

> Minerva renders him more tall and fair,
> Curling in rings like daffadills his hair.

No anthology, however, can show the true merit of Mr. Morris' translation, whose real value does not depend on stray beauties, nor is revealed by chance selections, but lies in the absolute rightness and coherence of the whole, in its purity and justice of touch, its freedom from affectation and commonplace, its harmony of form and matter. It is sufficient to say that this is a poet's version of a poet, and for such surely we should be thankful. In these latter days of coarse and vulgar literature it is something to have made the great sea-epic of the South native and natural to our northern isle, something to have shown that our English speech may be a pipe through which Greek lips can blow, something to have taught Nausicäa to speak the same language as Perdita.

Dostoevsky's
The Insulted
and Injured*

Of the three great Russian novelists of our time, Tourgenieff is by far the finest artist. He has that spirit of exquisite selection, that delicate choice of detail, which is the essence of style; his work is entirely free from any personal intention; and by taking existence at its most fiery-coloured moments, he can distil into a few pages of perfect prose the moods and passions of many lives. Count Tolstoi's method is much larger and his field of vision more extended. He reminds us sometimes of Paul Veronese, and like that great painter can crowd, without overcrowding, the giant canvas on which he works. We may not at first gain from his books that artistic unity of impression which is Tourgenieff's chief charm, but once that we have mastered the details, the whole seems to have the grandeur and simplicity of an epic. Doistoieffski differs widely from both his rivals. He is not so fine an artist as Tourgenieff, for he deals more with the facts than with the effects of life; nor has he Tolstoi's largeness of vision and epic dignity; but he has qualities that are distinctively and absolutely his own, such as a fierce intensity of passion and concentration of impulse, a power of dealing with the deepest mysteries of psychology and the most hidden springs of life, and a realism that is pitiless in its fidelity, and terrible be-

* Unsigned review, entitled "A Batch of Novels," of Fyodor Dostoevsky, *Injury and Insult*, translated by Frederick Whishaw, and other books. *Pall Mall Gazette* XLV : 6902 (2 May 1887) 11.

cause it is true. Some time ago we had occasion to draw attention to his marvellous novel "Crime and Punishment," where in the haunt of impurity and vice a harlot and an assassin meet together to read the story of Lazarus and Dives, and the outcast girl leads the sinner to make atonement for his sin; nor is the book entitled "Injury and Insult" at all inferior to that great masterpiece. Mean and ordinary though the surroundings of the story may seem, the heroine Natasha is like one of the noble victims of Greek tragedy, she is Antigone with the passions of Phaedra, and it is impossible to approach her without a feeling of awe. Greek also is the gloom of Nemesis that hangs over each character, only it is Nemesis that does not stand outside of life, but is part of our own nature, and of the same material as life itself. Aleosha, the beautiful young lad whom Natasha follows to her doom, is a second Tito Melema, and has all Tito's charm, and grace, and fascination. Yet he is different. He would never have denied Baldassare in the square at Florence, nor lied to Romola about Tessa. He has a magnificent, momentary sincerity; a boyish unconsciousness of all that life signifies; an ardent enthusiasm for all that life cannot give. There is nothing calculating about him. He never thinks evil, he only does it. From a psychological point of view he is one of the most interesting characters of modern fiction, as from an artistic standpoint he is one of the most attractive. As we grow to know him, he stirs strange questions for us, and makes us feel that it is not the wicked only who do wrong, nor the bad alone who work evil. And by what a subtle objective method does Doistoieffski show us his characters! He never tickets them with a list, nor labels them with a description. We grow to know them very gradually, as we know people whom we meet in society, at first by little tricks of manner, personal appearance, fancies in dress and the like; and afterwards by their deeds and words; and even then they constantly elude us, for though Doistoieffski may lay bare for us the secrets of their nature, yet he never explains his personages away, they are always surprising us by something that they say or do, and keep to the end the eternal mystery of life. Irrespective of its value as a work of art, this novel possesses a deep autobiographical interest also, as the character of Vania, the poor student who loves Natasha through all her sin and shame, is Doistoieffski's study of himself. Goethe once had to delay the completion of one of his novels till experience had furnished him with new situations, but almost before he had arrived at manhood Doistoieffski knew life in its most real forms; poverty and suffering, pain and misery, prison, exile, and love were soon familiar to him, and by the lips of Vania he has told his own story. This note of personal feeling, this harsh reality of actual experience, undoubtedly gives the book something of its strange fervour and terrible passion, yet it has not made it egotistic; we see things from every point of view, and we feel, not that Fiction has been trammelled by fact, but that fact itself has become ideal and imaginative. Pitiless too though Doistoieffski is in his method, as an artist, yet as a man he is full of human pity for all, for those who do evil as well as for those who suffer it, for the selfish no less than for those whose lives are wrecked for others, and whose sacrifice is in vain. Since "Adam Bede," and *Le Pere Goriot*, no more powerful novel has been written than "Insult and Injury."

Mr. Mahaffy's New Book [*Greek Life and Thought*]*

Mr. Mahaffy's new book will be a great disappointment to everybody except the Paper-Unionists and the members of the Primrose League. His subject, the history of Greek life and thought from the age of Alexander to the Roman conquest, is extremely interesting, but the manner in which the subject is treated is quite unworthy of a scholar, nor can there be anything more depressing than Mr. Mahaffy's continual efforts to degrade history to the level of the ordinary political pamphlet of contemporary party warfare. There is, of course, no reason why Mr. Mahaffy should be called upon to express any sympathy with the aspirations of the old Greek cities for freedom and autonomy. The personal preferences of modern historians on these points are matters of no import whatsoever. But in his attempts to treat the Hellenic world as "Tipperary writ large," to use Alexander the Great as a means of whitewashing Mr. Smith, and to finish the battle of Chaeronea on the plains of Mitchelstown, Mr. Mahaffy shows an amount of political bias and literary blindness that is quite extraordinary. He might have made his book a work of solid and enduring interest, but he has chosen to give it a merely ephemeral value, and to substitute for the scientific temper of the true historian the prejudice, the flippancy, and the violence of the platform partisan. For the

* Unsigned review of J. P. Mahaffy, *Greek Life and Thought: from the Age of Alexander to the Roman Conquest*. Pall Mall Gazette XLVI : 7066 (9 November 1887) 3.

flippancy parallels can no doubt be found in some of Mr. Mahaffy's earlier books, but the prejudice and the violence are new, and their appearance is very much to be regretted. There is always something peculiarly impotent about the violence of a literary man. It seems to bear no reference to facts, for it is never kept in check by action. It is simply a question of adjectives and rhetoric, of exaggeration and over emphasis. Mr. Balfour is very anxious that Mr. William O'Brien should wear prison clothes, sleep on a plank bed, and be subjected to other indignities, but Mr. Mahaffy goes far beyond such mild measures as these, and begins his history by frankly expressing his regret that Demosthenes was not summarily put to death for his attempts to keep the spirit of patriotism alive among the citizens of Athens! Indeed, he has no patience with what he calls "the foolish and senseless opposition to Macedonia;" regards the revolt of the Spartans against "Alexander's Lord Lieutenant for Greece" as an example of "parochial politics;" indulges in Primrose League platitudes against a low franchise and the iniquity of allowing "every pauper" to have a vote; and tells us that the "demagogues" and "pretended patriots" were so lost to shame that they actually preached to the parasitic mob of Athens the doctrine of Autonomy—"not now extinct," Mr. Mahaffy adds regretfully—and propounded, as a principle of political economy, the curious idea that people should be allowed to manage their own affairs! As for the personal character of the despots, Mr. Mahaffy admits that if he had to judge by the accounts in the Greek historians, from Herodotus downwards, he "would certainly have said that the ineffaceable passion for autonomy, which marks every epoch of Greek history, and every canton within its limits, must have arisen from the excesses committed by the officers of foreign potentates, or local tyrants," but a careful study of the cartoons published in *United Ireland* has convinced him "that a ruler may be the soberest, the most conscientious, the most considerate, and yet have terrible things said of him by mere political malcontents." In fact, since Mr. Balfour has been caricatured Greek history must be entirely rewritten! This is the pass to which the distinguished professor of a distinguished university[1] has been brought. Nor can anything equal

[1] Trinity College, Dublin.—Ed.

Mr. Mahaffy's prejudice against the Greek patriots, unless it be his contempt for those few fine Romans who, sympathizing with Hellenic civilization and culture, recognized the political value of autonomy and the intellectual importance of a healthy national life. He mocks at what he calls their "vulgar mawkishness about Greek liberties," their "anxiety to redress historical wrongs," and congratulates his readers that this feeling was not intensified by the remorse that their own forefathers had been the oppressors. "Luckily," says Mr. Mahaffy, "the old Greeks had conquered Troy, and so the pangs of conscience which now so deeply affect a Gladstone and a Morley for the sins of their ancestors could hardly affect a Marcius or a Quinctius!" It is quite unnecessary to comment on the silliness and bad taste of passages of this kind, but it is interesting to note that the facts of history are too strong even for Mr. Mahaffy. In spite of his sneers at the provinciality of national feeling, and his vague panegyrics on cosmopolitan culture, he is compelled to admit (p. 403) that, "however patriotism may be superseded in stray individuals by larger benevolence, bodies of men who abandon it will only replace it by meaner motives," and cannot help expressing his regret that the better classes among the Greek communities were so entirely devoid of public spirit that they squandered "as idle absentees, or still older residents, the time and means given them to benefit their country," and failed to recognize their opportunity of founding a Hellenic Federal Empire. Even when he comes to deal with art, he cannot help admitting that the noblest sculpture of the time was that which expressed the spirit of the first great *national* struggle, the repulse of the Gallic hordes which overran Greece in 278 B.C., and that to the patriotic feeling evoked at this crisis we owe the Belvedere Apollo, the Artemis of the Vatican, the Dying Gaul, and the finest achievements of the Perganene [*sic*] school. In literature, also, Mr. Mahaffy is loud in his lamentations over what he considers to be the shallow society tendencies of the new comedy, and misses the fine freedom of Aristophanes, with his intense patriotism, his vital interest in politics, his large issues, and his delight in vigorous national life. He confesses the decay of oratory under the blighting influences of imperialism, and the sterility of those pedantic disquisitions upon style which are the inevitable consequence of the lack of healthy subject-matter. Indeed on the last page of his history Mr. Mahaffy makes a formal recantation of most of his political prejudices. He is still of opinion that Demosthenes should have been put to death for resisting the Macedonian invasion, but admits that the imperialism of Rome, which followed the imperialism of Alexander, produced incalculable mischief, beginning with intellectual decay, and ending with financial ruin. "The touch of Rome," he says, "numbed Greece and Egypt, Syria and Asia Minor, and if there are great buildings attesting the splendour of the Empire, where are the signs of intellectual and moral vigour, if we except that stronghold of nationality, the little land of Palestine?" This palinode is no doubt intended to give a plausible air of fairness to the book, but such a death-bed repentance comes too late, and makes the whole preceding history seem not fair, but foolish.

It is a relief to turn to the few chapters that deal directly with the social life and thought of the Greeks. Here Mr. Mahaffy is very pleasant reading indeed. His account of the colleges at Athens and Alexandria, for instance, is extremely interesting, and so is his estimate of the schools of Zeno, of Epicurus, and of Pyrrho. Excellent, too, in many points is the description of the literature and art of the period. We do not agree with Mr. Mahaffy in his panegyric of the Laocoon, and we are surprised to find a writer, who is very indignant at what he considers to be the modern indifference to Alexandrine poetry, gravely stating that no study is "more wearisome and profitless" than that of the Greek anthology. The criticism of the new comedy, also, seems to us somewhat pedantic. The aim of social comedy, in Menander no less than in Sheridan, is to mirror the manners, not to reform the morals of its day, and the censure of the Puritan, whether real or affected, is always out of place in literary criticism, and shows a want of recognition of the essential distinction between art and life. After all, it is only the Philistine who thinks of blaming Jack Absolute for his deception, Bob Acres for his cowardice, and Charles Surface for his extravagance, and there is very little use in airing one's moral sense at the expense of one's artistic appreciation. Valuable, also, though modernity of expression undoubtedly is, still it requires to be used with tact and judgment. There is no objection to Mr. Mahaffy's describing Philopoenen as the Garibaldi, and Antigonus Doson as the Victor Emmanuel of his age. Such comparisons have no doubt a certain cheap popular value. But, on the other hand, a phrase like "Greek Pre-raphaelitism" is rather awkward; not much is gained by dragging in an allusion to Mr. Shorthouse's "John Inglesant" in a description of the Argonautics of Apollonius Rhodius; and when we are told that the superb Pavilion erected in Alexandria by Ptolemy Philadelphus was "a sort of glorified Holborn Restaurant," we must say that the elaborate description of the building given in Athenaeus could have been summed up in a better and more intelligible epigram.

On the whole, however, Mr. Mahaffy's book may have the effect of drawing attention to a very important and interesting period in the history of Hellenism. We can only regret that, just as he has spoiled his account of Greek politics by a foolish partizan bias, so he should have marred the value of some of his remarks on literature by a bias that is quite unmeaning. It is uncouth and harsh to say that "the superannuated schoolboy who holds fellowships and masterships at English colleges" knows nothing of the period in question except what he reads in Theocritus, or that a man may be considered in England a distinguished Greek professor "who does not know a single date in Greek history between the death of Alexander and the battle of Cynoscephalae," and the statement that Lucian, Plutarch, and the Four Gospels are excluded from English school and college studies in consequence of the pedantry of "pure scholars, as they are pleased to call themselves," is of course quite inaccurate. In fact, not merely does Mr. Mahaffy miss the spirit of the true historian, but he often seems entirely devoid of the temper of the true man of letters. He is clever, and at times even brilliant, but he lacks reasonableness, moderation, style, and charm. He seems to have no sense of literary proportion, and as a rule spoils his case by overstating it. With all his passion for imperialism, there is something about Mr. Mahaffy that is, if not parochial, at least provincial, and we cannot say that this last book of his will add anything to his reputation either as a historian, a critic, or a man of taste.

84

The Poet's Corner[*]

"The Chronicle of Mites" is a mock-heroic poem about the inhabitants of a decaying cheese, who speculate about the origin of their species, and hold learned discussions upon the meaning of Evolution, and the Gospel according to Darwin. This cheese-epic is a rather unsavoury production, and the style is, at times, so monstrous and so realistic that the author should be called the Gorgon-Zola of literature.

* Unsigned review, entitled "The Poet's Corner," of (among other books) James Aitcheson, *The Chronicle of Mites*. *Pall Mall Gazette* XLVII : 7150 (15 February 1888) 2–3.

M. Caro
on George Sand*

The biography of a very great man from the pen of a very lady-like writer—this is the best description that we can give of M. Caro's life of George Sand. The late Professor of the Sorbonne could chatter charmingly about culture, and had all the fascinating insincerity of an accomplished phrase-maker; being an extremely superior person he had a great contempt for democracy and its doings, but he was always very popular with the Duchesses of the Faubourg, as there was nothing in history or in literature that he could not explain away for their edification; having never done anything remarkable he was naturally elected a member of the Academy, and he always remained loyal to the traditions of that thoroughly respectable and thoroughly pretentious institution. In fact, he was just the sort of man who should never have attempted to write a life of George Sand, or to interpret George Sand's genius. He was too feminine to appreciate the grandeur of that large womanly nature, too much of a dilettante to realize the masculine force of that strong and ardent mind. He never gets at the secret of George Sand, and never brings us near to her wonderful personality. He looks on her simply as a littérateur, as a writer of pretty stories of country life, and of charming, if somewhat exaggerated romances. But George Sand was much more than this. Beautiful as are

* Unsigned review of Elme Marie Caro, *George Sand*, translated by Gustave Masson. *Pall Mall Gazette* XLVII : 7200 (14 April 1888) 3.

such books as "Consuelo" and "Mauprat," "François le Champi," and "La Mare au Diable," yet in none of them is she adequately expressed, by none of them is she adequately revealed. As Mr. Matthew Arnold said, many years ago, "we do not know George Sand unless we feel the spirit which goes through her work as a whole." With this spirit, however, M. Caro has no sympathy. Mdme. Sand's doctrines are antediluvian, he tells us, her philosophy is quite dead, and her ideas of social regeneration are Utopian, incoherent, and absurd. The best thing for us to do is to forget these silly dreams, and to read "Teverino" and "Le Secrétaire Intime." Poor M. Caro! This spirit, which he treats with such airy flippancy, is the very leaven of modern life. It is remoulding the world for us, and fashioning our age anew. If it is antediluvian, it is so because the deluge is yet to come; if it is Utopian then Utopia must be added to our geographies. To what curious straits M. Caro is driven by his violent prejudices may be estimated by the fact that he tries to class George Sand's novels with the old *chansons de geste*, the stories of adventure characteristic of primitive literature, whereas in using fiction as a vehicle of thought, and romance as a means of influencing the social ideals of her age, George Sand was merely carrying out the traditions of Voltaire and Rousseau, of Diderot and of Chateaubriand. The novel, says M. Caro, must be allied either to poetry or to science. That it has found in philosophy one of its strongest allies seems not to have occurred to him. In an English critic such a view might possibly be excusable. Our greatest novelists, such as Fielding, Scott, and Thackeray, cared little for the philosophy of their age. But coming, as it does, from a French critic, the statement seems to show a strange want of recognition of one of the most important elements of French fiction. Nor, even in the narrow limits that he has imposed on himself, can M. Caro be said to be a very fortunate or felicitous critic. To take merely one instance out of many, he says nothing of George Sand's delightful treatment of art and the artist's life. And yet how exquisitely does she analyse each separate art, and present it to us in its relation to life! In "Consuelo" she tells us of music; in "Horace" of authorship; in "Le Chateau des Désertes" of acting; in "Les Maîtres Mosaïstes" of mosaic work; in "Le Chateau de Pictordu" of portrait-painting; and in "La Daniella" of the painting of landscape. What Mr. Ruskin and Mr. Browning have done for England, she did for France. She invented an art literature. It is unnecessary, however, to discuss any of M. Caro's minor failings, for the whole effect of the book, as far as it attempts to portray for us the scope and character of George Sand's genius, is entirely spoiled by the false attitude assumed from the beginning, and though the dictum may seem to many somewhat harsh and exclusive, we cannot help feeling that an absolute incapacity for appreciating the spirit of a great writer is no real qualification for writing a treatise on the subject. As for Mdme. Sand's private life, which is so intimately connected with her art (for like Goethe she had to live her romances before she could write them), M. Caro says hardly anything about it. He passes it over with a modesty that almost makes one blush, and for fear of wounding the susceptibilities of those *grandes dames*, whose passions M. Paul Bourget analyses with such subtlety, he transforms her mother, who was a typical French *grisette*, into "a very amiable and *spirituelle* milliner"! It must be admitted that Joseph Surface himself could hardly show greater tact and delicacy, though we ourselves must plead guilty to preferring Mdme. Sand's own description of her as an "enfant du vieux pavé de Paris."

As regards the English version, which is by M. Gustave Masson, it may be up to the intellectual requirements of the Harrow schoolboys, but it will hardly satisfy those who consider that accuracy, lucidity, and ease are essential to a good translation. Its carelessness is absolutely astounding, and it is difficult to understand how a publisher like Mr. Routledge could have allowed such a piece of work to issue from his press. "Il descend avec le sourire d'un Machiavel" appears as "he descends into the simile of a Machiavelli;" George Sand's remark to Flaubert about literary style, "tu la considères comme un but, elle n'est qu'un effet," is tranlsated, "you consider it an end, it is merely *an effort;*" and such a simple phrase as "ainsi le veut l'esthétique du roman" is converted into "so the aesthetes of the world would have it." "Il faudra relâcher mes économies" is "I will have to draw upon my savings," not "my economies will assuredly be relaxed;" "cassures resineuses" is not "cleavages full of rosin;" and

"Mme. Sand ne réussit que deux fois" is hardly "Mdme. Sand was not twice successful." "Querelles d'école" does not mean "school disputations;" "ceux qui se font une sorte d'esthétique de l'indifférence absolue," is not "those of which the aesthetics seem to be an absolute indifference;" "chimère" should not be translated "chimera," nor "lettres inédites" "inedited letters;" "ridicules" means absurdities, not "ridicules," and "qui pourra définir sa pensée?" is not "who can clearly despise her thought?" M. Masson comes to grief over even such a simple sentence as "elle s'étonna des fureurs qui accueillirent ce livre, ne comprenant pas que l'on haisse un auteur à travers son oeuvre," which he translates, "she was surprised at the storm which greeted this book, *not understanding that the author is hated through his work.*" Then passing over such phrases as "substituted by religion" instead of "replaced by religion," and "vulgarization" where "popularization" is meant, we come to that most irritating form of translation, the literal word-for-word style. The stream "excites itself by the declivity which it obeys" is one of M. Masson's finest achievements in this *genre,* and it is an admirable instance of the influence of schoolboys on their masters. However, it would be tedious to make a complete "catalogue of slips," so we will content ourselves by saying that M. Masson's translation is not merely quite unworthy of himself, but is also quite undeserved by the public. Nowadays even the public has its feelings.

[Poems by Henley and Sharp]*

"If I were king," says Mr. Henley in one of his most modest rondeaus,

> "Art should aspire, yet ugliness be dear;
> Beauty, the shaft, should speed with wit for feather;
> And love, sweet love, should never fall to sere,
>   If I were king."

And these lines contain, if not the best criticism of his own work, certainly a very complete statement of his aim and motive as a poet. His little "Book of Verse" (David Nutt) reveals to us an artist who is seeking to find new methods of expression, and who has not merely a delicate sense of beauty and a brilliant fantastic wit, but a real passion also for what is horrible, ugly, or grotesque. No doubt everything that is worthy of existence is worthy also of art—at least, one would like to think so—but while echo or mirror can repeat for us a beautiful thing, to artistically render a thing that is ugly requires the most exquisite alchemy of form, the most subtle magic of transformation. To me there is more of the cry of Marsyas than of the singing of Apollo in the earlier poems of Mr. Henley's volume, the "Rhymes and Rhythms in Hospital," as he calls

---

* Article entitled, "A Note on Some Modern Poets," *Woman's World* II : 14 (December 1888) 108–12.

them. But it is impossible to deny their power. Some of them
are like bright, vivid pastels; others like charcoal drawings, with
dull blacks and murky whites; others like etchings with deeply-
bitten lines, and abrupt contrasts, and clever colour-suggestions.
In fact, they are like anything and everything, except perfected
poems—that they certainly are not. They are still in the twilight. They are preludes, experiments, inspired jottings in a
note-book, and should be heralded by a design of "Genius making Sketches." Rhyme gives architecture as well as melody to
verse; it gives that delightful sense of limitation which in all
the arts is so pleasurable, and is, indeed, one of the secrets of
perfection; it will whisper, as a French critic has said, "things
unexpected and charming, things with strange and remote
relations to each other," and bind them together in indissoluble
bonds of beauty; and in his constant rejection of rhyme Mr.
Henley seems to me to have abdicated half his power. He is a
roi en exil who has thrown away some of the strings of his lute,
a poet who has forgotten the fairest part of his kingdom.

However, all work criticizes itself. Here is one of Mr. Henley's inspired jottings. According to the temperament of the
reader it will serve either as a model or as the reverse:—

"As with varnish red and glistening
  Dripped his hair; his feet were rigid;
  Raised, he settled stiffly sideways,
  You could see the hurts were spinal.

"He had fallen from an engine,
  And been dragged across the metals.
  It was hopeless, and they knew it,
  So they covered him and left him.

"As he lay, by fits half sentient,
  Inarticulately moaning,
  With his stockinged feet protruded
  Sharp and awkward from the blankets,

"To his bed there came a woman;
  Stood and looked, and sighed a little,
  And departed without speaking,
  As himself a few hours after.

> "I was told she was his sweetheart.
> They were on the eve of marriage.
> She was quiet as a statue,
> But her lip was gray and writhen."

In this poem the rhythm, and the music, such as it is, are obvious—perhaps a little too obvious. In the following I see nothing but ingeniously printed prose. It is a description—and a very accurate one—of a scene in a hospital ward. The medical students are supposed to be crowding round the doctor. What I quote is only a fragment, but the poem itself is a fragment:—

> "So shows the ring
> Seen, from behind, round a conjuror
> Doing his pitch in the street.
> High shoulders, low shoulders, broad shoulders, narrow ones,
> Round, square, and angular, serry and shove;
> While from within a voice,
> Gravely and weightily fluent,
> Sounds; and then ceases; and suddenly
> (Look at the stress of the shoulders!)
> Out of a quiver of silence,
> Over the hiss of the spray,
> Comes a low cry, and the sound
> Of breath quick intaken through teeth
> Clenched in resolve. And the master
> Breaks from the crowd, and goes,
> Wiping his hands,
> To the next bed, with his pupils
> Flocking and whispering behind him.

> "Now one can see.
> Case Number One
> Sits (rather pale) with his bed-clothes
> Stripped up, and showing his foot
> (Alas, for God's image!)
> Swaddled in wet white lint
> Brilliantly hideous with red."

Théophile Gautier once said that Flaubert's style was meant to be read, and his own style to be looked at. Mr. Henley's unrhymed rhythms form very dainty designs, from a typographical point of view. From the point of view of literature, they are a series of vivid concentrated impressions with a keen grip of fact, a terrible actuality, and an almost masterly power of picturesque presentation. But the poetic form—what of that?

Well, let us pass to the later poems, to the rondels and rondeaus, the sonnets and quatorzains, the echoes and the ballades. How brilliant and fanciful this is! The Toyokuni colour-print that suggested it could not be more delightful. It seems to have kept all the wilful fantastic charm of the original:—

> "Was I a Samurai renowned,
> Two-sworded, fierce, immense of bow?
> A histrion, angular and profound?
> A priest? a porter?—Child, although
> I have forgotten clean, I know
> That in the shade of Fujisan,
> What time the cherry-orchards blow,
> I loved you once in old Japan.
>
> "As here you loiter, flowing-gowned
> And hugely sashed, with pins a-row
> Your quaint head as with flamelets crowned,
> Demure, inviting—even so,
> When merry maids in Miyako
> To feel the sweet o' the year began,
> And green gardens to overflow,
> I loved you once in old Japan.
>
> "Clear shine the hills; the rice-fields round
> Two cranes are circling; sleepy and slow,
> A blue canal the lake's blue bound
> Breaks at the bamboo bridge; and lo!
> Touched with the sundown's spirit and glow,
> I see you turn, with flirted fan,
> Against the plum-tree's bloomy snow . . .
> I loved you once in old Japan!
>
> "ENVOY.
>
> "Dear, 'twas a dozen lives ago;
> But that I was a lucky man

> The Toyokuni here will show:
> I loved you—once—in old Japan!"

This rondel, too—how light it is, and graceful!—

> "We'll to the woods and gather may
> Fresh from the footprints of the rain;
> We'll to the woods, at every vein
> To drink the spirit of the day.
>
> "The winds of spring are out at play,
> The needs of spring in heart and brain.
> We'll to the woods and gather may
> Fresh from the footprints of the rain.
>
> "The world's too near her end, you say?
> Hark to the blackbird's mad refrain!
> It waits for her, the vast Inane?
> Then, girls, to help her on the way
> We'll to the woods and gather may."

There are fine verses, also, scattered through this little book; some of them very strong, as—

> "Out of the night that covers me,
>   Black as the pit from pole to pole.
> I thank whatever gods may be
>   For my unconquerable soul.
>
> "It matters not how strait the gate,
>   How charged with punishments the scroll,
> I am the master of my fate:
>   I am the captain of my soul."

Others with a true touch of romance, as—

> "Or ever the knightly years were gone
>   With the old world to the grave,
> I was a King in Babylon,
>   And you were a Christian slave."

And here and there we come across such felicitous phrases as—

"In the sand
The gold prow-griffin claws a hold."

Or—

"The spires
Shine and are changed."

And many other graceful or fanciful lines, even "the green sky's minor thirds" being perfectly right in its place, and a very refreshing bit of affectation in a volume where there is so much that is natural.

However, Mr. Henley is not to be judged by samples. Indeed, the most attractive thing in the book is no single poem that is in it, but the strong humane personality that stands behind both flawless and faulty work alike, and looks out through many masks, some of them beautiful, and some grotesque, and not a few mis-shapen. In the case of most of our modern poets, when we have analyzed them down to an adjective we can go no further, or we care to go no further, but with this book it is different. Through these reeds and pipes blows the very breath of life. It seems as if one could put one's hand upon the singer's heart and count its pulsations. There is something wholesome, virile, and sane about the man's soul. Anybody can be reasonable, but to be sane is not common; and sane poets are as rare as blue lilies, though they may not be quite so delightful.

"Let the great winds their worst and wildest blow,
    Or the gold weather round us mellow slow;
We have fulfilled ourselves, and we can dare,
And we can conquer, though we may not share
    In the rich quiet of the afterglow,
            What is to come,"

is the concluding stanza of the last rondeau—indeed, of the last poem in the collection, and the high serene temper displayed in these lines serves at once as keynote and keystone to the book. The very lightness and slightness of so much of the

95

work, its careless moods and casual fancies, seem to suggest a nature that is not primarily interested in art—a nature, like Sordello's, passionately enamoured of life, and to which lyre and lute are things of less importance. From this mere joy of living, this frank delight in experience for its own sake, this lofty indifference, and momentary unregretted ardours, come all the faults and all the beauties of the volume. But there is this difference between them—the faults are deliberate and the result of much study, the beauties have the air of fascinating impromptus. Mr. Henley's healthy, if sometimes misapplied, confidence in the myriad suggestions of life gives him his charm. He is made to sing along the highways, not to sit down and write. If he took himself more seriously his work would become trivial.

Mr. William Sharp takes himself very seriously, and has written a preface to his "Romantic Ballads and Poems of Phantasy" (Walter Scott), which is, on the whole, the most interesting part of his volume. We are all, it seems, far too cultured, and lack robustness. There are those amongst us, says Mr. Sharp, who would prefer a dexterously turned triolet to such apparently uncouth measures as "Thomas the Rhymer" or the ballad of "Clerk Saunders," and who "would rather listen to the drawing-room music of the Villanelle than to the wild harp-playing by the mill-dams o' Binnorie, or the sough of the night-wind o'er drumly Allan water." Such an expression as "the drawing-room music of the Villanelle" is not very happy, and I cannot imagine any one with the smallest pretensions to culture preferring a dexterously turned triolet to a fine imaginative ballad, as it is only the Philistine who ever dreams of comparing works of art that are absolutely different in motive, in treatment, and in form. If English Poetry is in danger—and, according to Mr. Sharp, the poor nymph is in a very critical state—what she has to fear is not the fascination of dainty metre or delicate form, but the predominance of the intellectual spirit over the spirit of beauty. Lord Tennyson dethroned Wordsworth as a literary influence, and later on Mr. Swinburne filled all the mountain valleys with echoes of his own song. The influence to-day is that of Mr. Browning. And as for the triolets, and the rondels, and the careful study of metrical subtleties, these things are merely the signs of a desire for perfection in small things, and of the recognition of poetry as an art. They have had certainly one good result—they have made our minor poets readable, and have not left us entirely at the mercy of geniuses.

But, says Mr. Sharp, every one is far too literary; even Rossetti is too literary. What we want is simplicity and directness of utterance; these should be the dominant characteristics of poetry. Well, is that quite so certain? Are simplicity and directness of utterance absolute essentials for poetry? I think not. They may be admirable for the drama, admirable for all those imitative forms of literature that claim to mirror life in its externals and its accidents, admirable for quiet narrative, admirable in their place; but their place is not everywhere. Poetry has many modes of music; she does not blow through one pipe alone. Directness of utterance is good, but so is the subtle recasting of thought into a new and delightful form. Simplicity is good, but complexity, mystery, strangeness, symbolism, obscurity even, these have their value. Indeed, properly speaking, there is no such thing as Style; there are merely styles, that is all.

One cannot help feeling also that everything that Mr. Sharp says in his preface was said at the beginning of the century by Wordsworth, only where Wordsworth called us back to nature Mr. Sharp invites us to woo romance. Romance, he tells us, is "in the air." A new romantic movement is imminent. "I anticipate," he says, "that many of our poets, especially those of the youngest generation, will shortly turn towards the ballad as a poetic vehicle, and that the next year or two will see much romantic poetry."

The ballad! Well, Mr. Andrew Lang some months ago signed the death-warrant of the ballade, and—though I hope that in this respect Mr. Lang resembles the Queen in "Alice in Wonderland," whose bloodthirsty orders were by general consent never carried into execution—it must be admitted that the number of ballades given to us by some of our poets was perhaps a little excessive. But the ballad? "Sir Patrick Spens," "Clerk Saunders," "Thomas the Rhymer"—are these to be our archetypes, our models, the sources of our inspiration? They are certainly great imaginative poems. In Chatterton's "Ballad of Charity," Coleridge's "Rhyme of the Ancient Mariner," the "La Belle Dame sans Merci" of Keats, the "Sister Helen" of Rossetti, we can see what marvellous works of art the spirit of old romance may fashion. But to preach a spirit is one thing, to propose a form is another. It is true that Mr. Sharp warns the rising generation against imitation. A ballad, he reminds them, does not necessarily denote a poem in quatrains and in antique language. But his own poems, as I think will be seen later on, are, in their way, warnings, and show the danger of suggesting any definite "poetic vehicle." And, further, are simplicity and directness of utterance really the dominant characteristics of these old imaginative ballads that Mr. Sharp so enthusiastically, and, in some particulars, so wisely praises? It does not seem to me to be so. We are always apt to think that the voices which sang at the dawn of poetry were simpler, fresher, and more natural than ours, and that the world which the early poets looked at, and through which they walked, had a kind of poetical quality of its own, and could pass, almost without changing, into song. The snow lies thick now upon Olympus, and its scarped sides are bleak and barren, but once, we fancy, the white feet of the Muses brushed the dew from the anemones in the morning, and at evening came Apollo to sing to the shepherds in the vale. But in this we are merely lending to other ages what we desire, or think we desire, for our own. Our historical sense is at fault. Every century that produces poetry is, so far, an artificial century, and the work that seems to us the most natural and simple product of its time is probably the result of the most deliberate and self-conscious effort. For Nature is always behind the age. It takes a great artist to be thoroughly modern.

Let us turn to the poems, which have really only the preface to blame for their somewhat late appearance. The best is undoubtedly "The Weird of Michael Scott," and these stanzas are a fair example of its power:—

> "Then Michael Scott laughed long and loud:
> 'Whan shone the mune ahint yon cloud

I speered the towers that saw my birth—
Lang, lang, sall wait my cauld grey shroud,
Lang cauld and weet my bed o' earth!'

"But as by Stair he rode full speed
His horse began to pant and bleed;
'Win hame, win hame, my bonnie mare,
Win hame if thou would'st rest and feed,
Win hame, we're nigh the House of Stair!'

"But with a shrill heart-bursten yell
The white horse stumbled, plunged, and fell,
And loud a summoning voice arose,
'Is't White-Horse Death that rides frae Hell,
Or Michael Scott that hereby goes?'

" 'Ah, Lord of Stair, I ken ye weel!
Avaunt or I your saul sall steal,
An' send ye howling through the wood
A wild man-wolf—aye ye maun reel
An' cry upon your Holy Rood!' "

There is a good deal of vigour, no doubt, in these lines; but one cannot help asking whether this is to be the common tongue of the future Renaissance of Romance. Are we all to talk Scotch, and to speak of the moon as the "mune," and the soul as the "saul"? I hope not. And yet if this Renaissance is to be a vital, living thing, it must have its linguistic side. Just as the spiritual development of music, and the artistic development of painting, have always been accompanied, if not occasioned, by the discovery of some new instrument or some fresh medium, so, in the case of any important literary movement, half of its strength resides in its language. If it does not bring with it a rich and novel mode of expression, it is doomed either to sterility or to imitation. Dialect, archaisms, and the like, will not do. Take, for instance, another poem of Mr. Sharp's, a poem which he calls "The Deith-Tide":—

"The weet saut wind is blawing
Upon the misty shore;
As like a stormy snawing

> The deid go streaming o'er:—
>   The wan drown'd deid sail wildly
>   Frae out each drumly wave:
>   It's O and O for the weary sea,
>   And O for a quiet grave."

This is simply a very clever *pastiche*, nothing more, and our language is not likely to be permanently enriched by such words as "weet," "saut," "blawing," and "snawing." Even "drumly," an adjective of which Mr. Sharp is so fond that he uses it both in prose and verse, seems to me to be hardly an adequate basis for a new romantic movement.

However, Mr. Sharp does not always write in dialect. "The Song of Allan" can be read without any difficulty, and "Phantasy" can be read with pleasure. They are both very charming poems in their way, and none the less charming because the cadences of the one recall "Sister Helen," and the motive of the other reminds us of "La Belle Dame sans Merci." But those who wish to thoroughly enjoy Mr. Sharp's poems should not read his preface; just as those who approve of the preface should avoid reading the poems. I cannot help saying that I think the preface a great mistake. The work that follows it is quite inadequate, and there seems little use in heralding a dawn that rose long ago, and proclaiming a Renaissance whose first-fruits, if we are to judge them by any high standard of perfection, are of so ordinary a character.

English Poetesses[*]

England has given to the world one great poetess—Elizabeth Barrett Browning. By her side Mr Swinburne would place Miss Christina Rossetti, whose New Year hymn he describes as so much the noblest of sacred poems in our language, that there is none which comes near it enough to stand second. "It is a hymn," he tells us, "touched as with the fire, and bathed as in the light of sunbeams, tuned as to chords and cadences of refluent sea-music beyond reach of harp and organ, large echoes of the serene and sonorous tides of heaven." Much as I admire Miss Rossetti's work, her subtle choice of words, her rich imagery, her artistic *naïveté*, wherein curious notes of strangeness and simplicity are fantastically blended together, I cannot but think that Mr Swinburne has, with noble and natural loyalty, placed her on too lofty a pedestal. To me, she is simply a very delightful artist in poetry. This is indeed something so rare that when we meet it we cannot fail to love it, but it is not everything. Beyond it and above it are higher and more sunlit heights of song, a larger vision, and an ampler air, a music at once more passionate and more profound, a creative energy that is born of the spirit, a winged rapture that is born of the soul, a force and fervour of mere utterance that has all the wonder of the prophet, and not a little of the consecration of the priest. Mrs Browning is unapproachable by any woman

* *Queen* LXXIV : 2189 (8 December 1888) 742–43.

who has ever touched lyre or blown through reed since the days of the great Æolian poetess. But Sappho, who, to the antique world, was a pillar of flame, is to us but a pillar of shadow. Of her poems, burnt with other most precious work by Byzantine Emperor and by Roman Pope, only a few fragments remain. Possibly they lie mouldering in the scented darkness of an Egyptian tomb, clasped in the withered hands of some long-dead lover. Some Greek monk at Athos may even now be poring over an ancient manuscript, whose crabbed characters conceal lyric or ode by her whom the Greeks spoke of as "the Poetess," just as they termed Homer "the Poet," who was to them the tenth Muse, the flower of the Graces, the child of Erôs, and the pride of Hellas—Sappho, with the sweet voice, the bright, beautiful eyes, the dark hyacinth-coloured hair. But, practically, the work of the marvellous singer of Lesbos is entirely lost to us. We have a few rose leaves out of her garden, that is all. Literature nowadays survives marble and bronze, but in old days, in spite of the Roman poet's noble boast, it was not so. The fragile clay vases of the Greek's still keep for us pictures of Sappho, delicately painted in black and red and white; but of her song we have only the echo of an echo.

Of all the women of history, Mrs Browning is the only one that we could name in any possible or remote conjunction with Sappho. Sappho was undoubtedly a far more flawless and perfect artist. She stirred the whole antique world more than Mrs Browning ever stirred our modern age. Never had Love such a singer. Even in the few lines that remain to us the passion seems to scorch and burn. But, as unjust Time, who has crowned her with the barren laurels of fame, has twined with them the dull poppies of oblivion, let us turn from the mere memory of a poetess to one whose song still remains to us as an imperishable glory of our literature; to her who heard the cry of the children from dark mine and crowded factory, and made England weep over its little ones; who, in the feigned sonnets from the Portug[u]ese, sang of the spiritual mystery of Love, and of the intellectual gifts that Love brings to the soul; who had faith in all that is worthy, and enthusiasm for all that is great, and pity for all that suffers; who wrote the "Vision of Poets," and "Casa Guidi Windows," and "Aurora Leigh."

As one, to whom I owe my love of poetry no less than my love of country, has said of her:

> Still on our ears
> The clear "Excelsior" from a woman's lip
> Rings out across the Apennines, although
> The woman's brow lies pale and cold in death
> With all the mighty marble dead in Florence.
> For while great songs can stir the hearts of men,
> Spreading their full vibrations through the world
> In ever-widening circles till they reach
> The Throne of God, and song becomes a prayer,
> And prayer brings down the liberating strength
> That kindles nations to heroic deeds,
> She lives—the great-souled poetess who saw
> From Casa Guidi windows Freedom dawn
> On Italy, and gave the glory back
> In sunrise hymns to all Humanity!

She lives indeed, and not alone in the heart of Shakespeare's England, but in the heart of Dante's Italy also. To Greek literature she owed her scholarly culture, but modern Italy created her human passion for Liberty. When she crossed the Alps she became filled with a new ardour, and from that fine, eloquent mouth, that we can still see in her portraits, broke forth such a noble and majestic outburst of lyrical song as had not been heard from woman's lips for more than two thousand years. It is pleasant to think that an English poetess was to a certain extent a real factor in bringing about that unity of Italy that was Dante's dream, and if Florence drove her great singer into exile, she at least welcomed within her walls the later singer that England had sent to her.

If one were asked the chief qualities of Mrs Browning's work, one would say, as Mr Swinburne said of Byron's, its sincerity and its strength. Faults it, of course, possesses. "She would rhyme moon to table," used to be said of her in jest; and certainly no more monstrous rhymes are to be found in all literature than some of those we come across in Mrs Browning's poems. But her ruggedness was never the result of carelessness.

It was deliberate, as her letters to Mr Horne show very clearly. She refused to sandpaper her muse. She disliked facile smoothness and artificial polish. In her very rejection of art she was an artist. She intended to produce a certain effect by certain means, and she succeeded; and her indifference to complete assonance in rhyme often gives a splendid richness to her verse, and brings into it a pleasurable element of surprise.

In philosophy she was a Platonist, in politics an Opportunist. She attached herself to no particular party. She loved the people when they were king-like, and kings when they showed themselves to be men. Of the real value and motive of poetry she had a most exalted ideal. "Poetry," she says, in the preface to one of her volumes, "has been as serious a thing to me as life itself; and life has been a very serious thing. There has been no playing at skittles for me in either. I never mistook pleasure for the final cause of poetry, nor leisure for the hour of the poet. I have done my work so far, not as mere hand and head work apart from the personal being, but as the completest expression of that being to which I could attain." It certainly is her completest expression, and through it she realizes her fullest perfection. "The poet," she says elsewhere, "is at once richer and poorer than he used to be; he wears better broadcloth, but speaks no more oracles." These words give us the keynote to her view of the poet's mission. He was to utter Divine oracles, to be at once inspired prophet and holy priest; and as such we may, I think, without exaggeration, conceive her. She was a Sibyl delivering a message to the world, sometimes through stammering lips, and once at least with blinded eyes, yet always with the true fire and fervour of lofty and unshaken faith, always with the great raptures of a spiritual nature, the high ardours of an impassioned soul. As we read her best poems we feel that, though Apollo's shrine be empty and the bronze tripod overthrown, and the vale of Delphi desolate, still the Pythia is not dead. In our own age she has sung for us, and this land gave her new birth. Indeed, Mrs Browning is the wisest of the Sibyls, wiser even than that mighty figure whom Michael Angelo has painted on the roof of the Sistine Chapel at Rome, poring over the scroll of mystery, and trying to decipher the secrets of Fate; for she realised that, while Knowledge is power, Suffering is part of Knowledge.

To her influence, almost as much as to the higher education of women, I would be inclined to attribute the really remarkable awakening of women's song that characterises the latter half of our century in England. No country has ever had so many poetesses at once. Indeed, when one remembers that the Greeks had only nine muses, one is sometimes apt to fancy that we have too many. And yet the work done by women in the sphere of poetry is really of a very high standard of excellence. In England we have always been prone to underrate the value of tradition in literature. In our eagerness to find a new voice and a fresh mode of music we have forgotten how beautiful Echo may be. We look first for individuality and personality, and these are, indeed, the chief characteristics of the masterpieces of our literature, either in prose or verse; but deliberate culture and a study of the best models, if united to an artistic temperament and a nature susceptible of exquisite impressions, may produce much that is admirable, much that is worthy of praise. It would be quite impossible to give a complete catalogue of all the women who since Mrs Browning's day have tried lute and lyre. Mrs Pfeiffer, Mrs Hamilton King, Mrs Augusta Webster, Graham Tomson, Miss Mary Robinson, Jean Ingelow, Miss May Kendall, Miss Nesbit, Miss May Probyn, Mrs Craik, Mrs Meynell, Miss Chapman, and many others have done really good work in poetry, either in the grave Dorian mode of thoughtful and intellectual verse, or in the light and graceful forms of old French song, or in the romantic manner of antique ballad, or in that "moment's monument," as Rossetti called it, the intense and concentrated sonnet. Occasionally one is tempted to wish that the quick artistic faculty that women undoubtedly possess developed itself somewhat more in prose and somewhat less in verse. Poetry is for our highest moods, when we wish to be with the gods, and in poetry nothing but the very best should satisfy us; but prose is for our daily bread, and the lack of good prose is one of the chief blots on our culture. French prose, even in the hands of the most ordinary writers, is always readable, but English prose is detestable. We have a few, a very few masters, such as they are. We have Carlyle, who should not be imitated; and Mr Pater, who, through the subtle perfection of his form, is inimitable absolutely; and Mr Froude, who is useful; and Mathew Arnold, who is a model; and Mr George Meredith, who is a warning; and Mr Lang, who is the divine amateur; and Mr Stevenson, who is the humane artist; and Mr Ruskin, whose rhythm and colour and fine rhetoric and marvellous music of words are entirely unattainable. But the general prose that one reads in magazines and in newspapers is terribly dull and cumbrous, heavy in movement and uncouth or exaggerated in expression. Possibly some day our women of letters will apply themselves more definitely to prose. Their light touch, and exquisite ear, and delicate sense of balance and proportion would be of no small service to us. I can fancy women bringing a new manner into our literature.

However, we have to deal here with women as poetesses, and it is interesting to note that, though Mrs Browning's influence undoubtedly contributed very largely to the development of this new song-movement, if I may so term it, still there seems to have been never a time during the last three hundred years when the women of this kingdom did not cultivate, if not the art, at least the habit, of writing poetry. Who the first English poetess was I cannot say. I believe it was the Abbess Juliana Berners, who lived in the fifteenth century; but I have no doubt that Mr Freeman would be able at a moment's notice to produce some wonderful Saxon or Norman poetess, whose works cannot be read without a glossary, and even with its aid are completely unintelligible. For my own part, I am content with the Abbess Juliana, who wrote enthusiastically about hawking; and after her I would mention Anne Askew, who in prison and on the eve of her fiery martydom wrote a ballad that has, at any rate, a pathetic and historical interest. Queen Elizabeth's "most sweet and sententious ditty" on Mary Stuart is highly praised by Puttenham, a contemporary critic, as an example of "Exargasia, or the Gorgeous in Literature," which somehow seems a very suitable epithet for such a great Queen's poems. The term she applies to the unfortunate Queen of Scots, "the daughter of debate" has, of course, long since passed into literature. The Countess of Pembroke, Sir Philip Sidney's sister, was much admired as a poetess in her day. In 1613 the "learned, virtuous, and truly noble ladie" Elizabeth Carew published a "Tragedie of Mariam, the Faire Queene of Jewry," and a few years later the "noble ladie Diana Primrose" wrote "A Chain of Pearl," which is a panegyric on the "peerless graces" of Gloriana. Mary Morpeth, the friend and admirer of Drummond of Hawthornden; Lady Mary Wroth, to whom Ben Jonson dedicated the "Alchemist;" and the Princess Elizabeth, the sister of Charles I, should also be mentioned. After the Restoration women applied themselves with still greater ardour to the study of literature and the practice of poetry. Margaret Duchess of Newcastle was a true woman of letters, and some of her verses are extremely pretty and graceful. Mrs Aphra Behn was the first Englishwoman who adopted literature as a regular profession. Mrs Katharine Philips, according to Mr Gosse, invented sentimentality. As she was praised by Dryden, and mourned by Cowley, let us hope she may be forgiven. Keats came across her poems at Oxford when he was writing "Endymion," and found in one of them "a most delicate fancy of the Fletcher kind;" but I fear that nobody reads the Matchless Orinda now. Of Lady Winchelsea's "Nocturnal Reverie" Wordsworth said that with the exception of Pope's "Windsor Forest," it was the only poem of the period intervening between "Paradise Lost" and Thompson's "Seasons" that contained a single new image of external nature. Lady Rachel Russell, who may be said to have inaugurated the letter-writing literature of England; Eliza Haywood, who is immortalised by the badness of her work, and has a niche in the Dunciad; and the Marchioness of Wharton, whose poems Waller said he admired, are very remarkable types, the finest of them being, of course, the first named, who was a woman of heroic mould and of a most noble dignity of nature. Indeed, though the English poetesses up to the time of Mrs Browning cannot be said to have produced any work of absolute genius, they are certainly interesting figures, fascinating subjects for study. Amongst them we find Lady Mary Wortley Montague, who had all the caprice of Cleopatra, and whose letters are delightful reading; Mrs Centlivre, who wrote one brilliant comedy; Lady Anne Barnard, whose "Auld Robin Gray" was described by Sir Walter Scott as "worth all the dialogues Corydon and Phillis have together spoken from the days of Theocritus downwards," and is certainly a very beautiful and touching poem; Esther Vanhomrigh and Hester Johnson, the Vanessa and the Stella of Dean Swift's life; Mrs Thrale, the friend of the great Lexicographer; the worthy Mrs Barbauld; the excellent Mrs Hannah More; the industrious Joanna Baillie; the admirable Mrs Chapone, whose "Ode to Solitude" always fills me with the wildest passion for society, and who will at least be remembered as the patroness of the establishment at which Becky Sharp was educated; Miss Anna Seward, who was called "the Swan of Lichfield;" poor L. E. L., whom Disraeli described in one of his clever letters to his sister as "the personification of Brompton—pink satin dress, white satin shoes, red cheeks, snub nose, and her hair *à la* Sappho;" Mrs Ratcliffe, who introduced the romantic novel, and has consequently much to answer for; the beautiful Duchess of Devonshire, of whom Gibbon said that she was "made for something better than a duchess;" the two wonderful sisters Lady Dufferin and Mrs Norton; Mrs Tighe, whose "Psyche" Keats read with pleasure; Constantia Grierson, a marvellous blue stocking in her time; Mrs Hemans; pretty, charming "Perdita," who flirted alternately with poetry and the Prince Regent, played divinely in "The Winter's Tale," was brutally attacked by Gifford, and has left us a pathetic little poem on the snowdrop; and Emily Bronte, whose poems are instinct with tragic power, and seem often on the verge of being great.

Old fashions in literature are not so pleasant as old fashions in dress. I like the costume of the age of powder better than the poetry of the age of Pope. But if one adopts the historical standpoint—and this is, indeed, the only standpoint from which we can ever form a fair estimate of work that is not absolutely of the highest order—we cannot fail to see that many of the English poetesses who preceded Mrs Browning were women of no ordinary talent, and that if the majority of them looked upon poetry simply as a department of *belles lettres,* so in most cases did their contemporaries. Since Mrs Browning's day our woods have become full of singing birds, and if I venture to ask them to apply themselves more to prose and less to song, it is not that I like poetical prose, but that I love the prose of poets.

London Models*

Professional models are a purely modern invention. To the Greeks, for instance, they were quite unknown. Mr. Mahaffy, it is true, tells us that Perikles used to present peacocks to the great ladies of Athenian society in order to induce them to sit to his friend Pheidias, and we know that Polygnotus introduced into his picture of the Trojan women the face of Elpinike, the celebrated sister of the great Conservative leader of the day, but those *grandes dames* clearly do not come under our category. As for the old masters, they undoubtedly made constant studies from their pupils and apprentices, and even their religious pictures are full of the portraits of their friends and relations, but they do not seem to have had the inestimable advantage of the existence of a class of people whose sole profession is to pose. In fact the model, in our sense of the word, is the direct creation of Academic Schools.

Every country now has its own models, except America. In New York, and even in Boston, a good model is so great a rarity that most of the artists are reduced to painting Niagara and millionaires. In Europe, however, it is different. Here we have plenty of models, and of every nationality. The Italian models are the best. The natural grace of their attitudes, as well as the wonderful picturesqueness of their colouring, makes them facile —often too facile—subjects for the painter's brush. The French

* *English Illustrated Magazine* VI : 64 (January 1889) 313–19.

models, though not so beautiful as the Italian, possess a quickness of intellectual sympathy, a capacity in fact of understanding the artist, which is quite remarkable. They have also a great command over the varieties of facial expression, are peculiarly dramatic, and can chatter the *argot* of the *atelier* as cleverly as the critic of the *Gil Blas*. The English models form a class entirely by themselves. They are not so picturesque as the Italian, nor so clever as the French, and they have absolutely no tradition, so to speak, of their order. Now and then some old veteran knocks at a studio door, and proposes to sit as Ajax defying the lightning, or as King Lear upon the blasted heath. One of them some time ago called on a popular painter who, happening at the moment to require his services, engaged him, and told him to begin by kneeling down in the attitude of prayer. "Shall I be Biblical or Shakespearean, sir?" asked the veteran. "Well—— Shakespearean," answered the artist, wondering by what subtle *nuance* of expression the model would convey the difference. "All right, sir," said the professor of posing, and he solemnly knelt down and began to wink with his left eye! This class however is dying out. As a rule the model, nowadays, is a pretty girl, from about twelve to twenty-five years of age, who knows nothing about art, cares less, and is merely anxious to earn seven or eight shillings a day without much trouble. English models rarely look at a picture, and never venture on any æsthetic theories. In fact they realize very completely Mr. Whistler's idea of the function of an art-critic, for they pass no criticisms at all. They accept all schools of art with the grand catholicity of the auctioneer, and sit to a fantastic young impressionist as readily as to a learned and laborious academician. They are neither for the Whistlerites, nor against them; the quarrel between the school of facts and the school of effects touches them not; idealistic and naturalistic are words that convey no meaning to their ears; they merely desire that the studio shall be warm, and the lunch hot, for all charming artists give their models lunch.

As to what they are asked to do they are equally indifferent. On Monday they will don the rags of a beggar-girl for Mr. Pumper, whose pathetic pictures of modern life draw such tears from the public, and on Tuesday they will pose in a peplum for Mr. Phœbus, who thinks that all really artistic subjects are necessarily B.C. They career gaily through all centuries and through all costumes, and, like actors, are only interesting when they are not themselves. They are extremely good-natured, and very accommodating. "What do you sit for?" said a young artist to a model who had sent him in her card (all models by the way have cards and a small black bag). "Oh, for anything you like sir," said the girl; "landscape if necessary!"

Intellectually, it must be acknowledged, they are Philistines, but physically they are perfect—at least some are. Though none of them can talk Greek, many can look Greek, which to a nineteenth-century painter is naturally of great importance. If they are allowed, they chatter a great deal, but they never say anything. Their observations are the only *banalités* heard in Bohemia. However, though they cannot appreciate the artist as an artist, they are quite ready to appreciate the artist as a man. They are very sensitive to kindness, respect, and generosity. A beautiful model who had sat for two years to one of our most distinguished English painters, got engaged to a street vendor of penny ices. On her marriage the painter sent her a pretty wedding present, and received in return a nice letter of thanks with the following remarkable postscript: "Never eat the green ices!"

When they are tired a wise artist gives them a rest. Then they sit in a chair and read penny dreadfuls, till they are roused from the tragedy of literature to take their place again in the tragedy of art. A few of them smoke cigarettes. This however is regarded by the other models as showing a want of seriousness, and is not generally approved of. They are engaged by the day and by the half-day. The tariff is a shilling an hour, to which great artists usually add an omnibus fare. The two best things about them are their extraordinary prettiness, and their extreme respectability. As a class they are very well behaved, particularly those who sit for the figure, a fact which is curious or natural according to the view one takes of human nature. They usually marry well, and sometimes they marry the artist. In neither case do they ever sit again. For an artist to marry his model is as fatal as for a *gourmet* to marry his cook, the one gets no sittings, and the other gets no dinners.

On the whole the English female models are very *naïve*, very natural, and very good-humoured. The virtues which the artist

111

values most in them are prettiness and punctuality. Every sensible model consequently keeps a diary of her engagements, and dresses neatly. The bad season is of course the summer, when the artists are out of town. However, of late years some artists have engaged their models to follow them, and the wife of one of our most charming painters has often had three or four models under her charge in the country, so that the work of her husband and his friends should not be interrupted. In France the models migrate *en masse* to the little seaport villages or forest hamlets where the painters congregate. The English models however wait patiently in London, as a rule, till the artists come back. Nearly all of them live with their parents, and help to support the house. They have every qualification for being immortalized in art except that of beautiful hands. The hands of the English model are nearly always coarse and red.

As for the male models, there is the veteran whom we have mentioned above. He has all the traditions of the grand style, and is rapidly disappearing with the school he represents. An old man who talks about Fuseli is of course unendurable, and besides patriarchs have ceased to be fashionable subjects. Then there is the true Academy model. He is usually a man of thirty, rarely good-looking, but a perfect miracle of muscles. In fact he is the apotheosis of anatomy, and is so conscious of his own splendour that he tells you of his tibia and his thorax, as if no one else had anything of the kind. Then come the Oriental models. The supply of these is limited, but there are always about a dozen in London. They are very much sought after as they can remain immobile for hours, and generally possess lovely costumes. However they have a poor opinion of English art, which they regard as something between a vulgar personality and a commonplace photograph. Next we have the Italian youth who has either come over specially to be a model, or takes to it when his organ is out of repair. He is often quite charming with his large melancholy eyes, his crisp hair, and his slim brown figure. It is true he eats garlic, but then he can stand like a faun and couch like a leopard, so he is forgiven. He is always full of pretty compliments, and has been known to have kind words of encouragement for even our greatest artists. As for the English lad of the same age he never sits at all. Apparently he does not regard the career of a model as a serious profession. In any case he is rarely if ever to be got hold of. English boys too are difficult to find. Sometimes an ex-model who has a son will curl his hair, and wash his face, and bring him the round of the studios, all soap and shininess. The young school don't like him, but the older school do, and when he appears on the walls of the Royal Academy he is called *The Infant Samuel.* Occasionally also an artist catches a couple of *gamins* in the gutter and asks them to come to his studio. The first time they always appear, but after that they don't keep their appointments. They dislike sitting still, and have a strong and perhaps natural objection to looking pathetic. Besides they are always under the impression that the artist is laughing at them. It is a sad fact, but there is no doubt that the poor are completely unconscious of their own picturesqueness. Those of them who can be induced to sit do so with the idea that the artist is merely a benevolent philanthropist who has chosen an eccentric method of distributing alms to the undeserving. Perhaps the School Board will teach the London *gamin* his own artistic value, and then they will be better models than they are now. One remarkable privilege belongs to the Academy model, that of extorting a sovereign from any newly elected Associate or R.A. They wait at Burlington House till the announcement is made, and then race to the hapless artist's house. The one who arrives first receives the money. They have of late been much troubled at the long distances they have had to run, and they look with strong disfavour on the election of artists who live at Hampstead or at Bedford Park, for it is considered a point of honour not to employ the underground railway, omnibuses, or any artificial means of locomotion. The race is to the swift.

Besides the professional posers of the studio there are the posers of the Row, the posers at afternoon teas, the posers in politics, and the circus-posers. All four classes are delightful, but only the last class is ever really decorative. Acrobats and gymnasts can give the young painter infinite suggestions, for they bring into their art an element of swiftness, of motion, and of constant change that the studio model necessarily lacks. What is interesting in these "slaves of the ring" is that with them Beauty is an unconscious result not a conscious aim, the result in fact of the mathematical calculation of curves and distances, of absolute precision of eye, of the scientific knowledge of the equilibrium of forces, and of perfect physical training. A good acrobat is always graceful though grace is never his object; he is graceful because he does what he has to do in the best way in which it can be done—graceful because he is natural. If an ancient Greek were to come to life now, which considering the probable severity of his criticisms would be rather trying to our conceit, he would be found far oftener at the circus than at the theatre. A good circus is an oasis of Hellenism in a world that reads too much to be wise, and thinks too much to be beautiful. If it were not for the running-ground at Eton, the towing-path at Oxford, the Thames swimming baths, and the yearly circuses, humanity would forget the plastic perfection of its own form, and degenerate into a race of short-sighted professors, and spectacled *précieuses!* Not that the circus-proprietors are, as a rule, conscious of their high mission. Do they not bore us with the *haute école*, and weary us with Shakespearean clowns? Still at least they give us acrobats, and the acrobat is an artist. The mere fact that he never speaks to the audience shows how well he appreciates the great truth that the aim of art is not to reveal personality but to please. The clown may be blatant, but the acrobat is always beautiful. He is an interesting combination of the spirit of Greek sculpture with the spangles of the modern costumier. He has even had his niche in the novels of our age, and if *Manette Salomon* be the unmasking of the model, *Les Frères Zemganno* is the apotheosis of the acrobat.

As regards the influence of the ordinary model on our English school of painting, it cannot be said that it is altogether good. It is of course an advantage for the young artist sitting in his studio to be able to isolate "a little corner of life," as the French say, from disturbing surroundings, and to study it under certain effects of light and shade. But this very isolation leads often to mere mannerism in the painter, and robs him of that broad acceptance of the general facts of life which is the very essence of art. Model-painting, in a word, while it may be the condition of art, is not by any means its aim. It is simply practice, not perfection. Its use trains the eye and the hand of the painter, its abuse produces in his work an effect of mere posing and prettiness. It is the secret of much of the artificiality of modern art, this constant posing of pretty people, and when art becomes artificial it becomes monotonous. Outside the little world of the studio, with its draperies and its *bric-à-brac*, lies the world of life with its infinite, its Shakespearian variety. We must, however[,] distinguish between the two kinds of models, those who sit for the figure and those who sit for the costume. The study of the first is always excellent, but the costume-model is becoming rather wearisome in modern pictures. It is really of very little use to dress up a London girl in Greek draperies and to paint her as a goddess. The robe may be the robe of Athens, but the face is usually the face of Brompton. Now and then, it is true, one comes across a model whose face is an exquisite anachronism, and who looks lovely and natural in the dress of any century but her own. This however is rather rare. As a rule models are absolutely *de nôtre siècle*, and should be painted as such. Unfortunately they are not, and as a consequence we are shown every year a series of scenes from fancy dress balls which are called historical pictures, but are little more than mediocre representations of modern people masquerading. In France they are wiser. The French painter uses the model simply for study, for the finished picture he goes direct to life.

However we must not blame the sitters for the shortcomings of the artists. The English models are a well-behaved and hard-working class, and if they are more interested in artists than they are in art, a large section of the public is in the same condition, and most of our modern exhibitions seem to justify its choice.

Poetry and
Prison*

Prison has had an admirable effect on Mr. Wilfrid Blunt as a poet. The "Love Sonnets of Proteus," in spite of their clever Musset-like modernities, and their swift brilliant wit, were but affected or fantastic at best. They were simply the records of passing moods and moments, of which some were sad, and others sweet, and not a few shameful. Their subject was not of high or serious import. They contained much that was wilful and weak. "In Vinculis," upon the other hand, is a book that stirs one by its fine sincerity of purpose, its lofty and impassioned thought, its depth and ardour of intense feeling. "Imprisonment," says Mr. Blunt in his preface, "is a reality of discipline most useful to the modern soul, lapped as it is in physical sloth and self-indulgence. Like a sickness or a spiritual retreat it purifies and ennobles; and the soul emerges from it stronger and more self-contained." To him, certainly, it has been a mode of purification. The opening sonnets, composed in the bleak cell of Galway gaol, and written down on the flyleaves of the prisoner's prayer-book, are full of things nobly conceived and nobly uttered, and show that though Mr. Balfour may enforce "plain living" by his prison regulations, he cannot prevent "high thinking," or in any way limit or constrain the freedom of a man's soul. They are, of course, intensely personal in ex-

* Unsigned review, entitled "Poetry and Prison: Mr. Wilfrid Blunt's *In Vinculis,* of Wilfrid Scawen Blunt, *In Vinculis,* and Andrew Lang, *Grass of Parnassus. Pall Mall Gazette* XLIX : 7425 (3 January 1889) 3.

pression. They could not fail to be so. But the personality that they reveal has nothing petty or ignoble about it. The petulant cry of the shallow egoist, which was the chief characteristic of the "Love Sonnets of Proteus," is not to be found here. In its place we have wild grief and terrible scorn, fierce rage and flame-like passion. Such a sonnet as the following comes out of the very fire of heart and brain:—

> God knows, 'twas not with a forereasoned plan
>   I left the easeful dwellings of my peace,
> And sought this combat with ungodly man,
>   And ceaseless still through years that do not cease
>   Have warred with powers and principalities;
> My natural soul, ere yet these strifes began,
>   Was as a sister diligent to please
> And loving all, and most the human clan.
>
> God knows it. And He knows how the world's tears
>   Touched me. And He is witness of my wrath,
> How it was kindled against murderers
>   Who slew for gold, and how upon their path
> I met them. Since which day the world in arms
> Strikes at my life with angers and alarms.

And this sonnet has all the strange strength of that despair which is but the prelude to a larger hope:—

> I thought to do a deed of chivalry,
>   An act of worth, which haply in her sight
> Who was my mistress should recorded be
>   And of the nations. And, when thus the fight
>   Faltered and men once bold with faces white
> Turned this and that way in excuse to flee,
>   I only stood, and by the foeman's might
> Was overborne and mangled cruelly.
>
> Then crawled I to her feet, in whose clear cause
>   I made this venture, and "Behold," I said,
>   "How I am wounded for thee in these wars."
>   But she, "Poor cripple, wouldst thou I should wed
> A limbless trunk?" and laughing turned from me:
>   Yet she was fair, and her name "Liberty."

The sonnet beginning

> A prison is a convent without God—
>   Poverty, Chastity, Obedience
> Its precepts are:—

is very fine, and this, written just after entering the gaol, is powerful:—

> Naked I came into the world of pleasure,
>   And naked come I to this house of pain.
> Here at the gate I lay down my life's treasure,
>   My pride, my garments, and my name with men.
>   The world and I henceforth shall be as twain,
> No sound of me shall pierce for good or ill
>   These walls of grief. Nor shall I hear the vain
> Laughter and tears of those who love me still.
>
> Within, what new life waits me? Little ease,
>   Cold lying, hunger, nights of wakefulness,
> Harsh orders given, no voice to soothe or please,
>   Poor thieves for friends, for books rules meaningless;
> This is the grave—nay hell. Yet, Lord of Might
> Still in Thy Light my spirit shall see light.

But indeed all the sonnets are worth reading, and "The Canon of Aughrim," the longest poem in the book, is a most masterly and dramatic description of the tragic life of the Irish peasant. Literature is not much indebted to Mr. Balfour for his sophistical "Defence of Philosophic Doubt," which is one of the dullest books we know, but it must be admitted that by sending Mr. Blunt to gaol he has converted a clever rhymer into an earnest and deep-thinking poet. The narrow confines of the prison-cell seem to suit the sonnet's "scanty plot of ground," and an unjust imprisonment for a noble cause strengthens as well as deepens the nature.

MR. ANDREW LANG'S 'GRASS OF PARNASSUS'

Whether or not Mr. Andrew Lang should be sent to prison, is another matter. We are inclined to think that he should not, except as a punishment for writing sonnets to Mr. Rider Haggard. His gay pleasant Muse, with her dainty if somewhat facile graces, her exquisite triviality, and her winsome irresponsible manner, would probably gain very little from such a dreary exile. When Leigh Hunt was in gaol he was allowed to console himself with a pretty wall-paper, but Mr. Balfour permits nothing but white-washed walls, and we are quite sure that Mr. Lang would find their monotony unbearable. Prison is for souls stronger than the soul revealed to us in the charming whisperings and musical echoes of the "Grass of Parnassus;" which, however, is a very fascinating little volume, in its way, and possesses many delicately-carved "ivories of speech," to borrow one of Mr. Pater's phrases. The translation of Rémy Belleau's well-known poem on April is excellent:—

> April with thy gracious wiles,
>   Like the smiles,
> Smiles of Venus; and thy breath
> Like her breath, the gods' delight,
>   (From their height
> They take the happy air beneath;)
>
> It is thou that, of thy grace,
>   From their place
> In the far-off isles dost bring
> Swallows over earth and sea,
>   Glad to be
> Messengers of thee and Spring.
>
> Daffodil and eglantine,
>   And woodbine,
> Lily, violet, and rose
> Plentiful in April fair,
>   To the air,
> Their pretty petals to unclose.

The assonance of "their" in the last line with "air" in the line preceding is not very pleasing, and indeed the word seems otiose, but the translation as a whole is admirably done. The version of poor Henri Murger's "Old Loves" is also very good. It is a little masterpiece of felicitous rendering, and the versions from the Greek anthology show the fine taste of a true scholar and man of letters. Where Mr. Lang pipes on his own reed, we like him less, and his sonnets are deficient in any fine central motive, and really show him at his worst. But such poems as "Colinette" and "The Singing Rose" are certainly wonderfully pretty. Mr. Lang has recently been christened "the Divine Amateur," and the little book that lies before us is a good instance of how well he deserves that graceful compliment. However, this book should not have been brought out in winter. It is made for summer. On a lazy June evening no more delightful companion could be found than a poet who has the sweetest of voices and absolutely nothing to say.

The Gospel According to Walt Whitman[*]

"No one will get at my verses who insists upon viewing them as a literary performance, or as aiming mainly towards art and aestheticism. 'Leaves of Grass' has been chiefly the outcropping of my own emotional and other personal nature—an attempt from first to last to put a *Person*, a human being (myself, in the latter half of the nineteenth century, in America) freely, fully and truly on record. I could not find any similar personal record in current literature that satisfied me." In these words Walt Whitman gives us the true attitude we should adopt towards his work, having indeed a much saner view of the value and meaning of that work than either his eloquent admirers or noisy detractors can boast of possessing. His last book, "November Boughs" as he calls it, published in the winter of the old man's life, reveals to us, not indeed a soul's tragedy, for its last note is one of joy and hope and noble and unshaken faith in all that is fine and worthy of such faith, but certainly the drama of a human soul, and puts on record with a simplicity that has in it both sweetness and strength the record of his spiritual development and of the aim and motive both of the manner and the matter of his work. His strange mode of expression is shown in these pages to have been the result of deliberate and self-conscious choice. The "barbaric yawp," which he

* Unsigned review of Walt Whitman, *November Boughs*. *Pall Mall Gazette* XLIX : 7444 (25 January 1889) 3.

sent over "the roofs of the world" so many years ago, and which wrung from Mr. Swinburne's lips such lofty panegyric in song and such loud clamorous censure in prose, appears here in what will be to many an entirely new light. For in his very rejection of art Walt Whitman is an artist. He tried to produce a certain effect by certain means and he succeeded. There is much method in which many have termed his madness, too much method indeed some may be tempted to fancy.

In the story of his life, as he tells it to us, we find him at the age of sixteen beginning a definite and philosophical study of literature:—

Summers and falls, I used to go off, sometimes for a week at a stretch, down in the country, or to Long Island's seashores—there in the presence of outdoor influences, I went over thoroughly the Old and New Testaments and absorb'd (probably to better advantage for me than in any library or indoor room—it makes such difference *where* you read) Shakspere, Ossian, the best translated versions I could get of Homer, Aeschylus, Sophocles, the old German Nibelungen, the ancient Hindoo poems, and one or two other masterpieces, Dante's among them. As it happen'd I read the latter mostly in an old wood. The Iliad I read first thoroughly on the peninsula of Orient, north-east end of Long Island, in a sheltered hollow of rocks and sand, with the sea on each side. (I have wondered since why I was not overwhelmed by those mighty masters. Likely because I read them, as described, in the full presence of Nature, under the sun, with the far-spreading landscapes and vistas, or the sea rolling in.)

Edgar Allan Poe's amusing bit of dogmatism that, for our occasions and for our day, there can be no such thing as a long poem, fascinated him: "The same thought had been haunting my mind before," he says, "but Poe's argument, though short, work'd the sum out and proved it to me:" and the English translation of the Bible seems to have suggested to him the possibility of a poetic form which while retaining the spirit of poetry would still be free from the trammels of rhyme and of a definite metrical system. Having thus to a certain degree settled upon what one might call the *technique* of Whitmanism, he began to brood upon the nature of that spirit that was to give life to the strange form. The central point of the poetry of the future seemed to him to be necessarily "an identical body and soul," a personality in fact, which personality he tells us frankly, "after many considerations and ponderings I deliberately settled should be myself." However for the true creation and revealing of this personality, at first only dimly felt, a new stimulus was needed. This came from the Civil War. After describing the many dreams and passions of his boyhood and early manhood he goes on to say:—

These, however, and much more might have gone on and come to naught (almost positively would have come to naught) if a sudden, vast, terrible, direct and indirect stimulus for new and national declamatory expression had not been given to me. It is certain I say, that, although I had made a start before, only from the occurrence of the Secession War, and what it showed me as by flashes of lightning, with the emotional depths it sounded and arous'd (of course, I don't mean in my own heart only, I saw it just as plainly in others, in millions) that only from the strong flare and provocation of that war's sights and scenes the final reasons-for-being of an autochthonic and passionate song definitely came forth. I went down to the war-fields of Virginia, lived thenceforward in camp, saw great battles—and the days and nights afterwards—partook of all the fluctuations, gloom, despair, hopes again aroused, courage evoked—death readily risked—the *cause* too— along and filling those agonistic and lurid following years, the real parturition years of the henceforth homogeneous Union. Without those three or four years and the experiences they gave, "Leaves of Grass" would not now be existing.

Having thus obtained the necessary stimulus for the quickening and awakening of the personal self, some day to be endowed with universality, he sought to find new notes of song, and passing beyond the mere passion for expression—he aimed at "Suggestiveness" first. "I round and finish little, if anything; and could not, consistently with my scheme. The reader will have his or her part to do, just as much as I have had mine. I seek less to state or display any theme of thought, and more to bring you, reader, into the atmosphere of the theme or thought —there to pursue your own flight." Another "impetus word" is

Comradeship, and other "word-signs" are Good Cheer, Content, and Hope. Individuality, especially, he sought for:—

I have allowed the stress of my poems from beginning to end to bear upon American individuality and assist it—not only because that is a great lesson in Nature, amid all her generalizing laws, but as a counterpoise to the levelling tendencies of Democracy—and for other reasons. Defiant of ostensible literary and other conventions, I avowedly chant "the great pride of a man in himself," and permit it to be more or less a *motif* of nearly all my verse. I think this pride indispensable to an American. I think it not inconsistent with obedience, humility, deference, and self-questioning.

*　　*　　*　　*　　*

A new theme also was to be found in the relation of the sexes, conceived in a natural, simple, and healthy form, and he protests against poor Mr. William Rossetti's attempt to Bowdlerize and expurgate his song.

From another point of view "Leaves of Grass" is avowedly the song of Sex, and Amativeness, and even Animality—though meanings that do not usually go with these words are behind all, and will duly emerge; and all are sought to be lifted into a different light and atmosphere. Of this feature intentionally palpable in a few lines, I shall only say the espousing principle of those lines so gives breath to my whole scheme that the bulk of the pieces might as well have been left unwritten were those lines omitted. . . . Universal as are certain facts and symptoms of communities there is nothing so rare in modern conventions and poetry as their normal recognizance. Literature is always calling in the doctor for consultation and confession, and always giving evasions and swathing suppressions in place of that "heroic nudity" on which only a genuine diagnosis can be built. And in respect to editions of "Leaves of Grass" in time to come (if there should be such) I take occasion now to confirm those lines with the settled convictions and deliberate renewals of thirty years, and to hereby prohibit, as far as mine can do so, any elision of them.

*　　*　　*　　*　　*

But beyond all these notes and moods and motives is the lofty spirit of a grand and free acceptance of all things that are worthy of existence. "I desired," he says, "to formulate a poem whose every thought or fact should indirectly or directly be or connive at an implicit belief in the wisdom, health, mystery, or beauty of every process, every concrete object, every human or other existence, not only consider'd from the point of view of all, but of each." His two final utterances are that really great poetry is always the result of a national spirit, and not the privilege of a polished and select few; and that the sweetest and strongest songs yet remain to be sung.

Such are the views contained in the opening essay, "A Backward Glance o'er Travel'd Roads," as he calls it: but there are many other essays in this fascinating volume, some on poets such as Burns and Lord Tennyson, for whom Walt Whitman has a profound admiration; some on old actors and singers, the elder Booth, Forrest, Alboni, and Mario being his special favourites; others on the native Indians, on the Spanish element in American nationality, on Western slang, on the poetry of the Bible, and on Abraham Lincoln. But Walt Whitman is at his best when he is analyzing his own work, and making schemes for the poetry of the future. Literature to him has a distinctly social aim. He seeks to build up the masses by "building up grand individuals." And yet literature itself must be preceded by noble forms of life. "The best literature is always the result of something far greater than itself—not the hero but the portrait of the hero. Before there can be recorded history or poem there must be the transaction." Certainly in Walt Whitman's views there is a largeness of vision, a healthy sanity, and a fine ethical purpose. He is not to be placed with the professional *littérateurs* of his country, Boston novelists, New York poets, and the like. He stands apart, and the chief value of his work is in its prophecy not in its performance. He has begun a prelude to larger themes. He is the herald to a new era. As a man he is the precursor of a fresh type. He is a factor in the heroic and spiritual evolution of the human being. If Poetry has passed him by, Philosophy will take note of him.

The New President [of the Royal Society of British Artists]*

In a little book that he calls "The Enchanted Island," Mr. Wyke Bayliss the new President of the Royal Society of British Artists has just given his gospel of art to the world. His predecessor in office had also a gospel of art, but it usually took the form of an autobiography. Mr. Whistler always spelt art, and we believe still spells it, with a capital "I." However, he was never dull. His brilliant wit, his caustic satire, and his amusing epigrams, or perhaps we should say epitaphs on his contemporaries made his views on art as delightful as they were misleading, and as fascinating as they were unsound. Besides, he introduced American humour into art criticism, and for this if for no other reason he deserves to be affectionately remembered. Mr. Wyke Bayliss, upon the other hand, is rather tedious. The last President never said much that was true, but the present President never says anything that is new, and if art be a fairy-haunted wood or an enchanted island, we must say that we prefer the old Puck to the fresh Prospero. Water is an admirable thing—at least, the Greeks said it was—and Mr. Ruskin is an admirable writer; but a combination of both is a little depressing.

Still, it is only right to add that Mr. Wyke Bayliss, at his best, writes very good English. Mr. Whistler, for some reason

* Unsigned review of Wyke Bayliss, *The Enchanted Island*. *Pall Mall Gazette* XLIX : 7445 (26 January 1889) 3.

or other, always adopted the phraseology of the minor prophets. Possibly it was in order to emphasize his well-known claims to verbal inspiration, or perhaps he thought with Voltaire that "Habakkuk est capable de tout," and wished to shelter himself under the shield of a definitely irresponsible writer none of whose prophecies, according to the French philosopher, have ever been fulfilled. The idea was clever enough at the beginning, but ultimately the manner became monotonous. The spirit of the Hebrews is excellent, but their mode of writing is not to be imitated, and no amount of American jokes will give it that modernity which is so essential to a good literary style. Admirable as are Mr. Whistler's fire-works on canvas, his fireworks in prose are abrupt, violent, and exaggerated. However, oracles, since the days of the Pythia, have never been remarkable for style, and the modest Mr. Wyke Bayliss is as much Mr. Whistler's superior as a writer, as he is his inferior as a painter and an artist. Indeed, some of the passages in this book are so charmingly written, and with such dexterous felicity of phrase that we cannot help feeling that the President of the British artists, like a still more Famous President of our day, can express himself far better through the medium of literature than he can through the medium of line and colour. This, however, only applies to Mr. Wyke Bayliss's prose. His poetry is very bad, and the sonnets at the end of the book are almost as mediocre as the drawings that accompany them. As we read them we cannot but regret that in this point at any rate Mr. Bayliss has not imitated the wise example of his predecessor, who with all his faults was never guilty of writing a line of poetry, and who is indeed quite incapable of doing anything of the kind.

As for the matter of Mr. Bayliss's discourse, his views on art must be admitted to be very commonplace and old fashioned. What is the use of telling artists that they should try and paint Nature as she really is? What Nature really is, is a question for metaphysics not for art. Art deals with appearances, and the eye of the man who looks at Nature, the vision in fact of the artist, is far more important to us than what he looks at. There is more truth in Corot's aphorism, that a landscape is simply the "mood of a man's mind," than there is in all Mr. Bayliss's laborious disquisitions on naturalism. Again, why does Mr. Bay-

liss waste a whole chapter in pointing out real or supposed re-
semblances between a book of his published twelve years ago
and an article by Mr. Palgrave which appeared recently in the
Nineteenth Century? Neither the book nor the article contains
anything of real interest, and as for the hundred or more parallel passages which Mr. Wyke Bayliss solemnly prints side by
side, most of them are like parallel lines and never meet. The
only original proposal that Mr. Bayliss has to offer us is that the
House of Commons should every year select some important
event from national and contemporary history, and hand it over
to the artists, who are to choose from among themselves a man
to make a picture of it. In this way Mr. Bayliss believes that
we could have the historic art, and suggests as examples of what
he means, a picture of Florence Nightingale in the hospital at
Scutari, a picture of the opening of the first London Board
school, and a picture of the Senate House at Cambridge with
the girl-graduate receiving a degree "that shall acknowledge her
to be as wise as Merlin himself, and leave her still as beautiful
as Vivien." This proposal is, of course, very well meant, but
to say nothing of the danger of leaving historic art at the mercy
of a majority in the House of Commons, who would naturally
vote for their own view of things, Mr. Bayliss does not seem to
realize that a great event is not necessarily a pictorial event.
"The decisive events of the world," as has been well said, "take
place in the intellect," and as for Board-schools, academic ceremonies, hospital wards, and the like they may well be left to
the artists of the illustrated papers, who do them admirably and
quite as well as they need be done. Indeed, the pictures of
contemporary events, Royal marriages, naval reviews and things
of this kind, that appear in the Academy every year, are always
extremely bad, while the very same subjects treated in black
and white in the *Graphic* or the *London News* are excellent.
Besides if we want to understand the history of a nation through
the medium of art it is to the imaginative and ideal arts that we
have to go, and not to the arts that are definitely imitative. The
visible aspect of life no longer contains for us the secret of life's
spirit. Probably it never did contain it. And if Mr. Barker's
"Waterloo Banquet," and Mr. Frith's "Marriage of the Prince
of Wales" are examples of healthy historic art, the less we have
of such art the better. However, Mr. Bayliss is full of the most

ardent faith, and speaks quite gravely of genuine portraits of St. John, St. Peter and St. Paul dating from the first century, and of the establishment by the Israelites of a school of art in the wilderness under the now little-appreciated Bezaleel. He is a pleasant picturesque writer, but he should not speak about art. Art is a sealed book to him.

[Yeats's *Fairy and Folk Tales*]*

"The various collectors of Irish folk-lore," says Mr. W. B. Yeats in his charming little book "Fairy and Folk Tales of the Irish Peasantry" (Walter Scott), "have, from our point of view one great merit, and, from the point of view of others, one great fault. They have made their work literature rather than science, and told us of the Irish peasantry rather than of the primitive history of mankind, or whatever else the folklorists are on the gad after. To be considered scientists, they should have tabulated all their tales in forms like grocers' bills—item the fairy king, item the fairy queen. Instead of this, they have caught the very voice of the people, the very pulse of life, each giving what was most noticed in his day. Croker and Lover, full of the ideas of the harum-scarum Irish gentility, saw everything humorised. The impulse of the Irish literature of their time came from a class that did not—mainly for political reasons—take the populace seriously, and imagined the country as a humorist's Arcadia; of its passion, its gloom, its tragedy, they knew nothing. What they did was not wholly false; they merely magnified an irresponsible type, found oftenest among boatmen, carmen, and gentlemen's servants, into the type of a whole nation, and created the stage-Irishman. The writings of 'Forty-eight and the Famine combined, burst their bubble. Their work had the dash

* From article entitled, "Some Literary Notes," *Woman's World* II:16 (February 1889) 221–24.

as well as the shallowness of an ascendent and idle class; and, in Croker, is touched everywhere with beauty, a gentle Arcadian beauty. Carleton, a peasant born, has in many of his stories, more especially in his ghost stories, a much more serious way with him, for all his humour. Kennedy, an old bookseller in Dublin, who seems to have had something of genuine belief in the fairies, comes next in time. He has far less literary faculty, but is wonderfully accurate, giving often the very words in which the stories were told. But the best book since Croker is Lady Wilde's 'Ancient Legends.' The humour has all given way to pathos and tenderness. We have here the innermost heart of the Celt in the moments he has grown to love through years of persecution, when, cushioning himself about with dreams, and hearing fairy songs in the twilight, he ponders on the soul and on the dead. Here is the Celt, only it is the Celt dreaming."

Into a volume of very moderate dimensions, and of extremely moderate price, Mr. Yeats has collected togther the most characteristic of our Irish folk-lore stories, grouping them together according to subject. First come the "Trooping Fairies." The peasants say that these are fallen angels who were not good enough to be saved, nor bad enough to be lost; but the Irish antiquarians see in them the gods of Pagan Ireland, who, when no longer worshipped or fed with offerings, dwindled away in the popular imagination, and are now only a few spans in height. Their chief occupations are feasting, fighting, making love, and playing the most beautiful music. They have only one industrious person among them, the *Leprachaun* (the Little Shoe-maker). It is his duty to repair their shoes when they wear them out with dancing. Mr. Yeats tells us that near the village of Ballisodare is an old woman who lived among them for seven years. When she came home she had no toes; she had danced them all off. On May Eve, every seventh year, they fight for the harvest, for the best ears of grain belong to them. An old man informed Mr. Yeats that he saw them fight once, and that they tore the thatch off a house. Had any one else been near they would merely have seen a great wind whirling everything into the air as it passed. When the wind drives the leaves and straws before it, that is the fairies, and the peasants take off their hats and say, "God bless them." When they are gay, they sing. Many of the most beautiful tunes of Ireland are only their music caught up by eavesdroppers. No prudent peasant would hum "The Pretty Girl Milking the Cow" near a fairy rath, for they are jealous, and do not like to hear their songs on clumsy mortal life. Blake once saw a fairy's funeral. But this, as Mr. Yeats points out, must have been an English fairy, for the Irish fairies never die; they are immortal.

Then come the "Solitary Fairies;" amongst them we find the little *Leprachaun* mentioned above. He has grown very rich, as he possesses all the treasure-crocks buried in war-time. In the early part of this century, according to Croker, they used to show in Tipperary a little shoe forgotten by the fairy shoemaker. Then there are two rather disreputable little fairies—the *Cluricaun*, who gets intoxicated in gentlemen's cellars; and "The Red Man," who plays unkind practical jokes. The *Fear-Gorta* (Man of Hunger) is an emaciated phantom who goes through the land in time of famine, begging an alms, and bringing good luck to the giver. The *Water-Sheerie* is own brother to the English Jack o' Lantern. The *Leanhaun Shee* (Fairy Mistress) seeks the love of mortals. If they refuse, she must be their slave; if they consent, they are hers, and can only escape by finding another to take their place. The fairy lives on their life, and they waste away. Death is no escape from her. She is the Gaelic Muse, for she gives inspiration to those she persecutes. The Gaelic poets die young, for she is restless, and will not let them remain long on earth. The *Pooka* is essentially an animal spirit, and some have considered him the forefather of Shakespeare's "Puck." He lives on solitary mountains and among old ruins "grown monstrous with much solitude," and is of the race of the nightmare. He has many shapes—is now a horse, now a goat, now an eagle. Like all spirits, he is only half in the world of form. The Banshee does not care much for our democratic levelling tendencies; she only loves old families, and despises the *parvenu* or the *nouveau riche*. When more than one Banshee is present, and they wail and sing in chorus, it is for the death of some holy or great one. An omen that sometimes accompanies the Banshee is an immense black coach, mounted by a coffin, and drawn by headless horses driven by a *Dullahan*. A *Dullahan* is

the most terrible thing in the world. In 1807 two of the sentries
stationed outside St. James's Park saw one climbing the railings,
and died of fright. Mr. Yeats suggests that they are possibly
descended from that Irish giant who swam across the Channel
with his head in his teeth.

Then come the stories of ghosts, of saints and priests, and of
giants. The ghosts live in a state intermediary between this
world and the next. They are held there by some earthly longing or affection, or some duty unfulfilled, or anger against the
living; they are those who are too good for hell and too bad for
heaven. Sometimes they take the form of insects, especially that
of butterflies. The author of "The Parochial Survey of Ireland"
heard a woman say to a child, who was chasing a butterfly,
"How do you know it is not the soul of your grandfather?" On
November Eve they are abroad, and dance with the fairies. As
for the saints and priests, there are no martyrs in the stories.
That ancient chronicler Giraldus Cambrensis taunted the Arch-
bishop of Cashel because no one in Ireland had received the
crown of martyrdom. "Our people may be barbarous," the prel-
ate answered, "but they have never lifted their hands against
God's saints; but now that a people have come amongst us
who know how to make them" (it was just after the English
invasion) "we shall have martyrs plentifully." The giants were
the old Pagan heroes of Ireland, who grew bigger and bigger,
just as the gods grew smaller and smaller. The fact is they did
not wait for offerings; they took them *vi et armis*.

Some of the prettiest stories are those that cluster round *Tir-
nán-Og*. This is the Country of the Young, "for age and death
have not found it, neither tears nor loud laughter have gone
near it." One man has gone there and returned. The bard Oisen
—who wandered away on a white horse, moving on the surface
of the foam with his fairy Niamh—lived there three hundred
years, and then returned in search of his comrades. The moment
his foot touched the earth his three hundred years fell on him,
and he was bowed double, and his beard swept the ground. He
described his sojourn in the Land of Youth to St. Patrick before
he died. Since then, according to Mr. Yeats, "many have seen
it in many places: some in the depths of lakes, and have heard

133

rising therefrom a vague sound of bells; more have seen it far off on the horizon, as they peered out from the western cliffs. Not three years ago a fisherman imagined that he saw it."

Mr. Yeats has certainly done his work very well. He has shown great critical capacity in his selection of the stories, and his little introductions are charmingly written. It is delightful to come across a collection of purely imaginative work, and Mr. Yeats has a very quick instinct in finding out the best and the most beautiful things in Irish folk-lore. I am also glad to see that he has not confined himself entirely to prose, but has included Allingham's lovely poem on the fairies:—

> "Up the airy mountain,
>   Down the rushy glen,
> We dare not go a-hunting
>   For fear of little men;
> Wee folk, good folk,
>   Trooping all together;
> Green jacket, red cap,
>   And white owl's feather.
>
> "Down along the rocky shore
>   Some make their home;
> They live on crispy pancakes
>   Of yellow tide-foam;
> Some in the reeds
>   Of the black mountain lake,
> With frogs for their watch-dogs
>   All night awake.
>
> "High on the hill-top
>   The old king sits,
> He is now so old and grey
>   He's nigh lost his wits.
> With a bridge of white mist
>   Colunkill he crosses
> On his stately journeys
>   From Slieveleague to Rosses;
> Or going up with music,
>   On cold starry nights,
> To sup with the Queen
>   Of the gay Northern Lights."

All lovers of fairy-tales and folk-lore should get this little book. "The Horned Women," "The Priest's Soul," and "Teig O'Kane," are really marvellous in their way; and, indeed, there is hardly a single story that is not worth reading and thinking over.

Mr. Froude's Blue Book [on Ireland]*

Blue Books are generally dull reading, but Blue Books on Ireland have always been interesting. They form the record of one of the great tragedies of modern Europe. In them England has written down her indictment against herself, and has given to the world the history of her shame. If in the last century she tried to govern Ireland with an insolence that was intensified by race-hatred and religious prejudice, she has sought to rule her in this century with a stupidity that is aggravated by good intentions. The last of these Blue Books, Mr. Froude's heavy novel, has appeared, however, somewhat too late. The society that he describes has long since passed away. An entirely new factor has appeared in the social development of the country, and this factor is the Irish-American, and his influence. To mature its powers, to concentrate its action, to learn the secret of its own strength and of England's weakness, the Celtic intellect has had to cross the Atlantic. At home it had but learned the pathetic weakness of nationality; in a strange land it realized what indomitable forces nationality possesses. What captivity was to the Jews, exile has been to the Irish. America and American influence has educated them. Their first practical leader is an Irish American.

But while Mr. Froude's book has no practical relation to

---

* Review (signed with initials only) of J. A. Froude, *The Two Chiefs of Dunboy*. Pall Mall Gazette XLIX : 7511 (13 April 1889) 3.

modern Irish politics, and does not offer any solution of the present question, it has a certain historical value. It is a vivid picture of Ireland in the latter half of the eighteenth century, a picture often false in its lights and exaggerated in its shadows, but a picture none the less. Mr. Froude admits the martyrdom of Ireland, but regrets that the martyrdom was not completely carried out. His ground of complaint against the executioner is not his trade, but his bungling. It is the bluntness, not the cruelty, of the sword that he objects to. Resolute government, that shallow shibboleth of those who do not understand how complex a thing the art of government is, is his posthumous panacea for past evils. His hero, Colonel Goring, has the words Law and Order ever on his lips, meaning by the one the enforcement of unjust legislation, and implying by the other the suppression of every fine natural aspiration. That the Government should enforce iniquity, and the governed submit to it, seems to be to Mr. Froude, as it certainly is to many others, the true ideal of political science. Like most pen-men he overrates the power of the sword. Where England has had to struggle she has been wise. Where physical strength has been on her side, as in Ireland, she has been made unwieldy by that strength. Her own strong hands have blinded her. She has had force, but no direction.

There is, of course, a story in Mr. Froude's novel. It is not simply a political disquisition. The interest of the tale, such as it is, centres round two men, Colonel Goring and Morty Sullivan, the Cromwellian and the Celt. These men are enemies by race, and creed, and feeling. The first represents Mr. Froude's cure for Ireland. He is a resolute Englishman, with strong Nonconformist tendencies, who plants an industrial colony on the coast of Kerry, and has deep-rooted objections to that illicit trade with France, which in the last century was the sole method by which the Irish people were enabled to pay their rents to their absentee land lords. Colonel Goring bitterly regrets that the Penal Laws against Catholics are not vigorously carried out. He is a *"Police* at any price" man:—

And this, said Goring scornfully, is what you call governing Ireland, hanging up your law like a scarecrow in the garden till

137

every sparrow has learned to make a jest of it. Your Popery Acts! Well, you borrow them from France. The French Catholics did not choose to keep the Huguenots among them, and recalled the Edict of Nantes. As they treated the Huguenots, so you said to all the world that you would treat the Papists. You borrowed from the French the very language of your statute, but they are not afraid to stand by their law, and you are afraid to stand by yours. You let the people laugh at it, and in teaching them to despise one law you teach them to despise all laws—God's and man's alike. I cannot say how it will end, but I can tell you this, that you are training up a race with the education which you are giving them that will astonish the world by and by.

Mr. Froude's resume of the History of Ireland is not without power, though it is far from being really accurate. The Irish, he tells us, had disowned the facts of life and the facts of life had proved the strongest. England, unable to tolerate anarchy so near their shores, consulted the Pope. The Pope gave them leave to interfere, and the Pope had the best of the bargain. For the English brought him in, and the Irish kept him there. England's first settlers were Norman nobles. They became more Irish than the Irish, and England found herself in this difficulty. To abandon Ireland would be discreditable, to rule it as a province would be contrary to English tradition. She then tried to rule by dividing, and failed. The Pope was too strong for her. At last she made her great political discovery. What Ireland wanted was evidently an entirely new population of the same race and the same religion as her own. The new policy was partly carried out:—

Elizabeth first, and then James, and then Cromwell replanted the island, introducing English, Scots, Huguenots, Flemings, Dutch, tens of thousands of families of vigorous and earnest Protestants who brought their industries along with them. Twice the Irish tried to drive out this new element. They failed. But England had no sooner accomplished her long task than she set herself to work to spoil it again. She destroyed the industries of her colonists by her trade laws. She set the Bishops to rob them of their religion . . . As for the gentry, the purpose for which they had been introduced into Ireland was unfulfilled. They were but alien intruders, who did nothing, who were allowed to do nothing. The time would come when an exasperated population would demand that the land should be given back to them, and England would then, perhaps, throw the gentry to the wolves, in the hope of a momentary peace. But her own turn would follow. She would be face to face with the old problem, either to make a new conquest or to retire with disgrace.

Political disquisitions of this kind, and prophecies after the event, are found all through Mr. Froude's book, and on almost every second page we come across aphorisms on the Irish character, on the teachings of Irish history, and on the nature of England's mode of government. Some of these represent Mr. Froude's own views, others are entirely dramatic, and introduced for the purpose of characterization. We append some specimens. As epigrams, they are not very felicitous, but they are interesting from some points of view.

Irish society grew up in happy recklessness. Insecurity added rest to enjoyment.

We Irish must either laugh or cry, and if we went in for crying, we should all hang ourselves.

Too close a union with the Irish had produced degeneracy both of character and creed in all the settlements of English.

We age quickly in Ireland with the whisky and the broken heads.

The Irish leaders cannot fight. They can make the country ungovernable, and keep an English army occupied in watching them.

No nation can ever achieve a liberty that will not be a curse to it, except by arms in the field.

The Irish are taught from their cradles that English rule is the cause of all their miseries. They were as ill off under their own chiefs; but they would bear from their natural leaders what they will not bear from us, and if we have not made their lot more wretched, we have not made it any better.

Patriotism? Yes! Patriotism of the Hibernian order. That the country has been badly treated, and is poor and miserable. This is the patriot's stock in trade. Does he want it mended? Not he. His own occupation would be gone.

Irish corruption is the twin brother of Irish eloquence.

England will not let us break the heads of our scoundrels: she will not break them herself: we are a free country, and must take the consequences.

139

The functions of the Anglo-Irish Government were to do what ought not to be done, and to leave undone what ought to be done.

The Irish race have always been noisy, useless, and ineffectual. They have produced nothing, they have done nothing which it is possible to admire. What they are that they have always been, and the only hope for them is that their ridiculous Irish nationality should be buried and forgotten.

The Irish are the best actors in the world.

Order is an exotic in Ireland. It has been imported from England, but it will not grow. It suits neither soil nor climate. If the English wanted order in Ireland, they should have left none of us alive.

When ruling powers are unjust, nature reasserts her rights.

Even anarchy has its advantages.

Nature keeps an accurate account. The longer a bill is left unpaid, the heavier the accumulation of interest.

You cannot live in Ireland without breaking laws on one side or another. *Pecca fortiter*, therefore, as Luther says.

The animal spirits of the Irish remained when all else was gone, and if there was no purpose in their lives they could at least enjoy themselves.

The Irish peasants can make the country hot for the Protestant gentlemen, but that is all they are fit for.

As we said before, if Mr. Froude intended his book to help the Tory Government to solve the Irish question he has entirely missed his aim. The Ireland of which he writes has disappeared. As a record, however, of the incapacity of a Teutonic to rule a Celtic people against their own wishes his book is not without value. It is dull, but dull books are very popular at present, and as people have grown a little tired of talking about "Robert Elsmere," they will probably take to discussing "The Two Chiefs of Dunboy." There are some who will welcome with delight the idea of solving the Irish question by doing away with the Irish people. There are others who will remember that Ireland has extended her boundaries, and that we have now to reckon with her not merely in the Old World but also in the New.

Ouida's New Novel [*Guilderoy*]*

Ouida is the last of the romantics. She belongs to the school of
Bulwer Lytton and George Sand, though she may lack the learning of the one, and the sincerity of the other. She tries to make
passion, imagination, and poetry, part of fiction. She still believes in heroes and in heroines. She is florid, and fervent, and
fanciful. Yet even she, the high-priestess of the impossible, is
affected by her age. Her last book, "Guilderoy" as she calls it,
is an elaborate psychological study of modern temperaments.
For her, it is realistic, and she has certainly caught much of the
tone and temper of the society of our day. Her people move
with ease and grace and indolence. The book may be described
as a study of the peerage from a poetical point of view. Those
who are tired of mediocre curates who have doubts, of serious
young ladies who has [*sic*] missions, and of the ordinary figure-
heads of most of the English fiction of our time, might turn
with pleasure, if not with profit, to this amazing romance. It is
a resplendent picture of our aristocracy. No expense has been
spared in gilding. For the comparatively small sum of £1 11s.
6d. one is introduced to the best society. The central figures are
exaggerated, but the background is admirable. In spite of everything, it gives one a sense of something like life.

What is the story? Well, we must admit that we have a faint
suspicion that Ouida has told it to us before. Lord Guilderoy,

---

* Unsigned review. *Pall Mall Gazette* XLIX : 7539 (17 May 1889) 3.

"whose name was as old as the days of Knut," falls madly in love, or fancies that he falls madly in love, with a rustic Perdita, a provincial Artemis who has "a Gainsborough face with wide-opened questioning eyes and tumbled auburn hair." She is poor but well born, being the only child of Mr. Vernon of Llanarth, a curious recluse, who is half a pedant and half Don Quixote. Guilderoy marries her, and tiring of her shyness, her lack of power to express herself, her want of knowledge of fashionable life, returns to an old passion for a wonderful creature called the Duchess of Soriá. Lady Guilderoy becomes ice: the Duchess becomes fire: at the end of the book Guilderoy is a pitiable object. He has to submit to be forgiven by one woman, and to endure to be forgotten by the other. He is thoroughly weak, thoroughly worthless, and the most fascinating person in the whole story. Then there is his sister Lady Sunbury, who is very anxious for Guilderoy to marry, and is quite determined to hate his wife. She is really a capital sketch. Ouida describes her as "one of those admirably virtuous women who are more likely to turn men away from the paths of virtue than the wickedest of sirens." She irritates herself, alienates her children, and infuriates her husband:—

"You are perfectly right; I know you are always right; I admit you are; but it is just that which makes you so damnably odious!" said Lord Sunbury once, in a burst of rage, in his town house, speaking in such stentorian tones that the people passing up Grosvenor-street looked up at his open windows, and a crossing-sweeper said to a match-seller, "My eye! ain't he giving it to the old gal like blazes."

The noblest character in the book is Lord Aubrey. As he is not a genius, he naturally behaves admirably on every occasion. He begins by pitying the neglected Lady Guilderoy, and ends by loving her, but he makes the great renunciation with considerable effect, and having induced Lady Guilderoy to receive back her husband he accepts "a distant and arduous Viceroyalty." He is Ouida's ideal of the true politician, for Ouida has apparently taken to the study of English politics. A great deal of her book is devoted to political disquisitions. She believes that the proper rulers of a country like ours are the aristocrats. Oligarchy has great fascinations for her. She thinks meanly of the people, and adores the House of Lords, and Lord Salisbury. Here are some of her views. We will not call them ideas:—

The House of Lords wants nothing of the nation, and therefore it is the only candid and disinterested guardian of the people's needs and resources. It has never withstood the real desire of the country: it has only stood between the country and its impetuous and evanescent follies.

A democracy cannot understand honour; how should it? The Caucus is chiefly made up of men who sand their sugar, put alum in their bread, forge bayonets and girders which bend like willow wands, send bad calico to India, and insure vessels at Lloyd's which they know will go to the bottom before they have been ten days at sea.

Lord Salisbury has often been accused of arrogance; people have never seen that what they mistook for arrogance was the natural, candid consciousness of a great noble that he is more capable of leading the country than most men composing it would be.

Democracy, after having made everything supremely hideous and uncomfortable for everybody, always ends by clinging to the coat tails of some successful general.

The professional politician may be honest, but his honesty is at best a questionable quality. The moment that a thing is a *metier*, it is wholly absurd to talk about any disinterestedness in the pursuit of it. To the professional politician national affairs are a manufacture into which he puts his audacity and his time, and out of which he expects to make so much percentage for his life time.

There is too great a tendency to govern the world by noise.

Ouida's aphorisms on women, love, and modern society are somewhat more characteristic:—

Women speak as though the heart were to be treated at will like a stone, or a bath.

Half the passions of men die early, because they are expected to be eternal.

It is the folly of life that lends charm to it.

What is the cause of half the misery of women? That their love is so much more tenacious than the man's: it grows stronger as his grows weaker.

To endure the country in England for long, one must have the rusticity of Wordsworth's mind, and boots and stockings as homely.

It is because men feel the necessity to explain that they drop into the habit of saying what is not true. Wise is the woman who never insists on an explanation.

Love can make its own world in a solitude *a deux*, but marriage cannot.

Nominally monogamous, all cultured society is polygamous; often even polyandrous.

Moralists say that a soul should resist passion. They might as well say that a house should resist an earthquake.

The whole world is just now on its knees in adoration before the poorer classes; all the cardinal virtues are taken for granted in them, and it is only property of any kind which is the sinner.

Men are not merciful to women's tears as a rule; and when it is a woman belonging to them who weeps, they only go out, and slam the door behind them.

Men always consider women unjust to them, when they fail to deify their weaknesses.

No passion, once broken, will ever bear renewal.

Feeling loses its force and its delicacy if we put it under the microscope too often.

Anything which is not flattery seems injustice to a woman.

When society is aware that you think it a flock of geese, it revenges itself by hissing loudly behind your back.

Of descriptions of scenery and art we have, of course, a large number, and it is impossible not to recognize the touch of the real Ouida manner in the following:—

It was an old palace; lofty, spacious, magnificent, and dull. Busts of dusky yellow marble, weird bronzes stretching out gaunt arms into the darkness, ivories brown with age, worn brocades with gold threads gleaming in them, and tapestries with strange and pallid figures of dead gods, were all half revealed and half obscured in the twilight. As he moved through them, a figure which looked almost as pale as the Adonis of the tapestry and was erect and motionless like the statue of the wounded Love, came before his sight out of the shadows. It was that of Gladys.

It is a manner full of exaggeration and over-emphasis, but with some remarkable rhetorical qualities, and a good deal of colour.

Ouida is fond of airing a smattering of culture, but she has a certain artistic insight into things, and though she is rarely true, she is never dull. "Guilderoy" with all its faults, which are great, and its absurdities, which are greater, is a book to be read.

Mr. Swinburne's Last Volume*

Mr. Swinburne once set his age on fire by a volume of very perfect and very poisonous poetry. Then he became revolutionary, and pantheistic, and cried out against those who sit in high places both in heaven and on earth. Then he invented Marie Stuart, and laid upon us the heavy burden of "Bothwell." Then he retired to the nursery, and wrote poems about children of a somewhat over-subtle character. He is now extremely patriotic, and manages to combine with his patriotism a strong affection for the Tory party. He has always been a great poet. But he has his limitations, the chief of which is, curiously enough, an entire lack of any sense of limit. His song is nearly always too loud for his subject. His magnificent rhetoric, nowhere more significant than in the volume that now lies before us, conceals rather than reveals. It has been said of him, and with truth, that he is a master of language, but with still greater truth it may be said that Language is his master. Words seem to dominate him. Alliteration tyrannizes over him. Mere sound often becomes his lord. He is so eloquent that whatever he touches becomes unreal.

Let us turn to the poem on the Armada:

The wings of the south-west wind are widened; the breath of his fervent lips,

* Unsigned review of Algernon Charles Swinburne, *Poems and Ballads. Third Series. Pall Mall Gazette* XLIX : 7574 (27 June 1889) 3.

More keen than a sword's edge; fiercer than fire, falls full on the
  plunging ships.
The pilot is he of their northward flight, their stay and their steers-
  man he;
A helmsman clothed with the tempest, and girdled with strength to
  constrain the sea.
And the host of them trembles and quails, caught fast in his hand
  as a bird in the toils;
For the wrath and joy that fulfil him are mightier than man's, whom
  he slays and spoils,
And vainly, with heart divided in sunder, and labour of wavering
  will,
The lord of their host takes counsel with hope if haply their star
  shine still.

Somehow, we seem to have heard all this before. Does it come
from the fact that of all poets who ever lived Mr. Swinburne
is the one who is the most limited in imagery? It must be admitted that he is so. He has wearied us with his monotony.
"Fire" and the "Sea" are the two words ever on his lips. We
must confess also that this shrill singing—marvellous as it is
—leaves us out of breath. Here is a passage from a poem called
"A Word with the Wind":

Be the sunshine bared or veiled, the sky superb or shrouded,
  Still the waters, lax and languid, chafed and foiled,
Keen and thwarted, pale and patient, clothed with fire or clouded
  Vex their heart in vain, or sleep like serpents coiled.
Thee they look for, blind and baffled, wan with wrath and weary
  Blown for ever back by winds that rock the bird:
Winds that seamews breast subdue the sea, and bid the dreary
  Waves be weak as hearts made sick with hope deferred.
Let the clarion sound from westward, let the south bear token
  How the glories of thy godhead sound and shine:
Bid the land rejoice to see the land-winds broad back broken,
  Bid the sea take comfort, bid the world be thine.

Verse of this kind may be justly praised for the sustained
strength and vigour of its metrical scheme. Its purely technical
excellence is extraordinary. But is it more than an oratorical
tour-de-force? Does it really convey much? Does it charm?

Could we return to it again and again with renewed pleasure? We think not. It seems to us empty.

Of course, we must not look to these poems for any revelation of human life. To be at one with the elements seems to be Mr. Swinburne's aim. He seeks to speak with the breath of wind and wave. The roar of the fire is ever in his ears. He puts his clarion to the lips of Spring and bids her blow, and the Earth wakes from her dreams and tells him her secret. He is the first lyric poet who has tried to make an absolute surrender of his own personality, and he has succeeded. We hear the song, but we never know the singer. We never even get near to him. Out of the thunder and splendour of words he himself says nothing. We have often had man's interpretation of Nature; now we have Nature's interpretation of man, and she has curiously little to say. Force and Freedom form her vague message. She deafens us with her clangours.

But Mr. Swinburne is not always riding the whirlwind, and calling out of the depths of the sea. Romantic ballads in Border dialect have not lost their fascination for him, and this last volume contains some very splendid examples of this curious artificial kind of poetry. The amount of pleasure one gets out of dialect is a matter entirely of temperament. To say "mither" instead of "mother" seems to many the acme of romance. There are others who are not quite as ready to believe in the pathos of provincialisms. There is, however, no doubt of Mr. Swinburne's mastery over the form, whether the form be quite legitimate or not. "The Weary Wedding" has the concentration and colour of a great drama, and the quaintness of its style lends it something of the power of a grotesque. The ballad of "The Witch-Mother," a medieval Medea who slays her children because her lord is faithless, is worth reading on account of its horrible simplicity. The "Bride's Tragedy" with its strange refrain of

> In, in, out and in,
> Blaws the wind and whirls the whin:

The "Jacobite's Exile,"

> O lordly flow the Loire and Seine,
>   And loud the dark Durance:
> But bonnier shine the braes of Tyne
>   Than a' the fields of France;
> And the waves of Till that speak sae still
>   Gleam goodlier where they glance:

"The Tyneside Widow," and "A Reiver's Neck-verse," are all poems of fine imaginative power, and some of them are terrible in their fierce intensity of passion. There is no danger of English poetry narrowing itself to a form so limited as the romantic ballad in dialect. It is too vital a growth for that. So we may welcome Mr. Swinburne's masterly experiments with the hope that things which are inimitable will not be imitated. The collection is completed by a few poems on children, some sonnets, a threnody on John William Inchbold, and a very lovely lyric entitled "The Interpreters."

> In human thought have all things habitation;
>   Our days
> Laugh, lower, and lighten past, and find no station
>   That stays.
>
> But thought and faith are mightier things than time
>   Can wrong,
> Made splendid once by speech, or made sublime
>   By song.
>
> Remembrance, though the tide of change that rolls
>   Wax hoary,
> Gives earth and heaven, for song's sake and the soul's,
>   Their glory.

Certainly "for song's sake" we should love Mr. Swinburne's work, cannot indeed help loving it, so marvellous a music-maker is he. But what of the soul? For the soul we must go elsewhere.

Yeats's *The Wanderings of Oisin**

Books of poetry by young writers are usually promissory notes that are never met. Now and then, however, one comes across a volume that is so far above the average that one can hardly resist the fascinating temptation of recklessly prophesying a fine future for its author. Such a volume Mr. Yeats's "Wanderings of Oisin" certainly is. Here we find nobility of treatment and nobility of subject matter, delicacy of poetic instinct, and richness of imaginative resource. Unequal and uneven much of the work must be admitted to be. Mr. Yeats does not try to "out-baby" Wordsworth, we are glad to say, but he occasionally succeeds in "out-glittering" Keats, and here and there in his book we come across strange crudities and irritating conceits. But when he is at his best he is very good. If he has not the grand simplicity of epic treatment, he has at least something of that largeness of vision that belongs to the epical temper. He does not rob of their stature the great heroes of Celtic mythology. He is very naïve, and very primitive, and speaks of his giants with the awe of a child. Here is a characteristic passage from the account of Oisin's return from the Island of Forgetfulness:—

* Unsigned review, entitled "Three New Poets: Yeats, Fitz Gerald, Le Gallienne," and two other books. *Pall Mall Gazette* XLIX : 7587 (12 July 1889) 3.

And I rode by the plains of the sea's edge, where all is barren and
    grey,
Grey sands on the green of the grasses and over the dripping trees,
Dripping and doubling landward, as though they would hasten away
Like an army of old men longing for rest from the moan of trees.

Long fled the foam-flakes around me, the winds fled out of the vast,
Snatching the bird in secret, nor knew I, embosomed apart,
When they froze the cloth on my body like armour riveted fast,
For Remembrance, lifting her leanness, keened in the gates of my
    heart.

Till fattening the winds of the morning, an odour of new-mown hay
Came, and my forehead fell low, and my tears like berries fell down;
Later a sound came, half lost in the sound of a shore far away,
From the great grass-barricade calling, and later the shore-weeds
    brown.

If I were as I once was, the gold hooves crushing the sand and the
    shells,
Coming forth from the sea like the morning with red lips murmur-
    ing a song,
Not coughing, my head on my knees, and praying, and wroth with
    the bells,
I would leave no saint's head on his body, though spacious his lands
    were and strong.

Making way from the kindling surges, I rode on a bridle path,
Much wondering to see upon all hands, of wattle and woodwork
    made,
Thy bell-mounted churches, and guardless the sacred cairn and the
    earth,
And a small and feeble populace stooping with mattock and spade.

In one or two places the music is faulty, the construction is
sometimes too involved, and the word "populace" in the last
line is rather infelicitous; but when all is said, it is impossible
not to feel in these stanzas the presence of the true poetic
spirit.

The Portrait
of Mr W. H.

I had been dining with Erskine in his pretty little house in Birdcage Walk, and we were sitting in the library over our coffee and cigarettes, when the question of literary forgeries happened to turn up in conversation. I cannot at present remember how it was that we struck upon this somewhat curious topic, as it was at that time, but I know we had a long discussion about Macpherson, Ireland, and Chatterton, and that with regard to the last I insisted that his so-called forgeries were merely the result of an artistic desire for perfect representation; that we had no right to quarrel with an artist for the conditions under which he chooses to present his work; and that all Art being to a certain degree a mode of acting, an attempt to realise one's own personality on some imaginative plane out of reach of the trammelling accidents and limitations of real life, to censure an artist for a forgery was to confuse an ethical with an æsthetical problem.

Erskine, who was a good deal older than I was, and had been listening to me with the amused deference of a man of forty, suddenly put his hand upon my shoulder and said to me, "What would you say about a young man who had a

* London, Methuen (1958); originally published 1921—early version in *Blackwood's Edinburgh Magazine*, July 1889.

strange theory about a certain work of art, believed in his theory, and committed a forgery in order to prove it?"

"Ah! that is quite a different matter," I answered.

Erskine remained silent for a few moments, looking at the thin grey threads of smoke that were rising from his cigarette. "Yes," he said, after a pause, "quite different."

There was something in the tone of his voice, a slight touch of bitterness perhaps, that excited my curiosity. "Did you ever know anybody who did that?" I cried.

"Yes," he answered, throwing his cigarette into the fire— "a great friend of mine, Cyril Graham. He was very fascinating, and very foolish, and very heartless. However, he left me the only legacy I ever received in my life."

"What was that?" I exclaimed laughing. Erskine rose from his seat, and going over to a tall inlaid cabinet that stood between the two windows, unlocked it, and came back to where I was sitting, carrying a small panel picture set in an old and somewhat tarnished Elizabethan frame.

It was a full-length portrait of a young man in late sixteenth-century costume, standing by a table, with his right hand resting on an open book. He seemed about seventeen years of age, and was of quite extraordinary personal beauty, though evidently somewhat effeminate. Indeed, had it not been for the dress and the closely cropped hair, one would have said that the face, with its dreamy, wistful eyes and its delicate scarlet lips, was the face of a girl. In manner, and especially in the treatment of the hands, the picture reminded one of François Clouet's later work. The black velvet doublet with its fantastically gilded points, and the peacock-blue background against which it showed up so pleasantly, and from which it gained such luminous value of colour, were quite in Clouet's style; and the two masks of Tragedy and Comedy that hung somewhat formally from the marble pedestal had that hard severity of touch—so different from the facile grace of the Italians— which even at the Court of France the great Flemish master never completely lost, and which in itself has always been a characteristic of the northern temper.

"It is a charming thing," I cried, "but who is this wonderful young man whose beauty Art has so happily preserved for us?"

"This is the portrait of Mr W. H.," said Erskine, with a sad smile. It might have been a chance effect of light, but it seemed to me that his eyes were swimming with tears.

"Mr W. H.!" I repeated; "who was Mr W. H.?"

"Don't you remember?" he answered; "look at the book on which his hand is resting."

"I see there is some writing there, but I cannot make it out," I replied.

"Take this magnifying-glass and try," said Erskine, with the same sad smile still playing about his mouth.

I took the glass, and moving the lamp a little nearer, I began to spell out the crabbed sixteenth-century handwriting. "To The Onlie Begetter Of These Insuing Sonnets." . . . "Good heavens!" I cried, "is this Shakespeare's Mr W. H.?"

"Cyril Graham used to say so," muttered Erskine.

"But it is not a bit like Lord Pembroke," I rejoined. "I know the Wilton portraits very well. I was staying near there a few weeks ago."

"Do you really believe then that the Sonnets are addressed to Lord Pembroke?" he asked.

"I am sure of it," I answered. "Pembroke, Shakespeare, and Mrs. Mary Fitton are the three personages of the Sonnets; there is no doubt at all about it."

"Well, I agree with you," said Erskine, "but I did not always think so. I used to believe—well, I suppose I used to believe in Cyril Graham and his theory."

"And what was that?" I asked, looking at the wonderful portrait, which had already begun to have a strange fascination for me.

"It is a long story," he murmured, taking the picture away from me—rather abruptly I thought at the time—"a very long story; but if you care to hear it, I will tell it to you."

"I love theories about the Sonnets," I cried; "but I don't think I am likely to be converted to any new idea. The matter has ceased to be a mystery to any one. Indeed, I wonder that it ever was a mystery."

"As I don't believe in the theory, I am not likely to convert you to it," said Erskine, laughing; "but it may interest you."

"Tell it to me, of course," I answered. "If it is half as delightful as the picture, I shall be more than satisfied."

"Well," said Erskine, lighting a cigarette, "I must begin by telling you about Cyril Graham himself. He and I were at the same house at Eton. I was a year or two older than he was, but we were immense friends, and did all our work and all our play together. There was, of course, a good deal more play than work, but I cannot say that I am sorry for that. It is always an advantage not to have received a sound commercial education, and what I learned in the playing fields at Eton has been quite as useful to me as anything I was taught at Cambridge. I should tell you that Cyril's father and mother were both dead. They had been drowned in a horrible yachting accident off the Isle of Wight. His father had been in the diplomatic service, and had married a daughter, the only daughter, in fact, of old Lord Crediton, who became Cyril's guardian after the death of his parents. I don't think that Lord Crediton cared very much for Cyril. He had never really forgiven his daughter for marrying a man who had no title. He was an extraordinary old aristocrat, who swore like a costermonger, and had the manners of a farmer. I remember seeing him once on Speech-day. He growled at me, gave me a sovereign, and told me not to grow up a 'damned Radical' like my father. Cyril had very little affection for him, and was only too glad to spend most of his holidays with us in Scotland. They never really got on together at all. Cyril thought him a bear, and he thought Cyril effeminate. He was effeminate, I suppose, in some things, though he was a capital rider and a capital fencer. In fact he got the foils before he left Eton. But he was very languid in his manner, and not a little vain of his good looks, and had a strong objection to football, which he used to say was a game only suitable for the sons of the middle classes. The two things that really gave him pleasure were poetry and acting. At Eton he was always dressing up and reciting Shakespeare, and when we went up to Trinity he became a member of the A.D.C. in his first term. I remember I was always very jealous of his acting. I was absurdly devoted to him; I suppose because we were so different in most things. I was a rather awkward, weakly lad, with huge feet, and horribly freckled. Freckles run in Scotch families just as gout does in English families. Cyril used to say that of the two he preferred the gout; but he always set an absurdly high value on personal appearance, and once read a paper before our Debating Society to prove that it was better to be good-looking than to be good. He certainly was wonderfully handsome. People who did not like him, philistines and college tutors, and young men reading for the Church, used to say that he was merely pretty; but there was a great deal more in his face than mere prettiness. I think he was the most splendid creature I ever saw, and nothing could exceed the grace of his movements, the charm of his manner. He fascinated everybody who was worth fascinating, and a great many people who were not. He was often wilful and petulant, and I used to think him dreadfully insincere. It was due, I think, chiefly to his inordinate desire to please. Poor Cyril! I told him once that he was contented with very cheap triumphs, but he only tossed his head, and smiled. He was horribly spoiled. All charming people, I fancy, are spoiled. It is the secret of their attraction.

"However, I must tell you about Cyril's acting. You know that no women are allowed to play at the A.D.C. At least they were not in my time. I don't know how it is now. Well, of course Cyril was always cast for the girls' parts, and when 'As You Like It' was produced he played Rosalind. It was a marvellous performance. You will laugh at me, but I assure you that Cyril Graham was the only perfect Rosalind I have ever seen. It would be impossible to describe to you the beauty, the delicacy, the refinement of the whole thing. It made an immense sensation, and the horrid little theatre, as it was then, was crowded every night. Even now when I read the play I can't help thinking of Cyril; the part might have been written for him, he played it with such extraordinary grace and distinction. The next term he took his degree, and came to London to read for the Diplomatic. But he never did any work. He spent his days in reading Shakespeare's Sonnets, and his evenings at the theatre. He was, of course, wild to go on the stage. It was all that Lord Crediton and I could do to prevent him. Perhaps, if he had gone on the stage he would be alive now. It is always a silly thing to give advice, but to give good advice is absolutely fatal. I hope you will never fall into that error. If you do, you will be sorry for it.

"Well, to come to the real point of the story, one afternoon I got a letter from Cyril asking me to come round to his rooms that evening. He had charming chambers in Piccadilly overlooking the Green Park, and as I used to go to see him almost every day, I was rather surprised at his taking the trouble to write. Of course I went, and when I arrived I found him in a state of great excitement. He told me that he had at last discovered the true secret of Shakespeare's Sonnets; that all the scholars and critics had been entirely on the wrong track; and that he was the first who, working purely by internal evidence, had found out who Mr W. H. really was. He was perfectly wild with delight, and for a long time would not tell me his theory. Finally, he produced a bundle of notes, took his copy of the Sonnets off the mantelpiece, and sat down and gave me a long lecture on the whole subject.

"He began by pointing out that the young man to whom Shakespeare addressed these strangely passionate poems must have been somebody who was a really vital factor in the development of his dramatic art, and that this could not be said of either Lord Pembroke or Lord Southampton. Indeed, whoever he was, he could not have been anybody of high birth, as was shown very clearly by Sonnet xxv, in which Shakespeare contrasts himself with men who are 'great princes' favourites'; says quite frankly—

> Let those who are in favour with their stars
> Of public honour and proud titles boast,
> Whilst I, whom fortune of such triumph bars,
> Unlooked for joy in that I honour most;

and ends the sonnet by congratulating himself on the mean state of him he so adored:

> Then happy I, that love and am beloved
> Where I may not remove nor be removed

This sonnet Cyril declared would be quite unintelligible if we fancied that it was addressed to either the Earl of Pembroke or the Earl of Southampton, both of whom were men of the highest position in England and fully entitled to be called 'great princes'; and he in corroboration of his view read me Sonnets CXXIV and CXXV, in which Shakespeare tells us that his love is not 'the child of state,' that it 'suffers not in smiling pomp,' but is 'builded far from accident.' I listened with a good deal of interest, for I don't think the point had ever been made before; but what followed was still more curious, and seemed to me at the time to dispose entirely of Pembroke's claim. We know from Meres that the Sonnets had been written before 1598, and Sonnet CIV informs us that Shakespeare's friendship for Mr W. H. had been already in existence for three years. Now Lord Pembroke, who was born in 1580, did not come to London till he was eighteen years of age, that is to say till 1598, and Shakespeare's acquaintance with Mr W. H. must have begun in 1594, or at the latest in 1595. Shakespeare, accordingly, could not have known Lord Pembroke until after the Sonnets had been written.

"Cyril pointed out also that Pembroke's father did not die until 1601; whereas it was evident from the line,

> You had a father, let your son say so,

that the father of Mr W. H. was dead in 1598; and laid great stress on the evidence afforded by the Wilton portraits which represent Lord Pembroke as a swarthy dark-haired man, while Mr W. H. was one whose hair was like spun gold, and whose face the meeting-place for the 'lily's white' and the 'deep vermilion in the rose'; being himself 'fair,' and 'red,' and 'white and red,' and of beautiful aspect. Besides it was absurd to imagine that any publisher of the time, and the preface is from the publisher's hand, would have dreamed of addressing William Herbert, Earl of Pembroke, as Mr W. H.; the case of Lord Buckhurst being spoken of as Mr Sackville being not really a parallel instance, as Lord Buckhurst, the first of that title, was plain Mr Sackville when he contributed to the 'Mirror for Magistrates,' while Pembroke, during his father's lifetime, was always known as Lord Herbert. So far for Lord Pembroke, whose supposed claims Cyril easily demolished while

I sat by in wonder. With Lord Southampton Cyril had even less difficulty. Southampton became at a very early age the lover of Elizabeth Vernon, so he needed no entreaties to marry; he was not beautiful; he did not resemble his mother, as Mr W. H. did—

> Thou art thy mother's glass, and she in thee
> Calls back the lovely April of her prime;

and, above all, his Christian name was Henry, whereas the punning sonnets (CXXXV and CXLIII) show that the Christian name of Shakespeare's friend was the same as his own—*Will*.

"As for the other suggestions of unfortunate commentators, that Mr W. H. is a misprint for Mr W. S., meaning Mr William Shakespeare; that 'Mr W. H. all' should be read 'Mr W. Hall'; that Mr W. H. is Mr William Hathaway; that Mr W. H. stands for Mr Henry Willobie, the young Oxford poet, with the initials of his name reversed; and that a full stop should be placed after 'wisheth,' making Mr W. H. the writer and not the subject of the dedication,—Cyril got rid of them in a very short time; and it is not worth while to mention his reasons, though I remember he sent me off into a fit of laughter by reading to me, I am glad to say not in the original, some extracts from a German commentator called Barnstorff, who insisted that Mr W. H. was no less a person than 'Mr William Himself.' Nor would he allow for a moment that the Sonnets are mere satires on the work of Drayton and John Davies of Hereford. To him, as indeed to me, they were poems of serious and tragic import, wrung out of the bitterness of Shakespeare's heart, and made sweet by the honey of his lips. Still less would he admit that they were merely a philosophical allegory, and that in them Shakespeare is addressing his Ideal Self, or Ideal Manhood, or the Spirit of Beauty, or the Reason, or the Divine Logos, or the Catholic Church. He felt, as indeed I think we all must feel, that the Sonnets are addressed to an individual,—to a particular young man whose personality for some reason seems to have filled the soul of Shakespeare with terrible joy and no less terrible despair.

"Having in this manner cleared the way, as it were, Cyril

asked me to dismiss from my mind any preconceived ideas I might have formed on the subject, and to give a fair and un-biased hearing to his own theory. The problem he pointed out was this: Who was that young man of Shakespeare's day who, without being of noble birth or even of noble nature, was ad-dressed by him in terms of such passionate adoration that we can but wonder at the strange worship, and are almost afraid to turn the key that unlocks the mystery of the poet's heart? Who was he whose physical beauty was such that it became the very corner-stone of Shakespeare's art; the very source of Shakespeare's inspiration; the very incarnation of Shakespeare's dreams? To look upon him as simply the object of certain love-poems was to miss the whole meaning of the poems: for the art of which Shakespeare talks in the Sonnets is not the art of the Sonnets themselves, which indeed were to him but slight and secret things—it is the art of the dramatist to which he is always alluding; and he to whom Shakespeare said—

> Thou art all my art, and dost advance
> As high as learning my rude ignorance,—

he to whom he promised immortality,

> Where breath most breathes, even in the mouths of men,—

he who was to him the tenth 'muse' and

> Ten times more in worth
> Than those old nine which rhymers invocate,

was surely none other than the boy-actor for whom he created Viola and Imogen, Juliet and Rosalind, Portia and Desdemona, and Cleopatra herself."

"The boy-actor of Shakespeare's plays?" I cried.

"Yes," said Erskine. "This was Cyril Graham's theory, evolved as you see purely from the Sonnets themselves, and depending for its acceptance not so much on demonstrable proof of formal evidence, but on a kind of spiritual and artistic sense, by which alone he claimed could the true meaning of the poems be discerned. I remember his reading to me that fine sonnet—

> How can my Muse want subject to invent,
> While thou dost breathe, that pour'st into my verse
> Thine own sweet argument, too excellent
> For every vulgar paper to rehearse
> O give thyself the thanks, if aught in me
> Worthy perusal stand against thy sight;
> For who's so dumb that cannot write to thee,
> When thou thyself dost give invention light?

—and pointing out how completely it corroborated his view; and indeed he went through all the Sonnets carefully, and showed, or fancied that he showed, that, according to his new explanation of their meaning, things that had seemed obscure, or evil, or exaggerated, became clear and rational, and of high artistic import, illustrating Shakespeare's conception of the true relations between the art of the actor and the art of the dramatist.

"It is of course evident that there must have been in Shakespeare's company some wonderful boy-actor of great beauty, to whom he intrusted the presentation of his noble heroines; for Shakespeare was a practical theatrical manager as well as an imaginative poet; and Cyril Graham had actually discovered the boy-actor's name. He was Will, or, as he preferred to call him, Willie Hughes. The Christian name he found of course in the punning sonnets, cxxxv and cxliii; the surname was, according to him, hidden in the seventh line of Sonnet xx, where Mr W. H. is described as—

> A man in hew, all *Hews* in his controwling.

"In the original edition of the Sonnets 'Hews' is printed with a capital letter and in italics, and this, he claimed, showed clearly that a play on words was intended, his view receiving a good deal of corroboration from those sonnets in which curious puns are made on the words 'use' and 'usury,' and from such lines as—

> Thou art as fair in knowledge as in hew.

Of course I was converted at once, and Willie Hughes became to me as real a person as Shakespeare. The only objection I made to the theory was that the name of Willie Hughes does not occur in the list of the actors of Shakespeare's company as it is printed in the first folio. Cyril, however, pointed out that the absence of Willie Hughes' name from this list really corroborated the theory, as it was evident from Sonnet LXXXVI, that he had abandoned Shakespeare's company to play at some a rival theatre, probably in some of Chapman's plays. It was in reference to this that in the great sonnet on Chapman Shakespeare said to Willie Hughes—

> But when your countenance filled up his line,
> Then lacked I matter; that enfeebled mine—

the expression 'when your countenance filled up his line' referring clearly to the beauty of the young actor giving life and reality and added charm to Chapman's verse, the same idea being also put forward in Sonnet LXXIX:

> Whilst I alone did call upon thy aid,
> My verse alone had all thy gentle grace,
> But now my gracious numbers are decayed,
> And my sick Muse doth give another place;

and in the immediately preceding sonnet, where Shakespeare says,

> Every alien pen hath got my *use*
> And under thee their poesy disperse,

the play upon words (use = Hughes) being of course obvious, and the phrase, 'under thee their poesy disperse,' meaning 'by your assistance as an actor bring their plays before the people.'

"It was a wonderful evening, and we sat up almost till dawn reading and re-reading the Sonnets. After some time, however, I began to see that before the theory could be placed before the world in a really perfected form, it was necessary to get some independent evidence about the existence of this young actor, Willie Hughes. If this could be once established, there could be no possible doubt about his identity with Mr W. H.; but otherwise the theory would fall to the ground. I put this forward very strongly to Cyril, who was a good deal annoyed at what he called my philistine tone of mind, and indeed was rather bitter upon the subject. However, I made him promise that in his own interest he would not publish his discovery till he had put the whole matter beyond the reach of doubt; and for weeks and weeks we searched the registers of City churches, the Alleyn MSS. at Dulwich, the Record Office, the books of the Lord Chamberlain—everything, in fact, that we thought might contain some allusion to Willie Hughes. We discovered nothing, of course, and each day the existence of Willie Hughes seemed to me to become more problematical. Cyril was in a dreadful state, and used to go over the whole question again and again, entreating me to believe; but I saw the one flaw in the theory, and I refused to be convinced till the actual existence of Willie Hughes, a boy-actor of the Elizabethan stage, had been placed beyond the reach of doubt or cavil.

"One day Cyril left town to stay with his grandfather, I thought at the time, but I afterwards heard from Lord Crediton that this was not the case; and about a fortnight afterwards I received a telegram from him, handed in at Warwick, asking me to be sure to come and dine with him in his chambers, that evening at eight o'clock. When I arrived, he said to me, 'The only apostle who did not deserve proof was St Thomas, and St Thomas was the only apostle who got it.' I asked him what he meant. He answered that he had been able not merely to establish the existence in the sixteenth century of a boy-actor of the name of Willie Hughes, but to prove by the most conclusive evidence that he was the Mr W. H. of the Sonnets. He would not tell me anything more at the time; but after dinner he solemnly produced the picture I showed you, and told me that he had discovered it by the merest chance nailed to the side of an old chest that he had bought at a farmhouse in Warwickshire. The chest itself, which was a very fine example of Elizabethan work, and thoroughly authentic, he had, of course, brought with him, and in the centre of the front panel the initials W. H. were undoubtedly carved. It was this monogram that had attracted his attention, and he told me that it was not till he had had the chest in his possession for several days that he had thought of making any careful examination of the inside. One morning, however, he saw that the right-hand side of the chest was much thicker than the other, and looking more closely, he discovered that a framed panel was clamped against it. On taking it out, he found it was the picture that is now lying on the sofa. It was very dirty, and covered with mould; but he managed to clean it, and, to his great joy, saw that he had fallen by mere chance on the one thing for which he had been looking. Here was an authentic portrait of Mr W. H. with his hand resting on the dedicatory page of the Sonnets, and on the corner of the picture could be faintly seen the name of the young man himself written in gold uncial letters on the faded *bleu de paon* ground, 'Master Will Hews.'

"Well, what was I to say? It is quite clear from Sonnet XLVII that Shakespeare had a portrait of Mr W. H. in his possession, and it seemed to me more than probable that here we had the very 'painted banquet' on which he invited his eye to feast; the actual picture that awoke his heart 'to heart's and eye's delight.' It never occurred to me for a moment that Cyril Graham was playing a trick on me, or that he was trying to prove his theory by means of a forgery."

"But is it a forgery?" I asked.

"Of course it is," said Erskine. "It is a very good forgery; but it is a forgery none the less. I thought at the time that Cyril was rather calm about the whole matter; but I remember he kept telling me that he himself required no proof of the kind, and that he thought the theory complete without it. I laughed at him, and told him that without it the entire theory would fall to the ground, and I warmly congratulated him on his marvellous discovery. We then arranged that the picture should be etched or facsimiled, and placed as the frontispiece to Cyril's edition of the Sonnets; and for three months we did nothing but go over each poem line by line, till we had settled every difficulty of text or meaning. One unlucky day I was in a print-shop in Holborn, when I saw upon the counter some extremely beautiful drawings in silver-point. I was so attracted by them that I bought them; and the proprietor of the place, a man called Rawlings, told me that they were done by a young painter of the name of Edward Merton, who was very clever, but as poor as a church mouse. I went to see Merton some days afterwards, having got his address from the print-seller, and found a pale, interesting young man, with a rather common-looking wife,—his model, as I subsequently learned. I told him how much I admired his drawings, at which he seemed very pleased, and I asked him if he would show me some of his other work. As we were looking over a portfolio, full of really very lovely things,—for Merton had a most delicate and delightful touch,—I suddenly caught sight of a drawing of the picture of Mr W. H. There was no doubt whatever about it. It was almost a facsimile,—the only difference being that the two masks of Tragedy and Comedy were not suspended from the marble table as they are in the picture but were lying on the floor at the young man's feet. 'Where on earth did you get that?' I asked. He grew rather confused, and said,—'Oh, that is nothing. I did not know it was in this portfolio. It is not a thing of any value.' 'It is what you did for Mr Cyril Graham,' exclaimed his wife; 'and if this gentleman wishes to buy it, let him have it.' 'For Mr Cyril Graham?' I repeated. 'Did you paint the picture of Mr W. H.?' 'I don't understand what you mean,' he answered growing very red. Well, the whole thing was quite dreadful. The wife let it all out. I gave her five pounds when I was going away. I can't bear to think of it, now; but of course I was furious. I went off at once to Cyril's chambers, waited there for three hours before he came in, with that horrid lie staring me in the face, and told him I had discovered his forgery. He grew very pale, and said,—'I did it purely for your sake. You would not be convinced in any other way. It does not affect the truth of the theory.' 'The truth of the theory!' I exclaimed; 'the less we talk about that the better. You never even believed in it yourself. If you had, you would not have committed a forgery to prove it.' High words passed between us; we had a fearful quarrel. I daresay I was unjust, and the next morning he was dead.'

"Dead!" I cried.

"Yes, he shot himself with a revolver. By the time I arrived, —his servant had sent for me at once,—the police were already there. He had left a letter for me, evidently written in the greatest agitation and distress of mind."

"What was in it?" I asked.

"Oh, that he believed absolutely in Willie Hughes; that the forgery of the picture had been done simply as a concession to me, and did not in the slightest degree invalidate the truth of the theory; and that in order to show me how firm and flawless his faith in the whole thing was, he was going to offer his life as a sacrifice to the secret of the Sonnets. It was a foolish, mad letter. I remember he ended by saying that he intrusted to me the Willie Hughes theory, and that it was for me to present it to the world, and to unlock the secret of Shakespeare's heart."

"It is a most tragic story," I cried, "but why have you not carried out his wishes?"

Erskine shrugged his shoulders. "Because it is a perfectly unsound theory from beginning to end," he answered.

"My dear Erskine," I exclaimed, getting up from my seat, "you are entirely wrong about the whole matter. It is the only perfect key to Shakespeare's Sonnets that has ever been made. It is complete in every detail. I believe in Willie Hughes."

"Don't say that," said Erskine, gravely; "I believe there is something fatal about the idea, and intellectually there is nothing to be said for it. I have gone into the whole matter, and I assure you the theory is entirely fallacious. It is plausible up to a certain point. Then it stops. For heaven's sake, my dear boy, don't take up the subject of Willie Hughes. You will break your heart over it."

"Erskine," I answered, "it is your duty to give this theory to the world. If you will not do it, I will. By keeping it back you wrong the memory of Cyril Graham, the youngest and the most splendid of all the martyrs of literature. I entreat you to do him this bare act of justice. He died for this thing,— don't let his death be in vain."

Erskine looked at me in amazement. "You are carried away by the sentiment of the whole story," he said. "You forget that a thing is not necessarily true because a man dies for it.

I was devoted to Cyril Graham. His death was a horrible blow
to me. I did not recover from it for years. I don't think I have
ever recovered from it. But Willie Hughes! There is nothing
in the idea of Willie Hughes. No such person ever existed.
As for bringing the matter before the world,—the world thinks
that Cyril Graham shot himself by accident. The only proof
of his suicide was contained in the letter to me, and of this
letter the public never heard anything. To the present day
Lord Crediton is under the impression that the whole thing
was accidental."

"Cyril Graham sacrificed his life to a great idea," I answered; "and if you will not tell of his martyrdom, tell at least
of his faith."

"His faith," said Erskine, "was fixed in a thing that was
false, in a thing that was unsound, in a thing that no Shakespearian scholar would accept for a moment. The theory would
be laughed at. Don't make a fool of yourself, and don't follow
a trail that leads nowhere. You start by assuming the existence
of the very person whose existence is the thing to be proved.
Besides, everybody knows that the Sonnets were addressed to
Lord Pembroke. The matter is settled once for all."

"The matter is not settled," I exclaimed. "I will take up the
theory where Cyril Graham left it, and I will prove to the
world that he was right."

"Silly boy!" said Erskine. "Go home, it is after three, and
don't think about Willie Hughes any more. I am sorry I
told you anything about it, and very sorry indeed that I should
have converted you to a thing in which I don't believe."

"You have given me the key to the greatest mystery of modern literature," I answered; "and I will not rest till I have made
you recognise, till I have made everybody recognise, that Cyril
Graham was the most subtle Shakespearian critic of our day."

I was about to leave the room when Erskine called me
back. "My dear fellow," he said, "let me advise you not to
waste your time over the Sonnets. I am quite serious. After all,
what do they tell us about Shakespeare? Simply that he was
the slave of beauty."

"Well, that is the condition of being an artist!" I replied.

There was a strange silence for a few moments. Then Erskine

got up, and looking at me with half closed eyes, said, "Ah! how you remind me of Cyril! He used to say just that sort of thing to me." He tried to smile, but there was a note of poignant pathos in his voice that I remember to the present day, as one remembers the tone of a particular violin that has charmed one, the touch of a particular woman's hand. The great events of life often leave one unmoved; they pass out of consciousness, and, when one thinks of them, become unreal. Even the scarlet flowers of passion seem to grow in the same meadow as the poppies of oblivion. We reject the burden of their memory, and have anodynes against them. But the little things, the things of no moment, remain with us. In some tiny ivory cell the brain stores the most delicate, and the most fleeting impressions.

As I walked home through St. James's Park, the dawn was just breaking over London. The swans were lying asleep on the smooth surface of the polished lake, like white feathers fallen upon a mirror of black steel. The gaunt Palace looked purple against the pale green sky, and in the garden of Stafford House the birds were just beginning to sing. I thought of Cyril Graham, and my eyes filled with tears.

II

It was past twelve o'clock when I awoke, and the sun was streaming in through the curtains of my room in long dusty beams of tremulous gold. I told my servant that I would not be at home to any one, and after I had discussed a cup of chocolate and a *petit-pain*, I took out of the library my copy of Shakespeare's Sonnets, and Mr Tyler's facsimile edition of the Quarto, and began to go carefully through them. Each poem seemed to me to corroborate Cyril Graham's theory. I felt as if I had my hand upon Shakespeare's heart, and was counting each separate throb and pulse of passion. I thought of the wonderful boy-actor, and saw his face in every line.

Previous to this, in my Lord Pembroke days, if I may so term them, I must admit that it had always seemed to me very difficult to understand how the creator of Hamlet and Lear and Othello could have addressed in such extravagant terms of praise and passion one who was merely an ordinary young nobleman of the day. Along with most students of Shakespeare, I had found myself compelled to set the Sonnets apart as things quite alien to Shakespeare's development as a dramatist, as things possibly unworthy of the intellectual side of his nature. But now that I began to realise the truth of Cyril Graham's theory, I saw that the moods and passions they mirrored were absolutely essential to Shakespeare's perfection as an artist writing for the Elizabethan stage, and that it was in the curious theatre conditions of that stage that the poems themselves had their origin. I remember what joy I had in feeling that these wonderful Sonnets,

> Subtle as Sphinx; as sweet and musical
> As bright Apollo's lute, strung with his hair,

were no longer isolated from the great æsthetic energies of Shakespeare's life, but were an essential part of his dramatic activity, and revealed to us something of the secret of his method. To have discovered the true name of Mr W. H. was comparatively nothing: others might have done that, had perhaps done it: but to have discovered his profession was a revolution in criticism.

Two sonnets, I remember, struck me particularly. In the first of these (LIII) Shakespeare, complimenting Willie Hughes on the versatility of his acting, on his wide range of parts, a range extending, as we know, from Rosalind to Juliet, and from Beatrice to Ophelia, says to him:—

> What is your substance, whereof are you made?
> That millions of strange shadows on you tend?
> Since everyone hath, every one, one shade,
> And you, but one, can every shadow lend—

lines that would be unintelligible if they were not addressed to an actor, for the word "shadow" had in Shakespeare's day a technical meaning connected with the stage. "The best in this kind are but shadows," says Theseus of the actors in the "Midsummer Night's Dream";

> Life's but a walking shadow, and poor player
> That struts and frets his hour upon the stage,

cries Macbeth in the moment of his despair, and there are many similar allusions in the literature of the day. This sonnet evidently belonged to the series in which Shakespeare discusses the nature of the actor's art, and of the strange and rare temperament that is essential to the perfect stage-player. "How is it," says Shakespeare to Willie Hughes, "that you have so many personalities?" and then he goes on to point out that his beauty is such that it seems to realise every form and phase of fancy, to embody each dream of the creative imagination,—an idea that is still further expanded in the sonnet that immediately follows, where, beginning with the fine thought,

> O, how much more doth beauty beauteous seem
> By that sweet ornament which *truth* doth give!

Shakespeare invites us to notice how the truth of acting, the truth of visible presentation on the stage, adds to the wonder of poetry, giving life to its loveliness, and actual reality to its ideal form. And yet, in Sonnet LXVII, Shakespeare calls upon Willie Hughes to abandon the stage with its artificiality, its unreal life of painted face and mimic costume, its immoral influences and suggestions, its remoteness from the true world of noble action and sincere utterance.

> Ah, wherefore with infection should he live,
> And with his presence grace impiety,
> That sin by him advantage should receive,
> And lace itself with his society?
> Why should false painting imitate his cheek,
> And steal dead seeing of his living hue?
> Why should poor beauty indirectly seek
> Roses of shadow, since his rose is true?

It may seem strange that so great a dramatist as Shakespeare, who realised his own perfection as an artist and his full humanity as a man on the ideal plane of stage-writing and stage-playing, should have written in these terms about the theatre; but we must remember that in Sonnets CX and CXI, Shakespeare shows us that he too was wearied of the world of puppets, and full of shame at having made himself "a motley to the view." Sonnet CXI is especially bitter:—

> O, for my sake do you with Fortune chide,
> The guilty goddess of my harmful deeds,
> That did not better for my life provide
> Than public means which public manners breeds.
> Thence comes it that my name receives a brand,
> And almost thence my nature is subdued
> To what it works in, like the dyer's hand:
> Pity me, then, and wish I were renewed—

and there are many signs of the same feeling elsewhere, signs familiar to all real students of Shakespeare.

One point puzzled me immensely as I read the Sonnets, and it was days before I struck on the true interpretation, which indeed Cyril Graham himself seemed to have missed. I could not understand how it was that Shakespeare set so high a value on his young friend marrying. He himself had married young and the result had been unhappiness, and it was not likely that he would have asked Willie Hughes to commit the same error. The boy-player of Rosalind had nothing to gain from marriage, or from the passions of real life. The early sonnets with their strange entreaties to love children seemed to be a jarring note.

The explanation of the mystery came on me quite suddenly and I found it in the curious dedication. It will be remembered that this dedication was as follows:—

> "TO.THE.ONLIE.BEGETTER.OF.
> THESE.INSUING.SONNETS.
> MR.W.H.ALL.HAPPINESSE.
> AND.THAT.ETERNITIE.
> PROMISED.BY.
> OUR.EVER-LIVING.POET.
> WISHETH.
> THE.WELL-WISHING.
> ADVENTURER.IN.
> SETTING.
> FORTH
> T.T."

Some scholars have supposed that the word "begetter" here means simply the procurer of the Sonnets for Thomas Thorpe the publisher; but this view is now generally abandoned, and the highest authorities are quite agreed that it is to be taken in the sense of inspirer, the metaphor being drawn from the analogy of physical life. Now I saw that the same metaphor was used by Shakespeare himself all through the poems, and this set me on the right track. Finally I made my great discovery. The marriage that Shakespeare proposes for Willie Hughes is the "marriage with his Muse," an expression which is definitely put forward in Sonnet LXXXII where, in the bitterness of his heart at the defection of the boy-actor for whom he had written his greatest parts, and whose beauty had indeed suggested them, he opens his complaint by saying—

> I grant thou wert not married to my Muse.

The children he begs him to beget are no children of flesh and blood, but more immortal children of undying fame. The whole cycle of the early sonnets is simply Shakespeare's invitations to Willie Hughes to go upon the stage and become a player. How barren and profitless a thing, he says, is this beauty of yours if it be not used:

> When forty winters shall besiege thy brow,
> And dig deep trenches in thy beauty's field,
> Thy youth's proud livery, so gazed on now,
> Will be a tattered weed, of small worth held:
> Then being asked where all thy beauty lies,
> Where all the treasure of thy lusty days,
> To say, within thine own deep-sunken eyes,
> Were an all-eating shame and thriftless praise.

You must create something in art: my verse "is thine and *born* of thee"; only listen to me, and I will

> *bring forth* eternal numbers to outlive long date,

and you shall people with forms of your own image the imaginary world of the stage. These children that you beget, he con-

tinues, will not wither away, as mortal children do, but you shall
live in them and in my plays: do but—

> Make thee another self, for love of me,
> That beauty still may live in thine or thee!

Be not afraid to surrender your personality, to give your "semblance to some other":

> To give away yourself keeps yourself still,
> And you must live, drawn by your own sweet skill.

I may not be learned in astrology, and yet, in those "constant
stars" your eyes,

> I read such art
> As truth and beauty shall together thrive,
> If from thyself to store thou wouldst convert.

What does it matter about others?

> Let those whom Nature hath not made for store,
> Harsh, featureless, and rude, barrenly perish:

With you it is different, Nature—

> carv'd thee for her seal, and meant thereby
> Thou shouldst print more, nor let that copy die.

Remember, too, how soon Beauty forsakes itself. Its action is
no stronger than a flower, and like a flower it lives and dies.
Think of "the stormy gusts of winter's day," of the "barren
edge of Death's eternal cold," and—

> ere thou be distilled,
> Make sweet some vial; treasure thou some place
> With beauty's treasure, ere it be self-killed.

Why, even flowers do not altogether die. When roses wither,

> Of their sweet deaths are sweetest odours made:

and you who are "my rose" should not pass away without leaving your form in Art. For Art has the very secret of joy.

> Ten times thyself were happier than thou art,
> If ten of thine ten times refigur'd thee.

You do not require the "bastard signs of fair," the painted face, the fantastic disguises of other actors:

> . . . the golden tresses of the dead,
> The right of sepulchres,

need not be shorn away for you. In you—

> . . those holy antique hours are seen,
> Without all ornament, itself and true,
> Making no summer of another's green.

All that is necessary is to "copy what in you is writ"; to place you on the stage as you are in actual life. All those ancient poets who have written of "ladies dead and lovely knights" have been dreaming of such a one as you, and:

> All their praises are but prophecies
> Of this our time, all you prefiguring.

For your beauty seems to belong to all ages and to all lands. Your shade comes to visit me at night, but, I want to look upon your "shadow" in the living day, I want to see you upon the stage. Mere description of you will not suffice:

> If I could write the beauty of your eyes,
> And in fresh numbers number all your graces,
> The age to come would say, "This poet lies;
> Such heavenly touches ne'er touched earthly faces."

It is necessary that "some child of yours," some artistic creation that embodies you, and to which your imagination gives life, shall present you to the world's wondering eyes. Your own thoughts are your children, offspring of sense and spirit; give some expression to them, and you shall find—

> Those children nursed, delivered from thy brain.

My thoughts, also, are my "children." They are of your begetting and my brain is:

> the womb wherein they grew.

For this great friendship of ours is indeed a marriage, it is the "marriage of true minds."

I collected together all the passages that seemed to me to corroborate this view, and they produced a strong impression on me, and showed me how complete Cyril Graham's theory really was. I also saw that it was quite easy to separate those lines in which Shakespeare speaks of the Sonnets themselves, from those in which he speaks of his great dramatic work. This was a point that had been entirely overlooked by all critics up to Cyril Graham's day. And yet it was one of the most important in the whole series of poems. To the Sonnets Shakespeare was more or less indifferent. He did not wish to rest his fame on them. They were to him his "slight Muse," as he calls them, and intended, as Meres tells us, for private circulation only among a few, a very few, friends. Upon the other hand he was extremely conscious of the high artistic value of his plays, and shows a noble self-reliance upon his dramatic genius. When he says to Willie Hughes:

> But thy eternal summer shall not fade,
> Nor lose possession of that fair thou owest;
> Nor shall Death brag thou wander'st in his shade,
> When in *eternal lines* to time thou growest:
> So long as men can breathe or eyes can see,
> So long lives this and this gives life to thee;—

the expression "eternal lines" clearly alludes to one of his plays that he was sending him at the time, just as the concluding couplet points to his confidence in the probability of his plays being always acted. In his address to the Dramatic Muse (Sonnets c and cı) we find the same feeling:

> Where art thou, Muse, that thou forget'st so long
> To speak of that which gives thee all thy might?
> Spend'st thou thy fury on some worthless song,
> Darkening thy power to lend base subjects light?

he cries, and he then proceeds to reproach the mistress of Tragedy and Comedy for her "neglect of truth in beauty dyed," and says:

> Because he needs no praise, wilt thou be dumb?
> Excuse not silence so; for 't lies in thee
> To make him much outlive a gilded tomb,
> And to be praised of ages yet to be.
> Then do thy office, Muse, I teach thee how,
> To make him seem long hence as he shows now.

It is, however, perhaps in Sonnet lv that Shakespeare gives to this idea its fullest expression. To imagine that the "powerful rhyme" of the second line refers to the sonnet itself was entirely to mistake Shakespeare's meaning. It seemed to me that it was extremely likely, from the general character of the sonnet, that a particular play was meant, and that the play was none other but "Romeo and Juliet."

> Not marble, nor the gilded monuments
> Of princes shall outlive this powerful rhyme;
> But you shall shine more bright in these contents
> Than unswept stone besmeared with sluttish time.
> When wasteful war shall statues overturn,
> And broils root out the work of masonry,
> Not Mars his sword nor war's quick fire shall burn
> The living record of your memory
> 'Gainst death and all-oblivious enmity
> Shall you pace forth; your praise shall still find room
> Even in the eyes of all posterity
> That wear this world out to the ending doom.
> So, till the judgment that yourself arise,
> You live in this, and dwell in lovers' eyes.

It was also very suggestive to note how here as elsewhere Shakespeare promised Willie Hughes immortality in a form that appealed to men's eyes—that is to say, in a spectacular form, in a play that is to be looked at.

For two weeks I worked hard at the Sonnets, hardly ever going out, and refusing all invitations. Every day I seemed to be discovering something new, and Willie Hughes became to me a kind of spiritual presence, an ever-dominant personality. I could almost fancy that I saw him standing in the shadow of my room, so well had Shakespeare drawn him, with his golden hair, his tender flower-like grace, his dreamy deep-sunken eyes, his delicate mobile limbs, and his white lily hands. His very name fascinated me. Willie Hughes! Willie Hughes! How musically it sounded! Yes; who else but he could have been the master-mistress of Shakespeare's passion,[1] the lord of his love to whom he was bound in vassalage,[2] the delicate minion of pleasure,[3] the rose of the whole world,[4] the herald of the spring,[5] decked in the proud livery of youth,[6] the lovely boy whom it was sweet music to hear,[7] and whose beauty was the very raiment of Shakespeare's heart,[8] as it was the keystone of his dramatic power? How bitter now seemed the whole tragedy of his desertion and his shame!—shame that he made sweet and lovely[9] by the mere magic of his personality, but that was none the less shame. Yet as Shakespeare forgave him, should not we forgive him also? I did not care to pry into the mystery of his sin or of the sin, if such it was, of the great poet who had so dearly loved him. "I am that I am," said Shakespeare in a sonnet of noble scorn,—

> I am that I am, and they that level
> At my abuses reckon up their own;

[1] Sonnet xx. 2.
[2] Sonnet xxvi. 1.
[3] Sonnet cxxvi. 9.
[4] Sonnet cix. 14.
[5] Sonnet i. 10.
[6] Sonnet ii. 3.
[7] Sonnet viii. 1.
[8] Sonnet xxii. 6.
[9] Sonnet xcv. 1.

> I may be straight, though they themselves be bevel;
> By their rank thoughts my deeds must not be shown.

Willie Hughes's abandonment of Shakespeare's theatre was a different matter, and I investigated it at great length. Finally I came to the conclusion that Cyril Graham had been wrong in regarding the rival dramatist of Sonnet LXXX as Chapman. It was obviously Marlowe who was alluded to. At the time the Sonnets were written, which must have been between 1590 and 1595, such an expression as "the proud full sail of his great verse" could not possibly have been used of Chapman's work, however applicable it might have been to the style of his later Jacobean plays. No; Marlowe was clearly the rival poet of whom Shakespeare spoke in such laudatory terms; the hymn he wrote in Willie Hughes' honour was the unfinished "Hero and Leander," and that

> Affable familiar ghost
> Which nightly gulls him with intelligence,

was the Mephistopheles of his Doctor Faustus. No doubt, Marlowe was fascinated by the beauty and grace of the boy-actor, and lured him away from the Blackfriars Theatre, that he might play the Gaveston of his "Edward II." That Shakespeare had some legal right to retain Willie Hughes in his own company seems evident from Sonnet LXXXVII, where he says:

> Farewell! thou art too dear for my possessing,
> And like enough thou know'st thy estimate:
> The *charter of thy worth* gives thee releasing;
> My *bonds* in thee are all determinate.
> For how do I hold thee but by thy granting?
> And for that riches where is my deserving?
> The cause of this fair gift in me is wanting,
> *And so my patent back again is swerving.*
> Thyself thou gav'st, thy own worth then not knowing,
> Or me, to whom thou gav'st it, else mistaking;
> So thy great gift, upon misprision growing,
> Comes home again, on better judgment making.
> Thus have I had thee, as a dream doth flatter,
> In sleep a king, but waking no such matter.

But him whom he could not hold by love, he would not hold by force. Willie Hughes became a member of Lord Pembroke's company, and perhaps in the open yard of the Red Bull Tavern, played the part of King Edward's delicate minion. On Marlowe's death, he seems to have returned to Shakespeare, who, whatever his fellow-partners may have thought of the matter, was not slow to forgive the wilfulness and treachery of the young actor.

How well, too, had Shakespeare drawn the temperament of the stage-player! Willie Hughes was one of those—

> That do not do the thing they most do show,
> Who, moving others, are themselves as stone.

He could act love, but could not feel it, could mimic passion without realising it.

> In many's looks the false heart's history
> Is writ in moods and frowns and wrinkles strange,

but with Willie Hughes it was not so. "Heaven," says Shakespeare, in a sonnet of mad idolatry—

> Heaven in thy creation did decree
> That in thy face sweet love should ever dwell;
> Whate'er thy thoughts or thy heart's workings be,
> Thy looks should nothing thence but sweetness tell.

In his "inconstant mind" and his "false heart" it was easy to recognise the insincerity that somehow seems inseparable from the artistic nature, as in his love of praise, that desire for immediate recognition that characterises all actors. And yet, more fortunate in this than other actors, Willie Hughes was to know something of immortality. Intimately connected with Shakespeare's plays, he was to live in them, and by their production.

> Your name from hence immortal life shall have,
> Though I, once gone, to all the world must die:
> The earth can yield me but a common grave,
> When you entombed in men's eyes shall lie.

> Your monument shall be my gentle verse,
> Which eyes not yet created shall o'er-read,
> And tongues to be your being shall rehearse,
> When all the breathers of this world are dead.

Nash with his venomous tongue had railed against Shakespeare for "reposing eternity in the mouth of a player," the reference being obviously to the Sonnets.

But to Shakespeare, the actor was a deliberate and self-conscious fellow worker who gave form and substance to a poet's fancy, and brought into Drama the elements of a noble realism. His silence could be as eloquent as words, and his gesture as expressive, and in those terrible moments of Titan agony or of god-like pain, when thought outstrips utterance, when the soul sick with excess of anguish stammers or is dumb, and the very raiment of speech is rent and torn by passion in its storm, then the actor could become, though it were but for a moment, a creative artist, and touch by his mere presence and personality those springs of terror and of pity to which tragedy appeals. This full recognition of the actor's art, and of the actor's power, was one of the things that distinguished the Romantic from the Classical Drama, and one of the things, consequently, that we owed to Shakespeare, who, fortunate in much, was fortunate also in this, that he was able to find Richard Burbage and to fashion Willie Hughes.

With what pleasure he dwelt upon Willie Hughes' influence over his audience—the "gazers" as he calls them; with what charm of fancy did he analyse the whole art! Even in the "Lover's Complaint" he speaks of his acting, and tells us that he was a nature so impressionable to the quality of dramatic situations that he could assume all "strange forms"—

> Of burning blushes, or of weeping water,
> Or swooning paleness:

explaining his meaning more fully later on where he tells us how Willie Hughes was able to deceive others by his wonderful power to—

> Blush at speeches rank, to weep at woes,
> Or to turn white and swoon at tragic shows.

It had never been pointed out before that the shepherd of this lovely pastoral, whose "youth in art and art in youth" are described with such subtlety of phrase and passion, was none other than the Mr W. H. of the Sonnets. And yet there was no doubt that he was so. Not merely in personal appearance are the two lads the same, but their natures and temperaments are identical. When the false shepherd whispers to the fickle maid—

> All my offences that abroad you see
> Are errors of the blood, none of mind;
> Love made them not:

when he says of his lovers,

> Harm have I done to them, but ne'er was harmed;
> Kept hearts in liveries, but mine own was free,
> And reigned, commanding in his monarchy:

when he tells us of the "deep-brained sonnets" that one of them had sent him, and cries out in boyish pride—

> The broken bosoms that to me belong
> Have emptied all their fountains in my well:

it is impossible not to feel that it is Willie Hughes who is speaking to us. "Deep-brained sonnets," indeed, had Shakespeare brought him, "jewels" that to his careless eyes were but as "trifles," though—

> each several stone,
> With wit well blazoned, smiled or made some moan;

and into the well of beauty he had emptied the sweet fountain of his song. That in both places it was an actor who was alluded to, was also clear. The betrayed nymph tells us of the "false fire" in her lover's cheek, of the "forced thunder" of his sighs, and of his "borrowed motion": of whom, indeed, but of an actor could it be said that to him "thought, characters, and words" were "merely Art," or that—

> To make the weeper laugh, the laugher weep,
> He had the dialect and different skill,
> Catching all passions in his craft of will?

The play on words in the last line is the same as that used in the punning sonnets, and is continued in the following stanza of the poem, where we are told of the youth who—

> did in the general bosom reign
> Of young, of old; and sexes both enchanted,

that there were those who—

> . . dialogued for him what he would say,
> Asked their own wills, and made their Wills obey.

Yes: the "rose-cheeked Adonis" of the Venus poem, the false shepherd of the "Lover's Complaint," the "tender churl," the "beauteous niggard" of the Sonnets, was none other but a young actor; and as I read through the various descriptions given of him, I saw that the love that Shakespeare bore him was as the love of a musician for some delicate instrument on which he delights to play, as a sculptor's love for some rare and exquisite material that suggests a new form of plastic beauty, a new mode of plastic expression. For all Art has its medium, its material, be it that of rhythmical words, or of pleasurable colour, or of sweet and subtly-divided sound; and, as one of the most fascinating critics of our day has pointed out, it is to the qualities inherent in each material, and special to it, that we owe the sensuous element in Art, and with all that in Art is essentially artistic. What then shall we say of the material that the Drama requires for its perfect presentation? What of the Actor, who is the medium through which alone the Drama can truly reveal itself? Surely, in that strange mimicry of life by the living which is the mode and method of theatric art, there are sensuous elements of beauty that none of the other arts possess. Looked at from one point of view, the common players of the saffron-strewn stage are Art's most complete, most satisfying instruments. There is no passion in bronze, nor motion in marble. The sculptor must surrender colour, and the painter fullness of form. The epos changes acts into words, and music changes words into tones. It is the Drama only that, to quote the fine saying of Gervinus, uses all means at once, and, appealing both to eye and ear, has at its disposal, and in its service, form and colour, tone, look, and word, the swiftness of motion, the intense realism of visible action.

It may be that in this very completeness of the instrument lies the secret of some weakness in the art. Those arts are happiest that employ a material remote from reality, and there is a danger in the absolute identity of medium and matter, the danger of ignoble realism and unimaginative imitation. Yet Shakespeare himself was a player, and wrote for players. He saw the possibilities that lay hidden in an art that up to his time had expressed itself but in bombast or in clowning. He has left us the most perfect rules for acting that have ever been written. He created parts that can be only truly revealed to us on the stage, wrote plays that need the theatre for their full realisation, and we cannot marvel that he so worshipped one who was the interpreter of his vision, as he was the incarnation of his dreams.

There was, however, more in his friendship than the mere delight of a dramatist in one who helps him to achieve his end. This was indeed a subtle element of pleasure, if not of passion, and a noble basis for an artistic comradeship. But it was not all that the Sonnets revealed to us. There was something beyond. There was the soul, as well as the language, of neo-Platonism.

"The fear of the Lord is the beginning of wisdom," said the stern Hebrew prophet: "The beginning of wisdom is Love," was the gracious message of the Greek. And the spirit of the Renaissance, which already touched Hellenism at so many points, catching the inner meaning of this phrase and divining its secret, sought to elevate friendship to the high dignity of the antique ideal, to make it a vital factor in the new culture, and a mode of self-conscious intellectual development. In 1492 appeared Marsilio Ficino's translation of the "Symposium" of Plato, and this wonderful dialogue, of all the Platonic dialogues perhaps the most perfect, as it is the most poetical, began to exercise a strange influence over men, and to colour their words and thoughts, and manner of living. In its subtle suggestions of sex in soul, in the curious analogies it draws between intellectual enthusiasm and the physical passion of love, in its dream of the incarnation of the Idea in a beautiful and living form, and of a real spiritual conception with a travail and a bringing to birth, there was something that fascinated the poets and scholars of the sixteenth century. Shakespeare, certainly, was fascinated by it, and had read the dialogue, if not in Ficino's translation, of which many copies found their way to England, perhaps in that French translation by Leroy to which Joachim du Bellay contributed so many graceful metrical versions. When he says to Willie Hughes,

> he that calls on thee, let him bring forth
> Eternal numbers to outlive long date,

he is thinking of Diotima's theory that Beauty is the goddess who presides over birth, and draws into the light of day the dim conceptions of the soul: when he tells us of the "marriage of true minds," and exhorts his friend to beget children that time cannot destroy, he is but repeating the words in which the prophetess tells us that "friends are married by a far nearer tie than those who beget mortal children, for fairer and more immortal are the children who are their common offspring." So, also, Edward Blount in his dedication of "Hero and Leander" talks of Marlowe's works as his "right children," being the "issue of his brain"; and when Bacon claims that "the best works and of greatest merit for the public have proceeded from the unmarried and childless men, which both in affection and means have married and endowed the public," he is paraphrasing a passage in the "Symposium."

Friendship, indeed, could have desired no better warrant for its permanence or its ardours than the Platonic theory, or creed, as we might better call it, that the true world was the world of ideas, and that these ideas took visible form and became incarnate in man, and it is only when we realise the influence of neo-Platonism on the Renaissance that we can understand the true meaning of the amatory phrases and words with which friends were wont, at this time, to address each other. There was a kind of mystic transference of the expressions of the physical sphere to a sphere that was spiritual, that was removed from gross bodily appetite, and in which the soul was Lord. Love had, indeed, entered the olive garden of the new Academe, but he wore the same flame-coloured raiment, and had the same words of passion on his lips.

Michael Angelo, the "haughtiest spirit in Italy" as he has been called, addresses the young Tommaso Cavalieri in such fervent and passionate terms that some have thought that the sonnets in question must have been intended for that noble lady, the widow of the Marchese di Pescara, whose white hand, when she was dying, the great sculptor's lips had stooped to kiss. But that it was to Cavalieri that they were written, and that the literal interpretation is the right one, is evident not merely from the fact that Michael Angelo plays with his name, as Shakespeare plays with the name of Willie Hughes, but from the direct evidence of Varchi, who was well acquainted with the young man, and who, indeed, tells us that he possessed "besides imcomparable personal beauty, so much charm of nature, such excellent abilities, and such a graceful manner, that he deserved, and still deserves, to be the better loved the more he is known." Strange as these sonnets may seem to us now, when rightly interpreted they merely serve to show with what intense and religious fervour Michael Angelo addressed himself to the worship of intellectual beauty, and how, to borrow a fine phrase from Mr Symonds, he pierced through the veil of flesh and sought the divine idea it imprisoned. In the sonnet written for Luigi del Riccio on the death of his friend, Cecchino Bracci, we can also trace, as Mr Symonds points out, the Platonic conception of love as nothing if not spiritual, and of beauty as a form that finds its immortality within the lover's soul. Cecchino was a lad who died at the age of seventeen, and when Luigi asked Michael Angelo to make a portrait of him, Michael Angelo answered, "I can only do so by drawing you in whom he still lives."

> If the beloved in the lover shine,
> Since Art without him cannot work alone,
> Thee must I carve, to tell the world of him.

The same idea is also put forward in Montaigne's noble essay on Friendship, a passion which he ranks higher than the love of brother for brother, or the love of man for woman. He tells us—I quote from Florio's translation, one of the books with which Shakespeare was familiar—how "perfect amitie" is indivisible, how it "possesseth the soule, and swaies it in all soveraigntie," and how "by the interposition of a spiritual beauty the desire of a spiritual conception is engendered in the beloved." He writes of an "internall beauty, of difficile knowledge, and abtruse discovery" that is revealed unto friends, and unto friends only. He mourns for the dead Etienne de la Boëtie, in accents of wild grief and inconsolable love. The learned Hubert Languet, the friend of Melanchthon and of the leaders of the reformed church, tells the young Philip Sidney how he kept his portrait by him some hours to feast his eyes upon it, and how his appetite was "rather increased than diminished by the sight," and Sidney writes to him, "the chief hope of my life, next to the everlasting blessedness of heaven, will always be the enjoyment of true friendship, and there you shall have the chiefest place." Later on there came to Sidney's house in London, one—some day to be burned at Rome, for the sin of seeing God in all things —Giordano Bruno, just fresh from his triumph before the University of Paris. "A filosofia è necessario amore" were the words ever upon his lips, and there was something in his strange ardent personality that made men feel that he had discovered the new secret of life. Ben Jonson writing to one of his friends subscribes himself "your true lover," and dedicates his noble eulogy on Shakespeare "To the memory of my Beloved." Richard Barnfield in his "Affectionate Shepherd" flutes on soft Virgilian reed the story of his attachment to some young Elizabethan of the day. Out of all the Eclogues, Abraham Fraunce selects the second for translation, and Fletcher's lines to Master W. C. show what fascination was hidden in the mere name of Alexis. It was no wonder then that Shakespeare had been stirred by a spirit that so stirred his age. There had been critics, like Hallam, who had regretted that the Sonnets had ever been written, who had seen in them something dangerous, something unlawful even. To them it would have been sufficient to answer in Chapman's noble words:

> There is no danger to a man that knows
> What Life and Death is: there's not any law
> Exceeds his knowledge: neither is it lawful
> That he should stoop to any other law.

But it was evident that the Sonnets needed no such defence as this, and that those who had talked of "the folly of excessive and misplaced affection" had not been able to interpret either language or the spirit of these great poems, so intimately connected with the philosophy and the art of their time. It is no doubt true that to be filled with an absorbing passion is to surrender the security of one's lover life, and yet in such surrender there may be gain, certainly there was for Shakespeare. When Pico della Mirandola crossed the threshold of the villa of Careggi, and stood before Marsilio Ficino in all the grace and comeliness of his wonderful youth, the aged scholar seemed to see in him the realisation of the Greek ideal, and determined to devote his remaining years to the translation of Plotinus, that new Plato, in whom, as Mr Pater reminds us, "the mystical element in the Platonic philosophy had been worked out to the utmost limit of vision and ecstasy." A romantic friendship with a young Roman of his day initiated Winckelmann into the secret of Greek art, taught him the mystery of its beauty and the meaning of its form. In Willie Hughes, Shakespeare found not merely a most delicate instrument for the presentation of his art, but the visible incarnation of his idea of beauty, and it is not too much to say that to this young actor, whose very name the dull writers of his age forgot to chronicle, the Romantic Movement of English Literature is largely indebted.

III

One evening I thought that I had really discovered Willie Hughes in Elizabethan literature. In a wonderfully graphic account of the last days of the great Earl of Essex, his chaplain, Thomas Knell, tells us that the night before the Earl died, "he called William Hewes, which was his musician, to play upon the virginals and to sing. 'Play,' said he, 'my song, Will Hewes, and I will sing it myself.' So he did it most joyfully, not as the howling swan, which, still looking down, waileth her end, but as a sweet lark, lifting up his hands and casting up his eyes to his God, with this mounted the crystal skies, and reached with his unwearied tongue the top of highest heavens." Surely the boy who played on the virginals to the dying father of Sidney's Stella was none other than the Will Hewes to whom Shakespeare dedicated the Sonnets, and who he tells us was himself sweet "music to hear." Yet Lord Essex died in 1576, when Shakespeare was but twelve years of age. It was impossible that his musician could have been the Mr W. H. of the Sonnets. Perhaps Shakespeare's young friend was the son of the player upon the virginals? It was at least something to have discovered that Will Hewes was an Elizabethan name. Indeed the name Hews seemed to have been closely connected with music and the stage. The first English actress was the lovely Margaret Hews, whom Prince Rupert so madly adored. What more probable than that between her and Lord Essex' musician had come the boy-actor of Shakespeare's plays? In 1587 a certain Thomas Hews brought out at Gray's Inn a Euripidean tragedy entitled "The Misfortunes of Arthur," receiving much assistance in the arrangement of the dumb shows from one Francis Bacon, then a student of law. Surely he was some near kinsman of the lad to whom Shakespeare said—

Take all my loves, my love, yea, take them all;

the "profitless usurer" of "unused beauty," as he describes him. But the proofs, the links—where were they? Alas! I could not find them. It seemed to me that I was always on the brink of

absolute verification, but that I could never really attain to it. I
thought it strange that no one had ever written a history of the
English boy-actors of the sixteenth and seventeenth centuries,
and determined to undertake the task myself, and to try to
ascertain their true relations to the drama. The subject was,
certainly, full of artistic interest. These lads had been the delicate reeds through which our poets had sounded their sweetest
strains, the gracious vessels of honour into which they had
poured the purple wine of their song. Foremost, naturally,
among them all had been the youth to whom Shakespeare had
intrusted the realisation of his most exquisite creations. Beauty
had been his, such as our age has never, or but rarely seen, a
beauty that seemed to combine the charm of both sexes, and
to have wedded, as the Sonnets tell us, the grace of Adonis
and the loveliness of Helen. He had been quick-witted, too, and
eloquent, and from those finely curved lips that the satirist had
mocked at had come the passionate cry of Juliet, and the bright
laughter of Beatrice, Perdita's flower-like words, and Ophelia's
wandering songs. Yet as Shakespeare himself had been but as a
god among giants, so Willie Hughes had only been one out of
many marvellous lads to whom our English Renaissance owed
something of the secret of its joy, and it appeared to me that
they also were worthy of some study and record.

In a little book with fine vellum leaves and damask silk cover
—a fancy of mine in those fanciful days—I accordingly collected such information as I could about them, and even now
there is something in the scanty record of their lives, in the
mere mention of their names, that attracts me. I seemed to
know them all: Robin Armin, the goldsmith's lad who was
lured by Tarlton to go on the stage: Sandford, whose performance of the courtezan Flamantia Lord Burleigh witnessed at
Gray's Inn: Cooke, who played Agrippina in the tragedy of
"Sejanus": Nat. Field, whose young and beardless portrait is
still preserved for us at Dulwich, and who in "Cynthia's Revels"
played the "Queen and Huntress chaste and fair": Gil. Carie,
who, attired as a mountain nymph, sang in the same lovely
masque Echo's song of mourning for Narcissus: Parsons, the
Salmacis of the strange pageant of "Tamburlaine": Will. Ostler,
who was one of "The Children of the Queen's Chapel," and

accompanied King James to Scotland: George Vernon, to whom the King sent a cloak of scarlet cloth, and a cape of crimson velvet: Alick Gough, who performed the part of Cænis, Vespasian's concubine, in Massingers' "Roman Actor," and three years later that of Acanthe, in the same dramatist's "Picture": Barrett, the heroine of Richards' tragedy of "Messalina": Dicky Robinson, "a very pretty fellow," Ben Jonson tells us, who was a member of Shakespeare's company, and was known for his exquisite taste in costume, as well as for his love of woman's apparel: Salathiel Pavy, whose early and tragic death Jonson mourned in one of the sweetest threnodies of our literature: Arthur Savile, who was one of "the players of Prince Charles," and took a girl's part in a comedy by Marmion: Stephen Hammerton, "a most noted and beautiful woman actor," whose pale oval face with its heavy-lidded eyes and somewhat sensuous mouth looks out at us from a curious miniature of the time: Hart, who made his first success by playing the Duchess in the tragedy of "The Cardinal," and who in a poem that is clearly modelled upon some of Shakespeare's Sonnets is described by one who had seen him as "beauty to the eye, and music to the ear": and Kynaston, of whom Betterton said that "it has been disputed among the judicious, whether any woman could have more sensibly touched the passions," and whose white hands and amber-coloured hair seem to have retarded by some years the introduction of actresses upon our stage.

The Puritans, with their uncouth morals and ignoble minds, had of course railed against them, and dwelt on the impropriety of boys disguising as women, and learning to affect the manners and passions of the female sex. Gosson, with his shrill voice, and Prynne, soon to be made earless for many shameful slanders, and others to whom the rare and subtle sense of abstract beauty was denied, had from pulpit and through pamphlet said foul or foolish things to their dishonour. To Francis Lenton, writing in 1629, what he speaks of as—

> loose action, mimic gesture
> By a poor boy clad in a princely vesture,

is but one of the many—

> tempting baits of hell
> Which draw more youth unto the damned cell
> Of furious lust, than all the devil could do
> Since he obtained his first overthrow.

Deuteronomy was quoted and the ill-digested learning of the period laid under contribution. Even our own time had not appreciated the artistic conditions of the Elizabethan and Jacobean drama. One of the most brilliant and intellectual actresses of this century had laughed at the idea of a lad of seventeen or eighteen playing Imogen, or Miranda, or Rosalind. "How could any youth, however gifted and specially trained, even faintly suggest these fair and noble women to an audience? . . . One quite pities Shakespeare, who had to put up with seeing his brightest creations marred, misrepresented, and spoiled." In his book on "Shakespeare's Predecessors" Mr John Addington Symonds also had talked of "hobbledehoys" trying to represent the pathos of Desdemona and Juliet's passion. Were they right? Are they right? I did not think so then. I do not think so now. Those who remember the Oxford production of the "Agamemnon," the fine utterance and marble dignity of the Clytemnestra, the romantic and imaginative rendering of the prophetic madness of Cassandra, will not agree with Lady Martin or Mr Symonds in their strictures on the conditions of the Elizabethan stage.

Of all the motives of dramatic curiosity used by our great playwrights, there is none more subtle or more fascinating than the ambiguity of the sexes. This idea, invented, as far as an artistic idea can be said to be invented, by Lyly, perfected and made exquisite for us by Shakespeare, seems to me to owe its origin, as it certainly owes its possibility of life-like presentation, to the circumstance that the Elizabethan stage, like the stage of the Greeks, admitted the appearance of no female performers. It is because Lyly was writing for the boy-actors of St Paul's that we have the confused sexes and complicated loves of Phillida and Gallathea: it is because Shakespeare was writing for Willie Hughes that Rosalind dons doublet and hose, and calls herself Ganymede, that Viola and Julia put on pages' dress, that Imogen steals away in male attire. To say that only a woman can portray the passions of a woman, and that therefore no boy can play Rosalind, is to rob the art of acting of all claim to objectivity, and to assign to the mere accident of sex what properly belongs to imaginative insight and creative energy. Indeed, if sex be an element in artistic creation, it might rather be urged that the delightful combination of wit and romance which characterises so many of Shakespeare's heroines was at least occasioned if it was not actually caused by the fact that the players of these parts were lads and young men, whose passionate purity, quick mobile fancy, and healthy freedom from sentimentality can hardly fail to have suggested a new and delightful type of girlhood or of womanhood. The very difference of sex between the player and the part he represented must also, as Professor Ward points out, have constituted "one more demand upon the imaginative capacities of the spectators," and must have kept them from that over-realistic identification of the actor with his *rôle*, which is one of the weak points in modern theatrical criticism.

This, too, must be granted, that it was to these boy-actors that we owe the introduction of those lovely lyrics that star the plays of Shakespeare, Dekker, and so many of the dramatists of the period, those "snatches of bird-like or god-like song," as Mr Swinburne calls them. For it was out of the choirs of the cathedrals and royal chapels of England that most of these lads came, and from their earliest years they had been trained in the singing of anthems and madrigals, and in all that concerns the subtle art of music. Chosen at first for the beauty of their voices, as well as for a certain comeliness and freshness of appearance, they were then instructed in gesture, dancing, and elocution, and taught to play both tragedies and comedies in the English as well as in the Latin language. Indeed, acting seems to have formed part of the ordinary education of the time, and to have been much studied not merely by the scholars of Eton and Westminster, but also by the students at the Universities of Oxford and Cambridge, some of whom went afterwards upon the public stage, as is becoming not uncommon in our own day. The great actors, too, had their pupils and apprentices, who were formally bound over to them by legal warrant, to whom they imparted the secrets of their craft, and who were so much

valued that we read of Henslowe, one of the managers of the
Rose Theatre, buying a trained boy of the name of James Bris-
towe for eight pieces of gold. The relations that existed between
the masters and their pupils seem to have been of the most
cordial and affectionate character. Robin Armin was looked
upon by Tarlton as his adopted son, and in a will dated "the
fourth daie of Maie, anno Domini 1605," Augustine Phillips,
Shakespeare's dear friend and fellow-actor, bequeathed to one
of his apprentices his "purple cloke, sword, and dagger," his
"base viall," and much rich apparel, and to another a sum of
money and many beautiful instruments of music, "to be delivered unto him at the expiration of his terme of yeres in his in-
denture of apprenticehood." Now and then, when some daring
actor kidnapped a boy for the stage, there was an outcry or an
investigation. In 1600, for instance, a certain Norfolk gentleman
of the name of Henry Clifton came to live in London in order
that his son, then about thirteen years of age, might have the
opportunity of attending the Bluecoat School, and from a petition which he presented to the Star Chamber, and which has
been recently brought to light by Mr Greenstreet, we learn
that as the boy was walking quietly to Christ Church cloister
one winter morning he was waylaid by James Robinson, Henry
Evans, and Nathaniel Giles, and carried off to the Blackfriars
Theatre, "amongste a companie of lewde and dissolute merce-
narie players," as his father calls them, in order that he might be
trained "in acting of parts in base playes and enterludes." Hearing of his son's misadventure, Mr Clifton went down at once to
the theatre, and demanded his surrender, but "the sayd Nathaniel
Giles, James Robinson and Henry Evans most arrogantlie then
and there answered that they had authoritie sufficient soe to
take any noble man's sonne in this land," and handing the
young schoolboy "a scrolle of paper, conteyning parte of one of
their said playes and enterludes," commanded him to learn it
by heart. Through a warrant issued by Sir John Fortescue, however, the boy was restored to his father the next day, and the
Court of Star Chamber seems to have suspended or cancelled
Evans' privileges.

The fact is that, following a precedent set by Richard III,
Elizabeth had issued a commission authorising certain persons

to impress into her service all boys who had beautiful voices that they might sing for her in her Chapel Royal, and Nathaniel Giles, her Chief Commissioner, finding that he could deal profitably with the managers of the Globe Theatre, agreed to supply them with personable and graceful lads for the playing of female parts, under colour of taking them for the Queen's service. The actors, accordingly, had a certain amount of legal warrant on their side, and it is interesting to note that many of the boys whom they carried off from their schools or homes, such as Salathiel Pavy, Nat. Field, and Alvery Trussell, became so fascinated by their new art that they attached themselves permanently to the theatre, and would not leave it.

Once it seemed as if girls were to take the place of boys upon the stage, and among the christenings chronicled in the registers of St. Giles', Cripplegate, occurs the following strange and suggestive entry: "Comedia, base-born, daughter of Alice Bowker and William Johnson, one of the Queen's plaiers, 10 Feb. 1589." But the child upon whom such high hopes had been built died at six years of age, and when, later on, some French actresses came over and played at Blackfriars, we learn that they were "hissed, hooted, and pippin-pelted from the stage." I think that, from what I have said above, we need not regret this in any way. The essentially male culture of the English Renaissance found its fullest and most perfect expression by its own method, and in its own manner.

I remember I used to wonder, at this time, what had been the social position and early life of Willie Hughes before Shakespeare had met with him. My investigations into the history of the boy-actors had made me curious of every detail about him. Had he stood in the carved stall of some gilded choir, reading out of a great book painted with square scarlet notes and long black key-lines? We know from the Sonnets how clear and pure his voice was, and what skill he had in the art of music. Noble gentlemen, such as the Earl of Leicester and Lord Oxford, had companies of boy-players in their service as part of their household. When Leicester went to the Netherlands in 1585 he brought with him a certain "Will" described as a "plaier". Was this Willie Hughes? Had he acted for Leicester at Kenilworth, and was it there that Shakespeare had first known him? Or was he, like Robin Armin, simply a lad of low degree, but possessing some strange beauty and marvellous fascination? It was evident from the early sonnets that when Shakespeare first came across him he had no connection whatsoever with the stage, and that he was not of high birth has already been shewn. I began to think of him not as the delicate chorister of a Royal Chapel, not as a petted minion trained to sing and dance in Leicester's stately masque, but as some fair-haired English lad whom in one of London's hurrying streets, or on Windsor's green silent meadows, Shakespeare had seen and followed, recognising the artistic possibilities that lay hidden in so comely and gracious a form, and divining by a quick and subtle instinct what an actor the lad would make could he be induced to go upon the stage. At this time Willie Hughes' father was dead, as we learn from Sonnet XIII, and his mother, whose remarkable beauty he is said to have inherited, may have been induced to allow him to become Shakespeare's apprentice by the fact that boys who played female characters were paid extremely large salaries, larger salaries, indeed, than were given to grown-up actors. Shakespeare's apprentice, at any rate, we know that he became, and we know what a vital factor he was in the development of Shakespeare's art. As a rule, a boy-actor's capacity for representing girlish parts on the stage lasted but for a few years at most. Such characters as Lady Macbeth, Queen Constance and Volumnia, remained of course always within the reach of those who had true dramatic genius and noble presence. Absolute youth was not necessary here, not desirable even. But with Imogen, and Perdita, and Juliet, it was different. "Your beard has begun to grow, and I pray God your voice be not cracked," says Hamlet mockingly to the boy-actor of the strolling company that came to visit him at Elsinore; and certainly when chins grew rough and voices harsh much of the charm and grace of the performance must have gone. Hence comes Shakespeare's passionate preoccupation with the youth of Willie Hughes, his terror of old age and wasting years, his wild appeal to time to spare the beauty of his friend:

> Make glad and sorry seasons as thou fleet'st,
> And do whate'er thou wilt, swift-footed time,

> To the wide world and all her fading sweets;
> But I forbid thee one most heinous crime:
> O carve not with thy hours my Love's fair brow
> Nor draw no lines there with thine antique pen;
> Him in thy course untainted do allow
> For beauty's pattern to succeeding men.

Time seems to have listened to Shakespeare's prayers, or perhaps Willie Hughes had the secret of perpetual youth. After three years he is quite unchanged:

> To me, fair friend, you never can be old,
> For as you were when first your eye I eyed,
> Such seems your beauty still. Three winters' cold
> Have from the forests shook three summers' pride,
> Three beauteous springs to yellow autumn turned,
> In process of the seasons have I seen,
> Three April perfumes in three hot Junes burned,
> Since first I saw you fresh which yet are green.

More years pass over, and the bloom of his boyhood seems to be still with him. When, in "The Tempest," Shakespeare, through the lips of Prospero, flung away the wand of his imagination and gave his poetic sovereignty into the weak, graceful hands of Fletcher, it may be that the Miranda who stood wondering by was none other than Willie Hughes himself, and in the last sonnet that his friend addressed to him, the enemy that is feared is not Time but Death.

> O thou, my lovely boy, who in thy power
> Dost hold time's fickle glass, his sickle hour;
> Who hast by waning grown, and therein show'st
> Thy lovers withering as thy sweet self grow'st;
> If Nature, sovereign mistress over wrack,
> As thou goest onwards, still will pluck thee back,
> She keeps thee to this purpose, that her skill
> May Time disgrace and wretched minutes kill.
> Yet fear her, O thou minion of her pleasure!
> She may detain, but not still keep, her treasure.
> Her audit, though delay'd, answer'd must be,
> And her quietus is to render thee.

IV

It was not for some weeks after I had begun my study of the subject that I ventured to approach the curious group of Sonnets (CXXVII–CLII) that deal with the dark woman who, like a shadow or thing of evil omen, came across Shakespeare's great romance, and for a season stood between him and Willie Hughes. They were obviously printed out of their proper place and should have been inserted between Sonnets XXXIII and XL. Psychological and artistic reasons necessitated this change, a change which I hope will be adopted by all future editors, as without it an entirely false impression is conveyed of the nature and final issue of this noble friendship.

Who was she, this black-browed, olive-skinned woman, with her amorous mouth "that Love's own hand did make," her "cruel eye," and her "foul pride," her strange skill on the virginals and her false, fascinating nature? An over-curious scholar of our day had seen in her a symbol of the Catholic Church, of that Bride of Christ who is "black but comely." Professor Minto, following in the footsteps of Henry Brown, had regarded the whole group of Sonnets as simply "exercises of skill undertaken in a spirit of wanton defiance and derision of the commonplace." Mr Gerald Massey, without any historical proof or probability, had insisted that they were addressed to the celebrated Lady Rich, the Stella of Sir Philip Sidney's sonnets, the Philoclea of his "Arcadia," and that they contained no personal revelation of Shakespeare's life and love, having been written in Lord Pembroke's name and at his request. Mr Tyler had suggested that they referred to one of Queen Elizabeth's maids-of-honour, by name Mary Fitton. But none of these explanations satisfied the conditions of the problem. The woman that came between Shakespeare and Willie Hughes was a real woman, black-haired, and married, and of evil repute. Lady Rich's fame was evil enough, it is true, but her hair was of—

fine threads of finest gold,
In curled knots man's thought to hold,

and her shoulders like "white doves perching." She was, as King James said to her lover, Lord Mountjoy, "a fair woman with a black soul." As for Mary Fitton, we know that she was unmarried in 1601, the time when her amour with Lord Pembroke was discovered, and besides, any theories that connected Lord Pembroke with the Sonnets were, as Cyril Graham had shewn, put entirely out of court by the fact that Lord Pembroke did not come to London till they had been actually written and read by Shakespeare to his friends.

It was not, however, her name that interested me. I was content to hold with Professor Dowden that "To the eyes of no diver among the wrecks of time will that curious talisman gleam." What I wanted to discover was the nature of her influence over Shakespeare, as well as the characteristics of her personality. Two things were certain: she was much older than the poet, and the fascination that she exercised over him was at first purely intellectual. He began by feeling no physical passion for her. "I do not love thee with mine eyes," he says:

> Nor are mine ears with thy tongue's tune delighted;
> Nor tender feeling to base touches prone,
> Nor taste, nor smell, desire to be invited
> To any sensual feast with thee alone.

He did not even think her beautiful:

> My mistress' eyes are nothing like the sun;
> Coral is far more red than her lips' red:
> If snow be white, why then her breasts are dun;
> If hairs be wires, black wires grow on her head.

He had his moments of loathing for her, for, not content with enslaving the soul of Shakespeare, she seems to have sought to snare the senses of Willie Hughes. Then Shakespeare cries aloud,—

> Two loves I have of comfort and despair,
> Which like two spirits do suggest me still:
> The better angel is a man right fair,
> The worser spirit a woman colour'd ill.

> To win me soon to hell, my female evil
> Tempteth my better angel from my side,
> And would corrupt my saint to be a devil,
> Wooing his purity with her foul pride.

Then he sees her as she really is, the "bay where all men ride," the "wide world's common place," the woman who is in the "very refuse" of her evil deeds, and who is "as black as hell, as dark as night." Then it is that he pens that great sonnet upon Lust ("Th' expense of spirit in a waste of shame"), of which Mr Theodore Watts says rightly that it is the greatest sonnet ever written. And it is then, also, that he offers to mortgage his very life and genius to her if she will but restore to him that "sweetest friend" of whom she had robbed him.

To compass this end he abandons himself to her, feigns to be full of an absorbing and sensuous passion of possession, forges false words of love, lies to her, and tells her that he lies.

> My thoughts and my discourse as madmen's are,
> At random from the truth vainly express'd;
> For I have sworn thee fair, and thought thee bright,
> Who art as black as hell, as dark as night.

Rather than suffer his friend to be treacherous to him, he will himself be treacherous to his friend. To shield his purity, he will himself be vile. He knew the weakness of the boy-actor's nature, his susceptibility to praise, his inordinate love of admiration, and deliberately set himself to fascinate the woman who had come between them.

It is never with impunity that one's lips say Love's Litany. Words have their mystical power over the soul, and form can create the feeling from which it should have sprung. Sincerity itself, the ardent, momentary sincerity of the artist, is often the unconscious result of style, and in the case of those rare temperaments that are exquisitely susceptible to the influences of language, the use of certain phrases and modes of expression can stir the very pulse of passion, can send the red blood coursing through the veins, and can transform into a strange sensuous energy what in its origin had been mere æsthetic impulse, and desire of art. So, at least, it seems to have been with Shakespeare. He begins by pretending to love, wears a lover's apparel and has a lover's words upon his lips. What does it matter? It is only acting, only a comedy in real life. Suddenly he finds that what his tongue had spoken his soul had listened to, and that the raiment that he had put on for disguise is a plague-stricken and poisonous thing that eats into his flesh, and that he cannot throw away. Then comes Desire, with its many maladies, and Lust that makes one love all that one loathes, and Shame, with its ashen face and secret smile. He is enthralled by this dark woman, is for a season separated from his friend, and becomes the "vassal-wretch" of one whom he knows to be evil and perverse and unworthy of his love, as of the love of Willie Hughes. "O, from what power," he says,—

>   hast thou this powerful might,
> With insufficiency my heart to sway?
> To make me give the lie to my true sight,
> And swear that brightness does not grace the day?
> Whence hast thou this becoming of things ill,
> That in the very refuse of thy deeds
> There is such strength and warranties of skill
> That, in my mind, thy worst all best exceeds?

He is keenly conscious of his own degradation, and finally, realising that his genius is nothing to her compared to the physical beauty of the young actor, he cuts with a quick knife the bond that binds him to her, and in this bitter sonnet bids her farewell:—

> In loving thee thou know'st I am forsworn,
> But thou art twice forsworn, to me love swearing;
> In act thy bed-vow broke, and new faith torn,
> In vowing new hate after new love bearing.
> But why of two oaths' breach do I accuse thee,
> When I break twenty? I am perjur'd most;
> For all my vows are oaths but to misuse thee,
> And all my honest faith in thee is lost:
> For I have sworn deep oaths of thy deep kindness,
> Oaths of thy love, thy truth, thy constancy;

> And, to enlighten thee, gave eyes to blindness,
> Or made them swear against the thing they see;
> For I have sworn thee fair; more perjur'd I,
> To swear against the truth so foul a lie!

His attitude towards Willie Hughes in the whole matter shews at once the fervour and the self-abnegation of the great love he bore him. There is a poignant touch of pathos in the close of this sonnet:

> Those pretty wrongs that liberty commits,
> When I am sometime absent from thy heart,
> Thy beauty and thy years full well befits,
> For still temptation follows where thou art.
> Gentle thou art, and therefore to be won,
> Beauteous thou art, therefore to be assailed;
> And when a woman woos, what woman's son
> Will sourly leave her till she have prevailed?
> Ay me! but yet thou mightst my seat forbear,
> And chide thy beauty and thy straying youth,
> Who lead thee in their riot even there
> Where thou art forc'd to break a two-fold truth,—
> Hers, by thy beauty tempting her to thee,
> Thine, by thy beauty being false to me.

But here he makes it manifest that his forgiveness was full and complete:

> No more be griev'd at that which thou hast done:
> Roses have thorns, and silver fountains mud;
> Clouds and eclipses stain both moon and sun,
> And loathsome canker lives in sweetest bud.
> All men make faults, and even I in this,
> Authorising thy trespass with compare,
> Myself corrupting, salving thy amiss,
> Excusing thy sins more than thy sins are;
> For to thy sensual fault I bring in sense,—
> Thy adverse party is thy advocate,—
> And 'gainst myself a lawful plea commence:
> Such civil war is in my love and hate,
> That I an accessary needs must be
> To that sweet thief which sourly robs from me.

Shortly afterwards Shakespeare left London for Stratford (Sonnets XLIII–LII), and when he returned Willie Hughes seems to have grown tired of the woman who for a little time had fascinated him. Her name is never mentioned again in the Sonnets, nor is there any allusion made to her. She had passed out of their lives.

But who was she? And, even if her name has not come down to us, were there any allusions to her in contemporary literature? It seems to me that although better educated than most of the women of her time, she was not nobly born, but was probably the profligate wife of some old and wealthy citizen. We know that women of this class, which was then first rising into social prominence, were strangely fascinated by the new art of stage playing. They were to be found almost every afternoon at the theatre, when dramatic performances were being given, and "The Actors' Remonstrance" is eloquent on the subject of their amours with the young actors.

Cranley in his "Amanda" tells us of one who loved to mimic the actor's disguises, appearing one day "embroidered, laced, perfumed, in glittering show . . . as brave as any Countess," and the next day, "all in mourning, black and sad," now in the grey cloak of a country wench, and now "in the neat habit of a citizen." She was a curious woman, "more changeable and wavering than the moon," and the books that she loved to read were Shakespeare's "Venus and Adonis," Beaumont's "Salmacis and Hermaphroditus," amorous pamphlets, and "songs of love and sonnets exquisite." These sonnets, that were to her the "bookes of her devotion," were surely none other but Shakespeare's own, for the whole description reads like the portrait of the woman who fell in love with Willie Hughes, and, lest we should have any doubt on the subject, Cranley, borrowing Shakespeare's play on words, tells us that, in her "proteus-like strange shapes," she is one who—

Changes hews with the chameleon.

Manningham's Table-book, also, contains a clear allusion to the same story. Manningham was a student at the Middle Temple with Sir Thomas Overbury and Edmund Curle, whose chambers he seems to have shared; and his Diary is still preserved among the Harleian MSS. at the British Museum, a small duodecimo book written in a fair and tolerably legible hand, and containing many unpublished anecdotes about Shakespeare, Sir Walter Raleigh, Spenser, Ben Jonson and others. The dates, which are inserted with much care, extend from January 1600–1 to April 1603, and under the heading "March 13, 1601," Manningham tells us that he heard from a member of Shakespeare's company that a certain citizen's wife being at the Globe Theatre one afternoon, fell in love with one of the actors, and "grew so farre in liking with him, that before shee went from the play shee appointed him to come that night unto hir," but that Shakespeare "overhearing their conclusion" anticipated his friend and came first to the lady's house, "went before and was entertained," as Manningham puts it, with some added looseness of speech which it is unnecessary to quote.

It seemed to me that we had here a common and distorted version of the story that is revealed to us in the Sonnets, the story of the dark woman's love for Willie Hughes, and Shakespeare's mad attempt to make her love him in his friend's stead. It was not, of course, necessary to accept it as absolutely true in every detail. According to Manningham's informant, for instance, the name of the actor in question was not Willie Hughes, but Richard Burbage. Tavern gossip, however, is proverbially inaccurate, and Burbage was, no doubt, dragged into the story to give point to the foolish jest about William the Conqueror and Richard the Third, with which the entry in Manningham's Diary ends. Burbage was our first great tragic actor, but it needed all his genius to counterbalance the physical defects of low stature and corpulent figure under which he laboured, and he was not the sort of man who would have fascinated the dark woman of the Sonnets, or would have cared to be fascinated by her. There was no doubt that Willie Hughes was referred to, and the private diary of a young law student of the time thus curiously corroborated Cyril Graham's wonderful guess at the secret of Shakespeare's great romance. Indeed, when taken in conjunction with "Amanda," Manningham's Table-book seemed to me to be an extremely strong link in the chain of evidence, and to place the new interpretation of the

Sonnets on something like a secure historic basis, the fact that Cranley's poem was not published till after Shakespeare's death being really rather in favour of this view, as it was not likely that he would have ventured during the lifetime of the great dramatist to revive the memory of this tragic and bitter story.

This passion for the dark lady also enabled me to fix with still greater certainty the date of the Sonnets. From internal evidence, from the characteristics of language, style, and the like, it was evident that they belonged to Shakespeare's early period, the period of "Love's Labour's Lost" and "Venus and Adonis." With the play, indeed, they are intimately connected. They display the same delicate euphuism, the same delight in fanciful phrase and curious expression, the artistic wilfulness and studied graces of the same "fair tongue, conceit's expositor," Rosaline, the—

> whitely wanton with a velvet brow,
> With two pitch-balls stuck in her face for eyes,

who is born "to make black fair," and whose "favour turns the fashion of the days," is the dark lady of the Sonnets who makes black "beauty's successive heir." In the comedy as well as in the poems we have that half-sensuous philosophy that exalts the judgment of the senses "above all slower, more toilsome means of knowledge," and Berowne is perhaps, as Walter Pater suggests, a reflex of Shakespeare himself "when he has just become able to stand aside from and estimate the first period of his poetry."

Now though "Love's Labour's Lost" was not published till 1598, when it was brought out "newlie corrected and augmented" by Cuthbert Burby, there is no doubt that it was written and produced on the stage at a much earlier date, probably, as Professor Dowden points out, in 1588–9. If this be so, it is clear that Shakespeare's first meeting with Willie Hughes must have been in 1585, and it is just possible that this young actor may, after all, have been in his boyhood the musician of Lord Essex.

It is clear, at any rate, that Shakespeare's love for the dark lady must have passed away before 1594. In this year there appeared, under the editorship of Hadrian Dorell, that fascinating poem, or series of poems, "Willobie his Avisa," which is described by Mr Swinburne as the one contemporary book which has been supposed to throw any direct or indirect light on the mystic matter of the Sonnets. In it we learn how a young gentleman of St. John's College, Oxford, by name Henry Willobie, fell in love with a woman so "fair and chaste" that he called her Avisa, either because such beauty as hers had never been seen, or because she fled like a bird from the snare of his passion, and spread her wings for flight when he ventured but to touch her hand. Anxious to win his mistress, he consults his familiar friend W. S., "who not long before had tried the curtesy of the like passion, and was now newly recovered of the like infection." Shakespeare encouraged him in the siege that he is laying to the Castle of Beauty, telling him that every woman is to be wooed, and every woman to be won; views this "loving comedy" from far off, in order to see "whether it would sort to a happier end for this new actor than it did for the old player," and "enlargeth the wound with the sharpe razor of a willing conceit," feeling the purely æsthetic interest of the artist in the moods and emotions of others. It is unnecessary, however, to enter more fully into this curious passage in Shakespeare's life, as all that I wanted to point out was that in 1594 he had been cured of his infatuation for the dark lady, and had already been acquainted for at least three years with Willie Hughes.

My whole scheme of the Sonnets was now complete, and, by placing those that refer to the dark lady in their proper order and position, I saw the perfect unity and completeness of the whole. The drama—for indeed they formed a drama and a soul's tragedy of fiery passion and of noble thought—is divided into four scenes or acts. In the first of these (Sonnets I–XXXII) Shakespeare invites Willie Hughes to go upon the stage as an actor, and to put to the service of Art his wonderful physical beauty, and his exquisite grace of youth, before passion has robbed him of the one, and time taken from him the other. Willie Hughes, after a time, consents to be a player in Shakespeare's company, and soon becomes the very centre and keynote of his inspiration. Suddenly, in one red-rose July (Sonnets XXXIII–LII, LXI, and CXXVII–CLII) there comes to the Globe The-

atre a dark woman with wonderful eyes, who falls passionately
in love with Willie Hughes. Shakespeare, sick with the malady
of jealousy, and made mad by many doubts and fears, tries to
fascinate the woman who had come between him and his
friend. The love, that is at first feigned, becomes real, and he
finds himself enthralled and dominated by a woman whom he
knows to be evil and unworthy. To her the genius of a man is
as nothing compared to a boy's beauty. Willie Hughes becomes
for a time her slave and the toy of her fancy, and the second
act ends with Shakespeare's departure from London. In the
third act her influence has passed away. Shakespeare returns to
London, and renews his friendship with Willie Hughes, to
whom he promises immortality in his plays. Marlowe, hearing
of the wonder and grace of the young actor, lures him away
from the Globe Theatre to play Gaveston in the tragedy of
"Edward II," and for the second time Shakespeare is separated
from his friend. The last act (Sonnets c–cxxvi) tells us of the
return of Willie Hughes to Shakespeare's company. Evil rumour
has now stained the white purity of his name, but Shakespeare's
love still endures and is perfect. Of the mystery of this love, and
of the mystery of passion, we are told strange and marvellous
things, and the Sonnets conclude with an envoi of twelve lines,
whose motive is the triumph of Beauty over Time, and of Death
over Beauty.

And what had been the end of him who had been so dear to
the soul of Shakespeare, and who by his presence and passion
had given reality to Shakespeare's art? When the Civil War
broke out, the English actors took the side of their king, and
many of them, like Robinson foully slain by Major Harrison at
the taking of Basing House, laid down their lives in the king's
service. Perhaps on the trampled heath of Marston, or on the
bleak hills of Naseby, the dead body of Willie Hughes had
been found by some of the rough peasants of the district, his
gold hair "dabbled with blood," and his breast pierced with
many wounds. Or it may be that the Plague, which was very
frequent in London at the beginning of the seventeenth century,
and was indeed regarded by many of the Christians as a judgment sent on the city for its love of "vaine plaies and idolatrous
shewes," had touched the lad while he was acting, and he had

crept home to his lodging to die there alone, Shakespeare being far away at Stratford, and those who had flocked in such numbers to see him, the "gazers" whom, as the Sonnets tell us, he had "led astray," being too much afraid of contagion to come near him. A story of this kind was current at the time about a young actor, and was made much use of by the Puritans in their attempts to stifle the free development of the English Renaissance. Yet, surely, had this actor been Willie Hughes, tidings of his tragic death would have been speedily brought to Shakespeare as he lay dreaming under the mulberry tree in his garden at New Place, and in an elegy as sweet as that written by Milton on Edward King, he would have mourned for the lad who had brought such joy and sorrow into his life, and whose connection with his art had been of so vital and intimate a character. Something made me feel certain that Willie Hughes had survived Shakespeare, and had fulfilled in some measure the high prophecies the poet had made about him, and one evening the true secret of his end flashed across me.

He had been one of those English actors who in 1611, the year of Shakespeare's retirement from the stage, went across sea to Germany and played before the great Duke Henry Julius of Brunswick, himself a dramatist of no mean order, and at the Court of that strange Elector of Brandenburg, who was so enamoured of beauty that he was said to have bought for his weight in amber the young son of a travelling Greek merchant, and to have given pageants in honour of his slave, all through that dreadful famine year of 1606–7, when the people died of hunger in the very streets of the town, and for the space of seven months there was no rain. The Library at Cassel contains to the present day a copy of the first edition of Marlowe's "Edward II," the only copy in existence, Mr Bullen tells us. Who could have brought it to that town, but he who had created the part of the king's minion, and for whom indeed it had been written? Those stained and yellow pages had once been touched by his white hands. We also know that "Romeo and Juliet," a play specially connected with Willie Hughes, was brought out at Dresden, in 1613, along with "Hamlet" and "King Lear," and certain of Marlowe's plays, and it was surely to none other than Willie Hughes himself that in 1617 the death-mask of

Shakespeare was brought by one of the suite of the English ambassador, pale token of the passing away of the great poet who had so dearly loved him. Indeed there was something peculiarly fitting in the idea that the boy-actor, whose beauty had been so vital an element in the realism and romance of Shakespeare's art, had been the first to have brought to Germany the seed of the new culture, and was in his way the precursor of the *Aufklärung* or Illumination of the eighteenth century, that splendid movement which, though begun by Lessing and Herder, and brought to its full and perfect issue by Goethe was in no small part helped on by a young actor—Friedrich Schroeder —who awoke the popular consciousness, and by means of the feigned passions and mimetic methods of the stage showed the intimate, the vital, connection between life and literature. If this was so,—and there was certainly no evidence against it,— it was not improbable that Willie Hughes was one of those English comedians (*mimi quidam ex Britannia*, as the old chronicle calls them), who were slain at Nuremberg in a sudden uprising of the people, and were secretly buried in a little vineyard outside the city by some young men "who had found pleasure in their performances, and of whom some had sought to be instructed in the mysteries of the new art." Certainly no more fitting place could there be for him to whom Shakespeare said "thou art all my art," than this little vineyard outside the city walls. For was it not from the sorrows of Dionysos that Tragedy sprang? Was not the light laughter of Comedy, with its careless merriment and quick replies, first heard on the lips of the Sicilian vine-dressers? Nay, did not the purple and red stain of the wine-froth on face and limbs give the first suggestion of the charm and fascination of disguise?—the desire for self-concealment, the sense of the value of objectivity, thus showing itself in the rude beginnings of the art. At any rate, wherever he lay—whether in the little vineyard at the gate of the Gothic town, or in some dim London churchyard amidst the roar and bustle of our great city—no gorgeous monument marked his resting place. His true tomb, as Shakespeare saw, was the poet's verse, his true monument the permanence of the drama. So had it been with others whose beauty had given a new creative impulse to their age. The ivory body of the Bithynian slave rots in the green ooze of the Nile, and on the yellow hills of the Cerameicus is strewn the dust of the young Athenian; but Antinous lives in sculpture, and Charmides in philosophy.

v

A young Elizabethan, who was enamoured of a girl so white that he named her Alba, has left on record the impression produced on him by one of the first performances of "Love's Labour's Lost." Admirable though the actors were, and they played "in cunning wise," he tells us, especially those who took the lover's parts, he was conscious that everything was "feigned," that nothing came "from the heart," that though they appeared to grieve they "felt no care," and were merely presenting "a show in jest." Yet, suddenly, this fanciful comedy of unreal romance became to him, as he sat in the audience, the real tragedy of his life. The moods of his own soul seemed to have taken shape and substance, and to be moving before him. His grief had a mask that smiled, and his sorrow wore gay raiment. Behind the bright and quickly-changing pageant of the stage, he saw himself, as one sees one's image in a fantastic glass. The very words that came to the actors' lips were wrung out of his pain. Their false tears were of his shedding.

There are few of us who have not felt something akin to this. We become lovers when we see Romeo and Juliet, and Hamlet makes us students. The blood of Duncan is upon our hands, with Timon we rage against the world, and when Lear wanders out upon the heath the terror of madness touches us. Ours is the white sinlessness of Desdemona, and ours, also, the sin of Iago. Art, even the art of fullest scope and widest vision, can never really show us the external world. All that it shows us is our own soul, the one world of which we have any real cognizance. And the soul itself, the soul of each one of us, is to each one of us a mystery. It hides in the dark and broods, and consciousness cannot tell us of its workings. Consciousness, indeed, is quite inadequate to explain the contents of personality. It is Art, and Art only, that reveals us to ourselves.

We sit at the play with the woman we love, or listen to the music in some Oxford garden, or stroll with our friend through the cool galleries of the Pope's house at Rome, and suddenly we become aware that we have passions of which we have never dreamed, thoughts that make us afraid, pleasures whose secret has been denied to us, sorrows that have been hidden from our tears. The actor is unconscious of our presence: the musician is thinking of the subtlety of the fugue, of the tone of his instrument; the marble gods that smile so curiously at us are made of insensate stone. But they have given form and substance to what was within us; they have enabled us to realise our personality; and a sense of perilous joy, or some touch or thrill of pain, or that strange self-pity that man so often feels for himself, comes over us and leaves us different.

Some such impression the Sonnets of Shakespeare had certainly produced on me. As from opal dawns to sunsets of withered rose I read and re-read them in garden or chamber, it seemed to me that I was deciphering the story of a life that had once been mine, unrolling the record of a romance that, without my knowing it, had coloured the very texture of my nature, had dyed it with strange and subtle dyes. Art, as so often happens, had taken the place of personal experience. I felt as if I had been initiated into the secret of that passionate friendship, that love of beauty and beauty of love, of which Marsilio Ficino tells us, and of which the Sonnets, in their noblest and purest significance, may be held to be the perfect expression.

Yes: I had lived it all. I had stood in the round theatre with its open roof and fluttering banners, had seen the stage draped with black for a tragedy, or set with gay garlands for some brighter show. The young gallants came out with their pages, and took their seats in front of the tawny curtain that hung from the satyr-carved pillars of the inner scene. They were insolent and debonair in their fantastic dresses. Some of them wore French lovelocks, and white doublets stiff with Italian embroidery of gold thread, and long hose of blue or pale yellow silk. Others were all in black, and carried huge plumed hats. These affected the Spanish fashion. As they played at cards, and blew thin wreaths of smoke from the tiny pipes that the pages lit for them, the truant prentices and idle schoolboys that thronged the yard mocked them. But they only smiled at each other. In the side boxes some masked women were sitting. One of them was waiting with hungry eyes and bitten lips for the drawing back of the curtain. As the trumpet sounded for the third time she leant forward, and I saw her olive skin and raven's-wing hair. I knew her. She had marred for a season the great friendship of my life. Yet there was something about her that fascinated me.

The play changed according to my mood. Sometimes it was "Hamlet." Taylor acted the Prince, and there were many who wept when Ophelia went mad. Sometimes it was "Romeo and Juliet." Burbage was Romeo. He hardly looked the part of the young Italian, but there was a rich music in his voice, and passionate beauty in every gesture. I saw "As You Like It," and "Cymbeline," and "Twelfth Night," and in each play there was some one whose life was bound up into mine, who realised for me every dream, and gave shape to every fancy. How gracefully he moved! The eyes of the audience were fixed on him.

And yet it was in this century that it had all happened. I had never seen my friend, but he had been with me for many years, and it was to his influence that I had owed my passion for Greek thought and art, and indeed all my sympathy with the Hellenic spirit. (Φιλοσοφεῖν μετ' ἐρῶτος!) How that phrase had stirred me in my Oxford days! I did not understand then why it was so. But I knew now. There had been a presence beside me always. Its silver feet had trod night's shadowy meadows, and the white hands had moved aside the trembling curtains of the dawn. It had walked with me through the grey cloisters, and when I sat reading in my room, it was there also. What though I had been unconscious of it? The soul had a life of its own, and the brain its own sphere of action. There was something within us that knew nothing of sequence or extension, and yet, like the philosopher of the Ideal City, was the spectator of all time and of all existence. It had senses that quickened, passions that came to birth, spiritual ecstasies of contemplation, ardours of fiery-coloured love. It was we who were unreal, and our conscious life was the least important part of our development. The soul, the secret soul, was the only reality.

How curiously it had all been revealed to me! A book of Sonnets, published nearly three hundred years ago, written by a dead hand and in honour of a dead youth, had suddenly explained to me the whole story of my soul's romance. I remembered how once in Egypt I had been present at the opening of a frescoed coffin that had been found in one of the basalt tombs at Thebes. Inside there was the body of a young girl swathed in tight bands of linen, and with a gilt mask over her face. As I stooped down to look at it, I had seen that one of the little withered hands held a scroll of yellow papyrus covered with strange characters. How I wished now that I had had it read to me! It might have told me something more about the soul that hid within me, and had its mysteries of passion of which I was kept in ignorance. Strange, that we knew so little about ourselves, and that our most intimate personality was concealed from us! Were we to look in tombs for our real life, and in art for the legend of our days?

Week after week, I pored over these poems, and each new form of knowledge seemed to me a mode of reminiscence. Finally, after two months had elapsed, I determined to make a strong appeal to Erskine to do justice to the memory of Cyril Graham, and to give to the world his marvellous interpretation of the Sonnets—the only interpretation that thoroughly explained the problem. I have not any copy of my letter, I regret to say, nor have I been able to lay my hand upon the original; but I remember that I went over the whole ground, and covered sheets of paper with passionate reiteration of the arguments and proofs that my study had suggested to me.

It seemed to me that I was not merely restoring Cyril Graham to his proper place in literary history, but rescuing the honour of Shakespeare himself from the tedious memory of a commonplace intrigue. I put into the letter all my enthusiasm. I put into the letter all my faith.

No sooner, in fact, had I sent it off than a curious reaction came over me. It seemed to me that I had given away my capacity for belief in the Willie Hughes theory of the Sonnets, that something had gone out of me, as it were, and that I was perfectly indifferent to the whole subject. What was it that had happened? It is difficult to say. Perhaps, by finding perfect expression for a passion, I had exhausted the passion itself. Emotional forces, like the forces of physical life, have their positive limitations. Perhaps the mere effort to convert any one to a theory involves some form of renunciation of the power of credence. Influence is simply a transference of personality, a mode of giving away what is most precious to one's self, and its exercise produces a sense, and, it may be, a reality of loss. Every disciple takes away something from his master. Or perhaps I had become tired of the whole thing, wearied of its fascination, and, my enthusiasm having burnt out, my reason was left to its own unimpassioned judgment. However it came about, and I cannot pretend to explain it, there was no doubt that Willie Hughes suddenly became to me a mere myth, an idle dream, the boyish fancy of a young man who, like most ardent spirits, was more anxious to convince others than to be himself convinced.

I must admit that this was a bitter disappointment to me. I had gone through every phase of this great romance. I had lived with it, and it had become part of my nature. How was it that it had left me? Had I touched upon some secret that my soul desired to conceal? Or was there no permanence in personality? Did things come and go through the brain, silently, swiftly, and without footprints, like shadows through a mirror? Were we at the mercy of such impressions as Art or Life chose to give us? It seemed to me to be so.

It was at night-time that this feeling first came to me. I had sent my servant out to post the letter to Erskine, and was seated at the window looking out at the blue and gold city. The moon had not yet risen, and there was only one star in the sky, but the streets were full of quick-moving and flashing lights, and the windows of Devonshire House were illuminated for a great dinner to be given to some of the foreign princes then visiting London. I saw the scarlet liveries of the royal carriages, and the crowd hustling about the sombre gates of the courtyard.

Suddenly, I said to myself: "I have been dreaming, and all my life for these two months has been unreal. There was no such person as Willie Hughes." Something like a faint cry of pain came to my lips as I began to realise how I had deceived myself, and I buried my face in my hands, struck with a sor-

row greater than any I had felt since boyhood. After a few
moments I rose, and going into the library took up the Sonnets, and began to read them. But it was all to no avail. They
gave me back nothing of the feeling that I had brought to
them; they revealed to me nothing of what I had found hidden in their lines. Had I merely been influenced by the beauty
of the forged portrait, charmed by that Shelley-like face into
faith and credence? Or, as Erskine had suggested, was it the
pathetic tragedy of Cyril Graham's death that had so deeply
stirred me? I could not tell. To the present day I cannot understand the beginning or the end of this strange passage in my
life.

However, as I had said some very unjust and bitter things
to Erskine in my letter, I determined to go and see him as
soon as possible, and make my apologies to him for my be-
haviour. Accordingly, the next morning I drove down to Birdcage Walk, where I found him sitting in his library, with the
forged picture of Willie Hughes in front of him.

"My dear Erskine!" I cried, "I have come to apologise to
you."

"To apologise to me?" he said. "What for?"

"For my letter," I answered.

"You have nothing to regret in your letter," he said. "On
the contrary, you have done me the greatest service in your
power. You have shown me that Cyril Graham's theory is perfectly sound."

I stared at him in blank wonder.

"You don't mean to say that you believe in Willie Hughes?"
I exclaimed.

"Why not?" he rejoined. "You have proved the thing to
me. Do you think I cannot estimate the value of evidence?"

"But there is no evidence at all," I groaned, sinking into
a chair. "When I wrote to you I was under the influence of
a perfectly silly enthusiasm. I had been touched by the story
of Cyril Graham's death, fascinated by his artistic theory,
enthralled by the wonder and novelty of the whole idea. I see
now that the theory is based on a delusion. The only evidence
for the existence of Willie Hughes is that picture in front of

you, and that picture is a forgery. Don't be carried away by mere sentiment in this matter. Whatever romance may have to say about the Willie Hughes theory, reason is dead against it."

"I don't understand you," said Erskine, looking at me in amazement. "You have convinced me by your letter that Willie Hughes is an absolute reality. Why have you changed your mind? Or is all that you have been saying to me merely a joke?"

"I cannot explain it to you," I rejoined, "but I see now that there is really nothing to be said in favour of Cyril Graham's interpretation. The Sonnets may not be addressed to Lord Pembroke. They probably are not. But for heaven's sake don't waste your time in a foolish attempt to discover a young Elizabethan actor who never existed, and to make a phantom puppet the centre of the great cycle of Shakespeare's Sonnets."

"I see that you don't understand the theory," he replied.

"My dear Erskine," I cried, "not understand it! Why, I feel as if I had invented it. Surely my letter shows you that I not merely went into the whole matter, but that I contributed proofs of every kind. The one flaw in the theory is that it presupposes the existence of the person whose existence is the subject of dispute. If we grant that there was in Shakespeare's company a young actor of the name of Willie Hughes, it is not difficult to make him the object of the Sonnets. But as we know that there was no actor of this name in the company of the Globe Theatre, it is idle to pursue the investigation further."

"But that is exactly what we don't know," said Erskine. "It is quite true that his name does not occur in the list given in the first folio; but, as Cyril pointed out, that is rather a proof in favour of the existence of Willie Hughes than against it, if we remember his treacherous desertion of Shakespeare for a rival dramatist. Besides," and here I must admit that Erskine made what seems to me now a rather good point, though, at the time, I laughed at it, "there is no reason at all why Willie Hughes should not have gone upon the stage under an assumed name. In fact it is extremely probable that he did so. We know that there was a very strong prejudice against the theatre in his day, and nothing is more likely than that his family insisted upon his adopting some *nom de plume*. The editors of the first folio would naturally put him down under his stage name, the name by which he was best known to the public, but the Sonnets were of course an entirely different matter, and in the dedication to them the publisher very properly addresses him under his real initials. If this be so, and it seems to me the most simple and rational explanation of the matter, I regard Cyril Graham's theory as absolutely proved."

"But what evidence have you?" I exclaimed, laying my hand on his. "You have no evidence at all. It is a mere hypothesis. And which of Shakespeare's actors do you think that Willie Hughes was? The 'pretty fellow' Ben Jonson tells us of, who was so fond of dressing up in girls' clothes?"

"I don't know," he answered rather irritably. "I have not had time to investigate the point yet. But I feel quite sure that my theory is the true one. Of course it is a hypothesis, but then it is a hypothesis that explains everything, and if you had been sent to Cambridge to study science, instead of to Oxford to dawdle over literature, you would know that a hypothesis that explains everything is a certainty."

"Yes, I am aware that Cambridge is a sort of educational institute," I murmured. "I am glad I was not there."

"My dear fellow," said Erskine, suddenly turning his keen grey eyes on me, "you believe in Cyril Graham's theory, you believe in Willie Hughes, you know that the Sonnets are addressed to an actor, but for some reason or other you won't acknowledge it."

"I wish I could believe it," I rejoined. "I would give anything to be able to do so. But I can't. It is a sort of moonbeam theory, very lovely, very fascinating, but intangible. When one thinks that one has got hold of it, it escapes one. No: Shakespeare's heart is still to us 'a closet never pierc'd with crystal eyes,' as he calls it in one of the sonnets. We shall never know the true secret of the passion of his life."

Erskine sprang from the sofa, and paced up and down the

room. "We know it already," he cried, "and the world shall know it some day."

I had never seen him so excited. He would not hear of my leaving him, and insisted on my stopping for the rest of the day.

We argued the matter over for hours, but nothing that I could say could make him surrender his faith in Cyril Graham's interpretation. He told me that he intended to devote his life to proving the theory, and that he was determined to do justice to Cyril Graham's memory. I entreated him, laughed at him, begged of him, but it was to no use. Finally we parted, not exactly in anger, but certainly with a shadow between us. He thought me shallow, I thought him foolish. When I called on him again, his servant told me that he had gone to Germany. The letters that I wrote to him remained unanswered.

Two years afterwards, as I was going into my club, the hall porter handed me a letter with a foreign postmark. It was from Erskine, and written at the Hôtel d'Angleterre, Cannes. When I had read it, I was filled with horror, though I did not quite believe that he would be so mad as to carry his resolve into execution. The gist of the letter was that he had tried in every way to verify the Willie Hughes theory, and had failed, and that as Cyril Graham had given his life for this theory, he himself had determined to give his own life also to the same cause. The concluding words of the letter were these: "I still believe in Willie Hughes; and by the time you receive this I shall have died by my own hand for Willie Hughes' sake: for his sake, and for the sake of Cyril Graham, whom I drove to his death by my shallow scepticism and ignorant lack of faith. The truth was once revealed to you, and you rejected it. It comes to you now, stained with the blood of two lives.—do not turn away from it."

It was a horrible moment. I felt sick with misery, and yet I could not believe that he would really carry out his intention. To die for one's theological opinions is the worst use a man can make of his life; but to die for a literary theory! It seemed impossible.

I looked at the date. The letter was a week old. Some unfortunate chance had prevented my going to the club for several days, or I might have got it in time to save him. Perhaps it was not too late. I drove off to my rooms, packed up my things, and started by the night mail from Charing Cross. The journey was intolerable. I thought I would never arrive.

As soon as I did, I drove to the Hôtel d'Angleterre. It was quite true. Erskine was dead. They told me that he had been buried two days before in the English cemetery. There was something horribly grotesque about the whole tragedy. I said all kinds of wild things, and the people in the hall looked curiously at me.

Suddenly Lady Erskine, in deep mourning, passed across the vestibule. When she saw me she came up to me, murmured something about her poor son, and burst into tears. I led her into her sitting room. An elderly gentleman was there, reading a newspaper. It was the English doctor.

We talked a great deal about Erskine, but I said nothing about his motive for committing suicide. It was evident that he had not told his mother anything about the reason that had driven him to so fatal, so mad an act. Finally Lady Erskine rose and said, "George left you something as a memento. It was a thing he prized very much. I will get it for you."

As soon as she had left the room I turned to the doctor and said, "What a dreadful shock it must have been for Lady Erskine! I wonder that she bears it as well as she does."

"Oh, she knew for months past that it was coming," he answered.

"Knew it for months past!" I cried. "But why didn't she stop him? Why didn't she have him watched? He must have been out of his mind."

The doctor stared at me. "I don't know what you mean," he said.

"Well," I cried, "if a mother knows that her son is going to commit suicide—"

"Suicide!" he answered. "Poor Erskine did not commit suicide. He died of consumption. He came here to die. The moment I saw him I knew that there was no chance. One lung was almost gone, and the other was very much affected.

Three days before he died he asked me was there any hope. I told him frankly that there was none, and that he had only a few days to live. He wrote some letters, and was quite resigned, retaining his senses to the last."

I got up from my seat, and going over to the open window I looked out on the crowded promenade. I remember that the brightly-coloured umbrellas and gay parasols seemed to me like huge fantastic butterflies fluttering by the shore of a blue-metal sea, and that the heavy odour of violets that came across the garden made me think of that wonderful sonnet in which Shakespeare tells us that the scent of these flowers always reminded him of his friend. What did it all mean? Why had Erskine written me that extraordinary letter? Why when standing at the very gate of death had he turned back to tell me what was not true? Was Hugo right? Is affectation the only thing that accompanies a man up the steps of the scaffold? Did Erskine merely want to produce a dramatic effect? That was not like him. It was more like something I might have done myself. No: he was simply actuated by a desire to reconvert me to Cyril Graham's theory, and he thought that if I could be made to believe that he too had given his life for it, I would be deceived by the pathetic fallacy of martyrdom. Poor Erskine! I had grown wiser since I had seen him. Martyrdom was to me merely a tragic form of scepticism, an attempt to realise by fire what one had failed to do by faith. No man dies for what he knows to be true. Men die for what they want to be true, for what some terror in their hearts tells them is not true. The very uselessness of Erskine's letter made me doubly sorry for him. I watched the people strolling in and out of the cafés, and wondered if any of them had known him. The white dust blew down the scorched sunlit road, and the feathery palms moved restlessly in the shaken air.

At that moment Lady Erskine returned to the room carrying the fatal portrait of Willie Hughes. "When George was dying, he begged me to give you this," she said. As I took it from her, her tears fell on my hand.

This curious work of art hangs now in my library, where it is very much admired by my artistic friends, one of whom has etched it for me. They have decided that it is not a Clouet, but an Ouvry. I have never cared to tell them its true history, but sometimes, when I look at it, I think there is really a great deal to be said for the Willie Hughes theory of Shakespeare's Sonnets.

A Chinese Sage
[Chuang Tsŭ]*

An eminent Oxford theologian once remarked that his only
objection to modern progress was that it progressed forward
instead of backward—a view that so fascinated a certain artistic
undergraduate that he promptly wrote an essay upon some unnoticed analogies between the development of ideas and the
movements of the common sea-crab. I feel sure THE SPEAKER
will not be suspected of holding this dangerous heresy of retro-
gression even by its most enthusiastic friends. But I must candidly admit that I have come to the conclusion that the most
caustic criticism of modern life I have met with for some time
is that contained in the writings of the learned Chuang Tsŭ,
recently translated into the vulgar tongue by Mr. Herbert
Giles, Her Majesty's Consul at Tamsui.

The spread of popular education has no doubt made the name
of this great thinker quite familiar to the general public, but
for the sake of the few and the over-cultured, I feel it my duty
to state definitely who he was, and to give a brief outline of the
character of his philosophy.

Chuang Tsŭ, whose name must carefully be pronounced as it
is not written, was born in the fourth century before Christ, by
the banks of the Yellow River, in the Flowery Land; and portraits of the wonderful sage seated on the flying dragon of con-

---

* Review of Chuang Tsŭ, translated from the Chinese by Herbert A.
Giles, *Speaker* I : 6 (8 February 1890) 144–46.

templation may still be found on the simple tea-trays and
pleasing screens of many of our most respectable suburban
households. The honest ratepayer and his healthy family have
no doubt often mocked at the dome-like forehead of the philosopher, and laughed over the strange perspective of the landscape that lies beneath him. If they really knew who he was,
they would tremble. For Chuang Tsŭ spent his life in preach-
ing the great creed of Inaction, and in pointing out the uselessness of all useful things. "Do nothing, and everything will
be done," was the doctrine which he inherited from his great
master Lao Tsŭ. To resolve action into thought, and thought
into abstraction, was his wicked transcendental aim. Like the
obscure philosopher of early Greek speculation, he believed in
the identity of contraries; like Plato, he was an idealist, and
had all the idealist's contempt for utilitarian systems; he was a
mystic like Dionysius, and Scotus Erigena, and Jacob Böhme,
and held, with them and with Philo, that the object of life
was to get rid of self-consciousness, and to become the unconscious vehicle of a higher illumination. In fact, Chuang Tsŭ
may be said to have summed up in himself almost every mood
of European metaphysical or mystical thought, from Hera-
kleitus down to Hegel. There was something in him of the
Quietist also; and in his worship of Nothing he may be said to
have in some measure anticipated those strange dreamers of
medieval days who, like Tauler and Master Eckhart, adored
the *purum nihil* and the Abyss. The great middle classes of this
country, to whom, as we all know, our prosperity, if not our
civilization, is entirely due, may shrug their shoulders over all
this, and ask, with a certain amount of reason, what is the
identity of contraries to them, and why they should get rid of
that self-consciousness which is their chief characteristic. But
Chuang Tsŭ was something more than a metaphysician and
an illuminist. He sought to destroy society, as we know it, as
the middle classes know it; and the sad thing is that he combines with the passionate eloquence of a Rousseau the scientific
reasoning of a Herbert Spencer. There is nothing of the sentimentalist in him. He pities the rich more than the poor, if he
ever pities at all, and prosperity seems to him as tragic a thing
as suffering. He has nothing of the modern sympathy with

failures, nor does he propose that the prizes should always be given on moral grounds to those who come in last in the race. It is the race itself that he objects to; and as for active sympathy, which has become the profession of so many worthy people in our own day, he thinks that trying to make others good is as silly an occupation as "beating a drum in a forest in order to find a fugitive." It is a mere waste of energy. That is all. While as for a thoroughly sympathetic man, he is, in the eyes of Chuang Tsǔ, simply a man who is always trying to be somebody else, and so misses the only possible excuse for his own existence.

Yes; incredible as it may seem, this curious thinker looked back with a sigh of regret to a certain Golden Age when there were no competitive examinations, no wearisome educational systems, no missionaries, no penny dinners for the people, no Established Churches, no Humanitarian Societies, no dull lectures about one's duty to one's neighbour, and no tedious sermons about any subject at all. In those ideal days, he tells us, people loved each other without being conscious of charity, or writing to the newspapers about it. They were upright, and yet they never published books upon Altruism. As every man kept his knowledge to himself, the world escaped the curse of scepticism; and as every man kept his virtues to himself, nobody meddled in other people's business. They lived simple and peaceful lives, and were contented with such food and raiment as they could get. Neighbouring districts were in sight, and "the cocks and dogs of one could be heard in the other," yet the people grew old and died without ever interchanging visits. There was no chattering about clever men, and no laudation of good men. The intolerable sense of obligation was unknown. The deeds of humanity left no trace, and their affairs were not made a burden for posterity by foolish historians.

In an evil moment the Philanthropist made his appearance, and brought with him the mischievous idea of Government. "There is such a thing," says Chuang Tsǔ, "as leaving mankind alone: there has never been such a thing as governing mankind." All modes of government are wrong. They are unscientific, because they seek to alter the natural environment of man; they are immoral, because, by interfering with the individual, they produce the most aggressive forms of egotism; they are ignorant, because they try to spread education; they are self-destructive, because they engender anarchy. "Of old," he tells us, "the Yellow Emperor first caused charity and duty to one's neighbour to interfere with the natural goodness of the heart of man. In consequence of this, Yao and Shun wore the hair off their legs in endeavouring to feed their people. They disturbed their internal economy in order to find room for artificial virtues. They exhausted their energies in framing laws, and they were failures." Man's heart, our philosopher goes on to say, may be "forced down or stirred up," and in either case the issue is fatal. Yao made the people too happy, so they were not satisfied. Chieh made them too wretched, so they grew discontented. Then everyone began to argue about the best way of tinkering up society. "It is quite clear that something must be done," they said to each other, and there was a general rush for knowledge. The results were so dreadful that the Government of the day had to bring in Coercion, and as a consequence of this "virtuous men sought refuge in mountain caves, while rulers of state sat trembling in ancestral halls." Then, when everything was in a state of perfect chaos, the Social Reformers got up on platforms, and preached salvation from the ills that they and their system had caused. The poor Social Reformers! "They know not shame, nor what it is to blush," is the verdict of Chuang Tsŭ upon them.

The economic question, also, is discussed by this almond-eyed sage at great length, and he writes about the curse of capital as eloquently as Mr. Hyndman. The accumulation of wealth is to him the origin of evil. It makes the strong violent, and the weak dishonest. It creates the petty thief, and puts him in a bamboo cage. It creates the big thief, and sets him on a throne of white jade. It is the father of competition, and competition is the waste, as well as the destruction, of energy. The order of nature is rest, repetition, and peace. Weariness and war are the results of an artificial society based upon capital; and the richer this society gets, the more thoroughly bankrupt it really is, for it has neither sufficient rewards for the good nor sufficient punishments for the wicked. There is also this to be remembered—that the prizes of the world degrade a man as much as the world's punishments. The age is rotten with its worship of success. As for education, true wisdom can neither be learnt nor taught. It is a spiritual state, to which he who lives in harmony with nature attains. Knowledge is shallow if we compare it with the extent of the unknown, and only the unknowable is of value. Society produces rogues, and education makes one rogue cleverer than another. That is the only result of School Boards. Besides, of what possible philosophic importance can education be, when it simply serves to make each man differ from his neighbour? We arrive ultimately at a chaos of opinions, doubt everything, and fall into the vulgar habit of arguing; and it is only the intellectually lost who ever argue. Look at Hui Tzu. "He was a man of many ideas. His works would fill five carts. But his doctrines were paradoxical." He said that there were feathers in an egg, because there were feathers on a chicken; that a dog could be a sheep, because all names were arbitrary; that there was a moment when a swiftly flying arrow was neither moving nor at rest; that if you took a stick a foot long, and cut it in half every day, you would never come to the end of it; and that a bay horse and a dun cow were three, because taken separately they were two, and taken together they were one, and one and two made up three. "He was like a man running a race with his own shadow, and making a noise in order to drown the echo. He was a clever gad-fly, that was all. What was the use of him?"

Morality is, of course, a different thing. It went out of fashion, says Chuang Tsŭ, when people began to moralise. Men ceased then to be spontaneous and to act on intuition. They became priggish and artificial, and were so blind as to have a definite purpose in life. Then came Governments and Philanthropists, those two pests of the age. The former tried to coerce people into being good, and so destroyed the natural goodness of man. The latter were a set of aggressive busybodies who caused confusion wherever they went. They were stupid enough to have principles, and unfortunate enough to act up to them. They all came to bad ends, and showed that universal altruism is as bad in its results as universal egotism. They "tripped people up over charity, and fettered them with duties to their neighbours." They gushed over music, and fussed over ceremonies.

As a consequence of all this, the world lost its equilibrium, and has been staggering ever since.

Who, then, according to Chuang Tsŭ, is the perfect man? And what is his manner of life? The perfect man does nothing beyond gazing at the universe. He adopts no absolute position. "In motion, he is like water. At rest, he is like a mirror. And, like Echo, he only answers when he is called upon." He lets externals take care of themselves. Nothing material injures him; nothing spiritual punishes him. His mental equilibrium gives him the empire of the world. He is never the slave of objective existences. He knows that, "just as the best language is that which is never spoken, so the best action is that which is never done." He is passive, and accepts the laws of life. He rests in inactivity, and sees the world become virtuous of itself. He does not try to "bring about his own good deeds." He never wastes himself on effort. He is not troubled about moral distinctions. He knows that things are what they are, and that their consequences will be what they will be. His mind is the "speculum of creation," and he is ever at peace.

All this is of course excessively dangerous, but we must remember that Chuang Tsŭ lived more than two thousand years ago, and never had the opportunity of seeing our unrivalled civilisation. And yet it is possible that, were he to come back to earth and visit us, he might have something to say to Mr. Balfour about his coercion and active misgovernment in Ireland; he might smile at some of our philanthropic ardours, and shake his head over many of our organised charities; the School Board might not impress him, nor our race for wealth stir his admiration; he might wonder at our ideals, and grow sad over what we have realised. Perhaps it is well that Chuang Tsŭ cannot return.

Meanwhile, thanks to Mr. Giles and Mr. Quaritch, we have his book to console us, and certainly it is a most fascinating and delightful volume. Chuang Tsŭ is one of the Darwinians before Darwin. He traces man from the germ, and sees his unity with nature. As an anthropologist he is excessively interesting, and he describes our primitive arboreal ancestor living in trees through his terror of animals stronger than himself, and knowing only one parent, the mother, with all the accuracy of a lecturer at the Royal Society. Like Plato, he adopts the dialogue as his mode of expression, "putting words into other people's mouths," he tells us, "in order to gain breadth of view." As a story-teller he is charming. The account of the visit of the respectable Confucius to the great Robber Chê is most vivid and brilliant, and it is impossible not to laugh over the ultimate discomfiture of the sage, the barrenness of whose moral platitudes is ruthlessly exposed by the successful brigand. Even in his metaphysics, Chuang Tsŭ is intensely humorous. He personifies his abstractions, and makes them act plays before us. The Spirit of the Clouds, when passing eastward through the expanse of air, happened to fall in with the Vital Principle. The latter was slapping his ribs and hopping about: whereupon the Spirit of the Clouds said, "Who are you, old man, and what are you doing?" "Strolling!" replied the Vital Principle, without stopping, for all activities are ceaseless. "I want to *know* something," continued the Spirit of the Clouds. "Ah!" cried the Vital Principle, in a tone of disapprobation, and a marvellous conversation follows, that is not unlike the dialogue between the Sphinx and the Chimæra in Flaubert's curious drama. Talking animals, also, have their place in Chuang Tsŭ's parables and stories, and through myth and poetry and fancy his strange philosophy finds musical utterance.

Of course it is sad to be told that it is immoral to be consciously good, and that doing anything is the worst form of idleness. Thousands of excellent and really earnest philanthropists would be absolutely thrown upon the rates if we adopted the view that nobody should be allowed to meddle in what does not concern them. The doctrine of the uselessness of all useful things would not merely endanger our commercial supremacy as a nation, but might bring discredit upon many prosperous and serious-minded members of the shop-keeping classes. What would become of our popular preachers, our Exeter Hall orators, our drawing-room evangelists, if we said to them, in the words of Chuang Tsŭ, "Mosquitoes will keep a man awake all night with their biting, and just in the same way this talk of charity and duty to one's neighbour drives us nearly crazy. Sirs, strive to keep the world to its own original simplicity, and, as the wind bloweth where it listeth, so let

Virtue establish itself. Wherefore this undue energy?" And what would be the fate of governments and professional politicians if we came to the conclusion that there is no such thing as governing mankind at all? It is clear that Chuang Tsŭ is a very dangerous writer, and the publication of his book in English, two thousand years after his death, is obviously premature, and may cause a great deal of pain to many thoroughly respectable and industrious persons. It may be true that the ideal of self-culture and self-development, which is the aim of his scheme of life, and the basis of his scheme of philosophy, is an ideal somewhat needed by an age like ours, in which most people are so anxious to educate their neighbours that they have actually no time left in which to educate themselves. But would it be wise to say so? It seems to me that if we once admitted the force of any one of Chuang Tsŭ's destructive criticisms we should have to put some check on our national habit of self-glorification; and the only thing that ever consoles man for the stupid things he does is the praise he always gives himself for doing them. There may, however, be a few who have grown wearied of that strange modern tendency that sets enthusiasm to do the work of the intellect. To these, and such as these, Chuang Tsŭ will be welcome. But let them only read him. Let them not talk about him. He would be disturbing at dinner-parties, and impossible at afternoon teas, and his whole life was a protest against platform speaking. "The perfect man ignores self; the divine man ignores action; the true sage ignores reputation." These are the principles of Chuang Tsŭ.

Mr. Pater's Last Volume
[*Appreciations*]*

When I first had the privilege—and I count it a very high one
—of meeting Mr. Walter Pater, he said to me, smiling, "Why
do you always write poetry? Why do you not write prose? Prose
is so much more difficult."

It was during my undergraduate days at Oxford; days of
lyrical ardours and of studious sonnet-writing; days when one
loved the exquisite intricacy and musical repetitions of the
ballade, and the villanelle with its linked long-drawn echoes
and its curious completeness; days when one solemnly sought to
discover the proper temper in which a triolet should be written;
delightful days, in which, I am glad to say, there was far more
rhyme than reason.

I may frankly confess now that at the time I did not quite
comprehend what Mr. Pater really meant; and it was not till I
had carefully studied his beautiful and suggestive essays on the
Renaissance that I fully realised what a wonderful self-conscious
art the art of English prose-writing really is, or may be made to
be. Carlyle's stormy rhetoric, Ruskin's winged and passionate
eloquence, had seemed to me to spring from enthusiasm rather
than from art. I don't think I knew then that even prophets
correct their proofs. As for Jacobean prose, I thought it too
exuberant; and Queen Anne prose appeared to me terribly bald,
and irritatingly rational. But Mr. Pater's essays became to me

* *Speaker* I : 12 (22 March 1890) 319–20.

"the golden book of spirit and sense, the holy writ of beauty."
They are still this to me. It is possible, of course, that I may
exaggerate about them. I certainly hope that I do; for where
there is no exaggeration there is no love, and where there is no
love there is no understanding. It is only about things that do
not interest one, that one can give a really unbiassed opinion;
and this is no doubt the reason why an unbiassed opinion is
always absolutely valueless.

But I must not allow this brief notice of Mr. Pater's new
volume to degenerate into an autobiography. I remember being
told in America that whenever Margaret Fuller wrote an essay
upon Emerson the printers had always to send out to borrow
some additional capital "I's," and I feel it right to accept this
transatlantic warning.

"Appreciations," in the fine Latin sense of the word, is the
title given by Mr. Pater to his book, which is an exquisite collection of exquisite essays, of delicately wrought works of art—
some of them being almost Greek in their purity of outline and
perfection of form, others mediæval in their strangeness of
colour and passionate suggestion, and all of them absolutely
modern, in the true meaning of the term modernity. For he to
whom the present is the only thing that is present, knows nothing of the age in which he lives. To realise the nineteenth
century, one must realise every century that has preceded it,
and that has contributed to its making. To know anything
about oneself, one must know all about others. There must be
no mood with which one cannot sympathise, no dead mode of
life that one cannot make alive. The legacies of heredity may
make us alter our views of moral responsibility, but they cannot but intensify our sense of the value of Criticism; for the
true critic is he who bears within himself the dreams and
ideas and feelings of myriad generations, and to whom no
form of thought is alien, no emotional impulse obscure.

Perhaps the most interesting, and certainly the least successful, of the essays contained in the present volume is that
on "Style." It is the most interesting because it is the work
of one who speaks with the high authority that comes from
the noble realisation of things nobly conceived. It is the least
successful, because the subject is too abstract. A true artist

like Mr. Pater, is most felicitous when he deals with the concrete, whose very limitations give him finer freedom, while they necessitate more intense vision. And yet what a high ideal is contained in these few pages! How good it is for us, in these days of popular education and facile journalism, to be reminded of the real scholarship that is essential to the perfect writer, who, "being a true lover of words for their own sake, a minute and constant observer of their physiognomy," will avoid what is mere rhetoric, or ostentatious ornament, or negligent misuse of terms, or ineffective surplusage, and will be known by his tact of omission, by his skilful economy of means, by his selection and self-restraint, and perhaps above all by that conscious artistic structure which is the expression of mind in style. I think I have been wrong in saying that the subject is too abstract. In Mr. Pater's hands it becomes very real to us indeed, and he shows us how, behind the perfection of a man's style, must lie the passion of a man's soul.

As one passes to the rest of the volume, one finds essays on Wordsworth and on Coleridge, on Charles Lamb and on Sir Thomas Browne, on some of Shakespeare's plays and on the English kings that Shakespeare fashioned, on Dante Rossetti, and on William Morris. As that on Wordsworth seems to be Mr. Pater's last work, so that on the singer of the "Defence of Guenevere" is certainly his earliest, or almost his earliest, and it is interesting to mark the change that has taken place in his style. This change is, perhaps, at first sight not very apparent. In 1868 we find Mr. Pater writing with the same exquisite care for words, with the same studied music, with the same temper, and something of the same mode of treatment. But, as he goes on, the architecture of the style becomes richer and more complex, the epithet more precise and intellectual. Occasionally one may be inclined to think that there is, here and there, a sentence which is somewhat long, and possibly, if one may venture to say so, a little heavy and cumbersome in movement. But if this be so, it comes from those side-issues suddenly suggested by the idea in its progress, and really revealing the idea more perfectly; or from those felicitous after-thoughts that give a fuller completeness to the central scheme, and yet convey something of the charm of chance; or from a desire to suggest the secondary shades of meaning with all their accumulating effect, and to avoid, it may be, the violence and harshness of too definite and exclusive an opinion. For in matters of art, at any rate, thought is inevitably coloured by emotion, and so is fluid rather than fixed, and, recognising its dependence upon moods and upon the passion of fine moments, will not accept the rigidity of a scientific formula or a theological dogma. The critical pleasure, too, that we receive from tracing, through what may seem the intricacies of a sentence, the working of the constructive intelligence, must not be overlooked. As soon as we have realised the design, everything appears clear and simple. After a time, these long sentences of Mr. Pater's come to have the charm of an elaborate piece of music, and the unity of such music also.

I have suggested that the essay on Wordsworth is probably the most recent bit of work contained in this volume. If one might choose between so much that is good, I should be inclined to say it is the finest also. The essay on Lamb is curiously suggestive; suggestive, indeed, of a somewhat more tragic, more sombre figure, than men have been wont to think of in connection with the author of the Essays of Elia. It is an interesting aspect under which to regard Lamb, but perhaps he himself would have had some difficulty in recognising the portrait given of him. He had, undoubtedly, great sorrows, or motives for sorrow, but he could console himself at a moment's notice for the real tragedies of life by reading any one of the Elizabethan tragedies, provided it was in a folio edition. The essay on Sir Thomas Browne is delightful, and has the strange, personal, fanciful charm of the author of the "Religio Medici;" Mr. Pater often catching the colour and accent and tone of whatever artist, or work of art, he deals with. That on Coleridge, with its insistence on the necessity of the cultivation of the relative, as opposed to the absolute spirit in philosophy and in ethics, and its high appreciation of the poet's true position in our literature, is in style and substance a very blameless work. Grace of expression, and delicate subtlety of thought and phrase, characterise the essays on Shakespeare. But the essay on Wordsworth has a spiritual beauty of its own. It appeals, not to the ordinary Wordsworthian with his uncritical temper, and his gross confusion of ethical with æsthetical problems, but rather to those who desire to separate the gold from the dross, and to reach at the true Wordsworth through the mass of tedious and prosaic work that bears his name, and that serves often to conceal him from us. The presence of an alien element in Wordsworth's art, is, of course, recognised by Mr. Pater but he touches on it merely from the psychological point of view, pointing out how this quality of higher and lower moods gives the effect in his poetry "of a power not altogether his own, or under his control"; a power which comes and goes when it wills, "so that the old fancy which made the poet's art an enthusiasm, a form of divine possession, seems almost true of him." Mr. Pater's earlier essays had their *purpurei panni*, so eminently suitable for quotation, such as the famous passage on Monna Lisa, and that other in which Botticelli's strange conception of the Virgin is so strangely set forth. From the present volume it is difficult to select any one passage in preference to another as specially characteristic of Mr. Pater's treatment. This, however, is worth quoting at length. It contains a truth eminently useful for our age:—

That the end of life is not action but contemplation—*being* as distinct from *doing*—a certain disposition of the mind: is, in some shape or other, the principle of all the higher morality. In poetry, in art, if you enter into their true spirit at all, you touch this principle in a measure; these, by their very sterility, are a type of beholding for the mere joy of beholding. To treat life in the spirit of art is to make life a thing in which means and ends are identified: to encourage such treatment, the true moral significance of art and poetry. Wordsworth, and other poets who have been like him in ancient or more recent times, are the masters, the experts, in this art of impassioned contemplation. Their work is not to teach lessons, or enforce rules, or even to stimulate us to noble ends, but to withdraw the thoughts for a while from the mere machinery of life, to fix them, with appropriate emotions, on the spectacle of those great facts in man's existence which no machinery affects, "on the great and universal passions of men, the most general and interesting of their occupations, and the entire world of nature"—on "the operations of the elements and the appearances of the visible universe, on storm and sunshine, on the revolutions of the seasons, on cold and heat, on loss of friends and kindred, on injuries and resentments, on gratitude and hope, on fear and sorrow." To witness this spectacle with appropriate emotions is the aim of all culture; and of these emotions poetry like Wordsworth's is a great nourisher and stimulant. He sees nature full of sentiment and excitement; he sees men and women as parts of nature, passionate, excited, in strange grouping and connection with the grandeur and beauty of the natural world:—images, in his own words, "of man suffering, amid awful forms and powers."

Certainly the real secret of Wordsworth has never been better expressed. After having read and re-read Mr. Pater's essay—for it requires re-reading—one returns to the poet's work with a new sense of joy and wonder, and with something of eager and impassioned expectation. And perhaps this might be roughly taken as the test or touchstone of the finest criticism.

Finally, one cannot help noticing the delicate instinct that has gone to fashion the brief epilogue that ends this delightful volume. The difference between the classical and romantic spirits in art has often, and with much over-emphasis, been discussed. But with what a light sure touch does Mr. Pater write of it. How subtle and certain are his distinctions! If imaginative prose be really special art of this century, Mr. Pater must rank amongst our century's most characteristic artists. In certain things he stands almost alone. The age has produced wonderful prose styles, turbid with individualism, and violent with excess of rhetoric. But in Mr. Pater, as in Cardinal Newman, we find the union of personality with perfection. He has no rival in his own sphere, and he has escaped disciples. And this, not because he has not been imitated, but because in art so fine as his there is something that, in its essence, is inimitable.

Preface to
*The Picture of Dorian Gray**

The artist is the creator of beautiful things.

    To reveal art and conceal the artist is art's aim.

The critic is he who can translate into another manner or a new material his impression of beautiful things.

    The highest as the lowest form of criticism is a mode of autobiography.

Those who find ugly meanings in beautiful things are corrupt without being charming. This is a fault.

    Those who find beautiful meanings in beautiful things are the cultivated. For these there is hope.

They are the elect to whom beautiful things mean only Beauty.

    There is no such thing as a moral or an immoral book. Books are well written, or badly written. That is all.

The nineteenth century dislike of Realism is the rage of Caliban seeing his own face in a glass.

    The nineteenth century dislike of Romanticism is the rage of Caliban not seeing his own face in a glass.

    The moral life of man forms part of the

* 1891.

subject-matter of the artist, but the morality of art consists in the perfect use of an imperfect medium.

No artist desires to prove anything. Even things that are true can be proved.

No artist has ethical sympathies. An ethical sympathy in an artist is an unpardonable mannerism of style.

No artist is ever morbid. The artist can express everything.

Thought and language are to the artist instruments of an art.

Vice and virtue are to the artist materials for an art.

From the point of view of form, the type of all the arts is the art of the musician. From the point of view of feeling, the actor's craft is the type.

All art is at once surface and symbol.

Those who go beneath the surface do so at their peril.

Those who read the symbol do so at their peril.

It is the spectator, and not life, that art really mirrors.

Diversity of opinion about a work of art shows that the work is new, complex, and vital.

When critics disagree the artist is in accord with himself.

We can forgive a man for making a useful thing as long as he does not admire it. The only excuse for making a useless thing is that one admires it intensely.

All art is quite useless.

Defense of
*Dorian Gray**

TO THE EDITOR OF

THE "ST JAMES'S GAZETTE"[1]

25 June [1890]   *16 Tite Street*

Sir, I have read your criticism of my story, *The Picture of Dorian Gray*, and I need hardly say that I do not propose to discuss its merits or demerits, its personalities or its lack of personality. England is a free country, and ordinary English criticism is perfectly free and easy. Besides, I must admit that, either from temperament or from taste, or from both, I am quite incapable of understanding how any work of art can be criticised from a moral standpoint. The sphere of art and the sphere of ethics are absolutely distinct and separate; and it is to the confusion between the two that we owe the appearance of Mrs

---

* Text from *The Letters of Oscar Wilde*, ed. Rupert Hart-Davis (London and New York, 1962).

[1] Wilde's only novel, *The Picture of Dorian Gray*, was first published on 20 June 1890, in the July number of *Lippincott's Monthly Magazine*, where it occupied pp. 3–100. It was extensively reviewed. The *St James's Gazette* printed a scurrilous notice on 24 June, under the heading "A Study in Puppydom." Its anonymous author was Samuel Henry Jeyes (1857–1911). The full text of all the important reviews of, and letters about, *Dorian Gray* is given in Stuart Mason's *Art and Morality* (1912). This letter of Wilde's was published on 26 June, under the heading MR OSCAR WILDE'S "BAD CASE."—Rupert Hart-Davis.

Grundy, that amusing old lady who represents the only original form of humour that the middle classes of this country have been able to produce. What I do object to most strongly is that you should have placarded the town with posters on which was printed in large letters: MR OSCAR WILDE'S LATEST ADVERTISEMENT; A BAD CASE.

Whether the expression "A Bad Case" refers to my book or to the present position of the Government, I cannot tell. What was silly and unnecessary was the use of the term "advertisement."

I think I may say without vanity—though I do not wish to appear to run vanity down—that of all men in England I am the one who requires least advertisement. I am tired to death of being advertised. I feel no thrill when I see my name in a paper. The chronicler does not interest me any more. I wrote this book entirely for my own pleasure, and it gave me very great pleasure to write it. Whether it becomes popular or not is a matter of absolute indifference to me. I am afraid, sir, that the real advertisement is your cleverly written article. The English public, as a mass, takes no interest in a work of art until it is told that the work in question is immoral, and your *réclame* will, I have no doubt, largely increase the sale of the magazine; in which sale, I may mention with some regret, I have no pecuniary interest.

I remain, sir, your obedient servant   OSCAR WILDE

TO THE EDITOR OF
THE ''ST JAMES'S GAZETTE''

26 *June* [1890]   16 *Tite Street*

In your issue of today you state that my brief letter published in your columns is the "best reply" I can make to your article upon *Dorian Gray*. This is not so. I do not propose to fully discuss the matter here, but I feel bound to say that your article contains the most unjustifiable attack that has been made upon any man of letters for many years. The writer of it, who is quite incapable of concealing his personal malice, and so in some measure destroys the effect he wishes to produce, seems not to have the slightest idea of the temper in which a work of art should be approached. To say that such a book as mine should be "chucked into the fire" is silly. That is what one does with newspapers.

Of the value of pseudo-ethical criticism in dealing with artistic work I have spoken already. But as your writer has ventured into the perilous grounds of literary criticism I ask you to allow me, in fairness not merely to myself but to all men to whom literature is a fine art, to say a few words about his critical method.

He begins by assailing me with much ridiculous virulence because the chief personages in my story are "puppies." They *are* puppies. Does he think that literature went to the dogs when Thackeray wrote about puppydom? I think that puppies are extremely interesting from an artistic as well as from a psychological point of view. They seem to me to be certainly far more interesting than prigs; and I am of opinion that Lord Henry Wotton is an excellent corrective of the tedious ideal shadowed forth in the semi-theological novels of our age.

He then makes vague and fearful insinuations about my grammar and my erudition. Now, as regards grammar, I hold that, in prose at any rate, correctness should always be subordinate to artistic effect and musical cadence; and any peculiarities of syntax that may occur in *Dorian Gray* are deliberately intended, and are introduced to show the value of the artistic theory in question. Your writer gives no instance of any such peculiarity. This I regret, because I do not think that any such instances occur.

As regards erudition, it is always difficult, even for the most modest of us, to remember that other people do not know quite as much as one does oneself. I myself frankly admit I cannot imagine how a casual reference to Suetonius and Petronius Arbiter can be construed into evidence of a desire to impress an unoffending and ill-educated public by an assumption of superior knowledge. I should fancy that the most ordinary of scholars is perfectly well acquainted with the *Lives of the Caesars* and with the *Satyricon*. The *Lives of the Caesars*, at any rate, forms part of the curriculum at Oxford for those who take the

Honour School of *Literæ Humaniores*; and as for the *Satyricon*, it is popular even among passmen, though I suppose they are obliged to read it in translations.

The writer of the article then suggests that I, in common with that great and noble artist Count Tolstoi, take pleasure in a subject because it is dangerous. About such a suggestion there is this to be said. Romantic art deals with the exception and with the individual. Good people, belonging as they do to the normal, and so, commonplace, type, are artistically uninteresting. Bad people are, from the point of view of art, fascinating studies. They represent colour, variety and strangeness. Good people exasperate one's reason; bad people stir one's imagination. Your critic, if I must give him so honourable a title, states that the people in my story have no counterpart in life; that they are, to use his vigorous if somewhat vulgar phrase, "mere catchpenny revelations of the non-existent." Quite so. If they existed they would not be worth writing about. The function of the artist is to invent, not to chronicle. There are no such people. If there were I would not write about them. Life by its realism is always spoiling the subject-matter of art. The supreme pleasure in literature is to realise the non-existent.

And finally, let me say this. You have reproduced, in a journalistic form, the comedy of *Much Ado about Nothing*, and have, of course, spoilt it in your reproduction. The poor public, hearing, from an authority so high as your own, that this is a wicked book that should be coerced and suppressed by a Tory Government, will, no doubt, rush to it and read it. But, alas! they will find that it is a story with a moral. And the moral is this: All excess, as well as all renunciation, brings its own punishment. The painter, Basil Hallward, worshipping physical beauty far too much, as most painters do, dies by the hand of one in whose soul he has created a monstrous and absurd vanity. Dorian Gray, having led a life of mere sensation and pleasure, tries to kill conscience, and at that moment kills himself. Lord Henry Wotton seeks to be merely the spectator of life. He finds that those who reject the battle are more deeply wounded than those who take part in it. Yes; there is a terrible moral in *Dorian Gray*—a moral which the prurient will not be able to find in it, but which will be revealed to all whose minds

are healthy. Is this an artistic error? I fear it is. It is the only
error in the book.

27 June [*1890*]   *16 Tite Street*

Sir, As you still keep up, though in a somewhat milder form
than before, your attacks on me and my book, you not merely
confer on me the right, but you impose upon me the duty, of
reply.

You state, in your issue of today, that I misrepresented you
when I said that you suggested that a book so wicked as mine
should be "suppressed and coerced by a Tory Government."
Now you did not propose this, but you did suggest it. When you
declared that you do not know whether or not the Government
will take action about my book, and remark that the authors of
books much less wicked have been proceeded against in law,
the suggestion is quite obvious. In your complaint of misrepresentation you seem to me, sir, to have been not quite candid.
However, as far as I am concerned, the suggestion is of no importance. What is of importance is that the editor of a paper
like yours should appear to countenance the monstrous theory
that the Government of a country should exercise a censorship
over imaginative literature. This is a theory against which I, and
all men of letters of my acquaintance, protest most strongly;
and any critic who admits the reasonableness of such a theory
shows at once that he is quite incapable of understanding what
literature is, and what are the rights that literature possesses. A
Government might just as well try to teach painters how to
paint, or sculptors how to model, as attempt to interfere with
the style, treatment and subject-matter of the literary artist;
and no writer, however eminent or obscure, should ever give
his sanction to a theory that would degrade literature far more
than any didactic or so-called immoral book could possibly do.

You then express your surprise that "so experienced a literary gentleman" as myself should imagine that your critic was animated by any feeling of personal malice towards him. The phrase "literary gentleman" is a vile phrase; but let that pass. I accept quite readily your assurance that your critic was simply criticising a work of art in the best way that he could; but I feel that I was fully justified in forming the opinion of him that I did. He opened his article by a gross personal attack on myself. This, I need hardly say, was an absolutely unpardonable error of critical taste. There is no excuse for it, except personal malice; and you, sir, should not have sanctioned it. A critic should be taught to criticise a work of art without making any reference to the personality of the author. This, in fact, is the beginning of criticism. However, it was not merely his personal attack on me that made me imagine that he was actuated by malice. What really confirmed me in my first impression was his reiterated assertion that my book was tedious and dull. Now, if I were criticising my book, which I have some thoughts of doing, I think I would consider it my duty to point out that it is far too crowded with sensational incident, and far too paradoxical in style, as far, at any rate, as the dialogue goes. I feel that from a standpoint of art these are two defects in the book. But tedious and dull the book is not. Your critic has cleared himself of the charge of personal malice, his denial and yours being quite sufficient in the matter; but he has only done so by a tacit admission that he has really no critical instinct about literature and literary work, which, in one who writes about literature, is, I need hardly say, a much graver fault than malice of any kind.

Finally, sir, allow me to say this. Such an article as you have published really makes one despair of the possibility of any general culture in England. Were I a French author, and my book brought out in Paris, there is not a single literary critic in France, on any paper of high standing, who would think for a moment of criticising it from an ethical standpoint. If he did so, he would stultify himself, not merely in the eyes of all men of letters, but in the eyes of the majority of the public. You have yourself often spoken against Puritanism. Believe me, sir, Puritanism is never so offensive and destructive as when it deals with art matters. It is there that its influence is radically wrong. It is this Puritanism, to which your critic has given expression, that is always marring the artistic instinct of the English. So far from encouraging it, you should set yourself against it, and should try to teach your critics to recognise the essential difference between art and life. The gentleman who criticised my book is in a perfectly hopeless confusion about it, and your attempt to help him out by proposing that the subject-matter of art should be limited does not mend matters. It is proper that limitations should be placed on action. It is not proper that limitations should be placed on art. To art belong all things that are and all things that are not, and even the editor of a London paper has no right to restrain the freedom of art in the selection of subject-matter.

I now trust, sir, that these attacks on me and on my book will cease. There are forms of advertisement that are unwarranted and unwarrantable.

I am, sir, your obedient servant,   OSCAR WILDE

TO THE EDITOR OF
THE ''ST JAMES'S GAZETTE''

28 June [1890]   *16 Tite Street*

Sir, In your issue of this evening you publish a letter from "A London Editor" which clearly insinuates in the last paragraph that I have in some way sanctioned the circulation of an expression of opinion, on the part of the proprietors of *Lippincott's Magazine,* of the literary and artistic value of my story of *The Picture of Dorian Gray.*

Allow me, sir, to state that there are no grounds for this insinuation. I was not aware that any such document was being circulated; and I have written to the agents, Messrs Ward & Lock—who cannot, I feel sure, be primarily responsible for its appearance—to ask them to withdraw it at once. No publisher should ever express an opinion of the value of what he publishes. That is a matter entirely for the literary critic to decide. I must admit, as one to whom contemporary literature is constantly submitted for criticism, that the only thing that ever prejudices me against a book is the lack of literary style; but I can quite understand how any ordinary critic would be strongly prejudiced against a work that was accompanied by a premature and unnecessary panegyric from the publisher. A publisher is simply a useful middle-man. It is not for him to anticipate the verdict of criticism.

I may, however, while expressing my thanks to the "London Editor" for drawing my attention to this, I trust, purely American method of procedure, venture to differ from him in one of his criticisms. He states that he regards the expression "complete," as applied to a story, as a specimen of the "adjectival exuberance of the puffer!" Here, it seems to me, he sadly exaggerates. What my story is, is an interesting problem. What my story is not, is a "novelette," a term which you have more than once applied to it. There is no such word in the English language as novelette. It should never be used. It is merely part of the slang of Fleet Street.

In another part of your paper, sir, you state that I received your assurance of the lack of malice in your critic "somewhat grudgingly." This is not so. I frankly said that I accepted that assurance "quite readily," and that your own denial and that of your own critic were "sufficient." Nothing more generous could have been said. What I did feel was that you saved your critic from the charge of malice by convicting him of the unpardonable crime of lack of literary instinct. I still feel that. To call my book an ineffective attempt at allegory that, in the hands of Mr Anstey, might have been made striking, is absurd. Mr Anstey's sphere in literature and my sphere are different—very widely different.

You then gravely ask me what rights I imagine literature possesses. That is really an extraordinary question for the editor of a newspaper such as yours to ask. The rights of literature, sir, are the rights of intellect.

I remember once hearing M. Renan say that he would sooner live under a military despotism than under the despotism of the Church, because the former merely limited the freedom of action, while the latter limited the freedom of mind. You say that a work of art is a form of action. It is not. It is the highest mode of thought.

In conclusion, sir, let me ask you not to force on me this continued correspondence, by daily attacks. It is a trouble and a nuisance. As you assailed me first, I have a right to the last word. Let that last word be the present letter, and leave my book, I beg you, to the immortality that it deserves.

I am, sir, your obedient servant, OSCAR WILDE

TO THE EDITOR OF
THE "DAILY CHRONICLE"

30 June [1890] *16 Tite Street*

Sir, Will you allow me to correct some errors into which your critic has fallen in his review of my story, *The Picture of Dorian Gray*, published in today's issue of your paper?

Your critic states, to begin with, that I make desperate attempts to "vamp up" a moral in my story. Now, I must candidly confess that I do not know what "vamping" is. I see, from time to time, mysterious advertisements in the newspapers about "How to Vamp," but what vamping really means remains a mystery to me—a mystery that, like all other mysteries, I hope some day to explore.

However, I do not propose to discuss the absurd terms used by modern journalism. What I want to say is that, so far from wishing to emphasise any moral in my story, the real trouble I experienced in writing the story was that of keeping the extremely obvious moral subordinate to the artistic and dramatic effect.

When I first conceived the idea of a young man selling his soul in exchange for eternal youth—an idea that is old in the history of literature, but to which I have given new form—I felt that, from an aesthetic point of view, it would be difficult to keep the moral in its proper secondary place; and even now I do not feel quite sure that I have been able to do so. I think the moral too apparent. When the book is published in a volume I hope to correct this defect.

As for what the moral is, your critic states that it is this—that when a man feels himself becoming "too angelic" he should rush out and make a "beast of himself!" I cannot say that I consider this a moral. The real moral of the story is that all excess, as well as all renunciation, brings its punishment, and this moral is so far artistically and deliberately suppressed that it does not enunciate its law as a general principle, but realises itself purely in the lives of individuals, and so becomes simply a dramatic element in a work of art, and not the object of the work of art itself.

Your critic also falls into error when he says that Dorian Gray, having a "cool, calculating, conscienceless character," was inconsistent when he destroyed the picture of his own soul, on the ground that the picture did not become less hideous after he had done what, in his vanity, he had considered his first good action. Dorian Gray has not got a cool, calculating, conscienceless character at all. On the contrary, he is extremely impulsive, absurdly romantic, and is haunted all through his life by an exaggerated sense of conscience which mars his pleasures for him and warns him that youth and enjoyment are not everything in the world. It is finally to get rid of the conscience that had dogged his steps from year to year that he destroys the picture; and thus in his attempt to kill conscience Dorian Gray kills himself.

Your critic then talks about "obtusively cheap scholarship." Now, whatever a scholar writes is sure to display scholarship in the distinction of style and the fine use of language; but my story contains no learned or pseudo-learned discussions, and the only literary books that it alludes to are books that any fairly educated reader may be supposed to be acquainted with, such as the *Satyricon* of Petronius Arbiter, or Gautier's *Emaux et Camées*. Such books as Alphonso's *Clericalis Disciplina* belong not to culture, but to curiosity. Anybody may be excused for not knowing them.

Finally, let me say this—the aesthetic movement produced certain colours, subtle in their loveliness and fascinating in their almost mystical tone. They were, and are, our reaction against the crude primaries of a doubtless more respectable but certainly less cultivated age. My story is an essay on decorative art. It reacts against the crude brutality of plain realism. It is poisonous if you like, but you cannot deny that it is also perfect, and perfection is what we artists aim at.

I remain, sir, your obedient servant   OSCAR WILDE

TO THE EDITOR OF
THE ''SCOTS OBSERVER''

9 *July 1890*   *16 Tite Street, Chelsea*

Sir, You have published a review of my story, *The Picture of Dorian Gray*. As this review is grossly unjust to me as an artist, I ask you to allow me to exercise in your columns my right of reply.

Your reviewer, sir, while admitting that the story in question is "plainly the work of a man of letters," the work of one who has "brains, and art, and style," yet suggests, and apparently in all seriousness, that I have written it in order that it should be read by the most depraved members of the criminal and illiterate classes. Now, sir, I do not suppose that the criminal and illiterate classes ever read anything except newspapers. They are certainly not likely to be able to understand anything of mine. So let them pass, and on the broad question of why a man of letters writes at all let me say this. The pleasure that one has in creating a work of art is a purely personal pleasure, and it is for the sake of this pleasure that one creates. The artist works with his eye on the object. Nothing else interests him. What people are likely to say does not even occur to him. He is fascinated by what he has in hand. He is indifferent to others. I write because it gives me the greatest possible artistic pleasure to write. If my work pleases the few, I am gratified. If it does not, it causes me no pain. As for the mob, I have no desire to be a popular noveliest. It is far too easy.

Your critic then, sir, commits the absolutely unpardonable crime of trying to confuse the artist with his subject-matter.

247

For this, sir, there is no excuse at all. Of one who is the greatest figure in the world's literature since Greek days Keats remarked that he had as much pleasure in conceiving the evil as he had in conceiving the good. Let your reviewer, sir, consider the bearings of Keats's fine criticism, for it is under these conditions that every artist works. One stands remote from one's subject-matter. One creates it, and one contemplates it. The further away the subject-matter is, the more freely can the artist work. Your reviewer suggests that I do not make it sufficiently clear whether I prefer virtue to wickedness or wickedness to virtue. An artist, sir, has no ethical sympathies at all. Virtue and wickedness are to him simply what the colours on his palette are to the painter. They are no more, and they are no less. He sees that by their means a certain artistic effect can be produced, and he produces it. Iago may be morally horrible and Imogen stainlessly pure. Shakespeare, as Keats said, had as much delight in creating the one as he had in creating the other.

It was necessary, sir, for the dramatic development of this story to surround Dorian Gray with an atmosphere of moral corruption. Otherwise the story would have had no meaning and the plot no issue. To keep this atmosphere vague and indeterminate and wonderful was the aim of the artist who wrote the story. I claim, sir, that he has succeeded. Each man sees his own sin in Dorian Gray. What Dorian Gray's sins are no one knows. He who finds them has brought them.

In conclusion, sir, let me say how really deeply I regret that you should have permitted such a notice as the one I feel constrained to write on to have appeared in your paper. That the editor of the *St James's Gazette* should have employed Caliban as his art-critic was possibly natural. The editor of the *Scots Observer* should not have allowed Thersites to make mows in his review. It is unworthy of so distinguished a man of letters. I am, etc.

OSCAR WILDE

[? 31] *July 1890*   16 *Tite Street*

Sir, In a letter dealing with the relations of art to morals recently published in your columns—a letter which I may say seems to me in many respects admirable, especially in its insistence on the rights of the artist to select his own subject-matter—Mr Charles Whibley suggests that it must be peculiarly painful for me to find that the ethical import of *Dorian Gray* has been so strongly recognized by the foremost Christian papers of England and America that I have been greeted by more than one of them as a moral reformer!

Allow me, sir, to reassure, on this point, not merely Mr Charles Whibley himself but also your no doubt anxious readers. I have no hesitation in saying that I regard such criticisms as a very gratifying tribute to my story. For if a work of art is rich, and vital, and complete, those who have artistic instincts will see its beauty, and those to whom ethics appeal more strongly than aesthetics will see its moral lesson. It will fill the cowardly with terror, and the unclean will see in it their own shame. It will be to each man what he is himself. It is the spectator, and not life, that art really mirrors.

And so, in the case of *Dorian Gray*, the purely literary critic, as in the *Speaker* and elsewhere, regards it as a "serious and fascinating work of art:" the critic who deals with art in its relation to conduct, as the *Christian Leader* and the *Christian World*, regards it as an ethical parable. *Light*, which I am told is the organ of the English mystics, regards it as "a work of high spiritual import." The *St James's Gazette*, which is seeking apparently to be the organ of the prurient, sees or pretends to see in it all kinds of dreadful things, and hints at Treasury prosecutions; and your Mr Charles Whibley genially says that he discovers in it "lots of morality." It is quite true that he goes on to say that he detects no art in it. But I do not think that it is fair to expect a critic to be able to see a work of art from every point of view. Even Gautier had his limitations just as much as Diderot had, and in modern England Goethes are rare. I can only assure Mr Charles Whibley that no moral apotheosis to which he has added the most modest contribution could possibly be a source of unhappiness to an artist.

I remain, sir, your obedient servant   OSCAR WILDE

TO THE EDITOR OF
THE "SCOTS OBSERVER"

13 August 1890   *16 Tite Street*

Sir, I am afraid I cannot enter into any newspaper discussion on the subject of art with Mr Whibley, partly because the writing of letters is always a trouble to me, and partly because I regret to say that I do not know what qualifications Mr Whibley possesses for the discussion of so important a topic. I merely noticed his letter because, I am sure without in any way intending it, he made a suggestion about myself personally that was quite inaccurate. His suggestion was that it must have been painful to me to find that a certain section of the public, as represented by himself and the critics of some religious publications, had insisted on finding what he calls "lots of morality" in my story of *The Picture of Dorian Gray*.

Being naturally desirous of setting your readers right on a question of such vital interest to the historian, I took the opportunity of pointing out in your columns that I regarded all such criticisms as a very gratifying tribute to the ethical beauty of the story, and I added that I was quite ready to recognise that it was not really fair to ask of any ordinary critic that he should be able to appreciate a work of art from every point of view. I still hold this opinion. If a man sees the artistic beauty of a thing, he will probably care very little for its ethical import. If his temperament is more susceptible to ethical than to aesthetic influences, he will be blind to questions of style, treatment, and the like. It takes a Goethe to see a work of art fully, completely, and perfectly, and I thoroughly agree with Mr Whibley when he says that it is a pity that Goethe never had an opportunity of reading *Dorian Gray*. I feel quite certain that he would have been delighted by it, and I only hope that some ghostly publisher is even now distributing shadowy copies in the Elysian fields, and that the cover of Gautier's copy is powdered with gilt asphodels.

You may ask me, sir, why I should care to have the ethical beauty of my story recognized. I answer, simply because it exists, because the thing is there. The chief merit of *Madame Bovary* is not the moral lesson that can be found in it, any more than the chief merit of *Salammbô* is its archaeology; but Flaubert was perfectly right in exposing the ignorance of those who called the one immoral and the other inaccurate; and not merely was he right in the ordinary sense of the word, but he was artistically right, which is everything. The critic has to educate the public; the artist has to educate the critic.

Allow me to make one more correction, sir, and I will have done with Mr Whibley. He ends his letter with the statement that I have been indefatigable in my public appreciation of my own work. I have no doubt that in saying this he means to pay me a compliment, but he really overrates my capacity, as well as my inclination for work. I must frankly confess that, by nature and by choice, I am extremely indolent. Cultivated idleness seems to me to be the proper occupation for man. I dislike newspaper controversies of any kind, and of the two hundred and sixteen criticisms of *Dorian Gray* that have passed from my library table into the wastepaper basket I have taken public notice of only three. One was that which appeared in the *Scots Observer*. I noticed it because it made a suggestion, about the intention of the author in writing the book, which needed correction. The second was an article in the *St James's Gazette*. It was offensively and vulgarly written, and seemed to me to require immediate and caustic censure. The tone of the article was an impertinence to any man of letters. The third was a meek attack in a paper called the *Daily Chronicle*. I think my writing to the *Daily Chronicle* was an act of pure wilfulness. In fact, I feel sure it was. I quite forget what they said. I believe they said that *Dorian Gray* was poisonous, and I thought that, on alliterative grounds, it would be kind to remind them that, however that may be, it is at any rate perfect. That was all. Of the other two hundred and thirteen criticisms I have taken no notice. Indeed, I have not read more than half of them. It is a sad thing, but one wearies even of praise.

As regards Mr Brown's letter, it is interesting only in so far as it exemplifies the truth of what I have said above on the question of the two obvious schools of critics. Mr Brown says frankly that he considers morality to be the "strong point" of my story. Mr Brown means well, and has got hold of a half-truth, but when he proceeds to deal with the book from the artistic standpoint he, of course, goes sadly astray. To class *Dorian Gray* with M. Zola's *La Terre* is as silly as if one were to class Musset's [Gautier's] *Fortunio* with one of the Adelphi melodramas. Mr Brown should be content with ethical appreciation. There he is impregnable.

Mr Cobban opens badly by describing my letter, setting Mr Whibley right on a matter of fact, as an "impudent paradox." The term "impudent" is meaningless, and the word "paradox" is misplaced. I am afraid that writing to newspapers has a deteriorating influence on style. People get violent, and abusive, and lose all sense of proportion, when they enter that curious journalistic arena in which the race is always to the noisiest. "Impudent paradox" is neither violent nor abusive, but it is not an expression that should have been used about my letter. However, Mr Cobban makes full atonement afterwards for what was, no doubt, a mere error of manner, by adopting the impudent paradox in question as his own, and pointing out that, as I had previously said, the artist will always look at the work of art from the standpoint of beauty of style and beauty of treatment, and that those who have not got the sense of beauty, or whose sense of beauty is dominated by ethical considerations, will always turn their attention to the subject-matter and make its moral import the test and touchstone of the poem, or novel, or picture, that is presented to them, while the newspaper critic will sometimes take one side and sometimes the other, according as he is cultured or uncultured. In fact, Mr Cobban converts the impudent paradox into a tedious truism, and, I dare say, in doing so does good service.

The English public like tediousness, and like things to be explained to them in a tedious way. Mr. Cobban has, I have no doubt, already repented of the unfortunate expression with which he has made his *début*, so I will say no more about it. As far as I am concerned he is quite forgiven.

And finally, sir, in taking leave of the *Scots Observer* I feel bound to make a candid confession to you. It has been suggested to me by a great friend of mine, who is a charming and distinguished man of letters, and not unknown to you personally[1] that there have been really only two people engaged in this terrible controversy, and that those two people are the editor of the *Scots Observer* and the author of *Dorian Gray*. At dinner this evening, over some excellent Chianti, my friend insisted that under assumed and mysterious names you had simply given dramatic expression to the views of some of the semi-educated classes in our community, and that the letters signed "H" were your own skilful, if somewhat bitter, caricature of the Philistine as drawn by himself. I admit that something of the kind had occurred to me when I read "H's" first letter—the one in which he proposed that the test of art should be the political opinions of the artist, and that if one differed from the artist on the question of the best way of misgoverning Ireland, one should always abuse his work. Still, there are such infinite varieties of Philistines, and North Britain is so renowned for seriousness, that I dismissed the idea as one unworthy of the editor of a Scotch paper. I now fear that I was wrong, and that you have been amusing yourself all the time by inventing little puppets and teaching them how to use big words. Well, sir, if it be so—and my friend is strong upon the point—allow me to congratulate you most sincerely on the cleverness with which you have reproduced that lack of literary style which is, I am told, essential for any dramatic and lifelike characterisation. I confess that I was completely taken in; but I bear no malice; and as you have no doubt been laughing at me in your sleeve, let me now join openly in the laugh, though it be a little against myself. A comedy ends when the secret is out. Drop your curtain, and put your dolls to bed. I

[1] Robert Ross, as Rupert Hart-Davis suggests.—Ed.

love Don Quixote, but I do not wish to fight any longer with marionettes, however cunning may be the master-hand that works their wires. Let them go, sir, on the shelf. The shelf is the proper place for them. On some future occasion you can re-label them and bring them out for our amusement. They are an excellent company, and go well through their tricks, and if they are a little unreal, I am not the one to object to unreality in art. The jest was really a good one. The only thing that I cannot understand is why you gave your marionettes such extraordinary and improbable names. I remain, sir, your obedient servant OSCAR WILDE

The Soul of Man under Socialism.*

The chief advantage that would result from the establishment of Socialism is, undoubtedly, the fact that Socialism would relieve us from that sordid necessity of living for others which, in the present condition of things, presses so hardly upon almost everybody. In fact, scarcely anyone at all escapes.

Now and then, in the course of the century, a great man of science, like Darwin; a great poet, like Keats; a fine critical spirit, like M. Renan; a supreme artist, like Flaubert, has been able to isolate himself, to keep himself out of reach of the clamorous claims of others, to stand "under the shelter of the wall," as Plato puts it, and so to realise the perfection of what was in him, to his own incomparable gain, and to the incomparable and lasting gain of the whole world. These, however, are exceptions. The majority of people spoil their lives by an unhealthy and exaggerated altruism—are forced, indeed, so to spoil them. They find themselves surrounded by hideous poverty, by hideous ugliness, by hideous starvation. It is inevitable that they should be strongly moved by all this. The emotions of man are stirred more quickly than man's intelligence; and, as I pointed out some time ago in an article on the function of criticism, it is much more easy to have sympathy with suffering than it is to have sympathy with thought. Accordingly,

* *Fortnightly Review* XLIX : 290 (February 1891) 292–319.

with admirable though misdirected intentions, they very seriously and very sentimentally set themselves to the task of remedying the evils that they see. But their remedies do not cure the disease: they merely prolong it. Indeed, their remedies are part of the disease.

They try to solve the problem of poverty, for instance, by keeping the poor alive or, in the case of a very advanced school, by amusing the poor.

But this is not a solution: it is an aggravation of the difficulty. *The proper aim is to try and reconstruct society on such a basis that poverty will be impossible.* And the altruistic virtues have really prevented the carrying out of this aim. Just as the worst slave-owners were those who were kind to their slaves, and so prevented the horror of the system being realised by those who suffered from it, and understood by those who contemplated it, so, in the present state of things in England, the people who do most harm are the people who try to do most good; and at last we have had the spectacle of men who have really studied the problem and know the life—educated men who live in the East-end—coming forward and imploring the community to restrain its altruistic impulses of charity, benevolence, and the like. They do so on the ground that such charity degrades and demoralizes. They are perfectly right. Charity creates a multitude of sins.

There is also this to be said. It is immoral to use private property in order to alleviate the horrible evils that result from the institution of private property. It is both immoral and unfair.

Under Socialism all this will, of course, be altered. There will be no people living in fetid dens and fetid rags, and bringing up unhealthy, hunger-pinched children in the midst of impossible and absolutely repulsive surroundings. The security of society will not depend, as it does now, on the state of the weather. If a frost comes we shall not have a hundred thousand men out of work, tramping about the streets in a state of disgusting misery, or whining to their neighbours for alms, or crowding round the doors of loathsome shelters to try and secure a hunch of bread and a night's unclean lodging. Each member of the society will share in the general prosperity and happiness of the society, and if a frost comes no one will practically be anything the worse.

Upon the other hand, *Socialism itself will be of value simply because it will lead to Individualism.*

Socialism, Communism, or whatever one chooses to call it, by converting private property into public wealth, and substituting cooperation for competition, will restore society to its proper condition of a thoroughly healthy organism, and insure the material well-being of each member of the community. It will, in fact, give Life its proper basis and its proper environment. But for the full development of Life to its highest mode of perfection, something more is needed. What is needed is Individualism. If the Socialism is Authoritarian; if there are Governments armed with economic power as they are now with political power; if, in a word, we are to have Industrial Tyrannies, then the last state of man will be worse than the first. At present, in consequence of the existence of private property, a great many people are enabled to develop a certain very limited amount of Individualism. They are either under no necessity to work for their living, or are enabled to choose the sphere of activity that is really congenial to them, and gives them pleasure. These are the poets, the philosophers, the men of science, the men of culture—in a word, the real men, the men who have realised themselves, and in whom all Humanity gains a partial realisation. Upon the other hand, there are a great many people who, having no private property of their own, and being always on the brink of sheer starvation, are compelled to do the work of beasts of burden, to do work that is quite uncongenial to them, and to which they are forced by the peremptory, unreasonable, degrading Tyranny of want. These are the poor, and amongst them there is no grace of manner, or charm of speech, or civilization, or culture, or refinement in pleasures, or joy of life. From their collective force Humanity gains much in material prosperity. But it is only the material result that it gains, and the man who is poor is in himself absolutely of no importance. He is merely the infinitesimal atom of a force that, so far from regarding him, crushes him: indeed, prefers him crushed, as in that case he is far more obedient.

Of course, it might be said that the Individualism generated under conditions of private property is not always, or even as a rule, of a fine or wonderful type, and that the poor, if they have not culture and charm, have still many virtues. Both these statements would be quite true. The possession of private property is very often extremely demoralising, and that is, of course, one of the reasons why Socialism wants to get rid of the institution. In fact, property is really a nuisance. Some years ago people went about the country saying that property has duties. They said it so often and so tediously that, at last, the church has begun to say it. One hears it now from every pulpit. It is perfectly true. Property not merely has duties, but has so many duties that its possession to any large extent is a bore. It involves endless claims upon one, endless attention to business, endless bother. If property had simply pleasures, we could stand it; but its duties make it unbearable. In the interest of the rich we must get rid of it. The virtues of the poor may be readily admitted, and are much to be regretted. We are often told that the poor are grateful for charity. Some of them are, no doubt, *but the best amongst the poor are never grateful.* They are ungrateful, discontented, disobedient, and rebellious. They are quite right to be so. Charity they feel to be a ridiculously inadequate mode of partial restitution, or a sentimental dole, usually accompanied by some impertinent attempt on the part of the sentimentalist to tyrannize over their private lives. Why should they be grateful for the crumbs that fall from the rich man's table? They should be seated at the board, and are beginning to know it. As for being discontented, a man who would not be discontented with such surroundings and such a low mode of life would be a perfect brute. Disobedience, in the eyes of any one who has read history, is man's original virtue. It is through disobedience that progress has been made, through disobedience and through rebellion. Sometimes the poor are praised for being thrifty. But to recommend thrift to the poor is both grotesque and insulting. It is like advising a man who is starving to eat less. For a town or country labourer to practise thrift would be absolutely immoral. Man should not be ready to show that he can live like a badly-fed animal. He should decline to live like that, and should either steal or go on the rates, which is considered by many to be a form of stealing. As for begging, it is safer to beg than to take, but it is finer to take than to beg. No: a poor man who is ungrateful, unthrifty, discontented, and rebellious is probably a real personality, and has much in him. He is at any rate a healthy protest. As for the virtuous poor, one can pity them, of course, but one cannot possibly admire them. They have made private terms with the enemy, and sold their birthright for very bad pottage. They must also be extraordinarily stupid. I can quite understand a man accepting laws that protect private property, and admit of its accumulation, as long as he himself is able under those conditions to realise some form of beautiful and intellectual life. But it is almost incredible to me how a man whose life is marred and made hideous by such laws can possibly acquiesce in their continuance.

However, the explanation is not really difficult to find. It is simply this. Misery and poverty are so absolutely degrading, and exercise such a paralysing effect over the nature of men, that no class is ever really conscious of its own suffering. They have to be told of it by other people, and they often entirely disbelieve them. What is said by great employers of labour against agitators is unquestionably true. Agitators are a set of interfering, meddling people, who come down to some perfectly contented class of the community, and sow the seeds of discontent amongst them. That is the reason why agitators are so absolutely necessary. Without them, in our incomplete state, there would be no advance towards civilization. Slavery was put down in America, not in consequence of any action on the part of the slaves, or even any express desire on their part that they should be free. It was put down entirely through the grossly illegal conduct of certain agitators in Boston and elsewhere, who were not slaves themselves, nor owners of slaves, nor had anything to do with the question really. It was, undoubtedly, the Abolitionists who set the torch alight, who began the whole thing. And it is curious to note that from the slaves themselves they received, not merely very little assistance, but hardly any sympathy even; and when at the close of the war the slaves found themselves free, found themselves indeed so absolutely free that they were free to starve, many of them bitterly regretted the new state of things. To the thinker, the most tragic fact in the whole of the French Revolution is not that Marie Antoinette was killed for being a queen, but that the starved peasant of the Vendee voluntarily went out to die for the hideous cause of feudalism.

It is clear, then, that no Authoritarian Socialism will do. For while under the present system a very large number of people can lead lives of a certain amount of freedom and expression and happiness, under an industrial-barrack system, or a system of economic tyranny, nobody would be able to have any such freedom at all. It is to be regretted that a portion of our community should be practically in slavery, but to propose to solve the problem by enslaving the entire community is childish. Every man must be left quite free to choose his own work. No form of compulsion must be exercised over him. If there is, his work will not be good for him, will not be good in itself, and will not be good for others. And by work I simply mean activity of any kind.

I hardly think that any Socialist, nowadays, would seriously propose that an inspector should call every morning at each house to see that each citizen rose up and did manual labour for eight hours. Humanity has got beyond that stage, and reserves such a form of life for the people whom, in a very arbitrary manner, it chooses to call criminals. But I confess that many of the socialistic views that I have come across seem to me to be tainted with ideas of authority, if not of actual compulsion. Of course authority and compulsion are out of the question. All association must be quite voluntary. *It is only in voluntary associations that man is fine.*

But it may be asked how Individualism, which is now more or less dependent on the existence of private property for its development, will benefit by the abolition of such private property. The answer is very simple. It is true that, under existing conditions, a few men who have had private means of their own, such as Byron, Shelley, Browning, Victor Hugo, Baudelaire, and others, have been able to realise their personality more or less completely. Not one of these men ever did a single day's work for hire. They were relieved from poverty. They had an immense advantage. The question is whether it would be for the good of Individualism that such an advantage should be taken away. Let us suppose that it is taken away. What happens then to Individualism? How will it benefit?

It will benefit in this way. Under the new conditions Individualism will be far freer, far finer, and far more intensified than it is now. I am not talking of the great imaginatively-realised individualism of such poets as I have mentioned, but of the great actual Individualism latent and potential in mankind generally. For the recognition of private property has really harmed Individualism, and obscured it, by confusing a man with what he possesses. It has led Individualism entirely astray. It has made gain not growth its aim. So that man thought that the imporant thing was to have, and did not know that the important thing is to be. *The true perfection of man lies, not in what man has, but in what man is.* Private property has crushed true Individualism, and set up an Individualism that is false. It has debarred one part of the community from being individual by starving them. It has debarred the other part of the community from being individual by putting them on the wrong road, and encumbering them. Indeed, so completely has man's personality been absorbed by his possessions that the English law has always treated offences against a man's property with far more severity than offences against his person, and property is still the test of complete citizenship. The industry necessary for the making money is also very demoralising. In a community like ours, where property confers immense distinction, social position, honour, respect, titles, and other pleasant things of the kind, man, being naturally ambitious, makes it his aim to accumulate this property, and goes on wearily and tediously accumulating it long after he has got far more than he wants, or can use, or enjoy, or perhaps even know of. Man will kill himself by over-work in order to secure property, and really, considering the enormous advantages that property brings, one is hardly surprised. One's regret is that society should be constructed on such a basis that man has been forced into a groove in which he cannot freely develop what is wonderful, and fascinating, and delightful in him—in which, in fact, he misses the true pleasure and joy of living. He is also, under existing conditions, very insecure. An enormously wealthy merchant may be—often is—at every moment of his life at the mercy of things that are not under his control. If the wind blows an extra point or so, or the weather suddenly changes, or some trivial thing happens, his ship may go down, his speculations may go wrong, and he finds himself a poor man, with his social position quite gone. Now, nothing should be able to harm a man except himself. Nothing should be able to rob a man at all. What a man really has, is what is in him. What is outside of him should be a matter of no importance.

With the abolition of private property, then, we shall have true beautiful, healthy Individualism. Nobody will waste his life in accumulating things, and the symbols for things. One will live. To live is the rarest thing in the world. Most people exist, that is all.

It is a question whether we have ever seen the full expression of a personality, except on the imaginative plane of art. In action, we never have. Cæsar, says Mommsen, was the complete and perfect man. But how tragically insecure was Cæsar! Wherever there is a man who exercises authority, there is a man who resists authority. Cæsar was very perfect, but his perfection travelled by too dangerous a road. Marcus Aurelius was the perfect man, says Renan. Yes; the great emperor was a perfect man. But how intolerable were the endless claims upon him! He staggered under the burden of the empire. He was conscious how inadequate one man was to bear the weight of that Titan and too vast orb. What I mean by a perfect man is one who develops under perfect conditions; one who is not wounded, or worried, or maimed, or in danger. *Most personalities have been obliged to be rebels. Half their strength has been wasted in friction.* Byron's personality, for instance, was terribly wasted in its battle with the stupidity, and hypocrisy, and Philistinism of the English. Such battles do not always intensify strength: they often exaggerate weakness. Byron was never able to give us what he might have given us. Shelley escaped better. Like Byron, he got out of England as soon as possible. But he was not so well known. If the English had had any idea of what a great poet he really was, they would have fallen on him with tooth and nail, and made his life as unbearable to him as they possibly could. But he was not a remarkable figure in society, and consequently he escaped, to a certain degree. Still, even in

Shelley the note of rebellion is sometimes too strong. The note of the perfect personality is not rebellion, but peace.

It will be a marvellous thing—the true personality of man—when we see it. It will grow naturally and simply, flower-like, or as a tree grows. It will not be at discord. It will never argue or dispute. It will not prove things. It will know everything. And yet it will not busy itself about knowledge. It will have wisdom. Its value will not be measured by material things. It will have nothing. And yet it will have everything, and whatever one takes from it, it will still have, so rich will it be. It will not be always meddling with others, or asking them to be like itself. It will love them because they will be different. And yet while it will not meddle with others it will help all, as a beautiful thing helps us, by being what it is. The personality of man will be very wonderful. It will be as wonderful as the personality of a child.

In its development it will be assisted by Christianity, if men desire that; but if men do not desire that, it will develop none the less surely. For it will not worry itself about the past, nor care whether things happened or did not happen. Nor will it admit any laws but its own laws; nor any authority but its own authority. Yet it will love those who sought to intensify it, and speak often of them. And of these Christ was one.

"Know Thyself" was written over the portal of the antique world. Over the portal of the new world, "Be thyself" shall be written. And the message of Christ to man was simply "Be thyself." That is the secret of Christ.

When Jesus talks about the poor he simply means personalities, just as when he talks about the rich he simply means people who have not developed their personalities. Jesus moved in a community that allowed the accumulation of private property just as ours does, and the gospel that he preached was not that in such a community it is an advantage for a man to live on scanty, unwholesome food, to wear ragged, unwholesome clothes, to sleep in horrid, unwholesome dwellings, and a disadvantage for a man to live under healthy, pleasant, and decent conditions. Such a view would have been wrong there and then, and would of course be still more wrong now and in England; for as man moves northwards the material necessities of life become of more vital importance, and our society is infinitely

263

more complex, and displays far greater extremes of luxury and pauperism than any society of the antique world. What Jesus meant, was this. He said to man, "You have a wonderful personality. Develop it. Be yourself. Don't imagine that your perfection lies in accumulating or possessing external things. Your perfection is inside of you. If only you could realise that, you would not want to be rich. Ordinary riches can be stolen from a man. Real riches cannot. In the treasury-house of your soul, there are infinitely precious things, that may not be taken from you. And so, try to so shape your life that external things will not harm you. And try also to get rid of personal property. It involves sordid preoccupation, endless industry, continual wrong. Personal property hinders Individualism at every step." It is to be noted that Jesus never says that impoverished people are necessarily good, or wealthy people necessarily bad. That would not have been true. Wealthy people are, as a class, better than impoverished people, more moral, more intellectual, more well-behaved. *There is only one class in the community that thinks more about money than the rich, and that is the poor.* The poor can think of nothing else. That is the misery of being poor. What Jesus does say is that man reaches his perfection, not through what he has, not even through what he does, but entirely through what he is. And so the wealthy young man who comes to Jesus is represented as a thoroughly good citizen, who has broken none of the laws of his state, none of the commandments of his religion. He is quite respectable, in the ordinary sense of that extraordinary word. Jesus says to him, "You should give up private property. It hinders you from realising your perfection. It is a drag within you, and not outside of you, that you will find what you really are, and what you really want." To his own friends he says the same thing. He tells them to be themselves, and not to be always worrying about other things. What do other things matter? Man is complete in himself. When they go into the world, the world will disagree with them. That is inevitable. The world hates Individualism. But this is not to trouble them. They are to be calm and self-centred. If a man takes their cloak, they are to give him their coat, just to show that material things are of no importance. If people abuse them, they are not to answer back. What does it signify? The things people say of a man do not alter a man. He is what he is. Public opinion is of no value whatsoever. Even if people employ actual violence, they are not to be violent in turn. That would be to fall to the same low level. After all, even in prison, a man can be quite free. His soul can be free. His personality can be untroubled. He can be at peace. And, above all things, they are not to interfere with other people or judge them in any way. Personality is a very mysterious thing. A man cannot always be estimated by what he does. He may keep the law, and yet be worthless. He may break the law, and yet be fine. He may be bad, without ever doing anything bad. He may commit a sin against society, and yet realise through that sin his true perfection.

There was a woman who was taken in adultery. We are not told the history of her love, but that love must have been very great; for Jesus said that her sins were forgiven her, not because she repented, but because her love was so intense and wonderful. Later on, a short time before his death, as he sat at a feast, the woman came in and poured costly perfumes on his hair. His friends tried to interfere with her, and said that it was an extravagance, and that the money that the perfume cost should have been expended on charitable relief of people in want, or something of that kind. Jesus did not accept that view. He pointed out that the material needs of Man were great and very permanent, but that the spiritual needs of Man were greater still, and that in one divine moment, and by selecting its own mode of expression, a personality might make itself perfect. The world worships the woman, even now, as a saint.

Yes; there are suggestive things in Individualism. Socialism annihilates family life, for instance. With the abolition of private property, marriage in its present form must disappear. This is part of the programme. Individualism accepts this and makes it fine. It converts the abolition of legal restraint into a form of freedom that will help the full development of personality, and make the love of man and woman more wonderful, more beautiful, and more ennobling. Jesus knew this. He rejected the claims of family life, although they existed in his day and community in a very marked form. "Who is my mother? Who are my brothers?" he said, when he was told that they wished to speak to him. When one of his followers asked leave to go and bury his father, "Let the dead bury the dead," was his terrible answer. He would allow no claim whatsoever to be made on personality.

And so he who would lead a Christ-like life is he who is perfectly and absolutely himself. He may be a great poet, or a great man of science; or a young student at a University, or one who watches sheep upon a moor; or a maker of dramas, like Shakespeare, or a thinker about God, like Spinoza; or a child who plays in a garden, or a fisherman who throws his nets into the sea. It does not matter what he is, as long as he realises the perfection of the soul that is within him. All imitation in morals and in life is wrong. Through the streets of Jerusalem at the present day crawls one who is mad and carries a wooden cross on his shoulders. He is a symbol of the lives that are marred by imitation. Father Damien was Christ-like when he went out to live with the lepers, because in such service he realised fully what was best in him. But he was not more Christ-like than Wagner, when he realised his soul in music; or than Shelley, when he realised his soul in song. There is no one type for man. There are as many perfections as their are imperfect men. And while to the claims of charity a man may yield and yet be free, to the claims of conformity no man may yield and remain free at all.

Individualism, then, is what through Socialism we are to attain to. As a natural result the State must give up all idea of government. It must give it up because, as a wise man once said many centuries before Christ, there is such a thing as leaving mankind alone; there is no such thing as governing mankind. *All modes of government are failures.* Despotism is unjust to everybody, including the despot, who was probably made for better things. Oligarchies are unjust to the many, and ochlocracies are unjust to the few. High hopes were once formed of democracy; but democracy means simply the bludgeoning of the people by the people for the people. It has been found out. I must say that it was high time, for all authority is quite degrading. It degrades those who exercise it, and degrades those over whom it is exercised. When it is violently, grossly, and cruelly used, it produces a good effect, by creating, or at any rate bringing out, the spirit of revolt and individualism that is to kill it. When it is used with a certain amount of kindness, and accompanied by prizes and rewards, it is dreadfully demoralizing. People, in that case, are less conscious of the horrible pressure that is being put on them, and so go through their lives in a sort of coarse comfort, like petted animals, without ever realising that they are probably thinking other people's thoughts, living by other people's standards, wearing practically what one may call other people's second-hand clothes, and never being themselves for a single moment. "He who would be free," says a fine thinker, "must not conform." And authority, by bribing people to conform, produces a very gross kind of over-fed barbarism amongst us.

With authority, punishment will pass away. This will be a great gain—a gain, in fact, of incalculable value. As one reads history, not in the expurgated editions written for schoolboys and passmen, but in the original authorities of each time, one is absolutely sickened, not by the crimes that the wicked have committed, but by the punishments that the good have inflicted; *and a community is infinitely more brutalised by the habitual employment of punishment, than it is by the occasional occurrence of crime.* It obviously follows that the more punishment is inflicted the more crime is produced, and most modern legislation has clearly recognised this, and has made it its task to diminish punishment as far as it thinks it can. Wherever it has really diminished it, the results have always been extremely good. The less punishment, the less crime. When there is not punishment at all, crime will either cease to exist, or if it occurs, will be treated by physicians as a very distressing form of dementia, to be cured by care and kindness. For what are called criminals nowadays are not criminals at all. Starvation, and not sin, is the parent of modern crime. That indeed is the reason why our criminals are, as a class, so absolutely uninteresting from any psychological point of view. They are not marvellous Macbeths and terrible Vautrins. They are merely what ordinary, respectable, commonplace people would be if they had not got enough to eat. When private property is abolished there will be no necessity for crime, no demand for it; it will cease to exist. Of course all crimes are not crimes against property, though such are the crimes that the English law, valuing what a man has more than what a man is, punishes with the harshest and most horrible severity, if we except the crime of murder, and regard death as worse than penal servitude, a point on which our criminals, I believe, disagree. But though a crime may not be against property, it may spring from the misery and rage and depression produced by our wrong system of property-holding, and so, when that system is abolished, will disappear. When each member of the community has sufficient for his wants, and is not interfered with by his neighbour, it will not be an object of any interest to him to interfere with anyone else. Jealousy, which is an extraordinary source of crime in modern life, is an emotion closely bound up with our conceptions of property, and under Socialism and Individualism will die out. It is remarkable that in communistic tribes jealousy is entirely unknown.

Now as the State is not to govern, it may be asked what the State is to do. The State is to be a voluntary association that will organize labour, and be the manufacturer and distributor of necessary commodities. *The State is to make what is useful. The individual is to make what is beautiful.* And as I have mentioned the word labour, I cannot help saying that a great deal of nonsense is being written and talked nowadays about the dignity of manual labour. There is nothing necessarily dignified about manual labour at all, and most of it is absolutely degrading. It is mentally and morally injurious to man to do anything in which he does not find pleasure, and many forms of labour are quite pleasureless activities, and should be regarded as such. To sweep a slushy crossing for eight hours on a day when the east wind is blowing is a disgusting occupation. To sweep it with mental, moral, or physical dignity seems to me to be impossible. To sweep it with joy would be appalling. Man is made for something better than disturbing dirt. All work of that kind should be done by a machine.

And I have no doubt that it will be so. Up to the present, man has been, to a certain extent, the slave of machinery, and there is something tragic in the fact that as soon as man had invented a machine to do his work he began to starve. This, however, is, of course, the result of our property system and our system of competition. One man owns a machine which does the work of five hundred men. Five hundred men are, in consequence, thrown out of employment, and having no work to do, become hungry and take to thieving. The one man secures the produce of the machine and keeps it, and has five hundred times as much as he should have, and probably, which is of much more importance, a great deal more than he really wants. Were that machine the property of all, every one would benefit by it. It would be an immense advantage to the community. All unintellectual labour, all monotonous, dull labour, all labour that deals with dreadful things, and involves unpleasant conditions, must be done by machinery. Machinery must work for us in coal mines, and do all sanitary services, and be the stoker of steamers, and clean the streets, and run messages on wet days, and do anything that is tedious or distressing. *At present machinery competes against man. Under proper conditions machinery will serve man.* There is no doubt at all that this is the future of machinery, and just as trees grow while the country gentleman is asleep, so while Humanity will be amusing itself, or enjoying cultivated leisure—which, and not labour, is the aim of man—or making beautiful things, or reading beautiful things, or simply contemplating the world with admiration and delight, machinery will be doing all the necessary and unpleasant work. The fact is, that civilization requires slaves. The Greeks were quite right there. Unless there are slaves to do the ugly, horrible, uninteresting work, culture and contemplation become almost impossible. Human slavery is wrong, insecure, and demoralising. On mechanical slavery, on the slavery of the machine, the future of the world depends. And when scientific men are no longer called upon to go down to a depressing East-end and distribute bad cocoa and worse blankets to starving people, they will have delightful leisure in which to devise wonderful and marvellous things for their own joy and the joy of everyone else. There will be great storages of force for every city, and for every house if required, and this force man will convert into heat, light, or motion, according to his needs. Is this Utopian? A map of the world that does not include Utopia is not worth even glancing at, for it leaves out the one country at which Humanity is always landing. And when Humanity lands there, it looks out, and, seeing a better country, sets sail. Progress is the realisation of Utopias.

Now, I have said that the community by means of organization of machinery will supply the useful things, and that the beautiful things will be made by the individual. This is not merely necessary, but it is the only possible way by which we can get either the one or the other. An individual who has to make things for the use of others, and with reference to their wants and their wishes, does not work with interest, and consequently cannot put into his work what is best in him. Upon the other hand, whenever a community or a powerful section of a community, or a government of any kind, attempts to dictate to the artist what he is to do, Art either entirely vanishes, or becomes stereotyped, or degenerates into a low and ignoble form of craft. *A work of art is the unique result of a unique temperament. Its beauty comes from the fact that the author is what he is. It has nothing to do with the fact that other people want what they want.* Indeed, the moment that an artist takes notice of what other people want, and tries to supply the demand, he ceases to be an artist, and becomes a dull or an amusing craftsman, an honest or a dishonest tradesman. He has no further claim to be considered as an artist. *Art is the most intense mode of individualism that the world has known.* I am inclined to say that it is the only real mode of individualism that the world has known. Crime, which, under certain conditions, may seem to have created individualism, must take cognizance of other people and interfere with them. It belongs to the sphere of action. But alone, without any reference to his neighbours, without any interference, the artist can fashion a beautiful thing; and if he does not do it solely for his own pleasure, he is not an artist at all.

And it is to be noted that it is the fact that Art is this intense form of individualism that makes the public try to exercise over it an authority that is as immoral as it is ridiculous, and as corrupting as it is contemptible. It is not quite their fault. The public has always, and in every age, been badly brought up. They are continually asking Art to be popular, to please their want of taste, to flatter their absurd vanity, to tell them what they have been told before, to show them what they ought to be tired of seeing, to amuse them when they feel heavy after eating too much, and to distract their thoughts when they are wearied of their own stupidity. *Now Art should never try to be popular. The public should try to make itself artistic.* There is a very wide difference. If a man of science were told that the results of his experiments, and the conclusions that he arrived at, should be of such a character that they would not upset the received popular notions on the subject, or disturb popular prejudice, or hurt the sensibilities of people who knew nothing about science; if a philosopher were told that he had a perfect right to speculate in the highest spheres of thought, provided that he arrived at the same conclusions as were held by those who had never thought in any sphere at all—well, nowadays the man of science and the philosopher would be considerably amused. Yet it is really a very few years since both philosophy and science were subjected to brutal popular control, to authority in fact—the authority of either the general ignorance of the community, or the terror and greed for power of an ecclesiastical or governmental class. Of course, we have to a very great extent got rid of any attempt on the part of the community, or the Church, or the Government, to interfere with the individualism of speculative thought, but the attempt to interfere with the individualism of imaginative art still lingers. In fact, it does more than linger: it is aggressive, offensive, and brutalizing.

In England, the arts that have escaped best are the arts in which the public take no interest. Poetry is an instance of what I mean. We have been able to have fine poetry in England because the public do not read it, and consequently do not influence it. The public like to insult poets because they are individual, but once they have insulted them they leave them alone. In the case of the novel and the drama, arts in which the public does take an interest, the result of the exercise of popular authority has been absolutely ridiculous. No country produces such badly written fiction, such tedious, common work in the novel-form, such silly, vulgar plays as in England. It must necessarily be so. The popular standard is of such a character that no artist can get to it. It is at once too easy and too difficult to be a popular novelist. It is too easy, because the requirements of the public as far as plot, style, psychology, treatment of life, and treatment of literature are concerned are within the reach of the very meanest capacity and the most uncultivated mind. It is too difficult, because to meet such requirements the artist would have to do violence to his temperament, would have to write not for the artistic joy of writing, but for the amusement of half-educated people, and so would have to suppress his individualism, forget his culture, annihilate his style, and surrender everything that is valuable in him. In the case of the drama, things are a little better: the theatre-going public like the obvious, it is true, but they do not like the tedious; and burlesque and farcical comedy, the two most popular forms, are distinct forms of art. Delightful work may be produced under burlesque and farcical conditions, and in work of this kind the artist in England is allowed very great freedom. It is when one comes to the higher forms of the drama that the result of popular control is seen. The one thing that the public dislike is novelty. Any attempt to extend the subject-matter of art is extremely distasteful to the public; and yet the vitality and progress of art depend in a large measure on the continual extension of subject-matter. The public dislike novelty because they are afraid of it. It represents to them a mode of Individualism, an assertion on the part of the artist that he selects his own subject, and treats it as he chooses. The public are quite right in their attitude. Art is Individualism, and Individualism is a disturbing and disintegrating force. Therein lies its immense value. For what it seeks to disturb is monotony of type, slavery of custom, tyranny of habit, and the reduction of man to the level of a machine. In Art, the public accept what has been, because they cannot alter it, not because they appreciate it. They swallow their classics whole, and never taste them. They endure them as the inevitable, and, as they cannot mar them, they mouth about them. Strangely enough, or not strangely, according to one's own views, this acceptance of the classics does a great deal of harm. The uncritical admiration of the Bible and Shakespeare in England is an instance of what I mean. With regard to the Bible, considerations of ecclesiastical authority enter into the matter, so that I need not dwell upon the point.

But in the case of Shakespeare it is quite obvious that the public really see neither the beauties nor the defects of his plays. If they saw the beauties, they would not object to the development of the drama; and if they saw the defects, they would not object to the development of the drama either. *The fact is, the public makes use of the classics of a country as a means of checking the progress of Art.* They degrade the classics into authorities. They use them as bludgeons for preventing the free expression of Beauty in new forms. They are always asking a writer why he does not write like somebody else, or a painter why he does not paint like somebody else, quite oblivious of the fact that if either of them did anything of the kind he would cease to be an artist. A fresh mode of Beauty is absolutely distasteful to them, and whenever it appears they get so angry and bewildered that they always use two stupid expressions—one is that the work of art is grossly unintelligible; the other, that the work of art is grossly immoral. What they mean by these words seems to me to be this. When they say a work is grossly unintelligible, they mean that the artist has said or made a beautiful thing that is new; when they describe a work as grossly immoral, they mean that the artist has said or made a beautiful thing that is true. The former expression has reference to style; the latter to subject matter. But they probably use the words very vaguely, as an ordinary mob will use ready-made paving-stones. *There is not a single real poet or prose-writer of this century, for instance, on whom the British public have not solemnly conferred diplomas of immorality,* and these diplomas practically take the place, with us, of what in France is the formal recognition of an Academy of Letters, and fortunately make the establishment of such an institution quite unnecessary in England. Of course the public are very reckless in their use of the word. That they should have called Wordsworth an immoral poet, was only to be expected. Wordsworth was a poet. But that they should have called Charles Kingsley an immoral novelist is extraordinary. Kingsley's prose was not of a very fine quality. Still, there is the word, and they use it as best they can. An artist is, of course, not disturbed by it. The true artist is a man who believes absolutely in himself, because he is absolutely himself. But I can fancy that if an artist produced a work of art in England that immediately on its appearance was recognised by the public, through their medium, which is the public press, as a work that was quite intelligible and highly moral, he would begin to seriously question whether in its creation he had really been himself at all, and consequently whether the work was not quite unworthy of him, and either of a thoroughly second-rate order, or of no artistic value whatsoever.

Perhaps, however, I have wronged the public in limiting them to such words as "immoral," "unintelligible," "exotic," and "unhealthy." There is one other word that they use. That word is "morbid." They do not use it often. The meaning of the word is so simple that they are not afraid of using it. Still, they use it sometimes, and, now and then, one comes across it in popular newspapers. It is, of course, a ridiculous word to apply to a work of art. For what is morbidity but a mood of emotion or a mode of thought that one cannot express? The public are all morbid, because the public can never find expression for anything. *The artist is never morbid. He expresses everything.* He stands outside his subject, and through its medium produces incomparable and artistic effects. To call an artist morbid because he deals with morbidity as his subject matter is as silly as if one called Shakespeare mad because he wrote *King Lear*.

On the whole, an artist in England gains something by being attacked. His individuality is intensified. He becomes more completely himself. Of course the attacks are very gross, very impertinent, and very contemptible. But then no artist expects grace from the vulgar mind, or style from the suburban intellect. Vulgarity and stupidity are two very vivid facts in modern life. One regrets them, naturally. But there they are. They are subjects for study, like everything else. And it is only fair to state, with regard to modern journalists, that they always apologise to one in private for what they have written against one in public.

Within the last few years two other adjectives, it may be mentioned, have been added to the very limited vocabulary of art-abuse that is at the disposal of the public. One is the word "unhealthy," the other is the word "exotic." The latter merely expresses the rage of the momentary mushroom against the immortal, entrancing, and exquisitely-lovely orchid. It is a tribute, but a tribute of no importance. The word "unhealthy," however, admits of analysis. It is a rather interesting word. In fact, it is so interesting that the people who use it do not know what it means.

What does it mean? What is a healthy, or an unhealthy work of art? All terms that one applies to a work of art, provided that one applies them rationally, have reference to either its style or its subject, or to both together. From the point of view of style, a healthy work of art is one whose style recognises the beauty of the material it employs, be that material one of words or of bronze, of colour or of ivory, and uses that beauty as a factor in producing the æsthetic effect. From the point of view of subject, a healthy work of art is one the choice whose subject is conditioned by the temperament of the artist, and comes directly out of it. In fine, a healthy work of art is one that has both perfection and personality. Of course, form and substance cannot be separated in a work of art; they are always one. But for purposes of analysis, and setting the wholeness of æsthetic impression aside for a moment, we can intellectually so separate them. An unhealthy work of art, on the other hand, is a work whose style is obvious, old-fashioned, and common, and whose subject is deliberately chosen, not because the artist has any pleasure in it, but because he thinks that the public will pay him for it. *In fact, the popular novel that the public calls healthy is always a thoroughly unhealthy production; and what the public call an unhealthy novel is always a beautiful and healthy work of art.*

I need hardly say that I am not, for a single moment, complaining that the public and the public press misuse these words. I do not see how, with their lack of comprehension of what Art is, they could possibly use them in the proper sense. I am merely pointing out the misuse; and as for the origin of the misuse and the meaning that lies behind it all, the explanation is very simple. It comes from the barbarous conception of authority. It comes from the natural inability of a community corrupted by authority to understand or appreciate Individualism. In a word, it comes from that monstrous and ignorant thing that is called Public Opinion, which bad and well-meaning as it is when it tries to control action, is infamous and of evil meaning when it tries to control Thought or Art.

Indeed, there is much more to be said in favour of the physical force of the public than there is in favour of the public's opinion. The former may be fine. The latter must be foolish. It is often said that force is no argument. That, however, entirely depends on what one wants to prove. Many of the most important problems of the last few centuries, such as the continuance of personal government in England, or of feudalism in France, have been solved entirely by means of physical force. The very violence of a revolution may make the public grand and splendid for a moment. It was a fatal day when the public discovered that the pen is mightier than the paving-stone, and can be made as offensive as the brickbat. They at once sought for the journalist, found him, developed him, and made him their industrious and well-paid servant. It is greatly to be regretted, for both their sakes. Behind the barricade there may be much that is noble and heroic. But what is there behind the leading-article but prejudice, stupidity, cant, and twaddle? And when these four are joined together they make a terrible force, and constitute the new authority.

In old days men had the rack. Now they have the press. That is an improvement certainly. But still it is very bad, and wrong, and demoralising. Somebody—was it Burke?—called journalism the fourth estate. That was true at the time, no doubt. But at the present moment it really is the only estate. It has eaten up the other three. The Lords Temporal say nothing, the Lords Spiritual have nothing to say, and the House of Commons has nothing to say and says it. We are dominated by Journalism. In America the President reigns for four years, and Journalism governs for ever and ever. Fortunately in America journalism has carried its authority to the grossest and most brutal extreme. As a natural consequence it has begun to create a spirit of revolt. People are amused by it, or disgusted by it, according to their temperaments. But it is no longer the real force it was. It is not seriously treated. In England, Journalism, not, except in a few well-known instances, having been carried to such excesses of brutality, is still a great factor, a really remarkable power. The tyranny that it proposes to exercise over people's private lives seems to me to be quite extraordinary. *The fact is, that the public have an insatiable curiosity to know everything, except what is worth knowing.* Journalism, conscious of this, and having tradesmanlike habits, supplies their demands. In centuries before ours the public nailed the ears of journalists to the pump. That was quite hideous. In this century journalists have nailed their own ears to the keyhole. That is much worse. And what aggravates the mischief is that the journalists who are most to blame are not the amusing journalists who write for what are called Society papers. The harm is done by the serious, thoughtful, earnest journalists, who solemnly, as they are doing at present, will drag before the eyes of the public some incident in the private life of a great statesman, of a man who is a leader of political thought as he is a creator of political force, and invite the public to discuss the incident, to exercise authority in the matter, to give their views, and not merely to give their views, but to carry them into action, to dictate to the man upon all other points, to dictate to his party, to dictate to his country, in fact to make themselves ridiculous, offensive, and harmful. The private lives of men and women should not be told to the public. The public have nothing to do with them at all. In France they manage these things better. There they do not allow the details of the trials that take place in the divorce courts to be published for the amusement or criticism of the public. All that the public are allowed to know is that the divorce has taken place and was granted on petition of one or other or both of the married parties concerned. In France, in fact, they limit the journalist, and allow the artist almost perfect freedom. *Here we allow absolute freedom to the journalist, and entirely limit the artist.* English public opinion, that is to say, tries to constrain and impede and warp the man who makes things that are beautiful in effect, and compels the journalist to retail things that are ugly, or disgusting, or revolting in fact, so that we have the most serious journalists in the world, and the most indecent newspapers. It is no exaggeration to talk of compulsion. There are possibly some journalists who take a real pleasure in publishing horrible things, or who, being poor, look to scandals as forming a sort of permanent basis for an income. But there are other journalists, I feel certain, men of education and cultivation, who really dislike publishing these things, who know that it is wrong to do so, and only do it because the unhealthy conditions under which their occupation is carried on oblige them to supply the public with what the public wants, and to compete with other journalists in making that supply as full and satisfying to the gross popular appetite as possible. It is a very degrading position for any body of educated men to be placed in, and I have no doubt that most of them feel it acutely.

However, let us leave what is really a very sordid side of the subject, and return to the question of popular control in the matter of Art, by which I mean Public Opinion dictating to the artist the form which he is to use, the mode in which he is to use it, and the materials with which he is to work. I have pointed out that the arts which have escaped best in England are the arts in which the public have not been interested. They are, however, interested in the drama, and as a certain advance has been made in the drama within the last ten or fifteen years, it is important to point out that this advance is entirely due to a few individual artists refusing to accept the popular want of taste as their standard, and refusing to regard Art as a mere matter of demand and supply. With his marvellous and vivid personality, with a style that has really a true colour-element in it, with his extraordinary power, not over mere mimicry but over imaginative and intellectual creation, Mr. Irving, had his sole object been to give the public what they wanted, could have produced the commonest plays in the commonest manner, and made as much success and money as a man could possibly desire. But his object was not that. His object was to realise his own perfection as an artist, under certain conditions, and in certain forms of Art. At first he appealed to the few: now he has educated the many. He has created in the public both taste and temperament. The public appreciate his artistic success immensely. I often wonder, however, whether the public understand that that success is entirely due to the fact that he did not accept their standard, but realised his own. With their standard the Lyceum would have been a sort of second-rate booth, as some of the popular theatres in London are at present. Whether they understand it or not the fact however remains, that taste and temperament have, to a certain extent, been created in the public, and that the public is capable of developing these qualities. The problem then is, why do not the public become more civilised? They have the capacity. What stops them?

The thing that stops them, it must be said again, is their desire to exercise authority over the artist and over works of art. To certain theatres, such as the Lyceum and the Haymarket, the public seem to come in a proper mood. In both of these theatres there have been individual artists, who have succeeded in creating in their audiences—and every theatre in London has its own audience—the temperament to which Art appeals. And what is that temperament? It is the temperament of receptivity. That is all.

If a man approaches a work of art with any desire to exercise authority over it and the artist, he approaches it in such a spirit that he cannot receive any artistic impression from it at all. *The work of art is to dominate the spectator: the spectator is not to dominate the work of art.* The spectator is to be receptive. He is to be the violin on which the master is to play. And the more completely he can suppress his own silly views, his own foolish prejudices, his own absurd ideas of what Art should be or should not be, the more likely he is to understand and appreciate the work of art in question. This is, of course, quite obvious in the case of the vulgar theatre-going public of English men and women. But it is equally true of what are called educated people. For an educated person's ideas of Art are drawn naturally from what Art has been, whereas the new work of art is beautiful by being what Art has never been; and to measure it by the standard of the past is to measure it by a standard on the rejection of which its real perfection depends. A temperament capable of receiving, through an imaginative medium, and under imaginative conditions, new and beautiful impressions is the only temperament that can appreciate a work of art. And true as this is in the case of the appreciation of sculpture and painting, it is still more true of the appreciation of such arts as the drama. For a picture and a statue are not at war with Time. They take no count of its succession. In one moment their unity may be apprehended. In the case of literature it is different. Time must be traversed before the unity of effect is realised. And so, in the drama, there may occur in the first act of the play something whose real artistic value may not be evident to the spectator till the third or fourth act is reached. Is the silly fellow to get angry and call out, and disturb the play, and annoy the artists? No. The honest man is to sit quietly, and know the delightful emotions of wonder, curiosity, and suspense. He is not to go to the play to lose a vulgar temper. He is to go to the play to realise an artistic temperament. He is to go to the play to gain an artistic temperament. He is not the arbiter of the work of art. He is one who is admitted to contemplate the work of art, and, if the work be fine, to forget in its contemplation all the egotism that mars him—the egotism of his ignorance, or the egotism of his information. This point about the drama is hardly, I think, sufficiently recognised. I can quite understand that were *Macbeth* produced for the first time before a modern London audience, many of the people present would strongly and vigorously object to the introduction of the witches in the first act, with their grotesque phrases and their ridiculous words. But when the play is over one realises that the laughter of the witches in *Macbeth* is as terrible as the laughter of madness in *Lear*, more terrible than the laughter of Iago in the tragedy of the Moor. No spectator of art needs a more perfect mood of receptivity than the spectator of a play. The moment he seeks to exercise authority he becomes the avowed enemy of Art and of himself. Art does not mind. It is he who suffers.

With the novel it is the same thing. Popular authority and the recognition of popular authority are fatal. Thackeray's *Esmond* is a beautiful work of art because he wrote it to please himself. In his other novels, in *Pendennis*, in *Philip*, in *Vanity Fair* even, at times, he is too conscious of the public, and spoils his work by appealing directly to the sympathies of the public, or by directly mocking at them. *A true artist takes no notice whatever of the public. The public are to him non-existent.* He has no poppied or honeyed cakes through which to give the monster sleep or sustenance. He leaves that to the popular novelist. One incomparable novelist we have now in England, Mr. George Meredith. There are better artists in France, but France has no one whose view of life is so large, so varied, so imaginatively true. There are tellers of stories in Russia who have a more vivid sense of what pain in fiction may be. But to him belongs philosophy in fiction. His people not merely live, but they live in thought. One can see them from myriad points of view. They are suggestive. There is soul in them and around them. They are interpretative and symbolic. And he who made them, those wonderful quickly-moving figures, made them for his own pleasure, and has never asked the public what they wanted, has never cared to know what they wanted, has never allowed the public to dictate to him or influence him in any way, but has gone on intensifying his own personality, and producing his own individual work. At first none came to him. That did not matter. Then the few came to him. That did not change him. The many have come now. He is still the same. He is an incomparable novelist.

With the decorative arts it is not different. The public clung with really pathetic tenacity to what I believe were the direct traditions of the Great Exhibition of international vulgarity, traditions that were so appalling that the houses in which people lived were only fit for blind people to live in. Beautiful things began to be made, beautiful colours came from the dyer's hand, beautiful patterns from the artist's brain, and the use of beautiful things and their value and importance were set forth. The public were really very indignant. They lost their temper. They said silly things. No one minded. No one was a whit the worse. No one accepted the authority of public opinion. And now it is almost impossible to enter any modern house without seeing some recognition of good taste, some recognition of the value of lovely surroundings, some sign of appreciation of beauty. In fact, people's houses are, as a rule, quite charming nowadays. People have been to a very great extent civilised. It is only fair to state, however, that the extraordinary success of the revolution in house-decoration and furniture and the like has not really been due to the majority of the public developing a very fine taste in such matters. It has been chiefly due to the fact that the craftsmen of things so appreciated the pleasure of making what was beautiful, and woke to such a vivid consciousness of the hideousness and vulgarity of what the public had previously wanted, that they simply starved the public out. It would be quite impossible at the present moment to furnish a room as rooms were furnished a few years ago, without going for everything to an auction of second-hand furniture from some third-rate lodging-house. The things are no longer made. However they may object to it, people must nowadays have something charming in their surroundings. Fortunately for them, their assumption of authority in these art-matters came to entire grief.

It is evident, then, that all authority in such things is bad. People sometimes inquire what form of government is most suitable for an artist to live under. To this question there is only one answer. *The form of government that is most suitable to the artist is no government at all.* Authority over him and his art is ridiculous. It has been stated that under despotisms artists have produced lovely work. This is not quite so. Artists have visited despots, not as subjects to be tyrannized over, but as wandering wonder-makers, as fascinating vagrant personalities, to be entertained and charmed and suffered to be at peace, and allowed to create. There is this to be said in favour of the despot, that he, being an individual, may have culture, while the mob, being a monster, has none. One who is an Emperor and King may stoop down to pick up a brush for a painter, but when the democracy stoops down it is merely to throw mud. And yet the democracy have not so far to stoop as the emperor. In fact, when they want to throw mud they have not to stoop at all. But there is no necessity to separate the monarch from the mob; all authority is equally bad.

There are three kinds of despots. There is the despot who tyrannizes over the body. There is the despot who tyrannizes over the soul. There is the despot who tyrannizes over soul and body alike. The first is called the Prince. The second is called the Pope. The third is called the People. The Prince may be cultivated. Many Princes have been. Yet in the Prince there is danger. One thinks of Dante at the bitter feast in Verona, of Tasso in Ferrara's madman's cell. It is better for the artist not to live with Princes. The Pope may be cultivated. Many Popes have been; the bad Popes have been. The bad Popes loved Beauty, almost as passionately, nay, with as much passion as the good Popes hated Thought. To the wickedness of the Papacy humanity owes much. The goodness of the Papacy owes a terrible debt to humanity. Yet, though the Vatican has kept the rhetoric of its thunders and lost the rod of its lightning, it is better for the artist not to live with Popes. It was a Pope who said of Cellini to a conclave of Cardinals that common laws and common authority were not made for men such as he; but it was a Pope who thrust Cellini into prison, and kept him there till he sickened with rage, and created unreal visions for himself, and saw the gilded sun enter his room, and grew so enamoured of it that he sought to escape, and crept out from tower to tower, and falling through dizzy air at dawn, maimed himself, and was by a vine-dresser covered with vine leaves, and carried in a cart to one who, loving beautiful things, had care of him. There is danger in Popes. And as for the People, what of them and their authority? Perhaps of them and their authority one has spoken enough. Their authority is a thing blind, deaf, hideous, grotesque, tragic, amusing, serious and obscene. It is impossible for the artist to live with the People. All despots bribe. The people bribe and brutalize. Who told them to exercise authority? They were made to live, to listen, and to love. Someone has done them a great wrong. They have marred themselves by imitation of their inferiors. They have taken the sceptre of the Prince. How should they use it? They have taken the triple tiara of the Pope. How should they carry its burden? They are as a clown whose heart is broken. They are as a priest whose soul is not yet born. Let all who love Beauty pity them. Though they themselves love not Beauty, yet let them pity themselves. Who taught them the trick of tyranny?

There are many other things that one might point out. One might point out how the Renaissance was great, because it sought to solve no social problem, and busied itself not about such things, but suffered the individual to develop freely, beautifully, and naturally, and so had great and individual artists, and great and individual men. One might point out how Louis XIV., by creating the modern state, destroyed the individualism of the artist, and made things monstrous in their monotony of repetition, and contemptible in their conformity to rule, and destroyed throughout all France all those fine freedoms of expression that had made tradition new in beauty, and new modes one with antique form. But the past is of no importance. The present is of no importance. It is with the future that we have to deal. For the past is what man should not have been. The present is what man ought not to be. The future is what artists are.

It will, of course, be said that such a scheme as is set forth here is quite unpractical, and goes against human nature. This is perfectly true. It is unpractical, and it goes against human nature. This is why it is worth carrying out, and that is why one proposes it. For what is a practical scheme? *A practical scheme is either a scheme that is already in existence, or a scheme that could be carried out under existing conditions.* But it is exactly the existing conditions that one objects to; and any scheme that could accept these conditions is wrong and foolish. The conditions will be done away with, and human nature will change. The only thing that one really knows about human nature is that it changes. Change is the one quality we can predicate of it. The systems that fail are those that rely on the permanency of human nature, and not on its growth and development. The error of Louis XIV. was that he thought human nature would always be the same. The result of his error was the French Revolution. It was an admirable result. All the results of the mistakes of governments are quite admirable.

It is to be noted also that Individualism does not come to man with any sickly cant about duty, which merely means doing what other people want because they want it; or any hideous cant about self-sacrifice, which is merely a survival of savage mutilation. *In fact, it does not come to man with any claims upon him at all. It comes naturally and inevitably out of man.* It is the point to which all development tends. It is the differentiation to which all organisms grow. It is the perfection that is inherent in every mode of life, and towards which every mode of life quickens. And so Individualism exercises no compulsion over man. On the contrary it says to man that he should suffer no compulsion to be exercised over him. It does not try to force people to be good. It knows that people are good when they are let alone. Man will develop Individualism out of himself. Man is now so developing Individualism. To ask whether Individualism is practical is like asking whether Evolution is practical. *Evolution is the law of*

life, and there is no evolution except towards Individualism.
Where this tendency is not expressed, it is a case of artificially-
arrested growth, or of disease, or of death.

Individualism will also be unselfish and unaffected. It has
been pointed out that one of the results of the extraordinary
tyranny of authority is that words are absolutely distorted from
their proper and simple meaning, and are used to express the
obverse of their right signification. What is true about Art is
true about Life. A man is called affected, now-a-days, if he
dresses as he likes to dress. But in doing that he is acting in a
perfectly natural manner. Affectation, in such matters, consists
in dressing according to the views of one's neighbour, whose
views, as they are the views of the majority, will probably be
extremely stupid. Or a man is called selfish if he lives in the
manner that seems to him most suitable for the full realisation of his own personality; if, in fact, the primary aim of his
life is self-development. But this is the way in which everyone
should live. *Selfishness is not living as one wishes to live, it is
asking others to live as one wishes to live.* And unselfishness is
letting other people's lives alone, not interfering with them.
Selfishness always aims at creating around it an absolute uniformity of type. Unselfishness recognizes infinite variety of
type as a delightful thing, accepts it, acquiesces in it, enjoys it.
It is not selfish to think for oneself. A man who does not think
for himself does not think at all. It is grossly selfish to require
of one's neighbour that he should think in the same way, and
hold the same opinions. Why should he? If he can think, he
will probably think differently. If he cannot think, it is monstrous to require thought of any kind from him. A red rose is
not selfish because it wants to be a red rose. It would be horribly selfish if it wanted all the other flowers in the garden to
be both red and roses. Under Individualism people will be quite
natural and absolutely unselfish, and will know the meanings
of the words, and realise them in their free, beautiful lives. Nor
will men be egotistic as they are now. For the egotist is he
who makes claims upon others, and the Individualist will not
desire to do that. It will not give him pleasure. When man
has realised Individualism, he will also realise sympathy and
exercise it freely and spontaneously. Up to the present man

has hardly cultivated sympathy at all. He has merely sympathy with pain, and sympathy with pain is not the highest form of sympathy. *All sympathy is fine, but sympathy with suffering is the least fine mode.* It is tainted with egotism. It is apt to become morbid. There is in it a certain element of terror for our own safety. We become afraid that we ourselves might be as the leper or as the blind, and that no man would have care of us. It is curiously limiting, too. One should sympathise with the entirety of life, not with life's sores and maladies merely, but with life's joy and beauty and energy and health and freedom. The wider sympathy is, of course, the more difficult. It requires more unselfishness. Anybody can sympathise with the sufferings of a friend, but it requires a very fine nature—it requires, in fact, the nature of a true Individualist—to sympathise with a friend's success. In the modern stress of competition and struggle for place, such sympathy is naturally rare, and is also very much stifled by the immoral ideal of uniformity of type and conformity to rule which is so prevalent everywhere, and is perhaps most obnoxious in England.

Sympathy with pain there will, of course, always be. It is one of the first instincts of man. The animals which are individual, the higher animals that is to say, share it with us. But it must be remembered that while sympathy with joy intensifies the sum of joy in the world, sympathy with pain does not really diminish the amount of pain. It may make man better able to endure evil, but the evil remains. Sympathy with consumption does not cure consumption; that is what Science does. And when Socialism has solved the problem of poverty, and Science solved the problem of disease, the area of the sentimentalists will be lessened, and the sympathy of man will be large, healthy, and spontaneous. Man will have joy in the contemplation of the joyous lives of others.

For it is through joy that the Individualism of the future will develop itself. *Christ made no attempt to reconstruct society, and consequently the Individualism that he preached to man could be realised only through pain or in solitude.* The ideals that we owe to Christ are the ideals of the man who abandons society entirely, or of the man who resists society absolutely. But man is naturally social. Even the Thebaid became peopled at last. And though the cenobite realises his personality, it is often an impoverished personality that he so realises. Upon the other hand, the terrible truth that pain is a mode through which man may realise himself exercised a wonderful fascination over the world. Shallow speakers and shallow thinkers in pulpits and on platforms often talk about the world's worship of pleasure, and whine against it. But it is rarely in the world's history that its ideal has been one of joy and beauty. The worship of pain has far more often dominated the world. Mediævalism, with its saints and martyrs, its love of self-torture, its wild passion for wounding itself, its gashing with knives, and its whipping with rods—Mediævalism is real Christianity, and the mediæval Christ is the real Christ. When the Renaissance dawned upon the world, and brought with it the new ideals of the beauty of life and the joy of living, men could not understand Christ. Even Art shows us that. The painters of the Renaissance drew Christ as a little boy playing with another boy in a palace or a garden, or lying back in his mother's arms, smiling at her, or at a flower, or at a bright bird; or as a noble stately figure moving nobly through the world; or as a wonderful figure rising in a sort of ecstasy from death to life. Even when they drew him crucified they drew him as a beautiful God on whom evil men had inflicted suffering. But he did not preoccupy them much. What delighted them was to paint the men and women whom they admired, and to show the loveliness of this lovely earth. They painted many religious pictures —in fact, they painted far too many, and the monotony of type and motive is wearisome, and was bad for art. It was the result of the authority of the public in art-matters, and is to be deplored. But their soul was not in the subject. Raphael was a great artist when he painted his portrait of the Pope. When he painted his Madonnas and infant Christs, he is not a great artist at all. Christ had no message for the Renaissance, which was wonderful because it brought an ideal at variance with his, and to find the presentation of the real Christ we must go to mediæval art. There he is one maimed and marred; one who is not comely to look on, because Beauty is a joy; one who is not in fair raiment, because that may be a joy also: he is a beggar who has a marvellous soul; he is a leper whose soul is divine;

he needs neither property nor health; he is a God realising his perfection through pain.

The evolution of man is slow. The injustice of man is great. It was necessary that pain should be put forward as a mode of self-realisation. Even now, in some places in the world, the message of Christ is necessary. No one who lived in modern Russia could possibly realise his perfection except by pain. A few Russian artists have realised themselves in Art, in a fiction that is mediæval in character, because its dominant note is the realisation of men through suffering. But for those who are not artists, and to whom there is no mode of life but the actual life of fact, pain is the only door to perfection. A Russian who lives happily under the present system of government in Russia must either believe that man has no soul, or that, if he has, it is not worth developing. A Nihilist who rejects all authority, because he knows authority to be evil, and who welcomes all pain, because through that he realises his personality, is a real Christian. To him the Christian ideal is a true thing.

And yet, Christ did not revolt against authority. He accepted the imperial authority of the Roman Empire and paid tribute. He endured the ecclesiastical authority of the Jewish Church, and would not repel its violence by any violence of his own. He had, as I said before, no scheme for the reconstruction of society. But the modern world has schemes. It proposes to do away with poverty and the suffering that it entails. It desires to get rid of pain, and the suffering that pain entails. It trusts to Socialism and to Science as its methods. What it aims at is an Individualism expressing itself through joy. This Individualism will be larger, fuller, lovelier than any Individualism has ever been. Pain is not the ultimate mode of perfection. It is merely provisional and a protest. It has reference to wrong, unhealthy, unjust surroundings. When the wrong, and the disease, and the injustice are removed, it will have no further place. It will have done its work. It was a great work, but it is almost over. Its sphere lessens every day.

Nor will man miss it. *For what man has sought for is, indeed, neither pain nor pleasure, but simply Life.* Man has sought to live intensely, fully, perfectly. When he can do so without exercising restraint on others, or suffering it ever, and his activities are all pleasurable to him, he will be saner, healthier, more civilized, more himself. Pleasure is Nature's test, her sign of approval. When man is happy, he is in harmony with himself and his environment. The new Individualism, for whose service Socialism, whether it wills it or not, is working, will be perfect harmony. It will be what the Greeks sought for, but could not, except in Thought, realise completely, because they had slaves, and fed them; it will be what the Renaissance sought for, but could not realise completely except in Art, because they had slaves, and starved them. It will be complete, and through it each man will attain to his perfection. The new Individualism is the new Hellenism.

Intentions[*]

Intentions[*]

THE DECAY OF LYING
An observation

A Dialogue.
Persons: Cyril and Vivian.
Scene: the library of a country house
in Nottinghamshire.

Cyril (coming in through the open window from the terrace). My dear Vivian, don't coop yourself up all day in the library. It is a perfectly lovely afternoon. The air is exquisite. There is a mist upon the woods, like the purple bloom upon a plum. Let us go and lie on the grass, and smoke cigarettes, and enjoy Nature.

Vivian. Enjoy Nature! I am glad to say that I have entirely lost that faculty. People tell us that Art makes us love Nature more than we loved her before; that it reveals her secrets to us; and that after a careful study of Corot and Constable we see things in her that had escaped our observation. My own experience is that the more we study Art, the less we care for Nature. What Art really reveals to us is Nature's lack of design,

---

* The four essays under this title were published together in 1891, but had all been published separately, the first two in January 1889, the third in July and September 1890, and the last in May 1885. All were much revised when they were collected.

her curious crudities, her extraordinary monotony, her absolutely unfinished condition. Nature has good intentions, of course, but, as Aristotle once said, she cannot carry them out. When I look at a landscape I cannot help seeing all its defects. It is fortunate for us, however, that Nature is so imperfect, as otherwise we should have had no art at all. Art is our spirited protest, our gallant attempt to teach Nature her proper place. As for the infinite variety of Nature, that is a pure myth. It is not to be found in Nature herself. It resides in the imagination, or fancy, or cultivated blindness of the man who looks at her.

Cyril. Well, you need not look at the landscape. You can lie on the grass and smoke and talk.

Vivian. But Nature is so uncomfortable. Grass is hard and lumpy and damp, and full of dreadful black insects. Why, even Morris' poorest workman could make you a more comfortable seat than the whole of Nature can. Nature pales before the furniture of "the street which from Oxford has borrowed its name," as the poet you love so much once vilely phrased it. I don't complain. If Nature had been comfortable, mankind would never have invented architecture, and I prefer houses to the open air. In a house we all feel of the proper proportions. Everything is subordinated to us, fashioned for our use and our pleasure. Egotism itself, which is so necessary to a proper sense of human dignity, is entirely the result of indoor life. Out of doors one becomes abstract and impersonal. One's individuality absolutely leaves one. And then Nature is so indifferent, so unappreciative. Whenever I am walking in the park here, I always feel that I am no more to her than the cattle that browse on the slope, or the burdock that blooms in the ditch. Nothing is more evident than that Nature hates Mind. Thinking is the most unhealthy thing in the world, and people die of it just as they die of any other disease. Fortunately, in England at any rate, thought is not catching. Our splendid physique as a people is entirely due to our national stupidity. I only hope we shall be able to keep this great historic bulwark of our happiness for many years to come; but I am afraid that we are beginning to be over-educated; at least everybody who is incapable of learning has taken to teaching

—that is really what our enthusiasm for education has come to. In the meantime, you had better go back to your wearisome uncomfortable Nature, and leave me to correct my proofs.

Cyril. Writing an article! That is not very consistent after what you have just said.

Vivian. Who wants to be consistent? The dullard and the doctrinaire, the tedious people who carry out their principles to the bitter end of action, to the *reductio ad absurdum* of practice. Not I. Like Emerson, I write over the door of my library the word "Whim." Besides, my article is really a most salutary and valuable warning. If it is attended to, there may be a new Renaissance of Art.

Cyril. What is the subject?

Vivian. I intend to call it "The Decay of Lying: A Protest."

Cyril. Lying! I should have thought that our politicians kept up that habit.

Vivian. I assure you that they do not. They never rise beyond the level of misrepresentation, and actually condescend to prove, to discuss, to argue. How different from the temper of the true liar, with his frank, fearless statements, his superb irresponsibility, his healthy, natural disdain of proof of any kind! After all, what is a fine lie? Simply that which is its own evidence. If a man is sufficiently unimaginative to produce evidence in support of a lie, he might just as well speak the truth at once. No, the politicians won't do. Something may, perhaps, be urged on behalf of the Bar. The mantle of the Sophist has fallen on its members. Their feigned ardours and unreal rhetoric are delightful. They can make the worse appear the better cause, as though they were fresh from Leontine schools, and have been known to wrest from reluctant juries triumphant verdicts of acquittal for their clients, even when those clients, as often happens, were clearly and unmistakeably innocent. But they are briefed by the prosaic, and are not ashamed to appeal to precedent. In spite of their endeavors, the truth will out. Newspapers, even, have degenerated. They may now be absolutely relied upon. One feels it as one wades through their columns. It is always the unreadable that occurs. I am afraid that there is not much to be said in favour of either the lawyer or the journalist. Besides, what I am pleading for is

Lying in art. Shall I read you what I have written? It might do you a great deal of good.

Cyril. Certainly, if you give me a cigarette. Thanks. By the way, what magazine do you intend it for?

Vivian. For the *Retrospective Review*. I think I told you that the elect had revived it.

Cyril. Whom do you mean by "the elect"?

Vivian. Oh, The Tired Hedonists of course. It is a club to which I belong. We are supposed to wear faded roses in our button-holes when we meet, and to have a sort of cult for Domitian. I am afraid you are not eligible. You are too fond of simple pleasures.

Cyril. I should be black-balled on the ground of animal spirits, I suppose?

Vivian. Probably. Besides, you are a little too old. We don't admit anybody who is of the usual age.

Cyril. Well, I should fancy you are all a good deal bored with each other.

Vivian. We are. That is one of the objects of the club. Now, if you promise not to interrupt too often, I will read you my article.

Cyril. You will find me all attention.

Vivian (*reading in a very clear, musical voice*). "The Decay of Lying: A Protest.—One of the chief causes that can be assigned for the curiously commonplace character of most of the literature of our age is undoubtedly the decay of Lying as an art, a science, and a social pleasure. The ancient historians gave us delightful fiction in the form of fact; the modern novelist presents us with dull facts under the guise of fiction. The Blue-Book is rapidly becoming his ideal both for method and manner. He has his tedious '*document humain*,' his miserable little '*coin de la création*,' into which he peers with his microscope. He is to be found at the Librairie Nationale, or at the British Museum, shamelessly reading up his subject. He has not even the courage of other people's ideas, but insists on going directly to life for everything, and ultimately, between encyclopædias and personal experience, he comes to the ground, having drawn his types from the family circle or from the weekly washerwoman, and having acquired an amount of useful information from which never, even in his most meditative moments, can he thoroughly free himself.

"The loss that results to literature in general from this false ideal of our time can hardly be overestimated. People have a careless way of talking about a 'born liar,' just as they talk about a 'born poet.' But in both cases they are wrong. Lying and poetry are arts—arts, as Plato saw, not unconnected with each other—and they require the most careful study, the most disinterested devotion. Indeed, they have their technique, just as the more material arts of painting and sculpture have, their subtle secrets of form and colour, their craft-mysteries, their deliberate artistic methods. As one knows the poet by his fine music, so one can recognize the liar by his rich rhythmic utterance, and in neither case will the casual inspiration of the moment suffice. Here, as elsewhere, practice must precede perfection. But in modern days while the fashion of writing poetry has become far too common, and should, if possible, be discouraged, the fashion of lying has almost fallen into disrepute. Many a young man starts in life with a natural gift for exaggeration which, if nurtured in congenial and sympathetic surroundings, or by the imitation of the best models, might grow into something really great and wonderful. But, as a rule, he comes to nothing. He either falls into careless habits of accuracy——"

Cyril. My dear fellow!

Vivian. Please don't interrupt in the middle of a sentence. "He either falls into careless habits of accuracy, or takes to frequenting the society of the aged and the well-informed. Both things are equally fatal to his imagination, as indeed they would be fatal to the imagination of anybody, and in a short time he develops a morbid and unhealthy faculty of truth-telling, begins to verify all statements made in his presence, has no hesitation in contradicting people who are much younger than himself, and often ends by writing novels which are so like life that no one can possibly believe in their probability. This is no isolated instance that we are giving. It is simply one example out of many; and if something cannot be done to check, or at least to modify, our monstrous worship of facts, Art will become sterile, and Beauty will pass away from the land.

"Even Mr. Robert Louis Stevenson, that delightful master of delicate and fanciful prose, is tainted with this modern vice, for we know positively no other name for it. There is such a thing as robbing a story of its reality by trying to make it too true, and *The Black Arrow* is so inartistic as not to contain a single anachronism to boast of, while the transformation of Dr. Jekyll reads dangerously like an experiment out of the *Lancet*. As for Mr. Rider Haggard, who really has, or had once, the makings of a perfectly magnificent liar, he is now so afraid of being suspected of genius that when he does tell us anything marvellous, he feels bound to invent a personal reminiscence, and to put it into a footnote as a kind of cowardly corroboration. Nor are our other novelists much better. Mr. Henry James writes fiction as if it were a painful duty, and wastes upon mean motives and imperceptible 'points of view' his neat literary style, his felicitous phrases, his swift and caustic satire. Mr. Hall Caine, it is true, aims at the grandiose, but then he writes at the top of his voice. He is so loud that one cannot hear what he says. Mr. James Payn is an adept in the art of concealing what is not worth finding. He hunts down the obvious with the enthusiasm of a short-sighted detective. As one turns over the pages, the suspense of the author becomes almost unbearable. The horses of Mr. William Black's phaeton do not soar towards the sun. They merely frighten the sky at evening into violent chromolithographic effects. On seeing them approach, the peasants take refuge in dialect. Mrs. Oliphant prattles pleasantly about curates, lawn-tennis parties, domesticity, and other wearisome things. Mr. Marion Crawford has immolated himself upon the altar of local colour. He is like the lady in the French comedy who keeps talking about 'le beau ciel d'Italie.' Besides, he has fallen into a bad habit of uttering moral platitudes. He is always telling us that to be good is to be good, and that to be bad is to be wicked. At times he is almost edifying. *Robert Elsmere* is of course a masterpiece—a masterpiece of the 'genre ennuyeux,' the one form of literature that the English people seem to thoroughly enjoy. A thoughtful young friend of ours once told us that it reminded him of the sort of conversation that goes on at a meat tea in the house of a serious Nonconformist family, and we can quite believe it. Indeed it is only in England that such a book could be produced. England is the home of lost ideas. As for that great and daily increasing school of novelists for whom the sun always rises in the East-End, the only thing that can be said about them is that they find life crude, and leave it raw.

"In France, though nothing so deliberately tedious as *Robert Elsmere* has been produced, things are not much better. M. Guy de Maupassant, with his keen mordant irony and his hard vivid style, strips life of the few poor rags that still cover her, and shows us foul sore and festering wound. He writes lurid little tragedies in which everybody is ridiculous; bitter comedies at which one cannot laugh for very tears. M. Zola, true to the lofty principle that he lays down in one of his prunuci-amentos on literature, 'L'homme de génie n'a jamais d'esprit,' is determined to show that, if he has not got genius, he can at least be dull. And how well he succeeds! He is not without power. Indeed at times, as in *Germinal*, there is something almost epic in his work. But his work is entirely wrong from beginning to end, and wrong not on the ground of morals, but on the ground of art. From any ethical standpoint it is just what it should be. The author is perfectly truthful, and describes things exactly as they happen. What more can any moralist desire? We have no sympathy at all with the moral indignation of our time against M. Zola. It is simply the indignation of Tartuffe on being exposed. But from the standpoint of art, what can be said in favour of the author of *L'Assommoir*, *Nana*, and *Pot-Bouille*? Nothing. Mr. Ruskin once described the characters in George Eliot's novels as being like the sweepings of a Pentonville omnibus, but M. Zola's characters are much worse. They have their dreary vices, and their drearier virtues. The record of their lives is absolutely without interest. Who cares what happens to them? In literature we require distinction, charm, beauty, and imaginative power. We don't want to be harrowed and disgusted with an account of the doings of the lower orders. M. Daudet is better.

He has wit, a light touch, and an amusing style. But he has lately committed literary suicide. Nobody can possibly care for Delobelle with his 'Il faut lutter pour l'art,' or for Valmajour with his eternal refrain about the nightingale, or for the poet in *Jack* with his 'mots cruels,' now that we have learned from *Vingt Ans de ma Vie littéraire* that these characters were taken directly from life. To us they seem to have suddenly lost all their vitality, all the few qualities they ever possessed. The only real people are the people who never existed, and if a novelist is base enough to go to life for his personages he should at least pretend that they are creations, and not boast of them as copies. The justification of a character in a novel is not that other persons are what they are, but that the author is what he is. Otherwise the novel is not a work of art. As for M. Paul Bourget, the master of the *roman psychologique*, he commits the error of imagining that the men and women of modern life are capable of being infinitely analysed for an innumerable series of chapters. In point of fact what is interesting about people in good society—and M. Bourget rarely moves out of the Faubourg St. Germain, except to come to London,—is the mask that each one of them wears, not the reality that lies behind the mask. It is a humiliating confession, but we are all of us made out of the same stuff. In Falstaff there is something of Hamlet, in Hamlet there is not a little of Falstaff. The fat knight has his moods of melancholy, and the young prince his moments of coarse humour. Where we differ from each other is purely in accidentals: in dress, manner, tone of voice, religious opinions, personal appearance, tricks of habit, and the like. The more one analyses people, the more all reasons for analysis disappear. Sooner or later one comes to that dreadful universal thing called human nature. Indeed, as any one who has ever worked among the poor knows only too well, the brotherhood of man is no mere poet's dream, it is a most depressing and humiliating reality; and if a writer insists upon analysing the upper classes, he might just as well write of match-girls and costermongers at once." However, my dear Cyril, I will not detain you any further just here. I quite admit that modern novels have many good points. All I insist on is that, as a class, they are quite unreadable.

Cyril. That is certainly a very grave qualification, but I must say that I think you are rather unfair in some of your strictures. I like *The Deemster,* and *The Daughter of Heth,* and *Le Disciple,* and *Mr. Isaacs,* and as for *Robert Elsmere* I am quite devoted to it. Not that I can look upon it as a serious work. As a statement of the problems that confront the earnest Christian it is ridiculous and antiquated. It is simply Arnold's *Literature and Dogma* with the literature left out. It is as much behind the age as Paley's *Evidences,* or Colenso's method of Biblical exegesis. Nor could anything be less impressive than the unfortunate hero gravely heralding a dawn that rose long ago, and so completely missing its true significance that he proposes to carry on the business of the old firm under the new name. On the other hand, it contains several clever caricatures, and a heap of delightful quotations, and Green's philosophy very pleasantly sugars the somewhat bitter pill of the author's fiction. I also cannot help expressing my surprise that you have said nothing about the two novelists whom you are always reading, Balzac and George Meredith. Surely they are realists, both of them?

Vivian. Ah! Meredith! Who can define him? His style is chaos illumined by flashes of lightning. As a writer he has mastered everything except language: as a novelist he can do everything, except tell a story: as an artist he is everything, except articulate. Somebody in Shakespeare—Touchstone, I think —talks about a man who is always breaking his shins over his own wit, and it seems to me that this might serve as the basis for a criticism of Meredith's method. But whatever he is, he is not a realist. Or rather I would say that he is a child of realism who is not on speaking terms with his father. By deliberate choice he has made himself a romanticist. He has refused to bow the knee to Baal, and after all, even if the man's fine spirit did not revolt against the noisy assertions of realism, his style would be quite sufficient of itself to keep life at a respectful distance. By its means he has planted round his garden a hedge full of thorns, and red with wonderful roses. As for Balzac, he was a most remarkable combination of the artistic temperament with the scientific spirit. The latter he bequeathed to his disciples: the former was entirely his own. The difference be-

tween such a book as M. Zola's *L'Assommoir* and Balzac's
Illusions Perdues is the difference between unimaginative realism and imaginative reality. "All Balzac's characters," said
Baudelaire, "are gifted with the same ardour of life that animated himself. All his fictions are as deeply coloured as dreams.
Each mind is a weapon loaded to the muzzle with will. The
very scullions have genius." A steady course of Balzac reduces
our living friends to shadows, and our acquaintances to the
shadows of shades. His characters have a kind of fervent fiery-
coloured existence. They dominate us, and defy scepticism.
One of the greatest tragedies of my life is the death of
Lucien de Rubempré. It is a grief from which I have never been
able to completely rid myself. It haunts me in my moments of
pleasure. I remember it when I laugh. But Balzac is no more
a realist than Holbein was. He created life, he did not copy it.
I admit, however, that he set far too high a value on modernity
of form, and that, consequently, there is no book of his that,
as an artistic masterpiece, can rank with *Salammbô* or *Esmond*,
or *The Cloister and the Hearth*, or the *Vicomte de Bragelonne*.

Cyril. Do you object to modernity of form, then?

Vivian. Yes. It is a huge price to pay for a very poor result.
Pure modernity of form is always somewhat vulgarising. It
cannot help being so. The public imagine that, because they
are interested in their immediate surroundings, Art should be
interested in them also, and should take them as her subject-
matter. But the mere fact that they are interested in these
things makes them unsuitable subjects for Art. The only beautiful things, as somebody once said, are the things that do not
concern us. As long as a thing is useful or necessary to us, or
affects us in any way, either for pain or for pleasure, or appeals
strongly to our sympathies, or is a vital part of the environment
in which we live, it is outside the proper sphere of art. To art's
subject-matter we should be more or less indifferent. We
should, at any rate, have no preferences, no prejudices, no
partisan feeling of any kind. It is exactly because Hecuba is
nothing to us that her sorrows are such an admirable motive
for a tragedy. I do not know anything in the whole history of
literature sadder than the artistic career of Charles Reade.
He wrote one beautiful book, *The Cloister and the Hearth*, a

book as much above *Romola* as *Romola* is above *Daniel Deronda*, and wasted the rest of his life in a foolish attempt to be modern, to draw public attention to the state of our convict prisons, and the management of our private lunatic asylums. Charles Dickens was depressing enough in all conscience when he tried to arouse our sympathy for the victims of the poor-law administration; but Charles Reade, an artist, a scholar, a man with a true sense of beauty, raging and roaring over the abuses of contemporary life like a common pamphleteer or a sensational journalist, is really a sight for the angels to weep over. Believe me, my dear Cyril, modernity of form and modernity of subject-matter are entirely and absolutely wrong. We have mistaken the common livery of the age for the vesture of the Muses, and spend our days in the sordid streets and hideous suburbs of our vile cities when we should be out on the hillside with Apollo. Certainly we are a degraded race, and have sold our birthright for a mess of facts.

Cyril. There is something in what you say, and there is no doubt that whatever amusement we may find in reading a purely modern novel, we have rarely any artistic pleasure in re-reading it. And this is perhaps the best rough test of what is literature and what is not. If one cannot enjoy reading a book over and over again, there is no use reading it at all. But what do you say about the return to Life and Nature? This is the panacea that is always being recommended to us.

Vivian. I will read you what I say on that subject. The passage comes later on in the article, but I may as well give it to you now:—

"The popular cry of our time is 'Let us return to Life and Nature; they will recreate Art for us, and send the red blood coursing through her veins; they will shoe her feet with swiftness and make her hand strong.' But, alas! we are mistaken in our amiable and well-meaning efforts. Nature is always behind the age. And as for Life, she is the solvent that breaks up Art, the enemy that lays waste her house."

Cyril. What do you mean by saying that Nature is always behind the age?

Vivian. Well, perhaps that is rather cryptic. What I mean is this. If we take Nature to mean natural simple instinct as opposed to self-conscious culture, the work produced under this influence is always old-fashioned, antiquated, and out of date. One touch of Nature may make the whole world kin, but two touches of Nature will destroy any work of Art. If, on the other hand, we regard Nature as the collection of phenomena external to man, people only discover in her what they bring to her. She has no suggestions of her own. Wordsworth went to the lakes, but he was never a lake poet. He found in stones the sermons he had already hidden there. He went moralizing about the district, but his good work was produced when he returned, not to Nature but to poetry. Poetry gave him "Laodamia," and the fine sonnets, and the great Ode, such as it is. Nature gave him "Martha Ray" and "Peter Bell," and the address to Mr. Wilkinson's spade.

Cyril. I think that view might be questioned. I am rather inclined to believe in the "impulse from a vernal wood," though of course the artistic value of such an impulse depends entirely on the kind of temperament that receives it, so that the return to Nature would come to mean simply the advance to a great personality. You would agree with that, I fancy. However, proceed with your article.

Vivian (reading). "Art begins with abstract decoration with purely imaginative and pleasurable work dealing with what is unreal and non-existent. This is the first stage. Then Life becomes fascinated with this new wonder, and asks to be admitted into the charmed circle. Art takes life as part of her rough material, recreates it, and refashions it in fresh forms, is absolutely indifferent to fact, invents, imagines, dreams, and keeps between herself and reality the impenetrable barrier of beautiful style, of decorative or ideal treatment. The third stage is when Life gets the upper hand, and drives Art out into the wilderness. This is the true decadence, and it is from this that we are now suffering.

"Take the case of the English drama. At first in the hands of the monks Dramatic Art was abstract, decorative, and mythological. Then she enlisted Life in her service, and using some of life's external forms, she created an entirely new race of beings, whose sorrows were more terrible than any sorrow man has ever felt, whose joys were keener than lover's joys, who had the rage of the Titans and the calm of the gods, who had monstrous and marvellous sins, monstrous and marvellous virtues. To them she gave a language different from that of actual use, a language full of resonant music and sweet rhythm, made stately by solemn cadence, or made delicate by fanciful rhyme, jewelled with wonderful words, and enriched with lofty diction. She clothed her children in strange raiment and gave them masks, and at her bidding the antique world rose from its marble tomb. A new Cæsar stalked through the streets of risen Rome, and with purple sail and flute-led oars another Cleopatra passed up the river to Antioch. Old myth and legend and dream took shape and substance. History was entirely re-written, and there was hardly one of the dramatists who did not recognize that the object of Art is not simple truth but complex beauty. In this they were perfectly right. Art itself is really a form of exaggeration; and selection, which is the very spirit of art, is nothing more than an intensified mode of over-emphasis.

"But Life soon shattered the perfection of the form. Even in Shakespeare we can see the beginning of the end. It shows itself by the gradual breaking up of the blank-verse in the later plays, by the predominance given to prose, and by the over-importance assigned to characterisation. The passages in Shakespeare—and they are many—where the language is uncouth, vulgar, exaggerated, fantastic, obscene even, are entirely due to Life calling for an echo of her own voice, and rejecting the intervention of beautiful style, through which alone should Life be suffered to find expression. Shakespeare is not by any means a flawless artist. He is too fond of going directly to life, and borrowing life's natural utterance. He forgets that when Art surrenders her imaginative medium she surrenders everything. Goethe says, somewhere—

In der Beschränkung zeigt sich erst der Meister,

'It is in working within limits that the master reveals himself,' and the limitation, the very condition of any art is style. However, we need not linger any longer over Shakespeare's realism. *The Tempest* is the most perfect of palinodes. All that we desired to point out was, that the magnificent work of the Eliza-

bethan and Jacobean artists contained within itself the seeds
of its own dissolution, and that, if it drew some of its strength
from using life as rough material, it drew all its weakness from
using life as an artistic method. As the inevitable result of this
substitution of an imitative for a creative medium, this surrender of an imaginative form, we have the modern English melo-
drama. The characters in these plays talk on the stage exactly
as they would talk off it; they have neither aspirations nor aspirates; they are taken directly from life and reproduce its vulgarity down to the smallest detail; they present the gait, manner, costume, and accent of real people; they would pass
unnoticed in a third-class railway carriage. And yet how wearisome the plays are! They do not succeed in producing even
that impression of reality at which they aim, and which is their
only reason for existing. As a method, realism is a complete
failure.

"What is true about drama and the novel is no less true
about those arts that we call decorative arts. The whole history
of these arts in Europe is the record of the struggle between
Orientalism, with its frank rejection of imitation, its love of
artistic convention, its dislike to the actual representation of
any object in Nature, and our own imitative spirit. Wherever
the former has been paramount, as in Byzantium, Sicily, and
Spain, by actual contact, or in the rest of Europe by the influence of the Crusades, we have had beautiful and imaginative
work in which the visible things of life are transmuted into
artistic conventions, and the things that Life has not are invented and fashioned for her delight. But wherever we have returned to Life and Nature, our work has always become vulgar,
common, and uninteresting. Modern tapestry, with its aërial
effects, its elaborate perspective, its broad expanses of waste
sky, its faithful and laborious realism, has no beauty whatsoever.
The pictorial glass of Germany is absolutely detestable. We are
beginning to weave possible carpets in England, but only because we have returned to the method and spirit of the East.
Our rugs and carpets of twenty years ago, with their solemn
depressing truths, their inane worship of Nature, their sordid
reproductions of visible objects, have become, even to the Philistine, a source of laughter. A cultured Mahomedan once re-

marked to us, 'You Christians are so occupied in misinterpreting the fourth commandment that you have never thought of making an artistic application of the second.' He was perfectly right, and the whole truth of the matter is this: The proper school to learn art in is not Life but Art."

And now let me read you a passage which seems to me to settle the question very completely.

"It was not always thus. We need not say anything about the poets, for they, with the unfortunate exception of Mr. Wordsworth, have been really faithful to their high mission, and are universally recognized as being absolutely unreliable. But in the works of Herodotus, who, in spite of the shallow and ungenerous attempts of modern sciolists to verify his history, may justly be called the 'Father of Lies'; in the published speeches of Cicero and the biographies of Suetonius; in Tacitus at his best; in Pliny's *Natural History*; in Hanno's *Periplus*; in all the early chronicles; in the Lives of the Saints; in Froissart and Sir Thomas Mallory; in the travels of Marco Polo; in Olaus Magnus, and Aldrovandus, and Conrad Lycosthenes, with his magnificent *Prodigiorum et Ostentorum Chronicon*; in the autobiography of Benvenuto Cellini; in the memoirs of Casanuova; in Defoe's *History of the Plague*; in Boswell's *Life of Johnson*; in Napoleon's despatches, and in the works of our own Carlyle, whose *French Revolution* is one of the most fascinating historical novels ever written, facts are either kept in their proper subordinate position, or else entirely excluded on the general ground of dulness. Now, everything is changed. Facts are not merely finding a footing-place in history, but they are usurping the domain of Fancy, and have invaded the kingdom of Romance. Their chilling touch is over everything. They are vulgarising mankind. The crude commercialism of America, its materialising spirit, its indifference to the poetical side of things, and its lack of imagination and of high unattainable ideals, are entirely due to that country having adopted for its national hero a man, who according to his own confession, was incapable of telling a lie, and it is not too much to say that the story of George Washington and the cherry-tree has done more harm, and in a shorter space of time, than any other moral tale in the whole of literature."

Cyril. My dear boy!

Vivian. I assure you it is the case, and the amusing part of the whole thing is that the story of the cherry-tree is an absolute myth. However, you must not think that I am too despondent about the artistic future either of America or of our own country. Listen to this:—

"That some change will take place before this century has drawn to its close we have no doubt whatsoever. Bored by the tedious and improving conversation of those who have neither the wit to exaggerate nor the genius to romance, tired of the intelligent person whose reminiscences are always based upon memory, whose statements are invariably limited by probability, who is at any time liable to be corroborated by the merest Philistine who happens to be present, Society sooner or later must return to its lost leader, the cultured and fascinating liar. Who he was who first, without ever having gone out to the rude chase, told the wondering cavemen at sunset how he had dragged the Megatherium from the purple darkness of its jasper cave, or slain the Mammoth in single combat and brought back its gilded tusks, we cannot tell, and not one of our modern anthropologists, for all their much-boasted science, has had the ordinary courage to tell us. Whatever was his name or race, he certainly was the true founder of social intercourse. For the aim of the liar is simply to charm, to delight, to give pleasure. He is the very basis of civilized society, and without him a dinner party, even at the mansions of the great, is as dull as a lecture at the Royal Society, or a debate at the Incorporated Authors, or one of Mr. Burnand's farcical comedies.

"Nor will he be welcomed by society alone. Art, breaking from the prison-house of realism, will run to greet him, and will kiss his false, beautiful lips, knowing that he alone is in possession of the great secret of all her manifestations, the secret that Truth is entirely and absolutely a matter of style; while Life—poor, probable, uninteresting human life—tired of repeating herself for the benefit of Mr. Herbert Spencer, scientific historians, and the compilers of statistics in general, will follow meekly after him, and try to produce, in her own simple and untutored way, some of the marvels of which he talks.

"No doubt there will always be critics who, like a certain

writer in the *Saturday Review,* will gravely censure the teller of
fairy tales for his defective knowledge of natural history, who
will measure imaginative work by their own lack of any imaginative faculty, and will hold up their inkstained hands in horror
if some honest gentleman, who has never been farther than the
yew-trees of his own garden, pens a fascinating book of travels
like Sir John Mandeville, or, like great Raleigh, writes a whole
history of the world, without knowing anything whatsoever
about the past. To excuse themselves they will try and shelter
under the shield of him who made Prospero the magician, and
gave him Caliban and Ariel as his servants, who heard the Tri-
tons blowing their horns round the coral reefs of the Enchanted
Isle, and the fairies singing to each other in a wood near Athens,
who led the phantom kings in dim procession across the misty
Scottish heath, and hid Hecate in a cave with the weird sisters.
They will call upon Shakespeare—they always do—and will
quote that hackneyed passage about Art holding the mirror up
to Nature, forgetting that this unfortunate aphorism is deliberately said by Hamlet in order to convince the bystanders of
his absolute insanity in all art-matters."

Cyril. Ahem! Another cigarette, please.

Vivian. My dear fellow, whatever you may say, it is merely
a dramatic utterance, and no more represents Shakespeare's
real views upon art than the speeches of Iago represent his real
views upon morals. But let me get to the end of the passage:

"Art finds her own perfection within, and not outside of,
herself. She is not to be judged by any external standard of resemblance. She is a veil, rather than a mirror. She has flowers
that no forests know of, birds that no woodland possesses. She
makes and unmakes many worlds, and can draw the moon from
heaven with a scarlet thread. Hers are the 'forms more real
than living man,' and hers the great archetypes of which things
that have existence are but unfinished copies. Nature has, in
her eyes, no laws, no uniformity. She can work miracles at her
will, and when she calls monsters from the deep they come.
She can bid the almond tree blossom in winter, and send the
snow upon the ripe cornfield. At her word the frost lays its
silver finger on the burning mouth of June, and the winged
lions creep out from the hollows of the Lydian hills. The dryads

peer from the thicket as she passes by, and the brown fauns smile strangely at her when she comes near them. She has hawk-faced gods that worship her, and the centaurs gallop at her side."

Cyril. I like that. I can see it. Is that the end?

Vivian. No. There is one more passage, but it is purely practical. It simply suggests some methods by which we could revive this lost art of Lying.

Cyril. Well, before you read it to me, I should like to ask you a question. What do you mean by saying that life, "poor, probable, uninteresting human life," will try to reproduce the marvels of art? I can quite understand your objection to art being treated as a mirror. You think it would reduce genius to the position of a cracked looking-glass. But you don't mean to say that you seriously believe that Life imitates Art, that Life in fact is the mirror, and Art the reality?

Vivian. Certainly I do. Paradox though it may seem—and paradoxes are always dangerous things—it is none the less true that Life imitates art far more than Art imitates life. We have all seen in our own day in England how a certain curious and fascinating type of beauty, invented and emphasised by two imaginative painters, has so influenced Life that whenever one goes to a private view or to an artistic salon one sees, here the mystic eyes of Rossetti's dream, the long ivory throat, the strange square cut jaw, the loosened shadowy hair that he so ardently loved, there the sweet maidenhood of "The Golden Stair," the blossom-like mouth and weary loveliness of the "Laus Amoris," the passion-pale face of Andromeda, the thin hands and lithe beauty of the Vivien in "Merlin's Dream." And it has always been so. A great artist invents a type, and Life tries to copy it, to reproduce it in a popular form, like an enterprising publisher. Neither Holbein nor Vandyck found in England what they have given us. They brought their types with them, and Life with her keen imitative faculty set herself to supply the master with models. The Greeks, with their quick artistic instinct, understood this, and set in the bride's chamber the statue of Hermes or of Apollo, that she might bear children as lovely as the works of art that she looked at in her rapture or her pain. They knew that Life gains from Art not merely spirituality, depth of thought and feeling, soul-turmoil or soul-peace, but that she can form herself on the very lines and colours of art, and can reproduce the dignity of Pheidias as well as the grace of Praxiteles. Hence came their objection to realism. They disliked it on purely social grounds. They felt that it inevitably makes people ugly, and they were perfectly right. We try to improve the conditions of the race by means of good air, free sunlight, wholesome water, and hideous bare buildings for the better housing of the lower orders. But these things merely produce health, they do not produce beauty. For this, Art is required, and the true disciples of the great artist are not his studio-imitators, but those who become like his works of art, be they plastic as in the Greek days, or pictorial as in modern times; in a word, Life is Art's best, Art's only pupil.

As it is with the visible arts, so it is with literature. The most obvious and the vulgarest form in which this is shown is in the case of the silly boys who, after reading the adventures of Jack Sheppard or Dick Turpin, pillage the stalls of unfortunate apple-women, break into sweet-shops at night, and alarm old gentlemen who are returning home from the city by leaping out on them in suburban lanes, with black masks and unloaded revolvers. This interesting phenomenon, which always occurs after the appearance of a new edition of either of the books I have alluded to, is usually attributed to the influence of literature on the imagination. But this is a mistake. The imagination is essentially creative and always seeks for a new form. The boy-burglar is simply the inevitable result of life's imitative instinct. He is Fact, occupied as Fact usually is, with trying to reproduce Fiction, and what we see in him is repeated on an extended scale throughout the whole of life. Schopenhauer has analysed the pessimism that characterises modern thought, but Hamlet invented it. The world has become sad because a puppet was once melancholy. The Nihilist, that strange martyr who has no faith, who goes to the stake without enthusiasm, and dies for what he does not believe in, is a purely literary product. He was invented by Tourgénieff, and completed by Dostoieffski. Robespierre came out of the pages of Rousseau as surely as the People's Palace rose out of the *débris* of a novel. Literature always anticipates life. It does not copy it, but moulds it to its purpose. The nineteenth century, as we know it, is largely an invention of Balzac. Our Luciens de Rubempré, our Rastignacs, and De Marsays made their first appearance on the stage of the *Comédie Humaine*. We are merely carrying out, with footnotes and unnecessary additions, the whim or fancy or creative vision of a great novelist. I once asked a lady, who knew Thackeray intimately, whether he had had any model for Becky Sharp. She told me that Becky was an invention, but that the idea of the character had been partly suggested by a governess who lived in the neighbourhood of Kensington Square, and was the companion of a very selfish and rich old woman. I inquired what became of the governess, and she replied that, oddly enough, some years after the appearance of *Vanity Fair*, she ran away with the nephew of the lady with whom she was living, and for a short time made a great splash in society, quite in Mrs. Rawdon Crawley's style, and entirely by Mrs. Rawdon Crawley's methods. Ultimately she came to grief, disappeared to the Continent, and used to be occasionally seen at Monte Carlo and other gambling places. The noble gentleman from whom the same great sentimentalist drew Colonel Newcome died, a few months after *The Newcomes* had reached a fourth edition, with the word "Adsum" on his lips. Shortly after Mr. Stevenson published his curious psychological story of transformation, a friend of mine, called Mr. Hyde, was in the north of London, and being anxious to get to a railway station, took what he thought would be a short cut, lost his way, and found himself in a network of mean, evil-looking streets. Feeling rather nervous he began to walk extremely fast, when suddenly out of an archway ran a child right between his legs. It fell on the pavement, he tripped over it, and trampled upon it. Being of course very much frightened and a little hurt, it began to scream, and in a few seconds the whole street was full of rough people who came pouring out of the houses like ants. They surrounded him, and asked him his name. He was just about to give it when he suddenly remembered the opening incident in Mr. Stevenson's story. He was so filled with horror at having realized in his own person that terrible and well written scene, and at having done accidently, though in fact, what the Mr. Hyde of fiction had done with deliberate intent, that he ran away as hard as he could go. He was, however, very closely followed, and finally he took refuge in a surgery, the door of which happened to be open, where he explained to a young assistant, who happened to be there, exactly what had occurred. The humanitarian crowd were induced to go away on his giving them a small sum of money, and as soon as the coast was clear he left. As he passed out, the name on the brass door-plate of the surgery caught his eye. It was "Jekyll." At least it should have been.

Here the imitation, as far as it went, was of course accidental. In the following case the imitation was self-conscious. In the year 1879, just after I had left Oxford, I met at a reception at the house of one of the Foreign Ministers a woman of very curious exotic beauty. We became great friends, and were constantly together. And yet what interested most in her was not her beauty, but her character, her entire vagueness of character. She seemed to have no personality at all, but simply the possibility of many types. Sometimes she would give herself up entirely to art, turn her drawing-room into a studio, and spend two or three days a week at picture-galleries or museums. Then she would take to attending race-meetings, wear the most horsey clothes, and talk about nothing but betting. She abandoned religion for mesmerism, mesmerism for politics, and politics for the melodramatic excitements of philanthropy. In fact, she was a kind of Proteus, and as much a failure in all her transformations as was that wondrous sea-god when Odysseus laid hold of him. One day a serial began in one of the French magazines. At that time I used to read serial stories, and I well remember the shock of surprise I felt when I came to the description of the heroine. She was so like my friend that I brought her the magazine, and she recognized herself in it immediately, and seemed fascinated by the resemblance. I should tell you, by the way, that the story was translated from some dead Russian writer, so that the author had not taken his type from my friend. Well, to put the matter briefly, some months afterwards I was in Venice, and finding the magazine in the reading-room of the hotel, I took it up casually to see what had become of the heroine. It was a most piteous tale, as the girl had ended by running away with a man absolutely inferior to her, not merely in social station, but in character and intellect also. I wrote to my friend that evening about my views on John Bellini, and the admirable ices at Florio's, and the artistic value of gondolas, but added a postscript to the effect that her double in the story had behaved in a very silly manner. I don't know why I added that, but I remember I had a sort of dread over me that she might do the same thing. Before my letter had reached her, she had run away with a man who deserted her in six months. I saw her in 1884 in Paris, where she was living with her mother, and I asked her whether the story had had anything to do with her action. She told me that she had felt an absolutely irresistible impulse to follow the heroine step by step in her strange and fatal progress, and that it was with a feeling of real terror that she had looked forward to the last few chapters of the story. When they appeared, it seemed to her that she was compelled to reproduce them in life, and she did so. It was a most clear example of this imitative instinct of which I was speaking, and an extremely tragic one.

However, I do not wish to dwell any further upon individual instances. Personal experience is a most vicious and limited circle. All that I desire to point out is the general principle that Life imitates Art far more than Art imitates Life, and I feel sure that if you think seriously about it you will find that it is true. Life holds the mirror up to Art, and either reproduces some strange type imagined by painter or sculptor, or realizes in fact what has been dreamed in fiction. Scientifically speaking, the basis of life—the energy of life, as Aristotle would call it—is simply the desire for expression, and Art is always presenting various forms through which this expression can be attained. Life seizes on them and uses them, even if they be to her own hurt. Young men have committed suicide because Rolla did so, have died by their own hand because by his own hand Werther died. Think of what we owe to the imitation of Christ, of what we owe to the imitation of Cæsar.

Cyril. The theory is certainly a very curious one, but to make it complete you must show that Nature, no less than Life, is an imitation of Art. Are you prepared to prove that?

311

Vivian. My dear fellow, I am prepared to prove anything.

Cyril. Nature follows the landscape painter then, and takes her effects from him?

Vivian. Certainly. Where, if not from the Impressionists, do we get those wonderful brown fogs that come creeping down our streets, blurring the gas-lamps and changing the houses into monstrous shadows? To whom, if not to them and their master, do we owe the lovely silver mists that brood over our river, and turn to faint forms of fading grace curved bridge and swaying barge? The extraordinary change that has taken place in the climate of London during the last ten years is entirely due to this particular school of Art. You smile. Consider the matter from a scientific or a metaphysical point of view, and you will find that I am right. For what is Nature? Nature is no great mother who has borne us. She is our creation. It is in our brain that she quickens to life. Things are because we see them, and what we see, and how we see it, depends on the Arts that have influenced us. To look at a thing is very different from seeing a thing. One does not see anything until one sees its beauty. Then, and then only, does it come into existence. At present, people see fogs, not because there are fogs, but because poets and painters have taught them the mysterious loveliness of such effects. There may have been fogs for centuries in London. I dare say there were. But no one saw them, and so we do not know anything about them. They did not exist till Art had invented them. Now, it must be admitted, fogs are carried to excess. They have become the mere mannerism of a clique, and the exaggerated realism of their method gives dull people bronchitis. Where the cultured catch an effect, the uncultured catch cold. And so, let us be humane, and invite Art to turn her wonderful eyes elsewhere. She has done so already, indeed. That white quivering sunlight that one sees now in France, with its strange blotches of mauve, and its restless violet shadows, is her latest fancy, and, on the whole, Nature reproduces it quite admirably. Where she used to give us Corots and Daubignys, she gives us now exquisite Monets and entrancing Pisaros. Indeed there are moments, rare, it is true, but still to be observed from time to time, when Nature becomes absolutely modern. Of course she is not always to be relied upon. The fact is that she is in this unfortunate position. Art creates an incomparable and unique effect, and, having done so, passes on to other things. Nature, upon the other hand, forgetting that imitation can be made the sincerest form of insult, keeps on repeating this effect until we all become absolutely wearied of it. Nobody of any real culture, for instance, ever talks now-a-days about the beauty of a sunset. Sunsets are quite old-fashioned. They belong to the time when Turner was the last note in art. To admire them is a distinct sign of provincialism of temperament. Upon the other hand they go on. Yesterday evening Mrs. Arundel insisted on my going to the window, and looking at the glorious sky, as she called it. Of course I had to look at it. She is one of those absurdly pretty Philistines, to whom one can deny nothing. And what was it? It was simply a very second-rate Turner, a Turner of a bad period, with all the painter's worst faults exaggerated and overemphasized. Of course, I am quite ready to admit that Life very often commits the same error. She produces her false Renés and her sham Vautrins, just as Nature gives us, on one day a doubtful Cuyp, and on another a more than questionable Rousseau. Still, Nature irritates one more when she does things of that kind. It seems so stupid, so obvious, so unnecessary. A false Vautrin might be delightful. A doubtful Cuyp is unbearable. However, I don't want to be too hard on Nature. I wish the Channel, especially at Hastings, did not look quite so often like a Henry Moore, grey pearl with yellow lights, but then, when Art is more varied, Nature will, no doubt, be more varied also. That she imitates Art, I don't think even her worst enemy would deny now. It is the one thing that keeps her in touch with civilized man. But have I proved my theory to your satisfaction?

Cyril. You have proved it to my dissatisfaction, which is better. But even admitting this strange imitative instinct in Life and Nature, surely you would acknowledge that Art expresses the temper of its age, the spirit of its time, the moral and social conditions that surround it, and under whose influence it is produced.

Vivian. Certainly not! Art never expresses anything but itself. This is the principle of my new æsthetics; and it is this, more than that vital connection between form and substance, on which

313

Mr. Pater dwells, that makes music the type of all the arts. Of course, nations and individuals, with that healthy natural vanity which is the secret of existence, are always under the impression that it is of them that the Muses are talking, always trying to find in the calm dignity of imaginative art some mirror of their own turbid passions, always forgetting that the singer of life is not Apollo, but Marsyas. Remote from reality, and with her eyes turned away from the shadows of the cave, Art reveals her own perfection, and the wondering crowd that watches the opening of the marvellous, many-petalled rose fancies that it is its own history that is being told to it, its own spirit that is finding expression in a new form. But it is not so. The highest art rejects the burden of the human spirit, and gains more from a new medium or a fresh material than she does from any enthusiasm for art, or from any lofty passion, or from any great awakening of the human consciousness. She develops purely on her own lines. She is not symbolic of any age. It is the ages that are her symbols.

Even those who hold that Art is representative of time and place and people, cannot help admitting that the more imitative an art is, the less it represents to us the spirit of its age. The evil faces of the Roman emperors look out at us from the foul porphyry and spotted jasper in which the realistic artists of the day delighted to work, and we fancy that in those cruel lips and heavy sensual jaws we can find the secret of the ruin of the Empire. But it was not so. The vices of Tiberius could not destroy that supreme civilization, any more than the virtues of the Antonines could save it. It fell for other, for less interesting reasons. The sibyls and prophets of the Sistine may indeed serve to interpret for some that new birth of the emancipated spirit that we call the Renaissance; but what do the drunken boors and brawling peasants of Dutch art tell us about the great soul of Holland? The more abstract, the more ideal an art is, the more it reveals to us the temper of its age. If we wish to understand a nation by means of its art, let us look at its architecture or its music.

Cyril. I quite agree with you there. The spirit of an age may be best expressed in the abstract ideal arts, for the spirit itself is abstract and ideal. Upon the other hand, for the visible aspect of an age, for its look, as the phrase goes, we must of course go to the arts of imitation.

Vivian. I don't think so. After all, what the imitative arts really give us are merely the various styles of particular artists, or of certain schools of artists. Surely you don't imagine that the people of the Middle Ages bore any resemblance at all to the figures on mediæval stained glass, or in mediæval stone and wood carving, or on mediæval metal-work, or tapestries, or illuminated MSS. They were probably very ordinary-looking people, with nothing grotesque, or remarkable, or fantastic in their appearance. The Middle Ages, as we know them in art, are simply a definite form of style, and there is no reason at all why an artist with this style should not be produced in the nineteenth century. No great artist ever sees things as they really are. If he did, he would cease to be an artist. Take an example from our own day. I know that you are fond of Japanese things. Now, do you really imagine that the Jappanese people, as they are presented to us in art, have any existence? If you do, you have never understood Japanese art at all. The Japanese people are the deliberate self-conscious creation of certain individual artists. If you set a picture by Hokusai, or Hokkei, or any of the great native painters, beside a real Japanese gentleman or lady, you will see that there is not the slightest resemblance between them. The actual people who live in Japan are not unlike the general run of English people; that is to say, they are extremely commonplace, and have nothing curious or extraordinary about them. In fact the whole of Japan is a pure invention. There is no such country, there are no such people. One of our most charming painters went recently to the Land of the Chrysanthemum in the foolish hope of seeing the Japanese. All he saw, all he had the chance of painting, were a few lanterns and some fans. He was quite unable to discover the inhabitants, as his delightful exhibition at Messrs. Dowdeswell's Gallery showed only too well. He did not know that the Japanese people are, as I have said, simply a mode of style, an exquisite fancy of art. And so, if you desire to see a Japanese effect, you will not behave like a tourist and go to Tokio. On the contrary, you will stay at home, and steep yourself in the work of certain Japanese artists, and then, when you have absorbed the spirit of their style, and caught their imaginative manner of vision, you will go some afternoon and sit in the Park or stroll down Piccadilly, and if you cannot see an absolutely Japanese effect there, you will not see it anywhere. Or, to return again to the past, take as another instance the ancient Greeks. Do you think that Greek art ever tells us what the Greek people were like? Do you believe that the Athenian women were like the stately dignified figures of the Parthenon frieze, or like those marvellous goddesses who sat in the triangular pediments of the same building? If you judge from the art, they certainly were so. But read an authority, like Aristophanes for instance. You will find that the Athenian ladies laced tightly, wore high-heeled shoes, dyed their hair yellow, painted and rouged their faces, and were exactly like any silly fashionable or fallen creature of our own day. The fact is that we look back on the ages entirely through the medium of Art, and Art, very fortunately, has never once told us the truth.

Cyril. But modern portraits by English painters, what of them? Surely they are like the people they pretend to represent?

Vivian. Quite so. They are so like them that a hundred years from now no one will believe in them. The only portraits in which one believes are portraits where there is very little of the sitter, and a very great deal of the artist. Holbein's drawings of the men and women of his time impress us with a sense of their absolute reality. But this is simply because Holbein compelled life to accept his conditions, to restrain itself within his limitations, to reproduce his type, and to appear as he wished it to appear. It is style that makes us believe in a thing—nothing but style. Most of our modern portrait painters are doomed to absolute oblivion. They never paint what they see. They paint what the public sees, and the public never sees anything.

Cyril. Well, after that I think I should like to hear the end of your article.

Vivian. With pleasure. Whether it will do any good I really cannot say. Ours is certainly the dullest and most prosaic century possible. Why, even Sleep has played us false, and has closed up the gates of ivory, and opened the gates of horn. The dreams of the great middle classes of this country, as recorded in Mr. Myers's two bulky volumes on the subject and in the

Transactions of the Psychical Society, are the most depressing things that I have ever read. There is not even a fine nightmare among them. They are commonplace, sordid, and tedious. As for the Church I cannot conceive anything better for the culture of a country than the presence in it of a body of men whose duty it is to believe in the supernatural, to perform daily miracles, and to keep alive that mythopœic faculty which is so essential for the imagination. But in the English Church a man succeeds, not through his capacity for belief, but through his capacity for disbelief. Ours is the only Church where the sceptic stands at the altar, and where St. Thomas is regarded as the ideal apostle. Many a worthy clergyman, who passes his life in admirable works of kindly charity, lives and dies unnoticed and unknown; but it is sufficient for some shallow uneducated passman out of either University to get up in his pulpit and express his doubts about Noah's ark, or Balaam's ass, or Jonah and the whale, for half of London to flock to hear him, and to sit openmouthed in rapt admiration at his superb intellect. The growth of common sense in the English Church is a thing very much to be regretted. It is really a degrading concession to a low form of realism. It is silly, too. It springs from an entire ignorance of psychology. Man can believe the impossible, but man can never believe the improbable. However, I must read the end of my article:—

"What we have to do, what at any rate it is our duty to do, is to revive this old art of Lying. Much of course may be done, in the way of educating the public, by amateurs in the domestic circle, at literary lunches, and at afternoon teas. But this is merely the light and graceful side of lying, such as was probably heard at Cretan dinner parties. There are many other forms. Lying for the sake of gaining some immediate personal advantage, for instance—lying with a moral purpose, as it is usually called—though of late it has been rather looked down upon, was extremely popular with the antique world. Athena laughs when Odysseus tells her 'his words of sly devising,' as Mr. William Morris phrases it, and the glory of mendacity illumines the pale brow of the stainless hero of Euripidean tragedy, and sets among the noble women of the past the young bride of one of Horace's most exquisite odes. Later on, what at first had been merely a natural instinct was elevated into a self-conscious science. Elaborate rules were laid down for the guidance of mankind, and an important school of literature grew up round the subject. Indeed, when one remembers the excellent philosophical treaties of Sanchez on the whole question, one cannot help regretting that no one has ever thought of publishing a cheap and condensed edition of the works of that great casuist. A short primer, 'When to Lie and How,' if brought out in an attractive and not too expensive a form, would no doubt command a large scale, and would prove of real practical service to many earnest and deep-thinking people. Lying for the sake of the improvement of the young, which is the basis of home education, still lingers amongst us, and its advantages are so admirably set forth in the early books of Plato's *Republic* that it is unnecessary to dwell upon them here. It is a mode of lying for which all good mothers have peculiar capabilities, but it is capable of still further development, and has been sadly overlooked by the School Board. Lying for the sake of a monthly salary is of course well known in Fleet Street, and the profession of a political leader-writer is not without its advantages. But it is said to be a somewhat dull occupation, and it certainly does not lead to much beyond a kind of ostentatious obscurity. The only form of lying that is absolutely beyond reproach is Lying for its own sake, and the highest development of this is, as we have already pointed out, Lying in Art. Just as those who do not love Plato more than Truth cannot pass beyond the threshold of the Academe, so those who do not love Beauty more than Truth never know the inmost shrine of Art. The solid stolid British intellect lies in the desert sands like the Sphinx in Flaubert's marvellous tale, and fantasy, *La Chimère*, dances round it, and calls to it with her false, flute-toned voice. It may not hear her now, but surely some day, when we are all bored to death with the commonplace character of modern fiction, it will hearken to her and try to borrow her wings.

"And when that day dawns, or sunset reddens how joyous we shall all be! Facts will be regarded as discreditable, Truth will be found mourning over her fetters, and Romance, with her temper of wonder, will return to the land. The very aspect of the world will change to our startled eyes. Out of the sea will rise Behemoth and Leviathan, and sail round the high-pooped galleys, as they do on the delightful maps of those ages when books on geography were actually readable. Dragons will wander about the waste places, and the phœnix will soar from her nest of fire into the air. We shall lay our hands upon the basilisk, and see the jewel in the toad's head. Champing his gilded oats, the Hippogriff will stand in our stalls, and over our heads will float the Blue Bird singing of beautiful and impossible things, of things that are lovely and that never happen, of things that are not and that should be. But before this comes to pass we must cultivate the lost art of Lying."

Cyril. Then we must certainly cultivate it at once. But in order to avoid making any error I want you to tell me briefly the doctrines of the new æsthetics.

Vivian. Briefly, then, they are these. Art never expresses anything but itself. It has an independent life, just as Thought has, and develops purely on its own lines. It is not necessarily realistic in an age of realism, nor spiritual in an age of faith. So far from being the creation of its time, it is usually in direct opposition to it, and the only history that it preserves for us is the history of its own progress. Sometimes it returns upon its footsteps, and revives some antique form, as happened in the archaistic movement of late Greek Art, and in the pre-Raphaelite movement of our own day. At other times it entirely anticipates its age, and produces in one century work that it takes another century to understand, to appreciate, and to enjoy. In no case does it reproduce its age. To pass from the art of a time to the time itself is the great mistake that all historians commit.

The second doctrine is this. All bad art comes from returning to Life and Nature, and elevating them into ideals. Life and Nature may sometimes be used as part of Art's rough material, but before they are of any real service to art they must be translated into artistic conventions. The moment Art surrenders its imaginative medium it surrenders everything. As a method Realism is a complete failure, and the two things that every artist should avoid are modernity of form and modernity of subject-matter. To us, who live in the nineteenth century, any century is a suitable subject for art except our own. The only beautiful things are the things that do not concern us. It is, to have the pleasure of quoting myself, exactly because Hecuba is nothing to us that her sorrows are so suitable a motive for a tragedy. Besides, it is only the modern that ever becomes old-fashioned. M. Zola sits down to give us a picture of the Second Empire. Who cares for the Second Empire now? It is out of date. Life goes faster than Realism, but Romanticism is always in front of Life.

The third doctrine is that Life imitates Art far more than Art imitates Life. This results not merely from Life's imitative instinct, but from the fact that the self-conscious aim of Life is to find expression, and that Art offers it certain beautiful forms through which it may realize that energy. It is a theory that has never been put forward before, but it is extremely fruitful, and throws an entirely new light upon the history of Art.

It follows, as a corollary from this, that external Nature also imitates Art. The only effects that she can show us are effects that we have already seen through poetry, or in paintings. This is the secret of Nature's charm, as well as the explanation of Nature's weakness.

The final revelation is that Lying, the telling of beautiful untrue things, is the proper aim of Art. But of this I think I have spoken at sufficient length. And now let us go out on the terrace, where "droops the milk-white peacock like a ghost," while the evening star "washes the dusk with silver." At twilight nature becomes a wonderfully suggestive effect, and is not without loveliness, though perhaps its chief use is to illustrate quotations from the poets. Come! We have talked long enough.

PEN PENCIL AND POISON
A study in green

It has constantly been made a subject of reproach against artists and men of letters that they are lacking in wholeness and completeness of nature. As a rule this must necessarily be so. That very concentration of vision and intensity of purpose which is the characteristic of the artistic temperament is in itself a mode of limitation. To those who are pre-occupied with the beauty of form nothing else seems of much importance. Yet there are many exceptions to this rule. Rubens served as ambassador, and Goethe as state councillor, and Milton as Latin secretary to Cromwell. Sophocles held civic office in his own city; the humorists, essayists, and novelists of modern America seem to desire nothing better than to become the diplomatic representatives of their country; and Charles Lamb's friend, Thomas Griffiths Wainewright, the subject of this brief memoir, though of an extremely artistic temperament, followed many masters other than art, being not merely a poet and a painter, an art-critic, an antiquarian, and a writer of prose, an amateur of beautiful things, and a dilettante of things delightful, but also a forger of no mean or ordinary capabilities, and as a subtle and secret poisoner almost without rival in this or any age.

This remarkable man, so powerful with "pen, pencil, and posion," as a great poet of our own day has finely said of him, was born at Chiswick, in 1794. His father was the son of a distinguished solicitor of Gray's Inn and Hatton Garden. His mother was the daughter of the celebrated Dr. Griffiths, the editor and founder of the *Monthly Review*, the partner in another literary speculation of Thomas Davies, that famous bookseller of whom Johnson said that he was not a bookseller, but "a gentleman who dealt in books," the friend of Goldsmith and Wedgwood, and one of the most well-known men of his day. Mrs. Wainewright died, in giving him birth, at the early age of twenty-one, and an obituary notice in the *Gentleman's Magazine* tells us of her "amiable disposition and numerous accomplishments," and adds somewhat quaintly that "she is supposed to have understood the writings of Mr. Locke as well as perhaps any person of either sex now living." His father did not long survive his young wife, and the little child seems to have been brought up by his grandfather, and, on the death of the latter in 1803, by his uncle George Edward Griffiths, whom he subsequently poisoned. His boyhood was passed at Linden House, Turnham Green, one of those many fine Georgian mansions that have unfortunately disappeared before the inroads of the suburban builder, and to its lovely gardens and well-timbered park he owed that simple and impassioned love of nature which never left him all through his life, and which made him so peculiarly susceptible to the spiritual influences of Wordsworth's poetry. He went to school at Charles Burney's academy at Hammersmith. Mr. Burney was the son of the historian of music, and the near kinsman of the artistic lad who was destined to turn out his most remarkable pupil. He seems to have been a man of a good deal of culture, and in after years Mr. Wainewright often spoke of him with much affection as a philosopher, an archæologist, and an admirable teacher who, while he valued the intellectual side of education, did not forget the importance of early moral training. It was under Mr. Burney that he first developed his talent as an artist, and Mr. Hazlitt tells us that a drawing book which he used at school is still extant, and displays great talent and natural feeling. Indeed, painting was the first art that fascinated him. It was not till much later that he sought to find expression by pen or poison.

Before this, however, he seems to have been carried away by boyish dreams of the romance and chivalry of a soldier's life, and to have become a young guardsman. But the reckless dissipated life of his companions failed to satisfy the refined artistic temperament of one who was made for other things. In a short time he wearied of the service. "Art," he tells us, in words that still move many by their ardent sincerity and strange fervour, "Art touched her renegade; by her pure and high influences the noisome mists were purged; my feelings, parched, hot, and tarnished, were renovated with cool, fresh bloom, simple, beautiful to the simple-hearted." But Art was not the only cause of the change. "The writings of Wordsworth," he goes on to say, "did much towards calming the confusing whirl necessarily incident to sudden mutations. I wept over them tears of happiness and gratitude." He accordingly left the army, with its rough barrack-life and coarse mess-room tittle-tattle, and returned to Linden House, full of this new-born enthusiasm for culture. A severe illness, in which, to use his own words, he was "broken like a vessel of clay," prostrated him for a time. His delicately strung organization, however indifferent it might have been to inflicting pain on others, was itself most keenly sensitive to pain. He shrank from suffering as a thing that mars and maims human life, and seems to have wandered through that terrible valley of melancholia from which so many great, perhaps greater, spirits have never emerged. But he was young —only twenty-five years of age—and he soon passed out of the "dead black waters," as he called them, into the larger air of humanistic culture. As he was recovering from the illness that had led him almost to the gates of death, he conceived the idea of taking up literaure as an art. "I said with John Wood-vill," he cries, "it were a life of gods to dwell in such an ele-ment," to see, and hear, and write brave things:—

> "These high and gusty relishes of life
> Have no allayings of mortality."

It is impossible not to feel that in this passage we have the utterance of a man who had a true passion for letters. "To see, and hear, and write brave things," this was his aim.

Scott, the editor of the *London Magazine*, struck by the young man's genius, or under the influence of the strange fas-cination that he exercised on every one who knew him, invited him to write a series of articles on artistic subjects, and under a series of fanciful pseudonyms he began to contribute to the literature of his day. *Janus Weathercock, Egomet Bonmot,* and *Van Vinkvooms,* were some of the grotesque masks under which he chose to hide his seriousness, or to reveal his levity. A mask tells us more than a face. These disguises intensified his personality. In an incredibly short time he seems to have made his mark. Charles Lamb speaks of "kind, light-hearted Wainewright," whose prose is "capital." We hear of him en-tertaining Macready, John Forster, Maginn, Talfourd, Sir Wentworth Dilke, the poet John Clare, and others, at a *petit-dîner*. Like Disraeli, he determined to startle the town as a dandy, and his beautiful rings, his antique cameo breast-pin, and his pale lemon-coloured kid gloves, were well known, and indeed were regarded by Hazlitt as being the signs of a new manner in literature: while his rich curly hair, fine eyes, and ex-quisite white hands gave him the dangerous and delightful dis-tinction of being different from others. There was something in him of Balzac's Lucien de Rubempré. At times he reminds us of Julien Sorel. De Quincey saw him once. It was at a dinner at Charles Lamb's. "Amongst the company, all literary men, sat a murderer," he tells us, and he goes on to describe how on that day he had been ill, and had hated the face of man and woman, and yet found himself looking with intellectual interest across the table at the young writer beneath whose affectations of manner there seemed to him to lie so much unaffected sensibility, and speculates on "what sudden growth of another interest" would have changed his mood, had he known of what terrible sin the guest to whom Lamb paid so much attention was even then guilty.

His life-work falls naturally under the three heads suggested by Mr. Swinburne, and it may be partly admitted that, if we set aside his achievements in the sphere of poison, what he has actually left to us hardly justifies his reputation.

But then it is only the Philistine who seeks to estimate a personality by the vulgar test of production. This young dandy sought to be somebody, rather than to do something. He recognized that Life itself is an art, and has its modes of style no less than the arts that seek to express it. Nor is his work without interest. We hear of William Blake stopping in the Royal Academy before one of his pictures and pronouncing it to be "very fine." His essays are prefiguring of much that has since been realized. He seems to have anticipated some of those accidents of modern culture that are regarded by many as true essentials. He writes about La Gioconda, and early French poets and the Italian Renaissance. He loves Greek gems, and Persian carpets, and Elizabethan translations of *Cupid and Psyche*, and the *Hypnerotomachia*, and book-bindings, and early editions, and wide-margined proofs. He is keenly sensitive to the value of beautiful surroundings, and never wearies of describing to us the rooms in which he lived, or would have liked to live. He had that curious love of green, which in individuals is always the sign of a subtle artistic temperament, and in nations is said to denote a laxity, if not a decadence of morals. Like Baudelaire he was extremely fond of cats, and with Gautier, he was fascinated by that "sweet marble monster" of both sexes that we can still see at Florence and in the Louvre.

There is of course much in his descriptions, and his suggestions for decoration, that shows that he did not entirely free
himself from the false taste of his time. But it is clear that he
was one of the first to recognize what is, indeed, the very keynote of æsthetic eclecticism, I mean the true harmony of all
really beautiful things irrespective of age or place, of school or
manner. He saw that in decorating a room, which is to be, not
a room for show, but a room to live in, we should never aim at
any archæological reconstruction of the past, nor burden ourselves with any fanciful necessity for historical accuracy. In
this artistic perception he was perfectly right. All beautiful
things belong to the same age.

And so, in his own library, as he describes it, we find the
delicate fictile vase of the Greek, with its exquisitely painted
figures and the faint ΚΑΛΟΣ finely traced upon its side, and behind it hangs an engraving of the "Delphic Sibyl" of Michael
Angelo, or of the "Pastoral" of Giorgione. Here is a bit of
Florentine majolica, and here a rude lamp from some old Roman tomb. On the table lies a book of Hours, "cased in a
cover of solid silver gilt, wrought with quaint devices and
studded with small brilliants and rubies," and close by it "squats
a little ugly monster, a Lar, perhaps, dug up in the sunny fields
of corn-bearing Sicily." Some dark antique bronzes contrast
"with the pale gleam of two noble *Christi Crucifixi*, one carved
in ivory, the other moulded wax." He has his trays of Tassie's
gems, his tiny Louis-Quatorze *bonbonnière* with a miniature
by Petitot, his highly prized "brown-biscuit teapots, filagree-
worked," his citron morocco letter-case, and his "pomona-green"
chair.

One can fancy him lying there in the midst of his books and
casts and engravings, a true virtuoso, a subtle connoisseur, turning over his fine collection of Marc Antonios, and his Turner's
"Liber Studiorum," of which he was a warm admirer, or exam-
ining with a magnifier some of his antique gems and cameos,
"the head of Alexander on an onyx of two strata," or "that
superb *altissimo relievo* on cornelian, Jupiter Ægiochus." He
was always a great amateur of engravings, and gives some very
useful suggestions as to the best means of forming a collection.
Indeed, while fully appreciating modern art, he never lost sight

325

of the importance of reproductions of the great masterpieces of the past, and all that he says about the value of plaster casts is quite admirable.

As an art-critic he concerned himself primarily with the complex impressions produced by a work of art, and certainly the first step in æsthetic criticism is to realize one's own impressions. He cared nothing for abstract discussions on the nature of the Beautiful, and the historical method, which has since yielded such rich fruit, did not belong to his day, but he never lost sight of the great truth that Art's first appeal is neither to the intellect nor to the emotions, but purely to the artistic temperament, and he more than once points out that this temperament, this "taste," as he calls it, being unconsciously guided and made perfect by frequent contact with the best work, becomes in the end a form of right judgment. Of course there are fashions in art just as there are fashions in dress, and perhaps none of us can ever quite free ourselves from the influence of custom and the influence of novelty. He certainly could not, and he frankly acknowledges how difficult it is to form any fair estimate of contemporary work. But, on the whole, his taste was good and sound. He admired Turner and Constable at a time when they were not so much thought of as they are now, and saw that for the highest landscape art we require more than "mere industry and accurate transcription." Of Crome's "Heath Scene near Norwich" he remarks that it shows "how much a subtle observation of the elements, in their wild moods, does for a most uninteresting flat," and of the popular type of landscape of his day he says that it is "simply an enumeration of hill and dale, stumps of trees, shrubs, water, meadows, cottages, and houses; little more than topography, a kind of pictorial map-work; in which rainbows, showers, mists, haloes, large beams shooting through rifted clouds, storms, starlight, all the most valued materials of the real painter, are not." He had a thorough dislike of what is obvious or commonplace in art, and while he was charmed to entertain Wilkie at dinner, he cared as little for Sir David's pictures as he did for Mr. Crabbe's poems. With the imitative and realistic tendencies of his day he had no sympathy, and he tells us frankly that his great admiration for Fuseli was largely due to the fact that the little Swiss did not consider it necessary that an artist should only paint what he sees. The qualities that he sought for in a picture were composition, beauty and dignity of line, richness of colour, and imaginative power. Upon the other hand, he was not a doctrinaire. "I hold that no work of art can be tried otherwise than by laws deduced from itself: whether or not it be consistent with itself is the question." This is one of his excellent aphorisms. And in criticising painters so different as Landseer and Martin, Stothard and Etty, he shows that, to use a phrase now classical, he is trying "to see the object as in itself it really is."

However, as I pointed out before, he never feels quite at his ease in his criticisms of contemporary work. "The present," he says, "is about as agreeable a confusion to me as Ariosto on the first perusal. . . . Modern things dazzle me. I must look at them through Time's telescope. Elia complains that to him the merit of a MS. poem is uncertain; 'print,' as he excellently says, 'settles it.' Fifty years' toning does the same thing to a picture." He is happier when he is writing about Watteau and Lancret, about Rubens and Giorgione, about Rembrandt, Correggio, and Michael Angelo; happiest of all when he is writing about Greek things. What is Gothic touched him very little, but classical art and the art of the Renaissance were always dear to him. He saw what our English school could gain from a study of Greek models, and never wearies of pointing out to the young student the artistic possibilities that lie dormant in Hellenic marbles and Hellenic methods of work. In his judgments on the great Italian Masters, says De Quincey, "There seemed a tone of sincerity and of native sensibility, as in one who spoke for himself, and was not merely a copier from books." The highest praise that we can give to him is that he tried to revive style as a conscious tradition. But he saw that no amount of art-lectures or art congresses, or "plans for advancing the fine arts," will ever produce this result. The people, he says very wisely, and in the true spirit of Toynbee Hall, must always have "the best models constantly before their eyes."

As is to be expected from one who was a painter, he is often extremely technical in his art criticisms. Of Tintoret's "St. George delivering the Egyptian Princess from the Dragon" he remarks:—

"The robe of Sabra, warmly glazed with Prussian blue, is relieved from the pale greenish background by a vermilion scarf;
and the full hues of both are beautifully echoed, as it were, in a
lower key by the purple-lake coloured stuffs and bluish iron
armour of the saint, besides an ample balance to the vivid azure
drapery on the foreground in the indigo shades of the wild wood
surrounding the castle."

And elsewhere he talks learnedly of "a delicate Schiavone,
various as a tulip-bed, with rich broken tints," of "a glowing
portrait, remarkable for *morbidezza*, by the scarce Moroni," and
of another picture being "pulpy in the carnations."

But, as a rule, he deals with his impressions of the work as
an artistic whole, and tries to translate those impressions into
words, to give, as it were, the literary equivalent for the imaginative and mental effect. He was one of the first to develop
what has been called the art-literature of the nineteenth century, that form of literature which has found in Mr. Ruskin
and Mr. Browning its two most perfect exponents. His description of Lancret's *Repas Italien*, in which "a dark-haired girl,
'amorous of mischief,' lies on the daisy-powdered grass," is in
some respects very charming. Here is his account of "The Cru-
cifixion," by Rembrandt. It is extremely characteristic of his
style:—

"Darkness—sooty, portentous darkness—shrouds the whole
scene: only above the accursed wood, as if through a horrid rift
in the murky ceiling, a rainy deluge—'sleety-flaw, discoloured
water'—streams down amain, spreading a grisly spectral light,
even more horrible than the palpable night. Already the Earth
pants thick and fast! the darkened Cross trembles! the winds are
dropt—the air is stagnant—a muttering rumble growls underneath their feet, and some of that miserable crowd begin to fly
down the hill. The horses snuff the coming terror, and become
unmanageable through fear. The moment rapidly approaches when,
nearly torn asunder by His own weight, fainting with loss of
blood, which now runs in narrower rivulets from His slit veins,
His temples and breast drowned in sweat, and His black tongue
parched with the fiery death-fever, Jesus cries, 'I thirst.' The deadly
vinegar is elevated to Him.

"His head sinks, and the sacred corpse 'swings senseless of the cross.' A sheet of vermilion flame shoots sheer through the air and vanishes; the rocks of Carmel and Lebanon cleave asunder; the sea rolls on high from the sands its black weltering waves. Earth yawns, and the graves give up their dwellers. The dead and the living are mingled together in unnatural conjunction and hurry through the holy city. New prodigies await them there. The veil of the temple—the unpierceable veil—is rent asunder from top to bottom, and that dreaded recess containing the Hebrew mysteries —the fatal ark with the tables and seven-branched candelabrum— is disclosed by the light of unearthly flames to the God-deserted multitude.

"Rembrandt never *painted* this sketch, and he was quite right. It would have lost nearly all its charm in losing that perplexing veil of indistinctness which affords such ample range wherein the doubting imagination may speculate. At present it is like a thing in another world. A dark gulf is betwixt us. It is not tangible by the body. We can only approach it in the spirit."

In this passage, written, the author tells us, "in awe and reverence," there is much that is terrible, and very much that is quite horrible, but it is not without a certain crude form of power, or, at any rate, a certain crude violence of words, a quality which this age should highly appreciate, as it is its chief defect. It is pleasanter, however, to pass to this description of Giulio Romano's "Cephalus and Procris":—

"We should read Moschus's lament for Bion, the sweet shepherd, before looking at this picture, or study the picture as a preparation for the lament. We have nearly the same images in both. For either victim the high groves and forest dells murmur; the flowers exhale sad perfume from their buds; the nightingale mourns on the craggy lands, and the swallow in the long-winding vales; 'the satyrs, too, and fauns dark-veiled groan,' and the fountain nymphs within the wood melt into tearful waters. The sheep and goats leave their pasture; and oreads, 'who love to scale the most inaccessible tops of all uprightest rocks,' hurry down from the song of their wind-courting pines; while the dryads bend from the branches of the meeting trees, and the rivers moan for white Procris, 'with many-sobbing streams,'

"Filling the far-seen ocean with a voice."

The golden bees are silent on thymy Hymettus; and the knelling horn of Aurora's love no more shall scatter away the cold twilight on the top of Hymettus. The foreground of our subject is a grassy sunburnt bank, broken into swells and hollows like waves (a sort of land-breakers), rendered more uneven by many foot-tripping roots and stumps of trees stocked untimely by the axe, which are again throwing out light green shoots. This bank rises rather suddenly on the right to a clustering grove, penetrable to no star, at the entrance of which sits the stunned Thessalian king, holding between his knees that ivory-bright body which was, but an instant agone, parting the rough boughs with her smooth fore-head, and treading alike on thorns and flowers with jealousy-stung foot—now helpless, heavy, void of all motion, save when the breeze lifts her thick hair in mockery.

"From between the closely-neighboured boles astonished nymphs press forward with loud cries—

"And deerskin-vested satyrs, crowned with ivy twists, advance;
And put strange pity in their horned countenance."

"Laelaps lies beneath, and shows by his panting the rapid pace of death. On the other side of the group, Virtuous Love with 'vans dejected' holds forth the arrow to an approaching troop of sylvan people, fauns, rams, goats, satyrs, and satyr-mothers, press-ing their children tighter with their fearful hands, who hurry along from the left in a sunken path between the foreground and a rocky wall, on whose lowest ridge a brook-guardian pours from her urn her grief-telling waters. Above and more remote than the Ephidryad, another female, rending her locks, appears among the vine-festooned pillars of an unshorn grove. The centre of the picture is filled by shady meadows, sinking down to a river-mouth; beyond is 'the vast strength of the ocean stream,' from whose floor the ex-tinguisher of stars, rosy Aurora, drives furiously up her brine-washed steeds to behold the death-pangs of her rival."

Were this description carefully rewritten, it would be quite admirable. The conception of making a prose-poem out of paint is excellent. Much of the best modern literature springs from the same aim. In a very ugly and sensible age, the arts borrow, not from life, but from each other.

His sympathies, too, were wonderfully varied. In everything connected with the stage, for instance, he was always extremely interested, and strongly upheld the necessity for archæological accuracy in costume and scene-painting. "In art," he says in one of his essays, "whatever is worth doing at all is worth doing well"; and he points out that once we allow the intrusion of anachronisms, it becomes difficult to say where the line is to be drawn. In literature, again, like Lord Beaconsfield on a famous occasion, he was, "on the side of angels." He was one of the first to admire Keats and Shelley—"the tremulously-sensitive and poetical Shelley," as he calls him. His admiration for Wordsworth was sincere and profound. He thoroughly appreciated William Blake. One of the best copies of the "Songs of Innocence and Experience" that is now in existence was wrought specially for him. He loved Alain Chartier, and Ronsard, and the Elizabethan dramatists, and Chaucer and Chapman, and Petrarch. And to him all the arts were one. "Our critics," he remarks with much wisdom, "seem hardly aware of the identity of the primal seeds of poetry and painting, nor that any true advancement in the serious study of one art cogenerates a proportionate perfection in the other"; and he says elsewhere that if a man who does not admire Michael Angelo talks of his love for Milton, he is deceiving either himself or his listeners. To his fellow-contributors in the *London Magazine* he was always most generous, and praises Barry Cornwall, Allan Cunningham, Hazlitt, Elton, and Leigh Hunt without anything of the malice of a friend. Some of his sketches of Charles Lamb are admirable in their way, and, with the art of the true comedian, borrow their style from the subject:—

"What can I say of thee more than all know? that thou hadst the gaiety of a boy with the knowledge of a man: as gentle a heart as ever sent tears to the eyes.

"How wittily would he mistake your meaning, and put in a conceit most seasonably out of season. His talk without affectation was compressed, like his beloved Elizabethans, even unto obscurity. Like grains of fine gold, his sentences would beat out into whole sheets. He had small mercy on spurious fame, and a caustic observation on the *fashion for men of genius* was a standing dish. Sir Thomas Browne was a 'bosom cronie' of his; so was Burton, and old Fuller. In his amorous vein he dallied with that peerless Duchess of many-folio odour; and with the heyday comedies of Beaumont and Fletcher he induced light dreams. He would deliver critical touches on these, like one inspired, but it was good to let him choose his own game; if another began even on the acknowledged pets he was liable to interrupt, or rather append, in a mode difficult to define whether as misapprehensive or mischievous. One night at C———'s, the above dramatic partners were the temporary subject of chat. Mr. X. commended the passion and haughty style of a tragedy (I don't know which of them), but was instantly taken up by Elia, who told him '*That* was nothing; the lyrics were the high things—the lyrics!' "

One side of his literary career deserves especial notice. Modern journalism may be said to owe almost as much to him as to any man of the early part of this century. He was the pioneer of Asiatic prose, and delighted in pictorial epithets and pompous exaggerations. To have a style so gorgeous that it conceals the subject is one of the highest achievements of an important and much admired school of Fleet Street leader-writers, and this school *Janus Weathercock* may be said to have invented. He also saw that it was quite easy by continued reiteration to make the public interested in his own personality, and in his purely journalistic articles this extraordinary young man tells the world what he had for dinner, where he gets his clothes, what wines he likes, and in what state of health he is, just as if he were writing weekly notes for some popular newspaper of our own time. This being the least valuable side of his work, is the one that has had the most obvious influence. A publicist, now-a-days, is a man who bores the community with the details of the illegalities of his private life.

Like most artificial people he had a great love of nature. "I hold three things in high estimation," he says somewhere: "to sit lazily on an eminence that commands a rich prospect; to be shadowed by thick trees while the sun shines around me; and to enjoy solitude with the consciousness of neighbourhood. The country gives them all to me." He writes about his wandering over fragrant furze and heath repeating Collin's "Ode to Evening," just to catch the fine quality of the moment; about smothering his face "in a watery bed of cowslips, wet with May dews"; and about the pleasure of seeing the sweet-breathed kine "pass slowly homeward through the twilight," and hearing "the distant clank of the sheep-bell." One phrase of his, "the polyanthus glowed in its cold bed of earth, like a solitary picture of

Giorgione on a dark oaken panel," is curiously characteristic of his temperament, and this passage is rather pretty in its way—

"The short tender grass was covered with marguerites—'such that men called *daisies* in our town'—thick as stars on a summer's night. The harsh caw of the busy rooks came pleasantly mellowed from a high dusky grove of elms at some distance off, and at intervals was heard the voice of a boy scaring away the birds from the newly-sown seeds. The blue depths were the colour of the darkest ultramarine; not a cloud streaked the calm æther; only round the horizon's edge streamed a light, warm film of misty vapour, against which the near village with its ancient stone church showed sharply out with blinding whiteness. I thought of Wordworth's 'Lines written in March.' "

However, we must not forget that the cultivated young man who penned these lines, and who was so susceptible to Wordsworthian influences, was also, as I said at the beginning of this memoir, one of the most subtle and secret poisoners of this or any age. How he first became fascinated by this strange sin he does not tell us, and the diary in which he carefully noted the results of his terrible experiments and the methods that he adopted, has unfortunately been lost to us. Even in later days, too, he was always reticent on the matter, and preferred to speak about "The Excursion," and the "Poems founded on the Affections." There is no doubt, however, that the poison that he used was strychnine. In one of the beautiful rings of which he was so proud, and which served to show off the fine modelling of his delicate ivory hands, he used to carry crystals of the Indian *nux vomica*, a poison, one of his biographers tells us, "nearly tasteless, difficult of discovery, and capable of almost infinite dilution." His murders, says De Quincey, were more than were ever made known judicially. This is no doubt so, and some of them are worthy of mention. His first victim was his uncle, Mr. Thomas Griffiths. He poisoned him in 1829 to gain possession of Linden House, a place to which he had always been very much attached. In the August of the next year he poisoned Mrs. Abercrombie, his wife's mother, and in the following December he poisoned the lovely Helen Abercrombie, his sister-in-law. Why he murdered Mrs. Abercrombie is not ascertained. It may have been for a caprice, or to quicken some hideous sense of power that was in him, or because she suspected something, or for no reason. But the murder of Helen Abercrombie was carried out by himself and his wife for the sake of a sum of about 18,000*l.* for which they had insured her life in various offices. The circumstances were as follows. On the 12th of December, he and his wife and child came up to London from Linden House, and took lodgings at No. 12, Conduit Street, Regent Street. With them were the two sisters, Helen and Madeleine Abercrombie. On the evening of the 14th they all went to the play, and at supper that night Helen sickened. The next day she was extremely ill, and Dr. Locock, of Hanover Square, was called in to attend her. She lived till Monday, the 20th, when, after the doctor's morning visit, Mr. and Mrs. Wainewright brought her some poisoned jelly, and then went out for a walk. When they returned Helen Abercrombie was dead. She was about twenty years of age, a tall graceful girl with fair hair. A very charming red-chalk drawing of her by her brother-in-law is still in existence, and shows how much his style as an artist was influenced by Sir Thomas Lawrence, a painter for whose work he had always entertained a great admiration. De Quincey says that Mrs. Wainewright was not really privy to the murder. Let us hope that she was not. Sin should be solitary, and have no accomplices.

The insurance companies, suspecting the real facts of the case, declined to pay the policy on the technical ground of misrepresentation and want of interest, and, with curious courage, the poisoner entered an action in the Court of Chancery against the Imperial, it being agreed that one decision should govern all the cases. The trial, however, did not come on for five years, when, after one disagreement, a verdict was ultimately given in the companies' favour. The judge on the occasion was Lord Abinger. *Egomet Bonmot* was represented by Mr. Erle and Sir William Follet, and the Attorney-General and Sir Frederick Pollock appeared for the other side. The plaintiff, unfortunately, was unable to be present at either of the trials. The refusal of the companies to give him the 18,000*l.* had placed him in a position of most painful pecuniary embarrassment. Indeed, a few months after the murder of Helen Abercrombie, he had been actually arrested for debt in the streets of London while he was serenading the pretty daughter of one of his friends. This difficulty was got over at the time, but shortly afterwards he thought it better to go abroad till he could come to some practical arrangement with his creditors. He accordingly went to Boulogne on a visit to the father of the young lady in question, and while he was there induced him to insure his life with the Pelican Company for 3000*l.* As soon as the necessary formalities had been gone through and the policy executed, he dropped some crystals of strychnine into his coffee as they sat together one evening after dinner. He himself did not gain any monetary advantage by doing this. His aim was simply to revenge himself on the first office that had refused to pay him the price of his sin. His friend died the next day in his presence, and he left Boulogne at once for a sketching tour through the most picturesque parts of Brittany, and was for some time the guest of an old French gentleman, who had a beautiful country house at St. Omer. From this he moved to Paris, where he remained for several years, living in luxury, some say, while others talk of his "skulking with poison in his pocket, and being dreaded by all who knew him." In 1837 he returned to England privately. Some strange mad fascination brought him back. He followed a woman whom he loved.

It was the month of June, and he was staying at one of the hotels in Covent Garden. His sitting room was on the ground floor, and he prudently kept the blinds down for fear of being seen. Thirteen years before, when he was making his fine collection of majolica and Marc Antonios, he had forged the names of his trustees to a power of attorney, which enabled him to get possession of some of the money which he had inherited from his mother, and had brought into marriage settlement. He knew that this forgery had been discovered, and that by returning to England he was imperilling his life. Yet he returned. Should one wonder? It was said that the woman was very beautiful. Besides, she did not love him.

It was by a mere accident that he was discovered. A noise in the street attracted his attention, and, in his artistic interest in modern life, he pushed aside the blind for a moment. Some one outside called out "That's Wainewright, the Bank-forger." It was Forrester, the Bow Street runner.

On the 5th of July he was brought up at the Old Bailey. The following report of the proceedings appeared in the *Times*:—

"Before Mr. Justice Vaughan and Mr. Baron Alderson, Thomas Griffiths Wainewright, aged forty-two, a man of gentlemanly appearance, wearing mustachios, was indicted for forging and uttering a certain power of attorney for 2259*l*., with intent to defraud the Governor and Company of the Bank of England.

"There were five indictments against the prisoner, to all of which he pleaded not guilty, when he was arraigned before Mr. Serjeant Arabin in the course of the morning. On being brought before the judges, however, he begged to be allowed to withdraw the former plea, and then pleaded guilty to two of the indictments which were not of a capital nature.

"The counsel for the Bank having explained that there were three other indictments, but that the Bank did not desire to shed blood, the plea of guilty on the two minor charges was recorded, and the prisoner at the close of the session sentenced by the Recorder to transportation for life."

He was taken back to Newgate, preparatory to his removal to the colonies. In a fanciful passage in one of his early essays he had fancied himself "lying in Horsemonger Gaol under sentence of death" for having been unable to resist the temptation of stealing some Marc Antonios from the British Museum in order to complete his collection. The sentence now passed on him was to a man of his culture a form of death. He complained bitterly of it to his friends, and pointed out, with a good deal of reason, some people may fancy, that the money was practically his own, having come to him from his mother, and that the forgery, such as it was, had been committed thirteen years before, which to use his own phrase, was at least a *circonstance attenuante*. The permanence of personality is a very subtle metaphysical problem, and certainly the English law solves the question in an extremely rough-and-ready manner. There is, however, something dramatic in the fact that this heavy punishment was inflicted on him for what, if we remember his fatal influence on the prose of modern journalism, was certainly not the worst of all his sins.

While he was in gaol, Dickens, Macready, and Hablot Browne came across him by chance. They had been going over prisons of London, searching for artistic effects, and in Newgate they suddenly caught sight of Wainewright. He met them with a defiant stare, Forster tells us, but Macready was "horrified to recognize a man familiarly known to him in former years, and at whose table he had dined."

Others had more curiosity, and his cell was for some time a kind of fashionable lounge. Many men of letters went down to visit their old literary comrade. But he was no longer the kind light-hearted Janus whom Charles Lamb admired. He seems to have grown quite cynical.

To the agent of an insurance company who was visiting him one afternoon, and thought he would improve the occasion by pointing out that, after all[,] crime was a bad speculation, he replied: "Sir, you City men enter on your speculations and take the chances of them. Some of your speculations succeed, some fail. Mine happen to have failed, yours happen to have succeeded. That is the only difference, sir, between my visitor and me. But, sir, I will tell you one thing in which I have succeeded to the last. I have been determined through life to hold the position of a gentleman. I have always done so. I do so still. It is the custom of this place that each of the inmates of a cell shall take his morning's turn of sweeping it out. I occupy a cell with a bricklayer and a sweep, but they never offer me the broom!" When a friend reproached him with the murder of Helen Abercrombie he shrugged his shoulders and said, "Yes; it was a dreadful thing to do, but she had very thick ankles."

From Newgate he was brought to the hulks at Portsmouth, and sent from there in the *Susan* to Van Diemen's Land along with three hundred other convicts. The voyage seems to have been most distasteful to him, and in a letter written to a friend he spoke bitterly about the ignominy of "the companion of poets and artists" being compelled to associate with "country bumpkins." The phrase that he applies to his companions need not surprise us. Crime in England is rarely the result of sin. It is nearly always the result of starvation. There was probably no one on board in whom he would have found a sympathetic listener, or even a psychologically interesting nature.

His love of art, however, never deserted him. At Hobart Town he started a studio, and returned to sketching and portrait-painting, and his conversation and manners seem not to have lost their charm. Nor did he give up his habit of poisoning, and there are two cases on record in which he tried to make away with people who had offended him. But his hand seems to have lost is cunning. Both of his attempts were complete failures, and in 1844, being thoroughly dissatisfied with Tasmanian society, he presented a memorial to the governor of the settlement, Sir John Eardley Wilmot, praying for a ticket-of-leave. In it he speaks of himself as being "tormented by ideas struggling for outward form and realization, barred up from increase of knowledge, and deprived of the exercise of profitable or even of decorous speech." His request, however, was refused, and the associate of Coleridge consoled himself by making those marvellous *Paradis Artificiels* whose secret is only known to the eaters of opium. In 1852 he died of apoplexy, his sole living companion being a cat, for which he had evinced an extraordinary affection.

His crimes seem to have had an important effect upon his art. They gave a strong personality to his style, a quality that his early work certainly lacked. In a note to the Life of Dickens, Forster mentions that in 1847 Lady Blessington received from her brother, Major Power, who held a military appointment at Hobart Town, an oil portrait of a young lady from his clever brush; and it is said that "he had contrived to put the expression of his own wickedness into the portrait of a nice, kind-hearted girl." M. Zola, in one of his novels, tells us of a young man who, having committed a murder, takes to art, and paints greenish impressionist portraits of perfectly respectable people, all of which bear a curious resemblance to his victim. The development of Mr. Wainewright's style seems to me far more subtle and suggestive. One can fancy an intense personality being created out of sin.

This strange and fascinating figure that for a few years dazzled literary London, and made so brilliant a *début* in life and letters, is undoubtedly a most interesting study. Mr. W. Carew Hazlitt, his latest biographer, to whom I am indebted for many of the facts contained in his memoir, and whose little book is, indeed, quite invaluable in its way, is of opinion that his love of art and nature was a mere pretence and assumption, and others have denied to him all literary power. This seems to me a shallow, or at least a mistaken, view. The fact of a man being a poisoner is nothing against his prose. The domestic virtues are not the true basis of art, though they may serve as an excellent advertisement for second-rate artists. It is possible that De Quincey exaggerated his critical powers, and I cannot help saying again that there is much in his published works that is too familiar, too common, too journalistic, in the bad sense of that word. Here and there he is distinctly vulgar in expression, and he is always lacking in the self-restraint of the true artist. But for some of his faults we must blame the time in which he lived, and, after all, prose that Charles Lamb thought "capital" has no small historic interest. That he had a sincere love of art and nature seems to me quite certain. There is no essential incongruity between crime and culture. We cannot re-write the whole of history for the purpose of gratifying our moral sense of what should be.

Of course, he is far too close to our own time for us to be able to form any purely artistic judgment about him. It is impossible not to feel a strong prejudice against a man who might have poisoned Lord Tennyson, or Mr. Gladstone, or the Master of Balliol. But had the man worn a costume and spoken a language different from our own, had he lived in imperial Rome, or at the time of the Italian Renaissance, or in Spain in the seventeenth century, or in any land or any century but this century and this land, we would be quite able to arrive at a perfectly unprejudiced estimate of his position and value. I know that there are many historians, or at least writers on historical subjects, who still think it necessary to apply moral judgments to history, and who distribute their praise or blame with the solemn complacency of a successful schoolmaster. This, however, is a foolish habit, and merely shows that the moral instinct can be brought to such a pitch of perfection that it will make its appearance wherever it is not required. Nobody with the true historical sense ever dreams of blaming Nero, or scolding Tiberius or censuring Cæsar Borgia. These personages have become like the puppets of a play. They may fill us with terror, or horror, or wonder, but they do not harm us. They are not in immediate relation to us. We have nothing to fear from them. They have passed into the sphere of art and science, and neither art nor science knows anything of moral approval or disapproval. And so it may be some day with Charles Lamb's friend. At present I feel that he is just a little too modern to be treated in that fine spirit of disinterested curiosity to which we owe so many charming studies of the great criminals of the Italian Renaissance from the pens of Mr. John Addington Symonds, Miss A. Mary F. Robinson, Miss Vernon Lee, and other distinguished writers. However, Art has not forgotten him. He is the hero of Dickens's *Hunted Down*, the Varney of Bulwer's *Lucretia*; and it is gratifying to note that fiction has paid some homage to one who was so powerful with "pen, pencil, and poison." To be suggestive for fiction is to be of more importance than a fact.

THE CRITIC AS ARTIST
With some remarks upon the importance of doing nothing

A Dialogue. Part I.
Persons: Gilbert and Ernest.
Scene: the library of a house in Piccadilly, overlooking the Green Park.

Gilbert (at the Piano). My dear Ernest, what are you laughing at?

Ernest (looking up). At a capital story that I have just come across in this volume of Reminiscences that I have found on your table.

Gilbert. What is the book? Ah! I see. I have not read it yet. Is it good?

Ernest. Well, while you have been playing, I have been turning over the pages with some amusement, though, as a rule, I dislike modern memoirs. They are generally written by people who have either entirely lost their memories, or have never done anything worth remembering; which, however, is, no doubt, the true explanation of their popularity, as the English public always feels perfectly at its ease when a mediocrity is talking to it.

Gilbert. Yes: the public is wonderfully tolerant. It forgives everything except genius. But I must confess that I like all memoirs. I like them for their form, just as much as for their matter. In literature mere egotism is delightful. It is what fascinates us in the letters of personalities so different as Cicero and Balzac, Flaubert and Berlioz, Byron and Madame de Sévigné. Whenever we come across it, and, strangely enough, it is rather rare, we cannot but welcome it, and do not easily forget it. Humanity will always love Rousseau for having confessed his sins, not to a priest, but to the world, and the couchant nymphs that Cellini wrought in bronze for the castle of King Francis, the green and gold Perseus, even, that in the open Loggia at Florence shows the moon the dead terror that once turned life to stone, have not given it more pleasure than has that autobiography in which the supreme scoundrel of the Renaissance relates the story of his splendour and his shame. The opinions, the character, the achievements of the man, matter very little. He may be a sceptic like the gentle Sieur de Montaigne, or a saint like the bitter son of Monica, but when he tells his own secrets he can always charm our ears to listening and our lips to silence. The mode of thought that Cardinal Newman represented—if that can be called a mode of thought which seeks to solve intellectual problems by a denial of the supremacy of the intellect—may not, cannot, I think, survive. But the world will never weary of watching that troubled soul in its progress from darkness to darkness. The lonely church at Littlemore, where "the breath of the morning is damp, and worshippers are few," will always be dear to it, and whenever men see the yellow snapdragon blossoming on the wall of Trinity they will think of that gracious undergraduate who saw in the flower's sure recurrence a prophecy that he would abide for ever with the Benign Mother of his days—a prophecy that Faith, in her wisdom or her folly, suffered not to be fulfilled. Yes; auto-biography is irresistible. Poor, silly, conceited Mr. Secretary Pepys has chattered his way into the circle of the Immortals, and, conscious that indiscretion is the better part of valour, bustles about among them in that "shaggy purple gown with gold buttons and looped lace" which he is so fond of describing to us, perfectly at his ease, and prattling, to his own and our infinite pleasure, of the Indian blue petticoat that he bought for his wife, of the "good hog's harslet," and the "pleasant French fricassee of veal" that he loved to eat, of his game of bowls with Will Joyce, and his "gadding after beauties," and his reciting of *Hamlet* on a Sunday, and his playing of the viol on week days, and other wicked or trivial things. Even in actual life egotism is not without its attractions. When people talk to us about others they are usually dull. When they talk to us about themselves they are nearly always interesting, and if one could shut them up, when they become wearisome, as easily as one can shut up a book of which one has grown wearied, they would be perfect absolutely.

Ernest. There is much virtue in that If, as Touchstone would say. But do you seriously propose that every man should become his own Boswell? What would become of our industrious compilers of Lives and Recollections in that case?

Gilbert. What has become of them? They are the pest of the age, nothing more and nothing less. Every great man nowadays has his disciples, and it is always Judas who writes the biography.

Ernest. My dear fellow!

Gilbert. I am afraid it is true. Formerly we used to canonize our heroes. The modern method is to vulgarize them. Cheap editions of great books may be delightful, but cheap editions of great men are absolutely detestable.

Ernest. May I ask, Gilbert, to whom you allude?

Gilbert. Oh! to all our second-rate *litterateurs*. We are overrun by a set of people who, when poet or painter passes away, arrive at the house along with the undertaker, and forget that their one duty is to behave as mutes. But we won't talk about them. They are the mere body-snatchers of literature. The dust is given to one, and the ashes to another, and the soul is out of their reach. And now, let me play Chopin to you, or Dvorák? Shall I play you a fantasy by Dvorák? He writes passionate, curiously-coloured things.

Ernest. No; I don't want music at present. It is far too indefinite. Besides, I took the Baroness Bernstein down to dinner last night, and, though absolutely charming in every other respect, she insisted on discussing music as if it were actually written in the German language. Now, whatever music sounds like, I am glad to say that it does not sound in the smallest degree like German. There are forms of patriotism that are really quite degrading. No; Gilbert, don't play any more. Turn round and talk to me. Talk to me till the white-horned day comes into the room. There is something in your voice that is wonderful.

Gilbert (rising from the piano). I am not in a mood for talking to-night. How horrid of you to smile? I really am not. Where are the cigarettes? Thanks. How exquisite these single daffodils are! They seem to be made of amber and cool ivory. They are like Greek things of the best period. What was the story in the confessions of the remorseful Academician that made you laugh? Tell it to me. After playing Chopin, I feel as if I had been weeping over sins that I had never committed, and mourning over tragedies that were not my own. Music always seems to me to produce that effect. It creates for one a past of which one has been ignorant, and fills one with a sense of sorrows that have been hidden from one's tears. I can fancy a man who had led a perfectly commonplace life, hearing by chance some curious piece of music, and suddenly discovering that his soul, without his being conscious of it, had passed through terrible experiences, and known fearful joys, or wild romantic loves, or great renunciations. And so, tell me this story, Ernest. I want to be amused.

Ernest. Oh! I don't know that it is of any importance. But I thought it a really admirable illustration of the true value of ordinary art-criticism. It seems that a lady once gravely asked the remorseful Academician, as you call him, if his celebrated picture of "A Spring-Day at Whiteley's," or "Waiting for the Last Omnibus," or some subject of that kind, was all painted by hand?

Gilbert. And was it?

Ernest. You are quite incorrigible. But, seriously speaking, what is the use of art-criticism? Why cannot the artist be left alone, to create a new world if he wishes it, or, if not, to shadow forth the world which we already know, and of which, I fancy, we would each one of us be wearied if Art, with her fine spirit of choice and delicate instinct of selection, did not, as it were, purify it for us, and give to it a momentary perfection. It seems to me that the imagination spreads, or should spread, a solitude around it, and works best in silence and in isolation. Why should the artist be troubled by the shrill clamour of criticism? Why should those who cannot create take upon themselves to estimate the value of creative work? What can they know about it? If a man's work is easy to understand, an explanation is unnecessary. . . .

Gilbert. And if his work is incomprehensible, an explanation is wicked.

Ernest. I did not say that.

Gilbert. Ah! but you should have. Nowadays, we have so few mysteries left to us that we cannot afford to part with one of them. The members of the Browning Society, like the theologians of the Broad Church Party, or the authors of Mr. Walter Scott's Great Writers' Series, seems to me to spend their time in trying to explain their divinity away. Where one had hoped that Browning was a mystic, they have sought to show that he was simply inarticulate. Where one had fancied that he had something to conceal, they have proved that he had but little to reveal. But I speak merely of his incoherent work. Taken as a whole, the man was great. He did not belong to the Olympians, and had all the incompleteness of the Titan. He did not survey, and it was but rarely that he could sing. His work is marred by struggle, violence and effort, and he passed not from emotion to form, but from thought to chaos. Still, he was great. He has been called a thinker, and was certainly a man who was always thinking, and always thinking aloud; but it was not thought that fascinated him, but rather the processes by which thought moves. It was the machine he loved, not what the machine makes. The method by which the fool arrives at his folly was as dear to him as the ultimate wisdom of the wise. So much, indeed, did the subtle mechanism of mind fascinate him that he despised language, or looked upon it as an incomplete instrument of expression. Rhyme, that exquisite echo which in the Muse's hollow hill creates and answers its own voice; rhyme, which in the hands of the real artist becomes not merely a material element of metrical beauty, but a spiritual element of thought and passion also, waking a new mood, it may be, or stirring a fresh train of ideas, or opening by mere sweetness and suggestion of sound some golden door at which the Imagination itself had knocked in vain; rhyme, which can turn man's utterance to the speech of gods; rhyme, the one chord we have added to the Greek lyre, became in Robert Browning's hands a grotesque, misshapen thing, which at times made him masquerade in poetry as a low comedian, and ride Pegasus too often with his tongue in his cheek. There are moments when he wounds us by monstrous music. Nay, if he can only get his music by breaking the strings of his lute, he breaks them, and they snap in discord, and no Athenian tettix, making melody from tremulous wings, lights on the ivory horn to make the movement perfect, or the interval less harsh. Yet, he was great: and though he turned language into ignoble clay, he made from it men and women that live. He is the most Shakespearian creature since Shakespeare. If Shakespeare could sing with myriad lips, Browning could stammer through a thousand mouths. Even now, as I am speaking, and speaking not against him but for him, there glides through the room the pageant of his persons. There, creeps Fra Lippo Lippi with his cheeks still burning from some girl's hot kiss. There, stands dread Saul with the lordly male-sapphires gleaming in his turban. Mildred Tresham is there, and the Spanish monk, yellow with hatred, and Blougram, and Ben Ezra, and the Bishop of St. Praxed's. The spawn of Setebos gibbers in the corner, and Sebald, hearing Pippa pass by, looks on Ottima's haggard face, and loathes her and his own sin, and himself. Pale as the white satin of his doublet, the melancholy king watches with dreamy treacherous eyes too loyal Strafford pass forth to his doom, and Andrea shudders as he hears the cousins whistle in the garden, and bids his perfect wife go down. Yes, Browning was great.

And as what will he be remembered? As a poet? Ah, not as a poet! He will be remembered as a writer of fiction, as the most supreme writer of fiction, it may be, that we have ever had. His sense of dramatic situation was unrivalled, and, if he could not answer his own problems, he could at least put problems forth, and what more should an artist do? Considered from the point of view of a creator of character he ranks next to him who made Hamlet. Had he been articulate, he might have sat beside him. The only man who can touch the hem of his garment is George Meredith. Meredith is a prose Browning, and so is Browning. He used poetry as a medium for writing in prose.

Ernest. There is something in what you say, but there is not everything in what you say. In many points you are unjust.

Gilbert. It is difficult not to be unjust to what one loves. But let us return to the particular point at issue. What was it that you said?

Ernest. Simply this: that in the best days of art there were no art-critics.

Gilbert. I seem to have heard that observation before, Ernest. It has all the vitality of error and all the tediousness of an old friend.

Ernest. It is true. Yes: there is no use your tossing your head in that petulant manner. It is quite true. In the best days of art there were no art-critics. The sculptor hewed from the marble block the great white-limbed Hermes that slept within it. The waxers and gilders of images gave tone and texture to the statue, and the world, when it saw it, worshipped and was dumb. He poured the glowing bronze into the mould of sand, and the river of red metal cooled into noble curves and took the impress of the body of a god. With enamel or polished jewels he gave sight to the sightless eyes. The hyacinth-like curls grew crisp beneath his graver. And when, in some dim frescoed fane, or pillared sunlit portico, the child of Leto stood upon his pedestal, those who passed by, ἁβρῶς βαίνοντες διὰ λαμπροτάτου αἰθέρος, became conscious of a new influence that had come across their lives, and dreamily, or with a sense of strange and quickening joy, went to their homes or daily labour, or wandered, it may be, through the city gates to that nymph-haunted meadow where young Phædrus bathed his feet, and, lying there on the soft grass, beneath the tall wind-whispering planes and flowering *agnus castus*, began to think of the wonder of beauty, and grew silent with unaccustomed awe. In those days the artist was free. From the river valley he took the fine clay in his fingers, and with a little tool of wood or bone, fashioned it into forms so exquisite that the people gave them to the dead as their playthings, and we find them still in the dusty tombs on the yellow hillside by Tanagra, with the faint gold and the fading crimson still lingering about hair and lips and raiment. On a wall of fresh plaster, stained with bright sandyx or mixed with milk and saffron, he pictured one who trod with tired feet the purple white-starred fields of asphodel, one 'in whose eyelids lay the whole of the Trojan War,' Polyxena, the daughter of Priam; or figured Odysseus, the wise and cunning, bound by tight cords to the mast-step, that he might listen without hurt to the singing of the Sirens, or wandering by the clear river of Acheron, where the ghosts of fishes flitted over the pebbly bed; or showed the Persian in trews and mitre flying before the Greek at Marathon, or the galleys clashing their beaks of brass in the little Salaminian bay. He drew with silver-point and charcoal upon parchment and prepared cedar. Upon ivory and rose-coloured terra-cotta he painted with wax, making the wax fluid with juice of olives, and with heated irons making it firm. Panel and marble and linen canvas became wonderful as his brush swept across them; and life seeing her own image, was still, and dared not speak. All life, indeed, was his, from the merchants seated in the market-place to the cloaked shepherd lying on the hill; from the nymph hidden in the laurels and the faun that pipes at noon, to the king whom, in long green-curtained litter, slaves bore upon oil-bright shoulders, and fanned with peacock fans. Men and women, with pleasure or sorrow in their faces, passed before him. He watched them, and their secret became his. Through form and colour he recreated a world.

All subtle arts belonged to him also. He held the gem against the revolving disk, and the amethyst became the purple couch for Adonis, and across the veined sardonyx sped Artemis with her hounds. He beat out the gold into roses, and strung them together for necklace or armlet. He beat out the gold into wreaths for the conqueror's helmet, or into palmates for the Tyrian robe, or into masks for the royal dead. On the back of the silver mirror he graved Thetis borne by her Nereids, or love-sick Phædra with her nurse, or Persephone, weary of memory, putting poppies in her hair. The potter sat in his shed, and, flower-like from the silent wheel, the vase rose up beneath his hands. He decorated the base and stem and ears with pattern of dainty olive-leaf, or foliated acanthus, or curved and crested wave. Then in black or red he painted lads wrestling, or in the race: knights in full armour, with strange heraldic shields and curious visors, leaning from shell-shaped chariot over rearing steeds: the gods seated at the feast or working their miracles: the heroes in their victory or in their pain. Sometimes he would etch in thin vermilion lines upon a ground of white the languid bridegroom and his bride, with Eros hovering round them—an Eros like one of Donatello's angels, a little laughing thing with gilded or with azure wings. On the curved side he would write the name of his friend. ΚΑΛΟΣ ΑΛΚΙΒΙΑΔΗΣ or ΚΑΛΟΣ ΧΑΡΜΙΔΗΣ tells us the story of his days. Again, on the rim of the wide flat cup he would draw the stag browsing, or the lion at rest, as his fancy willed it. From the tiny perfume-bottle laughed Aphrodite at her toilet, and, with bare-limbed Mænads in his train, Dionysus danced round the wine-jar on naked must-stained feet, while, satyr-like, the old Silenus sprawled upon the bloated skins, or shook that magic spear which was tipped with a fretted fir-cone, and wreathed with dark ivy. And no one came to trouble the artist at his work. No irresponsible chatter disturbed him. He was not worried by opinions. By the Ilyssus, says Arnold somewhere, there was no Higginbotham. By the Ilyssus, my dear Gilbert, there were no silly art-congresses, bringing provincialism to the provinces and teaching the mediocrity how to mouth. By the Ilyssus there were no tedious magazines about art, in which the industrious prattle of what they do not understand. On the reed-grown banks of that little stream strutted no ridiculous journalism monopolizing the seat of judgment when it should be apologizing in the dock. The Greeks had no art-critics.

Gilbert. Ernest, you are quite delightful, but your views are terribly unsound. I am afraid that you have been listening to the conversation of someone older than yourself. That is always a dangerous thing to do, and if you allow it to degenerate into a habit, you will find it absolutely fatal to any intellectual development. As for modern journalism, it is not my business to defend it. It justifies its own existence by the great Darwinian principle of the survival of the vulgarest. I have merely to do with literature.

Ernest. But what is the difference between literature and journalism?

Gilbert. Oh! journalism is unreadable, and literature is not read. That is all. But with regard to your statement that the Greeks had no art-critics, I assure you that is quite absurd. It would be more just to say that the Greeks were a nation of art-critics.

Ernest. Really?

Gilbert. Yes, a nation of art-critics. But I don't wish to destroy the delightfully unreal picture that you have drawn of the relation of the Hellenic artist to the intellectual spirit of his age. To give an accurate description of what has never occurred is not merely the proper occupation of the historian, but the inalienable privilege of any man of parts and culture. Still less do I desire to talk learnedly. Learned conversation is either the affectation of the ignorant or the profession of the mentally unemployed. And, as for what is called improving conversation, that is merely the foolish method by which the still more foolish philanthropist feebly tries to disarm the just rancour of the criminal classes. No: let me play to you some mad scarlet thing by Dvorák. The pallid figures on the tapestry are smiling at us, and the heavy eyelids of my bronze Narcissus are folded in sleep. Don't let us discuss anything solemnly. I am but too conscious of the fact that we are born in an age when only the dull are treated seriously, and I live in terror of not being misunderstood. Don't degrade me into the position of giving you useful information. Education is an admirable thing, but it is well to remember from time to time that nothing that is worth knowing can be taught. Through the parted curtains of the window I see the moon like a clipped piece of silver. Like gilded bees the stars cluster round her. The sky is a hard hollow sapphire. Let us go out into the night. Thought is wonderful, but adventure is more wonderful still. Who knows but we may meet Prince Florizel of Bohemia, and hear the fair Cuban tell us that she is not what she seems?

Ernest. You are horribly wilful. I insist on your discussing this matter with me. You have said that the Greeks were a nation of art-critics. What art-criticism have they left us?

Gilbert. My dear Ernest, even if not a single fragment of art-criticism had come down to us from Hellenic or Hellenistic days, it would be none the less true that the Greeks were a nation of art-critics, and that they invented the criticism of art just as they invented the criticism of everything else. For, after all, what is our primary debt to the Greeks? Simply the critical spirit. And, this spirit, which they exercised on questions of religion and science, of ethics and metaphysics, of politics and education, they exercised on questions of art also, and, indeed, of the two supreme and highest arts, they have left us the most flawless system of criticism that the world has ever seen.

Ernest. But what are the two supreme and highest arts?

Gilbert. Life and Literature, life and the perfect expression of life. The principles of the former, as laid down by the Greeks, we may not realize in an age so marred by false ideals of our own. The principles of the latter, as they laid them down, are, in many cases, so subtle that we can hardly understand them. Recognizing that the most perfect art is that which most fully mirrors man in all his infinite variety, they elaborated the criticism of language, considered in the light of the mere material of that art, to a point to which we, with our accentual system of reasonable or emotional emphasis, can barely if at all attain; studying, for instance, the metrical movements of a prose as scientifically as a modern musician studies harmony and counterpoint, and, I need hardly say, with much keener æsthetic instinct. In this they were right, as they were right in all things. Since the introduction of printing, and the fatal development of the habit of reading amongst the middle and lower classes of this country, there has been a tendency in literature to appeal more and more to the eye, and less and less to the ear which is really the sense which, from the standpoint of pure art, it should seek to please, and by whose canons of pleasure it should abide always. Even the work of Mr. Pater, who is, on the whole, the most perfect master of English prose now creating amongst us, is often far more like a piece of mosaic than a passage in music, and seems, here and there, to lack the true rhythmical life of words and the fine freedom and richness of effect that such rhythmical life produces. We, in fact, have made writing a definite mode of composition, and have treated it as a form of elaborate design. The Greeks, upon the other hand, regarded writing simply as a method of chronicling. Their test was always the spoken word in its musical and metrical relations. The voice was the medium, and the ear the critic. I have sometimes thought that the story of Homer's blindness might be really an artistic myth, created in critical days, and serving to remind us, not merely that the great poet is always a seer, seeing less with the eyes of the body than he does with the eyes of the soul, but that he is a true singer also, building his song out of music, repeating each line over and over again to himself till he has caught the secret of its melody, chaunting in darkness the words that are winged with light. Certainly, whether this be so or not, it was to his blindness, as an occasion if not as a cause, that England's great poet owed much of the majestic movement and sonorous splendour of his later verse. When Milton could no longer write, he began to sing. Who would match the measures of *Comus* with the measures of *Samson Agonistes*, or of *Paradise Lost* or *Regained*? When Milton became blind he composed, as everyone should compose, with the voice purely, and so the pipe or reed of earlier days became that mighty many-stopped organ whose rich reverberant music has all the stateliness of Homeric verse, if it seeks not to have its swiftness, and is the one imperishable inheritance of English literature, sweeping through all the ages, because above them, and abiding with us ever, being immortal in its form. Yes: writing has done much harm to writers. We must return to the voice. That must be our test, and perhaps then we shall be able to appreciate some of the subtleties of Greek art-criticism.

As it now is, we cannot do so. Sometimes, when I have written a piece of prose that I have been modest enough to consider absolutely free from fault, a dreadful thought comes over me that I may have been guilty of the immoral effeminacy of using trochaic and tribrachic movements, a crime for which a learned critic of the Augustan age censures with most just severity the brilliant if somewhat paradoxical Hegesias. I grow cold when I think of it, and wonder to myself if the admirable ethical effect of the prose of that charming writer, who once in a spirit of reckless generosity towards the uncultivated portion of our community proclaimed the monstrous doctrine that conduct is three-fourths of life, will not some day be entirely annihilated by the discovery that the pæons have been wrongly placed.

Ernest. Ah! now you are flippant.

Gilbert. Who would not be flippant when he is gravely told that the Greeks had no art-critics? I can understand it being said that the constructive genius of the Greeks lost itself in criticism, but not that the race to whom we owe the critical spirit did not criticise. You will not ask me to give you a survey of Greek art criticism from Plato to Plotinus. The night is too lovely for that, and the moon, if she heard us, would put more ashes on her face than are there already. But think merely of one perfect little work of æsthetic criticism, Aristotle's *Treatise on Poetry*. It is not perfect in form, for it is badly written, consisting perhaps of notes jotted down for an art lecture, or of isolated fragments destined for some larger book, but in temper and treatment it is perfect absolutely. The ethical effect of art, its importance to culture, and its place in the formation of character, had been done once for all by Plato; but here we have art treated, not from the moral, but from the purely æsthetic point of view. Plato had, of course, dealt with many definitely artistic subjects, such as the importance of unity in a work of art, the necessity for tone and harmony, the æsthetic value of appearances, the relation of the visible arts to the external world, and the relation of fiction to fact. He first perhaps stirred in the soul of man that desire which we have not yet satisfied, the desire to know the connection between Beauty and Truth, and the place of Beauty in the moral and intellectual order of the Kosmos. The problems of idealism and realism, as he sets them forth, may seem to many to be somewhat barren of results in the metaphysical sphere of abstract being in which he places them, but transfer them to the sphere of art, and you will find that they are still vital and full of meaning. It may be that it is as a critic of Beauty that Plato is destined to live, and by altering the name of the sphere of his speculation we shall find a new philosophy. But Aristotle, like Goethe, deals with art primarily in its concrete manifestations, taking Tragedy, for instance, and investigating the material it uses, which is language, its subject-matter, which is life, the method by which it works, which is action, the conditions under which it reveals itself, which are those of theatric presentation, its logical structure, which is plot, and its final æsthetic appeal, which is to the sense of beauty realized through the passions of pity and awe. That purification and spiritualizing of the nature which he calls κάθαρσις is, as Goethe saw, essentially æsthetic, and is not moral, as Lessing fancied. Concerning himself primarily with the impression that the work of art produces, Aristotle sets himself to analyse that impression, to investigate its source, to see how it is engendered. As a physiologist and psychologist, he knows that the health of a function resides in energy. To have a capacity for a passion and not to realize it, is to make oneself incomplete and limited. The mimic spectacle of life that Tragedy affords cleanses the bosom of much 'perilous stuff,' and by presenting high and worthy objects for the exercise of the emotions purifies and spiritualizes the man; nay, not merely does is spiritualize him, but it initates him also into noble feelings of which he might else have known nothing, the word κάθαρσις having, it has sometimes seemed to me, a definite allusion to the rite of initiation, if indeed that be not, as I am occasionally tempted to fancy, its true and only meaning here. This is of course a mere outline of the book. But you see what a perfect piece of æsthetic criticism it is. Who indeed but a Greek could have analysed art so well? After reading it, one does not wonder any longer that Alexandria devoted itself so largely to art-criticism, and that we find the artistic temperaments of the day investigating every question of style and manner, discussing the great Academic schools of painting, for instance, such as the school of Sicyon, that sought to preserve the dignified traditions of the antique mode, or the realistic and impressionist schools, that aimed at reproducing actual life, or the elements of ideality in portrai-

353

ture, or the artistic value of the epic form in an age so modern as theirs, or the proper subject-matter for the artist. Indeed, I fear that the inartistic temperaments of the day busied themselves also in matters of literature and art, for the accusations of plagiarism were endless, and such accusations proceed either from the thin colourless lips of impotence, or from the grotesque mouths of those who, possessing nothing of their own, fancy that they can gain a reputation for wealth by crying out that they have been robbed. And I assure you, my dear Ernest, that the Greeks chattered about painters quite as much as people do nowadays, and had their private views, and shilling exhibitions, and Arts and Crafts guilds, and Pre-Raphaelite movements, and movements towards realism, and lectured about art, and wrote essays on art, and produced their art-historians, and their archæologists, and all the rest of it. Why, even the theatrical managers of travelling companies brought their dramatic critics with them when they went on tour, and paid them very handsome salaries for writing laudatory notices. Whatever, in fact, is modern in our life we owe to the Greeks. Whatever is an anachronism is due to mediævalism. It is the Greeks who have given us the whole system of art-criticism, and how fine their critical instinct was, may be seen from the fact that the material they criticised with most care was, as I have already said, language. For the material that painter or sculptor uses is meagre in comparison with that of words. Words have not merely music as sweet as that of viol and lute, colour as rich and vivid as any that makes lovely for us the canvas of the Venetian or the Spaniard, and plastic form no less sure and certain than that which reveals itself in marble or in bronze, but thought and passion and spirituality are theirs also, are theirs indeed alone. If the Greeks had criticised nothing but language, they would still have been the great art-critics of the world. To know the principles of the highest art, is to know the principles of the arts.

But I see that the moon is hiding behind a sulphur-coloured cloud. Out of a tawny mane of drift she gleams like a lion's eye. She is afraid that I will talk to you of Lucian and Longinus, of Quinctilian and Dionysius, of Pliny and Fronto and Pausanias, of all those who in the antique world wrote or lectured upon art-matters. She need not be afraid. I am tired of my expedition into the dim, dull abyss of facts. There is nothing left for me now but the divine μονόχρονος ἡδονή of another cigarette. Cigarettes have at least the charm of leaving one unsatisfied.

Ernest. Try one of mine. They are rather good. I get them direct from Cairo. The only use of our *attachés* is that they supply their friends with excellent tobacco. And as the moon has hidden herself, let us talk a little longer. I am quite ready to admit that I was wrong in what I said about the Greeks. They were, as you have pointed out, a nation of art-critics. I acknowledge it, and feel a little sorry for them. For the creative faculty is higher than the critical. There is really no comparison between them.

Gilbert. The antithesis between them is entirely arbitrary. Without the critical faculty, there is no artistic creation at all, worthy of the name. You spoke a little while ago of that fine spirit of choice and delicate instinct of selection by which the artist realizes life for us, and gives to it a momentary perfection. Well, that spirit of choice, that subtle tact of omission, is really the critical faculty in one of its most characteristic moods, and no one who does not possess this critical faculty can create anything at all in art. Arnold's definition of literature as a criticism of life, was not very felicitous in form, but it showed how keenly he recognized the importance of the critical element in all creative work.

Ernest. I should have said that great artists worked unconsciously, that they were "wiser than they knew," as, I think, Emerson remarks somewhere.

Gilbert. It is really not so, Ernest. All fine imaginative work is self-conscious and deliberate. No poet sings because he must sing. At least, no great poet does. A great poet sings because he chooses to sing. It is so now, and it has always been so. We are sometimes apt to think that the voices that sounded at the dawn of poetry were simpler, fresher, and more natural than ours, and that the world which the early poets looked at, and through which they walked, had a kind of poetical quality of its own, and almost without changing could pass into song. The snow lies thick now upon Olympus, and its steep scarped sides are bleak and barren, but once, we fancy, the white feet of the Muses brushed the dew from the anemones in the morning, and at evening came Apollo to sing to the shepherds in the vale. But in this we are merely lending to other ages what we desire, or think we desire, for our own. Our historical sense is at fault. Every century that produces poetry is, so far, an artificial century, and the work that seems to us to be the most natural and simple product of its time is always the result of the most self-conscious effort. Believe me, Ernest, there is no fine art without self-consciousness, and self-consciousness and the critical spirit are one.

Ernest. I see what you mean, and there is much in it. But surely you would admit that the great poems of the early world, the primitive, anonymous collective poems, were the result of the imagination of races, rather than of the imagination of individuals?

Gilbert. Not when they became poetry. Not when they received a beautiful form. For there is no art where there is no style, and no style where there is no unity, and unity is of the individual. No doubt Homer had old ballads and stories to deal with, as Shakespeare had chronicles and plays and novels from which to work, but they were merely his rough material. He took them, and shaped them into song. They become his, because he made them lovely. They were built out of music,

> And so not built at all,
> And therefore built for ever.

The longer one studies life and literature, the more strongly one feels that behind everything that is wonderful stands the individual, and that it is not the moment that makes the man, but the man who creates the age. Indeed, I am inclined to think that each myth and legend that seems to us to spring out of the wonder, or terror, or fancy of tribe and nation, was in its origin the invention of one single mind. The curiously limited number of the myths seems to me to point to this conclusion. But we must not go off into questions of comparative mythology. We must keep to criticism. And what I want to point out is this. An age that has no criticism is either an age in which art is immobile, hieratic, and confined to the reproduction of formal types, or an age that possesses no art at all. There have been critical ages that have not been creative, in the ordinary sense of the word, ages in which the spirit of man has sought to set in order the treasures of his treasure-house, to separate the gold from the silver, and the silver from the lead, to count over the jewels, and to give names to the pearls. But there has never been a creative age that has not been critical also. For it is the critical faculty that invents fresh forms. The tendency of creation is to repeat itself. It is to the critical instinct that we owe each new school that springs up, each new mould that art finds ready to its hand. There is really not a single form that art now uses that does not come to us from the critical spirit of Alexandria, where these forms were either stereotyped, or invented, or made perfect. I say Alexandria, not merely because it was there that the Greek spirit became most self-conscious, and indeed ultimately expired in scepticism and theology, but because it was to that city, and not to Athens, that Rome turned for her models, and it was through the survival, such as it was, of the Latin language that culture lived at all. When, at the Renaissance, Greek literature dawned upon Europe, the soil had been in some measure prepared for it. But, to get rid of the details of history, which are always wearisome and usually inaccurate, let us say generally, that the forms of art have been due to the Greek critical spirit. To it we owe the epic, the lyric, the entire drama in every one of its developments, including burlesque, the idyll, the romantic novel, the novel of adventure, the essay, the dialogue, the oration, the lecture, for which perhaps we should not forgive them, and the epigram, in all the wide meaning of that word. In fact, we owe it everything, except the sonnet, to which, however, some curious parallels of thought-movement may be traced in the Anthology, American journalism, to which no parallel can be found anywhere and the ballad in sham Scotch dialect, which one of our most industrious writers has recently proposed should be made the basis for a final and unanimous effort on the part of our second-rate poets to make themselves really romantic. Each new school, as it appears, cries out against criticism, but it is to the critical faculty in man that it owes its origin. The mere creative instinct does not innovate, but reproduces.

Ernest. You have been talking of criticism as an essential

357

part of the creative spirit, and I now fully accept your theory. But what of criticism outside creation? I have a foolish habit of reading periodicals, and it seems to me that most modern criticism is perfectly valueless.

Gilbert. So is most modern creative work also. Mediocrity weighing mediocrity in the balance, and incompetence applauding its brother—that is the spectacle which the artistic activity of England affords us from time to time. And yet, I feel I am a little unfair in this matter. As a rule, the critics— I speak, of course, of the higher class, of those in fact who write for the sixpenny papers—are far more cultured than the people whose work they are called upon to review. This is, indeed, only what one would expect, for criticism demands infinitely more cultivation than creation does.

Ernest. Really?

Gilbert. Certainly. Anybody can write a three-volumed novel. It merely requires a complete ignorance of both life and literature. The difficulty that I should fancy the reviewer feels is the difficulty of sustaining any standard. Where there is no style a standard must be impossible. The poor reviewers are apparently reduced to be the reporters of the police-court of literature, the chroniclers of the doings of the habitual criminals of art. It is sometimes said of them that they do not read all through the works they are called upon to criticise. They do not. Or at least they should not. If they did so, they would become confirmed misanthropes, or if I may borrow a phrase from one of the pretty Newnham graduates, confirmed woman-thropes for the rest of their lives. Nor is it necessary. To know the vintage and quality of a wine one need not drink the whole cask. It must be perfectly easy in half an hour to say whether a book is worth anything or worth nothing. Ten minutes are really sufficient, if one has the instinct for form. Who wants to wade through a dull volume? One tastes it, and that is quite enough—more than enough, I should imagine. I am aware that there are many honest workers in painting as well as in literature who object to criticism entirely. They are quite right. Their work stands in no intellectual relation to their age. It brings us no new element of pleasure. It suggests no fresh departure of thought, or passion, or beauty. It should not be spoken of. It should be left to the oblivion that it deserves.

Ernest. But, my dear fellow—excuse me for interrupting you —you seem to me to be allowing your passion for criticism to lead you a great deal too far. For, after all, even you must admit that it is much more difficult to do a thing than to talk about it.

Gilbert. More difficult to do a thing than to talk about it? Not at all. That is a gross popular error. It is very much more difficult to talk about a thing than to do it. In the sphere of actual life that is of course obvious. Anybody can make history. Only a great man can write it. There is no mode of action, no form of emotion, that we do not share with the lower animals. It is only by language that we rise above them, or above each other—by language, which is the parent, and not the child, of thought. Action, indeed, is always easy, and when presented to us in its most aggravated, because most continuous form, which I take to be that of real industry, becomes simply the refuge of people who have nothing whatsoever to do. No, Ernest, don't talk about action. It is a blind thing dependent on external influences, and moved by an impulse of whose nature it is unconscious. It is a thing incomplete in its essence, because limited by accident, and ignorant of its direction, being always at variance with its aim. Its basis is the lack of imagination. It is the last resource of those who know not how to dream.

Ernest. Gilbert, you treat the world as if it were a crystal ball. You hold it in your hand, and reverse it to please a wilful fancy. You do nothing but rewrite history.

Gilbert. The one duty we owe to history is to rewrite it. That is not the least of the tasks in store for the critical spirit. When we have fully discovered the scientific laws that govern life, we shall realize that the one person who has more illusions than the dreamer is the man of action. He, indeed, knows neither the origin of his deeds nor their results. From the field in which he thought that he had sown thorns, we have gathered our vintage, and the fig-tree that he planted for our pleasure is as barren as the thistle, and more bitter. It is because Humanity has never known where it was going that it has been able to find its way.

Ernest. You think, then, that in the sphere of action a conscious aim is a delusion?

Gilbert. It is worse than a delusion. If we lived long enough to see the results of our actions it may be that those who call themselves good would be sickened with a dull remorse, and those whom the world calls evil stirred by a noble joy. Each little thing that we do passes into the great machine of life which may grind our virtues to powder and make them worthless, or transform our sins into elements of a new civilization, more marvellous and more splendid than any that has gone before. But men are the slaves of words. They rage against Materialism, as they call it, forgetting that there has been no material improvement that has not spiritualized the world, and that there have been few, if any, spiritual awakenings that have not wasted the world's faculties in barren hopes, and fruitless aspirations, and empty or trammelling creeds. What is termed Sin is an essential element of progress. Without it the world would stagnate, or grow old, or become colourless. By its curiosity, Sin increases the experience of the race. Through its intensified assertion of individualism, it saves us from monotony of type. In its rejection of the current notions about morality, it is one with the higher ethics. And as for the virtues! What are the virtues? Nature, M. Renan tells us, cares little about chastity, and it may be that it is to the shame of the Magdalen, and not to their own purity, that the Lucretias of modern life owe their freedom from stain. Charity, as even those of whose religion it makes a formal part have been compelled to acknowledge, creates a multitude of evils. The mere existence of conscience, that faculty of which people prate so much nowadays, and are so ignorantly proud, is a sign of our imperfect development. It must be merged in instinct before we become fine. Self-denial is simply a method by which man arrests his progress, and self-sacrifice a survival of the mutilation of the savage, part of that old worship of pain which is so terrible a factor in the history of the world, and which even now makes its victims day by day, and has its altars in the land. Virtues! Who knows what the virtues are? Not you. Not I. Not anyone. It is well for our vanity that we slay the criminal, for if we suffered him to live he might show us what we had gained by his crime. It is well for his peace that the saint goes to his martyrdom. He is spared the sight of the horror of his harvest.

Ernest. Gilbert, you sound too harsh a note. Let us go back to the more gracious fields of literature. What was it you said? That it was more difficult to talk about a thing than to do it?

Gilbert (after a pause). Yes: I believe I ventured upon that simple truth. Surely you see now that I am right? When man acts he is a puppet. When he describes he is a poet. The whole secret lies in that. It was easy enough on the sandy plains by windy Ilion to send the notched arrow from the painted bow, or to hurl against the shield of hide and flame-like brass the long ash-handled spear. It was easy for the adulterous queen to spread the Tyrian carpets for her lord, and then, as he lay couched in the marble bath, to throw over his head the purple net, and call to her smooth-faced lover to stab through the meshes at the heart that should have broken at Aulis. For Antigone even, with Death waiting for her as her bridegroom, it was easy to pass through the tainted air at noon, and climb the hill, and strew with kindly earth the wretched naked corse that had no tomb. But what of those who wrote about these things? What of those who gave them reality, and made them live for ever? Are they not greater than the men and women they sing of? "Hector that sweet knight is dead," and Lucian tells us how in the dim underworld Menippus saw the bleaching skull of Helen, and marvelled that it was for so grim a favour that all those horned ships were launched, those beautiful mailed men laid low, those towered cities brought to dust. Yet, every day the swan-like daughter of Leda comes out on the battlements, and looks down at the tide of war. The greybeards wonder at her loveliness, and she stands by the side of the king. In his chamber of stained ivory lies her leman. He is polishing his dainty armour, and combing the scarlet plume. With squire and page, her husband passes from tent to tent. She can see his bright hair, and hears, or fancies that she hears, that clear cold voice. In the courtyard below, the son of Priam is buckling on his brazen cuirass. The white arms of Andromache are around his neck. He sets his helmet on the ground, lest their babe should be frightened. Behind the embroidered curtains of his pavilion sits Achilles, in perfumed raiment, while in harness of gilt and silver the friend of his soul arrays himself to go forth to the fight. From a curiously carven chest that his mother Thetis had brought to his ship-side, the Lord of the Myrmidons takes out that mystic chalice that the lip of man had never touched, and cleanses it with brimstone, and with fresh water cools it, and, having washed his hands, fills with black wine its burnished hollow, and spills the thick grape-blood upon the ground in honour of Him whom at Dodona barefooted prophets worshipped, and prays to Him, and knows not that he prays in vain, and that by the hands of two knights from Troy, Panthous' son, Euphorbus, whose love-locks were looped with gold, and the Priamid, the lion-hearted, Patroklus, the comrade of comrades, must meet his doom. Phantoms, are they? Heroes of mist and mountain? Shadows in a song? No: they are real. Action! What is action? It dies at the moment of its energy. It is a base concession to fact. The world is made by the singer for the dreamer.

Ernest. While you talk it seems to me to be so.

Gilbert. It is so in truth. On the mouldering citadel of Troy lies the lizard like a thing of green bronze. The owl has built her nest in the palace of Priam. Over the empty plain wander shepherd and goatherd with their flocks, and where, on the wine-surfaced, oily sea, οἶνοψ πόντος, as Homer calls it, copper-prowed and streaked with vermilion, the great galleys of the Danaoi came in their gleaming crescent; the lonely tunny-fisher sits in his little boat and watches the bobbing corks of his net. Yet, every morning the doors of the city are thrown open, and on foot, or in horse-drawn chariot, the warriors go forth to battle, and mock their enemies from behind their iron masks. All day long the fight rages, and when night comes the torches gleam by the tents, and the cresset burns in the hall. Those who live in marble or on painted panel, know of life but a single exquisite instant, eternal indeed in its beauty, but limited to one note of passion or one mood of calm. Those whom the poet makes live have their myriad emotions of joy and terror, of courage and despair, of pleasure and of suffering. The seasons come and go in glad or saddening pageant, and with winged or leaden feet the years pass by before them. They have their youth and their manhood, they are children, and they grow old. It is always dawn for St. Helena, as Veronese saw her at the window. Through the still morning air the angels bring her the symbol of God's pain. The cool breezes of the morning lift the gilt threads from her brow. On that little hill by the city of Florence, where the lovers of Giorgione are lying, it is always the solstice of noon, of noon made so languorous by summer suns that hardly can the slim naked girl dip into the marble tank the round bubble of clear glass, and the long fingers of the lute-player rest idly upon the chords. It is twilight always for the dancing nymphs whom Corot set free among the silver poplars of France. In eternal twilight they move, those frail diaphanous figures, whose tremulous white feet seem not to touch the dew-drenched grass they tread on. But those who walk in epos, drama, or romance, see through the labouring months the young moons wax and wane, and watch the night from evening unto morning star, and from sunrise unto sunsetting can note the shifting day with all its gold and shadow. For them, as for us, the flowers bloom and wither, and the Earth, that Green-tressed Goddess as Coleridge calls her, alters her raiment for their pleasure. The statue is concentrated to one moment of perfection. The image stained upon the canvas possesses no spiritual element of growth or change. If they know nothing of death, it is because they know little of life, for the secrets of life and death belong to those, and those only, whom the sequence of time affects, and who possess not merely the present but the future, and can rise or fall from a past of glory or of shame. Movement, that problem of the visible arts, can be truly realized by Literature alone. It is Literature that shows us the body in its swiftness and the soul in its unrest.

Ernest. Yes; I see now what you mean. But, surely, the higher you place the creative artist, the lower must the critic rank.

Gilbert. Why so?

Ernest. Because the best that he can give us will be but an echo of rich music, a dim shadow of clear-outlined form. It may, indeed, be that life is chaos, as you tell me that it is; that its martyrdoms are mean and its heroisms ignoble; and that it is the function of Literature to create, from the rough material of actual existence, a new world that will be more marvellous, more enduring, and more true than the world that common eyes look upon, and through which common natures seek to realize their perfection. But surely, if this new world has been made by the spirit and touch of a great artist, it will be a thing so complete and perfect that there will be nothing left for the critic to do. I quite understand now, and indeed admit most readily, that it is far more difficult to talk about a thing than to do it. But it seems to me that this sound and sensible maxim, which is really extremely soothing to one's feelings, and should be adopted as its motto by every Academy of Literature all over the world, applies only to the relations that exist between Art and Life, and not to any relations that there may be between Art and Criticism.

Gilbert. But, surely, Criticism is itself an art. And just as artistic creation implies the working of the critical faculty, and, indeed, without it cannot be said to exist at all, so Criticism is really creative in the highest sense of the word. Criticism is, in fact, both creative and independent.

Ernest. Independent?

Gilbert. Yes; independent. Criticism is no more to be judged by any low standard of imitation or resemblance than is the work of poet or sculptor. The critic occupies the same relation to the work of art that he criticises as the artist does to the visible world of form and colour, or the unseen world of passion and of thought. He does not even require for the perfection of his art the finest materials. Anything will serve his purpose. And just as out of the sordid and sentimental amours of the silly wife of a small country doctor in the squalid village of Yonville-l'Abbaye, near Rouen, Gustave Flaubert was able to create a classic, and make a masterpiece of style, so, from subjects of little or of no importance, such as the pictures in this year's Royal Academy, or in any year's Royal Academy for that matter, Mr. Lewis Morris's poems, M. Ohnet's novels, or the plays of Mr. Henry Arthur Jones, the true critic can, if it be his pleasure so to direct or waste his faculty of contemplation, produce work that will be flawless in beauty and instinct with intellectual subtlety. Why not? Dulness is always an irresistible temptation for brilliancy, and stupidity is the permanent *Bestia Trionfans* that calls wisdom from its cave. To an artist so creative as the critic, what does subject-matter signify? No more and no less than it does to the novelist and the painter. Like them, he can find his motives everywhere. Treatment is the test. There is nothing that has not in it suggestion or challenge.

Ernest. But is Criticism really a creative art?

Gilbert. Why should it not be? It works with materials, and puts them into a form that is at once new and delightful. What more can one say of poetry? Indeed, I would call criticism a creation within a creation. For just as the great artists, from Homer and Æschylus, down to Shakespeare and Keats, did not go directly to life for their subject-matter, but sought for it in myth, and legend and ancient tale, so the critic deals with materials that others have, as it were, purified for him, and to which imaginative form and colour have been already added. Nay, more, I would say that the highest Criticism, being the purest form of personal impression, is in its way more creative than creation, as it has least reference to any standard external to itself, and is, in fact, its own reason for existing, and, as the Greeks would put it, in itself, and to itself, an end. Certainly, it is never trammelled by any shackles of verisimilitude. No ignoble considerations of probability, that cowardly concession to the tedious repetitions of domestic or public life, affect it ever. One may appeal from fiction unto fact. But from the soul there is no appeal.

Ernest. From the soul?

Gilbert. Yes, from the soul. That is what the highest criticism really is, the record of one's own soul. It is more fascinating than history, as it is concerned simply with oneself. It is more delightful than philosophy, as its subject is concrete and not abstract, real and not vague. It is the only civilized form of autobiography, as it deals not with the events, but with the thoughts of one's life; not with life's physical accidents of deed or circumstance, but with the spiritual moods and imaginative passions of the mind. I am always amused by the silly vanity of those writers and artists of our day who seem to imagine that the primary function of the critic is to chatter about their second-rate work. The best that one can say of most modern creative art is that it is just a little less vulgar than reality, and so the critic, with his fine sense of distinction and sure instinct of delicate refinements, will prefer to look into the silver mirror or through the woven veil, and will turn his eyes away from the chaos and clamour of actual existence, though the mirror be tarnished and the veil be torn. His sole aim is to chronicle his own impressions. It is for him that pictures are painted, books written, and marble hewn into form.

Ernest. I seem to have heard another theory of Criticism.

Gilbert. Yes: it has been said by one whose gracious memory we all revere, and the music of whose pipe once lured Proserpina from her Sicilian fields, and made those white feet stir, and not in vain, the Cumnor cowslips, that the proper aim of Criticism is to see the object as in itself it really is. But this is a very serious error, and takes no cognizance of Criticism's most perfect form, which is in its essence purely subjective, and seeks to reveal its own secret and not the secret of another. For the highest Criticism deals with art not as expressive but as impressive purely.

Ernest. But is that really so?

Gilbert. Of course it is. Who cares whether Mr. Ruskin's views on Turner are sound or not? What does it matter? That mighty and majestic prose of his, so fervid and so fiery-coloured in its noble eloquence, so rich in its elaborate symphonic music, so sure and certain, at its best, in subtle choice of word and epithet, is at least as great a work of art as any of those wonderful sunsets that bleach or rot on their corrupted canvases in England's Gallery; greater indeed, one is apt to think at times, not merely because its equal beauty is more enduring, but on account of the fuller variety of its appeal, soul speaking to soul in those long-cadenced lines, not through form and colour alone, though through these, indeed, completely and without loss, but with intellectual and emotional utterance, with lofty passion and with loftier thought, with imaginative insight, and with poetic aim; greater, I always think, even as Literature is the greater art. Who, again, cares whether Mr. Pater has put into the portrait of Monna Lisa something that Lionardo never dreamed of? The painter may have been merely the slave of an archaic smile, as some have fancied, but whenever I pass into the cool galleries of the Palace of the Louvre, and stand before that strange figure "set in its marble chair in that cirque of fantastic rocks, as in some faint light under sea," I murmur to myself, "She is older than the rocks among which she sits; like the vampire, she has been dead many times, and learned the secrets of the grave; and has been a diver in deep seas, and keeps their fallen day about her; and trafficked for strange webs with Eastern merchants; and, as Leda, was the mother of Helen of Troy, and, as St. Anne, the mother of Mary; and all this has been to her but as the sound of lyres and flutes, and lives only in the delicacy with which it has moulded the changing lineaments, and tinged the eyelids and the hands." And I say to my friend, "The presence that thus so strangely rose beside the waters is expressive of what in the ways of a thousand years man had come to desire;" and he answers me, "Hers is the head upon which all 'the ends of the world are come,' and the eyelids are a little weary."

And so the picture becomes more wonderful to us than it really is, and reveals to us a secret of which, in truth, it knows nothing, and the music of the mystical prose is as sweet in our ears as was that flute-player's music that lent to the lips of La Gioconda those subtle and poisonous curves. Do you ask me what Lionardo would have said had anyone told him of this picture that "all the thoughts and experience of the world had etched and moulded there in that which they had of power to refine and make expressive the outward form, the animalism of Greece, the lust of Rome, the reverie of the Middle Age with its spiritual ambition and imaginative loves, the return of the Pagan world, the sins of the Borgias?" He would probably have answered that he had contemplated none of these things, but had concerned himself simply with certain arrangements of lines and masses, and with new and curious colour-harmonies of blue and green. And it is for this very reason that the criticism which I have quoted is criticism of the highest kind. It treats the work of art simply as a starting-point for a new creation. It does not confine itself—let us at least suppose so for the moment—to discovering the real intention of the artist and accepting that as final. And in this it is right, for the meaning of any beautiful created thing is, at least, as much in the soul of him who looks at it, as it was in his soul who wrought it. Nay, it is rather the beholder who lends to the beautiful thing its myriad meanings, and makes it marvellous for us, and sets it

367

in some new relation to the age, so that it becomes a vital portion of our lives, and a symbol of what we pray for, or perhaps of what, having prayed for, we fear that we may receive. The longer I study, Ernest, the more clearly I see that the beauty of the visible arts is, as the beauty of music, impressive primarily, and that it may be marred, and indeed often is so, by any excess of intellectual intention on the part of the artist. For when the work is finished it has, as it were, an independent life of its own, and may deliver a message far other than that which was put into its lips to say. Sometimes, when I listen to the overture to *Tannhäuser*, I seem indeed to see that comely knight treading delicately on the flower-strewn grass, and to hear the voice of Venus calling to him from the caverned hill. But at other times it speaks to me of a thousand different things, of myself, it may be, and my own life, or of the lives of others whom one has loved and grown weary of loving, or of the passions that man has known, or of the passions that man has not known, and so has sought for. To-night it may fill one with that EPΩΣ TΩN AΔΥNATΩN, that *Amour de l'Impossible*, which falls like a madness on many who think they live securely and out of reach of harm, so that they sicken suddenly with the poison of unlimited desire, and, in the infinite pursuit of what they may not obtain, grow faint and swoon or stumble. To-morrow, like the music of which Aristotle and Plato tell us, the noble Dorian music of the Greek, it may perform the office of a physician, and give us an anodyne against pain, and heal the spirit that is wounded, and "bring the soul into harmony with all right things." And what is true about music is true about all the arts. Beauty has as many meanings as man has moods. Beauty is the symbol of symbols. Beauty reveals everything, because it expresses nothing. When it shows us itself, it shows us the whole fiery-coloured world.

Ernest. But is such work as you have talked about really criticism?

Gilbert. It is the highest Criticism, for it criticises not merely the individual work of art, but Beauty itself, and fills with wonder a form which the artist may have left void, or not understood, or understood incompletely.

Ernest. The highest Criticism, then, is more creative than creation, and the primary aim of the critic is to see the object as in itself it really is not; that is your theory, I believe?

Gilbert. Yes, that is my theory. To the critic the work of art is simply a suggestion for a new work of his own, that need not necessarily bear any obvious resemblance to the thing it criticises. The one characteristic of a beautiful form is that one can put into it whatever one wishes, and see in it whatever one chooses to see; and the Beauty, that gives to creation its universal and æsthetic element, makes the critic a creator in his turn, and whispers of a thousand different things which were not present in the mind of him who carved the statue or painted the panel or graved the gem.

It is sometimes said by those who understand neither the nature of the highest Criticism nor the charm of the highest Art, that the pictures that the critic loves most to write about are those that belong to the anecdotage of painting, and that deal with scenes taken out of literature or history. But this is not so. Indeed, pictures of this kind are far too intelligible. As a class, they rank with illustrations, and even considered from this point of view are failures, as they do not stir the imagination, but set definite bounds to it. For the domain of the painter is, as I suggested before, widely different from that of the poet. To the latter belongs life in its full and absolute entirety; not merely the beauty that men look at, but the beauty that men listen to also; not merely the momentary grace of form or the transient gladness of colour, but the whole sphere of feeling, the perfect cycle of thought. The painter is so far limited that it is only through the mask of the body that he can show us the mystery of the soul; only through conventional images that he can handle ideas; only through its physical equivalents that he can deal with psychology. And how inadequately does he do it then, asking us to accept the torn turban of the Moor for the noble rage of Othello, or a dotard in a storm for the wild madness of Lear! Yet it seems as if nothing could stop him. Most of our elderly English painters spend their wicked and wasted lives in poaching upon the domain of the poets, marring their motives by clumsy treatment, and striving to render, by visible form or colour, the marvel of what is invisible, the splendour of what is not seen. Their pictures are, as a natural consequence, insufferably tedious. They have degraded the visible arts into the obvious arts, and the one thing not worth looking at is the obvious. I do not say that poet and painter may not treat of the same subject. They have always done so, and will always do so. But while the poet can be pictorial or not, as he chooses, the painter must be pictorial always. For a painter is limited, not to what he sees in nature, but to what upon canvas may be seen.

And so, my dear Ernest, pictures of this kind will not really fascinate the critic. He will turn from them to such works as make him brood and dream and fancy, to works that possess the subtle quality of suggestion, and seem to tell one that even from them there is an escape into a wider world. It is sometimes said that the tragedy of an artist's life is that he cannot realize his ideal. But the true tragedy that dogs the steps of most artists is that they realize their ideal too absolutely. For, when the ideal is realized, it is robbed of its wonder and its mystery, and becomes simply a new starting-point for an ideal that is other than itself. This is the reason why music is the perfect type of art. Music can never reveal its ultimate secret. This, also, is the explanation of the value of limitations in art. The sculptor gladly surrenders imitative colour, and the painter the actual dimensions of form, because by such renunciations they are able to avoid too definite a presentation of the Real, which would be mere imitation, and too definite a realization of the Ideal, which would be too purely intellectual. It is through its very incompleteness that Art becomes complete in beauty, and so addresses itself, not to the faculty of recognition nor to the faculty of reason, but to the æsthetic sense alone, which, while accepting both reason and recognition as stages of apprehension, subordinates them both to a pure synthetic impression of the work of art as a whole, and, taking whatever alien emotional elements the work may possess, uses their very complexity as a means by which a richer unity may be added to the ultimate impression itself. You see, then, how it is that the æsthetic critic rejects those obvious modes of art that have but one message to deliver, and having delivered it become dumb and sterile, and seeks rather for such modes as suggest reverie and mood, and by their imaginative beauty make all interpretations true and no interpretation final. Some resemblance, no doubt, the creative work of the critic will have to the work that has stirred him to creation, but it will be such resemblance as exists, not between Nature and the mirror that the painter of landscape or figure may be supposed to hold up to her, but between Nature and the work of the decorative artist. Just as on the flowerless carpets of Persia, tulip and rose blossom indeed and are lovely to look on, though they are not reproduced in visible shape or line; just as the pearl and purple of the sea-shell is echoed in the church of St. Mark at Venice; just as the vaulted ceiling of the wondrous chapel of Ravenna is made gorgeous by the gold and green and sapphire of the peacock's tail, though the birds of Juno fly not across it; so the critic reproduces the work that he criticises in a mode that is never imitative, and part of whose charm may really consist in the rejection of resemblance, and shows us in this way not merely the meaning but also the mystery of Beauty, and, by transforming each art into literature, solves once for all the problem of Art's unity.

But I see it is time for supper. After we have discussed some Chambertin and a few ortolans, we will pass on to the question of the critic considered in the light of the interpreter.

Ernest. Ah! you admit, then, that the critic may occasionally be allowed to see the object as in itself it really is.

Gilbert. I am not quite sure. Perhaps I may admit it after supper. There is a subtle influence in supper.

THE CRITIC AS ARTIST
With some remarks upon the importance of discussing everything

A Dialogue. Part II.
Persons: the same.
Scene: the same.

Ernest. The ortolans were delightful, and the Chambertin perfect. And now let us return to the point at issue.

Gilbert. Ah! don't let us do that. Conversation should touch everything, but should concentrate itself on nothing. Let us talk about *Moral Indignation, its Cause and Cure,* a subject on which I think of writing: or about *The Survival of Thersites,* as shown by the English comic papers; or about any topic that may turn up.

Ernest. No: I want to discuss the critic and criticism. You have told me that the highest criticism deals with art, not as expressive, but as impressive purely, and is consequently both creative and independent, is in fact an art by itself, occupying the same relation to creative work that creative work does to the visible world of form and colour, or the unseen world of passion and of thought. Well, now tell me, will not the critic be sometimes a real interpreter?

Gilbert. Yes; the critic will be an interpreter, if he chooses. He can pass from his synthetic impression of the work of art as a whole, to an analysis or exposition of the work itself, and in this lower sphere, as I hold it to be, there are many delightful things to be said and done. Yet his object will not always be to explain the work of art. He may seek rather to deepen its mystery, to raise round it, and round its maker, that mist of wonder which is dear to both gods and worshippers alike. Ordinary people are "terribly at ease in Zion." They propose to walk arm in arm with the poets, and have a glib ignorant way of saying "Why should we read what is written about Shakespeare and Milton? We can read the plays and the poems. That is enough." But an appreciation of Milton is, as the late Rector of Lincoln remarked once, the reward of consummate scholarship. And he who desires to understand Shakespeare truly must understand the relations in which Shakespeare stood to the Renaissance and the Reformation, to the age of Elizabeth and the age of James; he must be familiar with the history of the struggle for supremacy between the old classical forms and the new spirit of romance, between the school of Sidney, and Daniel, and Jonson, and the school of Marlowe and Marlowe's greater son; he must know the materials that were at Shakespeare's disposal, and the method in which he used them, and the conditions of theatric presentation in the sixteenth and seventeenth century, their limitations and their opportunities for freedom, and the literary criticism of Shakespeare's day, its aims and modes and canons; he must study the English language in its progress, and blank or rhymed verse in its various developments; he must study the Greek drama, and the connection between the art of the creator of the Agamemnon and the art of the creator of Macbeth; in a word, he must be able to bind Elizabethan London to the Athens of Pericles, and to learn Shakespeare's true position in the history of European drama and the drama of the world. The critic will certainly be an interpreter, but he will not treat Art as a riddling Sphinx, whose shallow secret may be guessed and revealed by one whose feet are wounded and who knows not his name. Rather, he will look upon Art as a goddess whose mystery it is his province to intensify, and whose majesty his privilege to make more marvellous in the eyes of men.

And here, Ernest, this strange thing happens. The critic will indeed be an interpreter, but he will not be an interpreter in the sense of one who simply repeats in another form a message that has been put into his lips to say. For, just as it is only by contact with the art of foreign nations that the art of a country gains that individual and separate life that we call nationality, so, by curious inversion, it is only by intensifying his own personality that the critic can interpret the personality and work of others, and the more strongly this personality enters into the interpretation the more real the interpretation becomes, the more satisfying, the more convincing, and the more true.

Ernest. I would have said that personality would have been a disturbing element.

Gilbert. No; it is an element of revelation. If you wish to understand others you must intensify your own individualism.

Ernest. What, then, is the result?

Gilbert. I will tell you, and perhaps I can tell you best by definite example. It seems to me that, while the literary critic stands of course first, as having the wider range, and larger vision, and nobler material, each of the arts has a critic, as it were, assigned to it. The actor is a critic of the drama. He shows the poet's work under new conditions, and by a method special to himself. He takes the written word, and action, gesture, and voice become the media of revelation. The singer, or the player

373

on lute and viol, is the critic of music. The etcher of a picture robs the painting of its fair colours, but shows us by the use of a new material its true colour-quality, its tones and values, and the relations of its masses, and so is, in his way, a critic of it, for the critic is he who exhibits to us a work of art in a form different from that of the work itself, and the employment of a new material is a critical as well as a creative element. Sculpture, too, has its critic, who may be either the carver of a gem, as he was in Greek days, or some painter like Mantegna, who sought to reproduce on canvas the beauty of plastic line and the symphonic dignity of processional bas-relief. And in the case of all these creative critics of art it is evident that personality is an absolute essential for any real interpretation. When Rubinstein plays to us the *Sonata Appassionata* of Beethoven, he gives us not merely Beethoven, but also himself, and so gives us Beethoven absolutely—Beethoven reinterpreted through a rich artistic nature, and made vivid and wonderful to us by a new and intense personality. When a great actor plays Shakespeare we have the same experience. His own individuality becomes a vital part of the interpretation. People sometimes say that actors give us their own Hamlets, and not Shakespeare's; and this fallacy—for it is a fallacy—is, I regret to say, repeated by that charming and graceful writer who has lately deserted the turmoil of literature for the peace of the House of Commons, I mean the author of *Obiter Dicta*. In point of fact, there is no such thing as Shakespeare's Hamlet. If Hamlet has something of the definiteness of a work of art, he has also all the obscurity that belongs to life. There are as many Hamlets as there are melancholies.

Ernest. As many Hamlets as there are melancholies?

Gilbert. Yes: and as art springs from personality, so it is only to personality that it can be revealed, and from the meeting of the two comes right interpretative criticism.

Ernest. The critic, then, considered as the interpreter, will give no less than he receives, and lend as much as he borrows?

Gilbert. He will be always showing us the work of art in some new relation to our age. He will always be reminding us that great works of art are living things—are, in fact, the only things that live. So much, indeed, will he feel this, that I am certain that, as civilization progresses and we become more highly organized, the elect spirits of each age, the critical and cultured spirits, will grow less and less interested in actual life, and *will seek to gain their impressions almost entirely from what Art has touched*. For Life is terribly deficient in form. Its catastrophes happen in the wrong way and to the wrong people. There is a grotesque horror about its comedies, and its tragedies seem to culminate in farce. One is always wounded when one approaches it. Things last either too long, or not long enough.

Ernest. Poor life! Poor human life! Are you not even touched by the tears that the Roman poet tells us are part of its essence?

Gilbert. Too quickly touched by them, I fear. For when one looks back upon the life that was so vivid in its emotional intensity, and filled with such fervent moments of ecstasy or of joy, it all seems to be a dream and an illusion. What are the unreal things, but the passions that once burned one like fire? What are the incredible things, but the things that one has faithfully believed? What are the improbable things? The things that one has done oneself. No, Ernest; life cheats us with shadows, like a puppet-master. We ask it for pleasure. It gives it to us, with bitterness and disappointment in its train. We come across some noble grief that we think will lend the purple dignity of tragedy to our days, but it passes away from us, and things less noble take its place, and on some grey windy dawn, or odorous eve of silence and of silver, we find ourselves looking with callous wonder, or dull heart of stone, at the trees of gold-flecked hair that we had once so wildly worshipped and so madly kissed.

Ernest. Life then is a failure?

Gilbert. From the artistic point of view, certainly. And the chief thing that makes life a failure from this artistic point of view is the thing that lends to life its sordid security, the fact that one can never repeat exactly the same emotion. How different it is in the world of Art! On a shelf of the bookcase behind you stands the *Divine Comedy*, and I know that, if I open it at a certain place, I shall be filled with a fierce hatred of some one who has never wronged me, or stirred by a great love for some one whom I shall never see. There is no mood or passion that Art cannot give us, and those of us who have discovered her secret can settle beforehand what our experiences are going to be. We can say to ourselves, "To-morrow, at dawn, we shall walk with grave Virgil through the valley of the shadow of death," and lo! the dawn finds us in the obscure wood, and the Mantuan stands by our side. We pass through the gate of the legend fatal to hope, and with pity or with joy behold the horror of another world. The hypocrites go by, with their painted faces and their cowls of gilded lead. Out of the ceaseless winds that drive them, the carnal look at us, and we watch the heretic rending his flesh, and the glutton lashed by the rain. We break the withered branches from the tree in the grove of the Harpies, and each dull-hued poisonous twig bleeds with red blood before us, and cries aloud with bitter cries. Out of a horn of fire Odysseus speaks to us, and when from his sepulchre of flame the great Ghibelline rises, the pride that triumphs over the torture of that bed becomes ours for a moment. Through the dim purple air fly those who have stained the world with the beauty of their sin, and in the pit of loathsome disease, dropsy-stricken and swollen of body into the semblance of a monstrous lute, lies Adamo di Brescia, the coiner of false coin. He bids us listen to his misery; we stop, and with dry and gaping lips he tells us how he dreams day and night of the brooks of clear water that in cool dewy channels gush down the green Casentine hills. Sinon, the false Greek of Troy, mocks at him. He smites him in the face and they wrangle. We are fascinated by their shame, and loiter, till Virgil chides us and leads us away to that city turreted by giants where great Nimrod blows his horn. Terrible things are in store for us, and we go to meet them in Dante's raiment and with Dante's heart. We traverse the marshes of the Styx, and Argenti swims to the boat through the slimy waves. He calls to us, and we reject him. When we hear the voice of his agony we are glad, and Virgil praises us for the bitterness of our scorn. We tread upon the cold crystal of Cocytus, in which traitors stick like straws in glass. Our foot strikes against the head of Bocca. He will not tell us his name, and we tear the hair in handfuls from the screaming skull. Alberigo prays us to break the ice upon his face that he may weep a little. We pledge our word to him, and when he has uttered his dolorous tale we deny the word that we have spoken, and pass from him; such cruelty being courtesy indeed, for who more base than he who has mercy for the condemned of God? In the jaws of Lucifer we see the man who sold Christ, and in the jaws of Lucifer the men who slew Cæsar. We tremble, and come forth to rebehold the stars.

In the land of Purgation the air is freer, and the holy mountain rises into the pure light of day. There is peace for us, and for those who for a season abide in it there is some peace also, though, pale from the poison of the Maremma, Madonna Pia passes before us, and Ismene, with the sorrow of earth still lingering about her, is there. Soul after soul makes us share in some repentance or some joy. He whom the mourning of his widow taught to drink the sweet wormwood of pain, tells us of Nella praying in her lonely bed, and we learn from the mouth of Buonconte how a single tear may save a dying sinner from the fiend. Sordello, that noble and disdainful Lombard, eyes us from afar like a couchant lion. When he learns that Virgil is one of Mantua's citizens, he falls upon his neck, and when he learns that he is the singer of Rome he falls before his feet. In that valley whose grass and flowers are fairer than cleft emerald and Indian wood, and brighter than scarlet and silver, they are singing who in the world were kings; but the lips of Rudolph of Hapsburg do not move to the music of the others, and Philip of France beats his breast and Henry of England sits alone. On and on we go, climbing the marvellous stair, and the stars become larger than their wont, and the song of the kings grows faint, and at length we reach the seven trees of gold and the garden of the Earthly Paradise. In a griffin-drawn chariot appears one whose brows are bound with olive, who is veiled in white, and mantled in green, and robed in a vesture that is coloured like live fire. The ancient flame wakes within us. Our blood quickens through terrible pulses. We recognize her. It is Beatrice, the woman we have worshipped. The ice congealed about our heart melts. Wild tears of anguish break from us, and we bow our forehead to the ground, for we know that we have sinned. When we have done penance, and are purified, and have drunk of the fountain of Lethe and bathed in the fountain of Eunoe, the mistress of our soul raises us to the Paradise of Heaven. Out of that eternal pearl, the moon, the face of

377

The Artist as Critic

Piccarda Donati leans to us. Her beauty troubles us for a moment, and when, like a thing that falls through water, she passes away, we gaze after her with wistful eyes. The sweet planet of Venus is full of lovers. Cunizza, the sister of Ezzelin, the lady of Sordello's heart, is there, and Folco, the passionate singer of Provence, who in sorrow for Azalais forsook the world, and the Canaanitish harlot whose soul was the first that Christ redeemed. Joachim of Flora stands in the sun, and, in the sun, Aquinas recounts the story of St. Francis and Bonaventure the story of St. Dominic. Through the burning rubies of Mars, Cacciaguida approaches. He tells us of the arrow that is shot from the bow of exile, and how salt tastes the bread of another, and how steep are the stairs in the house of a stranger. In Saturn the souls sing not, and even she who guides us dare not smile. On a ladder of gold the flames rise and fall. At last, we see the pageant of the Mystical Rose. Beatrice fixes her eyes upon the face of God to turn them not again. The beatific vision is granted to us; we know the Love that moves the sun and all the stars.

Yes, we can put the earth back six hundred courses and make ourselves one with the great Florentine, kneel at the same altar with him, and share his rapture and his scorn. And if we grow tired of an antique time, and desire to realize our own age in all its weariness and sin, are there not books that can make us live more in one single hour than life can make us live in a score of shameful years? Close to your hand lies a little volume, bound in some Nile-green skin that has been powdered with gilded nenuphars and smoothed with hard ivory. It is the book that Gautier loved, it is Baudelaire's masterpiece. Open it at that sad madrigal that begins

"Que m'importe que tu sois sage?
Sois belle! et sois triste!"

and you will find yourself worshipping sorrow as you have never worshipped joy. Pass on to the poem on the man who tortures himself, let its subtle music steal into your brain and colour your thoughts, and you will become for a moment what he was who wrote it; nay, not for a moment only, but for many barren moonlit nights and sunless sterile days will a despair that is not your own make its dwelling within you, and the misery of another gnaw your heart away. Read the whole book, suffer it to tell even one of its secrets to your soul, and your soul will grow eager to know more, and will feed upon poisonous honey, and seek to repent of strange crimes of which it is guiltless, and to make atonement for terrible pleasures that it has never known. And then, when you are tired of these flowers of evil, turn to the flowers that grow in the garden of Perdita, and in their dew-drenched chalices cool your fevered brow, and let their loveliness heal and restore your soul; or wake from his forgotten tomb the sweet Syrian, Meleager, and bid the lover of Heliodore make you music, for he too has flowers in his song, red pomegranate-blossoms, and irises that smell of myrrh, ringed daffodils and dark-blue hyacinths, and marjoram and crinkled ox-eyes. Dear to him was the perfume of the bean-field at evening, and dear to him the odorous eared-spikenard that grew on the Syrian hills, and the fresh green thyme, the wine-cup's charm. The feet of his love as she walked in the garden were like lilies set upon lilies. Softer than sleep-laden poppy petals were her lips, softer than violets and as scented. The flame-like crocus sprang from the grass to look at her. For her the slim narcissus stored the cool rain; and for her the anemones forgot the Sicilian winds that wooed them. And neither crocus, nor anemone, nor narcissus was as fair as she was.

It is a strange thing, this transference of emotion. We sicken with the same maladies as the poets, and the singer lends us his pain. Dead lips have their message for us, and hearts that have fallen to dust can communicate their joy. We run to kiss the bleeding mouth of Fantine, and we follow Manon Lescaut over the whole world. Ours is the love-madness of the Tyrian, and the terror of Orestes is ours also. There is no passion that we cannot feel, no pleasure that we may not gratify, and we can choose the time of our initiation and the time of our freedom also. Life! Life! Don't let us go to life for our fulfilment or our experience. It is a thing narrowed by circumstances, incoherent in its utterance, and without that fine correspondence of form and spirit which is the only thing that can satisfy the artistic and critical temperament. It makes us pay too high a price for its wares, and we purchase the meanest of its secrets at a cost that is monstrous and infinite.

Ernest. Must we go, then, to Art for everything?

Gilbert. For everything. Because Art does not hurt us. The tears that we shed at a play are a type of the exquisite sterile emotions that it is the function of Art to awaken. We weep, but we are not wounded. We grieve, but our grief is not bitter. In the actual life of man, sorrow, as Spinoza says somewhere, is a passage to a lesser perfection. But the sorrow with which Art fills us both purifies and initiates, if I may quote once more from the great art-critic of the Greeks. It is through Art, and through Art only, that we can realize our perfection; through Art, and through Art only, that we can shield ourselves from the sordid perils of actual existence. This results not merely from the fact that nothing that one can imagine is worth doing, and that one can imagine everything, but from the subtle law that emotional forces, like the forces of the physical sphere, are limited in extent and energy. One can feel so much, and no more. And how can it matter with what pleasure life tries to tempt one, or with what pain it seeks to maim and mar one's soul, if in the spectacle of the lives of those who have never existed one has found the true secret of joy, and wept away one's tears over their deaths who, like Cordelia and the daughter of Brabantio, can never die?

Ernest. Stop a moment. It seems to me that in everything that you have said there is something radically immoral.

Gilbert. All art is immoral.

Ernest. All art?

Gilbert. Yes. For emotion for the sake of emotion is the aim of art, and emotion for the sake of action is the aim of life, and of that practical organization of life that we call society. Society, which is the beginning and basis of morals, exists simply for the concentration of human energy, and in order to ensure its own continuance and healthy stability it demands, and no doubt rightly demands, of each of its citizens that he should contribute some form of productive labour to the common weal, and toil and travail that the day's work may be done. Society often forgives the criminal; it never forgives the dreamer. The beautiful sterile emotions that art excites in us, are hateful in its eyes, and so completely are people dominated by the tyranny of this dreadful social ideal that they are always coming shamelessly up to one at Private Views and other places that are open to the general public, and saying in a loud stentorian voice, "What are you doing?" whereas "What are you thinking?" is the only question that any single civilized being should ever be allowed to whisper to another. They mean well, no doubt, these honest beaming folk. Perhaps that is the reason why they are so excessively tedious. But some one should teach them that while, in the opinion of society, Contemplation is the gravest sin of which any citizen can be guilty, in the opinion of the highest culture it is the proper occupation of man.

Ernest. Contemplation?

Gilbert. Contemplation. I said to you some time ago that it was far more difficult to talk about a thing than to do it. Let me say to you now that to do nothing at all is the most difficult thing in the world, the most difficult and the most intellectual. To Plato, with his passion for wisdom, this was the noblest form of energy. To Aristotle, with his passion for knowledge, this was the noblest form of energy also. It was to this that the passion for holiness led the saint and the mystic of medieval days.

Ernest. We exist, then, to do nothing?

Gilbert. It is to do nothing that the elect exist. Action is limited and relative. Unlimited and absolute is the vision of him who sits at ease and watches, who walks in loneliness and dreams. But we who are born at the close of this wonderful age, are at once too cultured and too critical, too intellectually subtle and too curious of exquisite pleasures, to accept any speculations about life in exchange for life itself. To us the *citta divina* is colourless, and the *fruitio Dei* without meaning. Metaphysics do not satisfy our temperaments, and religious ecstasy is out of date. The world through which the Academic philosopher becomes "the spectator of all time and of all existence" is not really an ideal world, but simply a world of abstract ideas. When we enter it, we starve amidst the chill mathematics of thought. The courts of the city of God are not open to us now. Its gates are guarded by Ignorance, and to pass them we have to surrender all that in our nature is most divine. It is enough that our fathers believed. They have exhausted the faith-faculty of the species. Their legacy to us is the scepticism of which they were afraid. Had they put it into words, it might not live within us as thought. No, Ernest, no. We cannot go back to the saint. There is far more to be learned from the sinner. We cannot go back to the philosopher, and the mystic leads us astray. Who, as Mr. Pater suggests somewhere, would exchange the curve of a single rose-leaf for that formless intangible Being which Plato rates so high? What to us is the Illumination of Philo, the Abyss of Eckhart, the Vision of Böhme, the monstrous Heaven itself that was revealed to Swedenborg's blinded eyes? Such things are less than the yellow trumpet of one daffodil of the field, far less than the meanest of the visible arts; for, just as Nature is matter struggling into mind, so Art is mind expressing itself under the conditions of matter, and thus, even in the lowliest of her manifestations, she speaks to both sense and soul alike. To the æsthetic temperament the vague is always repellent. The Greeks were a nation of artists, because they were spared the sense of the infinite. Like Aristotle, like Goethe after he had read Kant, we desire the concrete, and nothing but the concrete can satisfy us.

Ernest. What then do you propose?

Gilbert. It seems to me that with the development of the critical spirit we shall be able to realize, not merely our own lives, but the collective life of the race, and so to make ourselves absolutely modern, in the true meaning of the word modernity. For he to whom the present is the only thing that is present, knows nothing of the age in which he lives. To realize the nineteenth century, one must realize every century that has preceded it and that has contributed to its making. To know anything about oneself, one must know all about others. There must be no mood with which one cannot sympathize, no dead mode of life that one cannot make alive. Is this impossible? I think not. By revealing to us the absolute mechanism of all action, and so freeing us from the self-imposed and trammelling burden of moral responsibility, the scientific principle of Heredity has become, as it were, the warrant for the contemplative life. It has shown us that we are never less free than when we try to act. It has hemmed us round with the nets of the hunter, and written upon the wall the prophecy of our doom. We may not watch it, for it is within us. We may not see it, save in a mirror that mirrors the soul. It is Nemesis without her mask. It is the last of the Fates, and the most terrible. It is the only one of the Gods whose real name we know.

And yet, while in the sphere of practical and external life it has robbed energy of its freedom and activity of its choice, in the subjective sphere, where the soul is at work, it comes to us, this terrible shadow, with many gifts in its hands, gifts of strange temperaments and subtle susceptibilities, gifts of wild ardours and chill moods of indifference, complex multiform gifts of thoughts that are at variance with each other, and passions that war against themselves. And so, it is not our own life that we live, but the lives of the dead, and the soul that dwells within us is no single spiritual entity, making us personal and individual, created for our service, and entering into us for our joy. It is something that has dwelt in fearful places, and in ancient sepulchres has made its abode. It is sick with many maladies, and has memories of curious sins. It is wiser than we are, and its wisdom is bitter. It fills us with impossible desires, and makes us follow what we know we cannot gain. One thing, however, Ernest, it can do for us. It can lead us away from surroundings whose beauty is dimmed to us by the mist of familiarity, or whose ignoble ugliness and sordid claims are marring the perfection of our development. It can help us to leave the age in which we were born, and to pass into other ages, and find ourselves not exiled from their air. It can teach us how to escape from our experience, and to realize the experiences of those who are greater than we are. The pain of Leopardi crying out against life becomes our pain. Theocritus blows on his pipe, and we laugh with the lips of nymph and shepherd. In the wolfskin of Pierre Vidal we flee before the hounds, and in the armour of Lancelot we ride from the bower of the Queen. We have whispered the secret of our love beneath the cowl of Abelard, and in the stained raiment of

Villon have put our shame into song. We can see the dawn through Shelley's eyes, and when we wander with Endymion the Moon grows amorous of our youth. Ours is the anguish of Atys, and ours the weak rage and noble sorrows of the Dane. Do you think that it is the imagination that enables us to live these countless lives? Yes: it is the imagination; and the imagination is the result of heredity. It is simply concentrated race-experience.

Ernest. But where in this is the function of the critical spirit?

Gilbert. The culture that this transmission of racial experiences makes possible can be made perfect by the critical spirit alone, and indeed may be said to be one with it. For who is the true critic but he who bears within himself the dreams, and ideas, and feelings of myriad generations, and to whom no form of thought is alien, no emotional impulse obscure? And who the true man of culture, if not he who by fine scholarship and fastidious rejection has made instinct self-conscious and intelligent, and can separate the work that has distinction from the work that has it not, and so by contact and comparison makes himself master of the secrets of style and school, and understands their meanings, and listens to their voices, and develops that spirit of disinterested curiosity which is the real root, as it is the real flower, of the intellectual life, and thus attains to intellectual clarity, and, having learned "the best that is known and thought in the world," lives—it is not fanciful to say so— with those who are the Immortals.

Yes, Ernest: the contemplative life, the life that has for its aim not *doing* but *being*, and not *being* merely, but *becoming* —that is what the critical spirit can give us. The gods live thus: either brooding over their own perfection, as Aristotle tells us, or, as Epicurus fancied, watching with the calm eyes of the spectator the tragi-comedy of the world that they have made. We, too, might live like them, and set ourselves to witness with appropriate emotions the varied scenes that man and nature afford. We might make ourselves spiritual by detaching ourselves from action, and become perfect by the rejection of energy. It has often seemed to me that Browning felt something of this. Shakespeare hurls Hamlet into active life, and makes him realize his mission by effort. Browning might have given us a Hamlet who would have realized his mission by thought. Incident and event were to him unreal or unmeaning. He made the soul the protagonist of life's tragedy, and looked on action as the one undramatic element of a play. To us, at any rate, the ΒΙΟΣ ΘΕΩΡΗΤΙΚΟΣ is the true ideal. From the high tower of Thought we can look out at the world. Calm, and self-centred, and complete, the æsthetic critic contemplates life, and no arrow drawn at a venture can pierce between the joints of his harness. He at least is safe. He has discovered how to live.

Is such a mode of life immoral? Yes: all the arts are immoral, except those baser forms of sensual or didactic art that seek to excite to action of evil or of good. For action of every kind belongs to the sphere of ethics. The aim of art is simply to create a mood. Is such a mode of life unpractical? Ah! it is not so easy to be unpractical as the ignorant Philistine imagines. It were well for England if it were so. There is no country in the world so much in need of unpractical people as this country of ours. With us, Thought is degraded by its constant association with practice. Who that moves in the stress and turmoil of actual existence, noisy politician, or brawling social reformer, or poor narrow-minded priest blinded by the sufferings of that unimportant section of the community among whom he has cast his lot, can seriously claim to be able to form a disinterested intellectual judgment about any one thing? Each of the professions means a prejudice. The necessity for a career forces every one to take sides. We live in the age of the overworked, and the undereducated; the age in which people are so industrious that they become absolutely stupid. And, harsh though it may sound, I cannot help saying that such people deserve their doom. The sure way of knowing nothing about life is to try to make oneself useful.

Ernest. A charming doctrine, Gilbert.

Gilbert. I am not sure about that, but it has at least the minor merit of being true. That the desire to do good to others produces a plentiful crop of prigs is the least of the evils of which it is the cause. The prig is a very interesting psychological study, and though of all poses a moral pose is the most offensive, still to have a pose at all is something. It is a formal recognition of the importance of treating life from a definite and reasoned standpoint. That Humanitarian Sympathy wars against Nature, by securing the survival of the failure, may make the man of science loathe its facile virtues. The political economist may cry out against it for putting the improvident on the same level as the provident, and so robbing life of the strongest, because most sordid, incentive to industry. But, in the eyes of the thinker, the real harm that emotional sympathy does is that it limits knowledge, and so prevents us from solving any single social problem. We are trying at present to stave off the coming crisis, the coming revolution as my friends the Fabianists call it, by means of doles and alms. Well, when the revolution or crisis arrives, we shall be powerless because we shall know nothing. And so, Ernest, let us not be deceived. England will never be civilized till she has added Utopia to her dominions. There is more than one of her colonies that she might with advantage surrender for so fair a land. What we want are unpractical people who see beyond the moment, and think beyond the day. Those who try to lead the people can only do so by following the mob. It is through the voice of one crying in the wilderness that the ways of the gods must be prepared.

But perhaps you think that in beholding for the mere joy of beholding, and contemplating for the sake of contemplation, there is something that is egotistic. If you think so, do not say so. It takes a thoroughly selfish age, like our own, to deify self-sacrifice. It takes a thoroughly grasping age, such as that in which we live, to set above the fine intellectual virtues, those shallow and emotional virtues that are an immediate practical benefit to itself. They miss their aim, too, these philanthropists and sentimentalists of our day, who are always chattering to one about one's duty to one's neighbour. For the development of the race depends on the development of the individual, and where self-culture has ceased to be the ideal, the intellectual standard is instantly lowered, and, often, ultimately lost. If you meet at dinner a man who has spent his life in educating himself—a rare type in our time, I admit, but still one occasionally to be met with—you rise from table richer, and conscious that a high ideal has for a moment touched and sanctified your days. But oh! my dear Ernest, to sit next a man who has spent his life in trying to educate others! What a dreadful experience that is! How appalling is that ignorance which is the inevitable result of the fatal habit of imparting opinions! How limited in range the creature's mind proves to be! How it wearies us, and must weary himself, with its endless repetitions and sickly reiteration! How lacking it is in any element of intellectual growth! In what a vicious circle it always moves!

Ernest. You speak with strange feeling, Gilbert. Have you had this dreadful experience, as you call it, lately?

Gilbert. Few of us escape it. People say that the schoolmaster is abroad. I wish to goodness he were. But the type of which, after all, he is only one, and certainly the least important, of the representatives, seems to me to be really dominating our lives; and just as the philanthropist is the nuisance of the ethical sphere, so the nuisance of the intellectual sphere is the man who is so occupied in trying to educate others, that he has never had any time to educate himself. No, Ernest, self-culture is the true ideal of man. Goethe saw it, and the immediate debt that we owe to Goethe is greater than the debt we owe to any man since Greek days. The Greeks saw it, and have left us, as their legacy to modern thought, the conception of the contemplative life as well as the critical method by which alone can that life be truly realized. It was the one thing that made the Renaissance great, and gave us Humanism. It is the one thing that could make our own age great also; for the real weakness of England lies, not in incomplete armaments or unfortified coasts, not in the poverty that creeps through sunless lanes, or the drunkenness that brawls in loathsome courts, but simply in the fact that her ideals are emotional and not intellectual.

I do not deny that the intellectual ideal is difficult of attainment, still less that it is, and perhaps will be for years to come, unpopular with the crowd. It is so easy for people to have sympathy with suffering. It is so difficult for them to have sympathy with thought. Indeed, so little do ordinary people understand what thought really is, that they seem to imagine that, when they have said that a theory is dangerous, they have pronounced its condemnation, whereas it is only such theories that have any true intellectual value. An idea that is not dangerous is unworthy of being called an idea at all.

Ernest. Gilbert, you bewilder me. You have told me that all art is, in its essence, immoral. Are you going to tell me now that all thought is, in its essence, dangerous?

Gilbert. Yes, in the practical sphere it is so. The security of society lies in custom and unconscious instinct, and the basis of the stability of society, as a healthy organism, is the complete absence of any intelligence amongst its members. The great majority of people being fully aware of this, rank themselves naturally on the side of that splendid system that elevates them to the dignity of machines, and rage so wildly against the intrusion of the intellectual faculty into any question that concerns life, that one is tempted to define man as a rational animal who always loses his temper when he is called upon to act in accordance with the dictates of reason. But let us turn from the practical sphere, and say no more about the wicked philanthropists, who, indeed, may well be left to the mercy of the almond-eyed sage of the Yellow River, Chuang Tsŭ the wise, who has proved that such well-meaning and offensive busy-bodies have destroyed the simple and spontaneous virtue that there is in man. They are a wearisome topic, and I am anxious to get back to the sphere in which criticism is free.

Ernest. The sphere of the intellect?

Gilbert. Yes. You remember that I spoke of the critic as being in his own way as creative as the artist, whose work, indeed, may be merely of value in so far as it gives to the critic a suggestion for some new mood of thought and feeling which he can realize with equal, or perhaps greater, distinction of form, and, through the use of a fresh medium of expression, make differently beautiful and more perfect. Well, you seemed to me to be a little sceptical about the theory. But perhaps I wronged you?

Ernest. I am not really sceptical about it, but I must admit that I feel very strongly that such work as you describe the critic producing—and creative such work must undoubtedly be admitted to be—is, of necessity, purely subjective, whereas the greatest work is objective always, objective and impersonal.

Gilbert. The difference between objective and subjective work is one of external form merely. It is accidental, not essential. All artistic creation is absolutely subjective. The very landscape that Corot looked at was, as he said himself, but a mood of his own mind; and those great figures of Greek or English drama that seem to us to possess an actual existence of their own, apart from the poets who shaped and fashioned them, are, in their ultimate analysis, simply the poets themselves, not as they thought they were, but as they thought they were not; and by such thinking came in strange manner, though but for a moment, really so to be. For out of ourselves we can never pass, nor can there be in creation what in the creator was not. Nay, I would say that the more objective a creation appears to be, the more subjective it really is. Shakespeare might have met Rosencrantz and Guildenstern in the white streets of London, or seen the serving-men of rival houses bite their thumbs at each other in the open square; but Hamlet came out of his soul, and Romeo out of his passion. They were elements of his nature to which he gave visible form, impulses that stirred so strongly within him that he had, as it were perforce, to suffer them to realize their energy, not on the lower plane of actual life, where they would have been trammelled and constrained and so made imperfect, but on that imaginative plane of art where Love can indeed find in Death its rich fulfilment, where one can stab the eavesdropper behind the arras, and wrestle in a new-made grave, and make a guilty king drink his own hurt, and see one's father's spirit, beneath the glimpses of the moon, stalking in complete steel from misty wall to wall. Action being limited would have left Shakespeare unsatisfied and unexpressed; and, just as it is because he did nothing that he has been able to achieve everything, so it is because he never speaks to us of himself in his plays that his plays reveal him to us absolutely, and show us his true nature and temperament far more completely than do those strange and exquisite sonnets, even, in which he bares to crystal eyes the secret closet of his heart. Yes, the objective form is the most subjective in matter. Man is least himself when he talks in his own person. Give him a mask, and he will tell you the truth.

389

The Artist as Critic

Ernest. The critic, then, being limited to the subjective form, will necessarily be less able to fully express himself than the artist, who has always at his disposal the forms that are impersonal and objective.

Gilbert. Not necessarily, and certainly not at all if he recognizes that each mode of criticism is, in its highest development, simply a mood, and that we are never more true to ourselves than when we are inconsistent. The æsthetic critic, constant only to the principle of beauty in all things, will ever be looking for fresh impressions, winning from the various schools the secret of their charm, bowing, it may be, before foreign altars, or smiling, if it be his fancy, at strange new gods. What other people call one's past has, no doubt, everything to do with them, but has absolutely nothing to do with oneself. The man who regards his past is a man who deserves to have no future to look forward to. When one has found expression for a mood, one has done with it. You laugh; but believe me it is so. Yesterday it was Realism that charmed one. One gained from it that *nouveau frisson* which it was its aim to produce. One analyzed it, explained it, and wearied of it. At sunset came the *Luministe* in painting, and the *Symboliste* in poetry, and the spirit of mediævalism, that spirit which belongs not to time but to temperament, woke suddenly in wounded Russia, and stirred us for a moment by the terrible fascination of pain. To-day the cry is for Romance, and already the leaves are tremulous in the valley, and on the purple hill-tops walks Beauty with slim gilded feet. The old modes of creation linger, of course. The artists reproduce either themselves or each other, with wearisome iteration. But Criticism is always moving on, and the critic is always developing.

Nor, again, is the critic really limited to the subjective form of expression. The method of the drama is his, as well as the method of the epos. He may use dialogue, as he did who set Milton talking to Marvel on the nature of comedy and tragedy, and made Sidney and Lord Brooke discourse on letters beneath the Penshurst oaks; or adopt narration, as Mr. Pater is fond of doing, each of whose Imaginary Portraits—is not that the title of the book?—presents to us, under the fanciful guise of fiction, some fine and exquisite piece of criticism, one on the painter Watteau, another on the philosophy of Spinoza, a third on the Pagan elements of the early Renaissance, and the last, and in some respects the most suggestive, on the source of that Aufklärung, that enlightening which dawned on Germany in the last century, and to which our own culture owes so great a debt. Dialogue, certainly, that wonderful literary form which, from Plato to Lucian, and from Lucian to Giordano Bruno, and from Bruno to that grand old Pagan in whom Carlyle took such delight, the creative critics of the world have always employed, can never lose for the thinker its attraction as a mode of expression. By its means he can both reveal and conceal himself, and give form to every fancy, and reality to every mood. By its means he can exhibit the object from each point of view, and show it to us in the round, as a sculptor shows us things, gaining in this manner all the richness and reality of effect that comes from those side issues that are suddenly suggested by the central idea in its progress, and really illumine the idea more completely, or from those felicitous after-thoughts that give a fuller completeness to the central scheme, and yet convey something of the delicate charm of chance.

Ernest. By its means, too, he can invent an imaginary antagonist, and convert him when he chooses by some absurdly sophistical argument.

Gilbert. Ah! it is so easy to convert others. It is so difficult to convert oneself. To arrive at what one really believes, one must speak through lips different from one's own. To know the truth one must imagine myriads of falsehoods. For what is Truth? In matters of religion, it is simply the opinion that has survived. In matters of science, it is the ultimate sensation. In matters of art, it is one's last mood. And you see now, Ernest, that the critic has at his disposal as many objective forms of expression as the artist has. Ruskin put his criticism into imaginative prose, and is superb in his changes and contradictions; and Browning put his into blank verse, and made painter and poet yield us their secret; and M. Renan uses dialogue, and Mr. Pater fiction, and Rossetti translated into sonnet-music the colour of Giorgione and the design of Ingres, and his own design and colour also, feeling, with the instinct of one who had many modes of utterance, that the ultimate art is literature, and the finest and fullest medium that of words.

Ernest. Well, now that you have settled that the critic has at his disposal all objective forms, I wish you would tell me what are the qualities that should characterize the true critic.

Gilbert. What would you say they were?

Ernest. Well, I should say that a critic should above all things be fair.

Gilbert. Ah! not fair. A critic cannot be fair in the ordinary sense of the word. It is only about things that do not interest one that one can give a really unbiassed opinion, which is no doubt the reason why an unbiassed opinion is always absolutely valueless. The man who sees both sides of a question, is a man who sees absolutely nothing at all. Art is a passion, and, in matters of art, Thought is inevitably coloured by emotion, and so is fluid rather than fixed, and, depending upon fine moods and exquisite moments, cannot be narrowed into the rigidity of a scientific formula or a theological dogma. It is to the soul that Art speaks, and the soul may be made the prisoner of the mind as well as of the body. One should, of course, have no prejudices; but, as a great Frenchman remarked a hundred years ago, it is one's business in such matters to have preferences, and when one has preferences one ceases to be fair. It is only an auctioneer who can equally and impartially admire all schools of Art. No: fairness is not one of the qualities of the true critic. It is not even a condition of criticism. Each form of Art with which we come in contact dominates us for the moment to the exclusion of every other form. We must surrender ourselves absolutely to the work in question, whatever it may be, if we wish to gain its secret. For the time, we must think of nothing else, can think of nothing else, indeed.

Ernest. The true critic will be rational, at any rate, will he not?

Gilbert. Rational? There are two ways of disliking art, Ernest. One is to dislike it. The other, to like it rationally. For Art, as Plato saw, and not without regret, creates in listener and spectator a form of divine madness. It does not spring from inspiration, but it makes others inspired. Reason is not the faculty to which it appeals. If one loves Art at all, one must love it beyond all other things in the world, and against such love, the reason, if one listened to it, would cry out. There is nothing sane about the worship of beauty. It is too splendid to be sane. Those of whose lives it forms the dominant note will always seem to the world to be pure visionaries.

Ernest. Well, at least, the critic will be sincere.

Gilbert. A little sincerity is a dangerous thing, and a great deal of it is absolutely fatal. The true critic will, indeed, always be sincere in his devotion to the principle of beauty, but he will seek for beauty in every age and in each school, and will never suffer himself to be limited to any settled custom of thought, or stereotyped mode of looking at things. He will realize himself in many forms, and by a thousand different ways, and will ever be curious of new sensations and fresh points of view. Through constant change, and through constant change alone, he will find his true unity. He will not consent to be the slave of his own opinions. For what is mind but motion in the intellectual sphere? The essence of thought, as the essence of life, is growth. You must not be frightened by words, Ernest. What people call insincerity is simply a method by which we can multiply our personalities.

Ernest. I am afraid I have not been fortunate in my suggestions.

Gilbert. Of the three qualifications you mentioned, two, sincerity and fairness, were, if not actually moral, at least on the border-land of morals, and the first condition of criticism is that the critic should be able to recognize that the sphere of Art and the sphere of Ethics are absolutely distinct and separate. When they are confused, Chaos has come again. They are too often confused in England now, and though our modern Puritans cannot destroy a beautiful thing, yet, by means of their extraordinary prurience, they can almost taint beauty for a moment. It is chiefly, I regret to say, through journalism that such people find expression. I regret it because there is much to be said in favour of modern journalism. By giving us the opinions of the uneducated, it keeps us in touch with the ignorance of the community. By carefully chronicling the current events of contemporary life, it shows us of what very little importance such events really are. By invariably discussing the unnecessary, it makes us understand what things are requisite for culture, and what are not. But it should not allow poor Tartuffe to write articles upon modern art. When it does this it stultifies itself. And yet Tartuffe's articles, and Chadband's notes do this good, at least. They serve to show how extremely limited is the area over which ethics, and ethical considerations, can claim to exercise influence. Science is out of the reach of morals, for her eyes are fixed upon eternal truths. Art is out of the reach of morals, for her eyes are fixed upon things beautiful and immortal and ever-changing. To morals belong the lower and less intellectual spheres. However, let these mouthing Puritans pass; they have their comic side. Who can help laughing when an ordinary journalist seriously proposes to limit the subject-matter at the disposal of the artist? Some limitation might well, and will soon, I hope, be placed upon some of our newspapers and newspaper writers. For they give us the bald, sordid, disgusting facts of life. They chronicle, with degrading avidity, the sins of the second-rate, and with the conscientiousness of the illiterate give us accurate and prosaic details of the doings of people of absolutely no interest whatsoever. But the artist, who accepts the facts of life, and yet transforms them into shapes of beauty, and makes them vehicles of pity or of awe, and shows their colour-element, and their wonder, and their true ethical import also, and builds out of them a world more real than reality itself, and of loftier and more noble import—who shall set limits to him? Not the apostles of that new Journalism which is but the old vulgarity "writ large." Not the apostles of that new Puritanism, which is but the whine of the hypocrite, and is both writ and spoken badly. The mere suggestion is ridiculous. Let us leave these wicked people, and proceed to the discussion of the artistic qualifications necessary for the true critic.

Ernest. And what are they? Tell me yourself.

Gilbert. Temperament is the primary requisite for the critic —a temperament exquisitely susceptible to beauty, and to the various impressions that beauty gives us. Under what conditions, and by what means, this temperament is engendered in race or individual, we will not discuss at present. It is sufficient to note that it exists, and that there is in us a beauty-sense, separate from the other senses and above them, separate from the reason and of nobler import, separate from the soul and of equal value—a sense that leads some to create, and others, the finer spirits as I think, to contemplate merely. But to be purified and made perfect, this sense requires some form of exquisite environment. Without this it starves, or is dulled. You remember that lovely passage in which Plato describes how a young Greek should be educated, and with what insistence he dwells upon the importance of surroundings, telling us how the lad is to be brought up in the midst of fair sights and sounds, so that the beauty of material things may prepare his soul for the reception of the beauty that is spiritual. Insensibly, and without knowing the reason why, he is to develop that real love of beauty which, as Plato is never weary of reminding us, is the true aim of education. By slow degrees there is to be engendered in him such a temperament as will lead him naturally and simply to choose the good in preference to the bad, and, rejecting what is vulgar and discordant, to follow by fine instinctive taste all that possesses grace and charm and loveliness. Ultimately, in its due course, this taste is to become critical and self-conscious, but at first it is to exist purely as a cultivated instinct, and "he who has received this true culture of the inner man will with clear and certain vision perceive the omissions and faults in art or nature, and with a taste that cannot err, while he praises, and finds his pleasure in what is good, and receives it into his soul, and so becomes good and noble, he will rightly blame and hate the bad, now in the days of his youth, even before he is able to know the reason why:" and so, when, later on, the critical and self-conscious spirit develops in him, he "will recognize and salute it as a friend with whom his education has made him long familiar." I need hardly say, Ernest, how far we in England have fallen short of this ideal, and I can imagine the smile that would illuminate the glossy face of the Philistine if one ventured to suggest to him that the true aim of education was the love of beauty, and that the methods by which education should work were the development of temperament, the cultivation of taste, and the creation of the critical spirit.

Yet, even for us, there is left some loveliness of environment, and the dulness of tutors and professors matters very little when one can loiter in the grey cloisters at Magdalen, and listen to some flute-like voice singing in Waynfleete's chapel, or lie in the green meadow, among the strange snake-spotted fritillaries, and watch the sunburnt noon smite to a finer gold the tower's gilded vanes, or wander up the Christ Church staircase beneath the vaulted ceiling's shadowy fans, or pass through the sculptured gateway of Laud's building in the College of St. John. Nor is it merely at Oxford, or Cambridge, that the sense of beauty can be formed and trained and perfected. All over England there is a Renaissance of the decorative Arts. Ugliness has had its day. Even in the houses of the rich there is taste, and the houses of those who are not rich have been made gracious and comely and sweet to live in. Caliban, poor noisy Caliban, thinks that when he has ceased to make mows at a thing, the thing ceases to exist. But if he mocks no longer, it is because he has been met with mockery, swifter and keener than his own, and for a moment has been bitterly schooled into that silence which should seal for ever his uncouth distorted lips. What has been done up to now, has been chiefly in the clearing of the way. It is always more difficult to destroy than it is to create, and when what one has to destroy is vulgarity and stupidity, the task of destruction needs not merely courage but also contempt. Yet it seems to me to have been, in a measure, done. We have got rid of what was bad. We have now to make what is beautiful. And though the mission of the æsthetic movement is to lure people to contemplate, not to lead them to create, yet, as the creative instinct is strong in the Celt, and it is the Celt who leads in art, there is no reason why in future years this strange Renaissance should not become almost as mighty in its way as was that new birth of Art that woke many centuries ago in the cities of Italy.

Certainly, for the cultivation of temperament, we must turn to the decorative arts: to the arts that touch us, not to the arts that teach us. Modern pictures are, no doubt, delightful to look at. At least, some of them are. But they are quite impossible to live with; they are too clever, too assertive, too intellectual. Their meaning is too obvious, and their method too clearly defined. One exhausts what they have to say in a very short time, and then they become as tedious as one's relations. I am very fond of the work of many of the Impressionist paint- ers of Paris and London. Subtlety and distinction have not yet left the school. Some of their arrangements and harmonies serve to remind one of the unapproachable beauty of Gautier's immortal *Symphonie en Blanc Majeur*, that flawless master- piece of colour and music which may have suggested the type as well as the titles of many of their best pictures. For a class that welcomes the incompetent with sympathetic eagerness, and that confuses the bizarre with the beautiful, and vulgarity with truth, they are extremely accomplished. They can do etchings that have the brilliancy of epigrams, pastels that are as fascinating as paradoxes, and as for their portraits, whatever the commonplace may say against them, no one can deny that they possess that unique and wonderful charm which belongs to works of pure fiction. But even the Impressionists, earnest and industrious as they are, will not do. I like them. Their white keynote, with its variations in lilac, was an era in colour. Though the moment does not make the man, the moment certainly makes the Impressionist, and for the moment in art, and the "moment's monument" as Rossetti phrased it, what may not be said? They are suggestive also. If they have not opened the eyes of the blind, they have at least given great en- couragement to the short-sighted, and while their leaders may have all the inexperience of old age, their young men are far too wise to be ever sensible. Yet they will insist on treating painting as if it were a mode of autobiography invented for the use of the illiterate, and are always prating to us on their coarse gritty canvases of their unnecessary selves and their un- necessary opinions, and spoiling by a vulgar over-emphasis that fine contempt of nature which is the best and only modest thing about them. One tires, at the end, of the work of individ- uals whose individuality is always noisy, and generally unin- teresting. There is far more to be said in favour of that newer school at Paris, the *Archaicistes*, as they call themselves, who, refusing to leave the artist entirely at the mercy of the weather, do not find the ideal of art in mere atmospheric effect, but seek rather for the imaginative beauty of design and the loveli- ness of fair colour, and rejecting the tedious realism of those who merely paint what they see, try to see something worth seeing, and to see it not merely with actual and physical vision, but with that nobler vision of the soul which is as far wider in spiritual scope as it is far more splendid in artistic purpose. They, at any rate, work under those decorative conditions that each art requires for its perfection, and have sufficient æsthetic instinct to regret those sordid and stupid limitations of absolute modernity of form which have proved the ruin of so many of the Impressionists. Still, the art that is frankly decorative is the art to live with. It is, of all visible arts, the one art that creates in us both mood and temperament. Mere colour, unspoiled by meaning, and unallied with definite form, can speak to the soul in a thousand different ways. The harmony that resides in the delicate proportions of lines and masses becomes mirrored in the mind. The repetitions of pattern give us rest. The marvels of design stir the imagination. In the mere loveliness of the materials employed there are latent elements of culture. Nor is this all. By its deliberate rejection of Nature as the ideal of beauty, as well as of the imitative method of the ordinary painter, decorative art not merely prepares the soul for the reception of true imaginative work, but develops in it that sense of form which is the basis of creative no less than of critical achievement. For the real artist is he who proceeds, not from feeling to form, but from form to thought and passion. He does not first conceive an idea, and then say to himself, "I will put my idea into a complex metre of fourteen lines," but, realizing the beauty of the sonnet-scheme, he conceives certain modes of music and methods of rhyme, and the mere form suggests what is to fill it and make it intellectually and emotionally complete. From time to time the world cries out against some charming artistic poet, because, to use its hackneyed and silly phrase, he has "nothing to say." But if he had something to say, he would probably say it, and the result would be tedious. It is just because he has no new message, that he can do beautiful work. He gains his inspiration from form, and from form purely, as an artist should. A real passion would ruin him. Whatever actually occurs is spoiled for art. All bad poetry springs from genuine feeling. To be natural is to be obvious, and to be obvious is to be inartistic.

Ernest. I wonder do you really believe what you say.

Gilbert. Why should you wonder? It is not merely in art that the body is the soul. In every sphere of life Form is the beginning of things. The rhythmic harmonious gestures of dancing convey, Plato tells us, both rhythm and harmony into the mind. Forms are the food of faith, cried Newman in one of those great moments of sincerity that made us admire and know the man. He was right, though he may not have known how terribly right he was. The Creeds are believed, not because they are rational, but because they are repeated. Yes: Form is everything. It is the secret of life. Find expression for a sorrow, and it will become dear to you. Find expression for a joy, and you intensify its ecstasy. Do you wish to love? Use Love's Litany, and the words will create the yearning from which the world fancies that they spring. Have you a grief that corrodes your heart? Steep yourself in the language of grief, learn its utterance from Prince Hamlet and Queen Constance, and you will find that mere expression is a mode of consolation, and that Form, which is the birth of passion, is also the death of pain. And so, to return to the sphere of Art, it is Form that creates not merely the critical temperament, but also the æsthetic instinct, that unerring instinct that reveals to one all things under their conditions of beauty. Start with the worship of form, and there is no secret in art that will not be revealed to you, and remember that in criticism, as in creation, temperament is everything, and that it is, not by the time of their production, but by the temperaments to which they appeal, that the schools of art should be historically grouped.

Ernest. Your theory of education is delightful. But what influence will your critic, brought up in these exquisite surroundings, possess? Do you really think that any artist is ever affected by criticism?

Gilbert. The influence of the critic will be the mere fact of his own existence. He will represent the flawless type. In him the culture of the century will see itself realized. You must not ask of him to have any aim other than the perfecting of himself. The demand of the intellect, as has been well said, is simply to feel itself alive. The critic may, indeed, desire to exercise influence; but, if so, he will concern himself not with the individual, but with the age, which he will seek to wake into consciousness, and to make responsive, creating in it new desires and appetites, and lending it his larger vision and his nobler moods. The actual art of to-day will occupy him less than the art of to-morrow, far less than the art of yesterday, and as for this or that person at present toiling away, what do the industrious matter? They do their best, no doubt, and consequently we get the worst from them. It is always with the best intentions that the worst work is done. And besides, my dear Ernest, when a man reaches the age of forty, or becomes a Royal Academician, or is elected a member of the Athenæum Club, or is recognized as a popular novelist, whose books are in great demand at suburban railway stations, one may have the amusement of exposing him, but one cannot have the pleasure of reforming him. And this is, I dare say, very fortunate for him; for I have no doubt that reformation is a much more painful process than punishment, is indeed punishment in its most aggravated and moral form—a fact which accounts for our entire failure as a community to reclaim that interesting phenomenon who is called the confirmed criminal.

Ernest. But may it not be that the poet is the best judge of poetry, and the painter of painting? Each art must appeal primarily to the artist who works in it. His judgment will surely be the most valuable?

Gilbert. The appeal of all art is simply to the artistic temperament. Art does not address herself to the specialist. Her claim is that she is universal, and that in all her manifestations she is one. Indeed, so far from its being true that the artist is the best judge of art, a really great artist can never judge of other people's work at all, and can hardly, in fact, judge of his own. That very concentration of vision that makes a man an artist, limits by its sheer intensity his faculty of fine appreciation. The energy of creation hurries him blindly on to his own goal. The wheels of his chariot raise the dust as a cloud around him. The gods are hidden from each other. They can recognize their worshippers. That is all.

Ernest. You say that a great artist cannot recognize the beauty of work different from his own.

Gilbert. It is impossible for him to do so. Wordsworth saw in *Endymion* merely a pretty piece of Paganism, and Shelley, with his dislike of actuality, was deaf to Wordsworth's message, being repelled by its form, and Byron, that great passionate human incomplete creature, could appreciate neither the poet of the cloud nor the poet of the lake, and the wonder of Keats was hidden from him. The realism of Euripides was hateful to Sophokles. Those droppings of warm tears had no music for him. Milton, with his sense of the grand style, could not understand the method of Shakespeare, any more than could Sir Joshua the method of Gainsborough. Bad artists always admire each other's work. They call it being large-minded and free from prejudice. But a truly great artist cannot conceive of life being shown, or beauty fashioned, under any conditions other than those that he has selected. Creation employs all its critical faculty within its own sphere. It may not use it in the sphere that belongs to others. It is exactly because a man cannot do a thing that he is the proper judge of it.

Ernest. Do you really mean that?

Gilbert. Yes, for creation limits, while contemplation widens, the vision.

Ernest. But what about technique? Surely each art has its separate technique?

Gilbert. Certainly: each art has its grammar and its materials. There is no mystery about either, and the incompetent can always be correct. But, while the laws upon which Art rests may be fixed and certain, to find their true realization they must be touched by the imagination into such beauty that they will seem an exception, each one of them. Technique is really personality. That is the reason why the artist cannot teach it, why the pupil cannot learn it, and why the æsthetic critic can understand it. To the great poet, there is only one method of music—his own. To the great painter, there is only one manner of painting—that which he himself employs. The æsthetic critic, and the æsthetic critic alone, can appreciate all forms and modes. It is to him that Art makes her appeal.

Ernest. Well, I think I have put all my questions to you. And now I must admit—

Gilbert. Ah! don't say that you agree with me. When people agree with me I always feel that I must be wrong.

Ernest. In that case I certainly won't tell you whether I agree with you or not. But I will put another question. You have explained to me that criticism is a creative art. What future has it?

Gilbert. It is to criticism that the future belongs. The subject-matter at the disposal of creation becomes every day more limited in extent and variety. Providence and Mr. Walter Besant have exhausted the obvious. If creation is to last at all, it can only do so on the condition of becoming far more critical than it is at present. The old roads and dusty highways have been traversed too often. Their charm has been worn away by plodding feet, and they have lost that element of novelty or surprise which is so essential for romance. He who would stir us now by fiction must either give us an entirely new background, or reveal to us the soul of man in its innermost workings. The first is for the moment being done for us by Mr. Rudyard Kipling. As one turns over the pages of his *Plain Tales from the Hills*, one feels as if one were seated under a palm-tree reading life by superb flashes of vulgarity. The bright colours of the bazaars dazzle one's eyes. The jaded, second-rate Anglo-Indians are in exquisite incongruity with their surroundings. The mere lack of style in the story-teller gives an odd journalistic realism to what he tells us. From the point of view of literature Mr. Kipling is a genius who drops his aspirates. From the point of view of life, he is a reporter who knows vulgarity better than any one has ever known it. Dickens knew its clothes and its comedy. Mr. Kipling knows its essence and its seriousness. He is our first authority on the second-rate, and has seen marvellous things through keyholes, and his backgrounds are real works of art. As for the second condition, we have had Browning, and Meredith is with us. But there is still much to be done in the sphere of introspection. People sometimes say that fiction is getting too morbid. As far as psychology is concerned, it has never been morbid enough. We have merely touched the surface of the soul, that is all. In one single ivory cell of the brain there are stored away things more marvellous and more terrible than even they have dreamed of, who, like the author of *Le Rouge et le Noir*, have sought to track the soul into its most secret places, and to make life confess its dearest sins. Still, there is a limit even to the number of untried backgrounds, and it is possible that a further development of the habit of introspection may prove fatal to that creative faculty to which it seeks to supply fresh material. I myself am inclined to think that creation is doomed. It springs from too primitive, too natural an impulse. However this may be, it is certain that the subject-matter at the disposal of creation is always diminishing, while the subject-matter of criticism increases daily. There are always new attitudes for the mind, and new points of view. The duty of imposing form upon chaos does not grow less as the world advances. There was never a time when Criticism was more needed than it is now. It is only by its means that Humanity can become conscious of the point at which it has arrived.

Hours ago, Ernest, you asked me the use of Criticism. You might just as well have asked me the use of thought. It is Criticism, as Arnold points out, that creates the intellectual atmosphere of the age. It is Criticism, as I hope to point out myself some day, that makes the mind a fine instrument. We, in our educational system, have burdened the memory with a load of unconnected facts, and laboriously striven to impart our laboriously-acquired knowledge. We teach people how to remember, we never teach them how to grow. It has never occurred to us to try and develop in the mind a more subtle quality of apprehension and discernment. The Greeks did this, and when we come in contact with the Greek critical intellect, we cannot but be conscious that, while our subject-matter is in every respect larger and more varied than theirs, theirs is the only method by which this subject-matter can be interpreted. England has done one thing; it has invented and established Public Opinion, which is an attempt to organize the ignorance of the community, and to elevate it to the dignity of physical force. But Wisdom has always been hidden from it. Considered as an instrument of thought, the English mind is coarse and undeveloped. The only thing that can purify it is the growth of the critical instinct.

It is Criticism, again, that, by concentration, makes culture possible. It takes the cumbersome mass of creative work, and distils it into a finer essence. Who that desires to retain any sense of form could struggle through the monstrous multitudinous books that the world has produced, books in which thought stammers or ignorance brawls? The thread that is to guide us across the wearisome labyrinth is in the hands of Criticism. Nay more, where there is no record, and history is either lost or was never written, Criticism can recreate the past for us from the very smallest fragment of language or art, just as surely as the man of science can from some tiny bone, or the mere impress of a foot upon a rock, recreate for us the winged dragon or Titan lizard that once made the earth shake beneath its tread, can call Behemoth out of his cave, and make Leviathan swim once more across the startled sea. Prehistoric history belongs to the philological and archæological critic. It is to him that the origins of things are revealed. The self-conscious deposits of an age are nearly always misleading. Through philological criticism alone we know more of the centuries of which no actual record has been preserved, than we do of the centuries that have left us their scrolls. It can do for us what can be done neither by physics nor metaphysics. It can give us the exact science of mind in the process of becoming. It can do for us what History cannot do. It can tell us what man thought before he learned how to write. You have asked me about the influence of Criticism. I think I have answered that question already; but there is this also to be said. It is Criticism that makes us cosmopolitan. The Manchester school tried to make men realize the brotherhood of humanity, by pointing out the commercial advantages of peace. It sought to degrade the wonderful world into a common market-place for the buyer and the seller. It addressed itself to the lowest instincts, and it failed. War followed upon war, and the tradesman's creed did not prevent France and Germany from clashing together in blood-stained battle. There are others of our own day who seek to appeal to mere emotional sympathies, or to the shallow dogmas of some vague system of abstract ethics. They have their Peace Societies, so dear to the sentimentalists, and their proposals for unarmed International Arbitration, so popular among those who have never read history. But mere emotional sympathy will not do. It is too variable, and too closely connected with the passions; and a board of arbitrators who, for the general welfare of the race, are to be deprived of the power of putting their decisions into execution, will not be of much avail. There is only one thing worse than Injustice, and that is Justice without her sword in her hand. When Right is not Might, it is Evil.

No: the emotions will not make us cosmopolitan, any more than the greed for gain could do so. It is only by the cultivation of the habit of intellectual criticism that we shall be able to rise superior to race prejudices. Goethe—you will not misunderstand what I say—was a German of the Germans. He loved his country—no man more so. Its people were dear to him; and he led them. Yet, when the iron hoof of Napoleon trampled upon vineyard and cornfield, his lips were silent. "How can one write songs of hatred without hating?" he said to Eckerman, "and how could I, to whom culture and barbarism are alone of importance, hate a nation which is among the most cultivated of the earth, and to which I owe so great a part of my own cultivation?" This note, sounded in the modern world by Goethe first, will become, I think, the starting point for the cosmopolitanism of the future. Criticism will annihilate race-prejudices, by insisting upon the unity of the human mind in the variety of its forms. If we are tempted to make war upon another nation, we shall remember that we are seeking to destroy an element of our own culture, and possibly its most important element. As long as war is regarded as wicked, it will always have its fascination. When it is looked upon as vulgar, it will cease to be popular. The change will, of course, be slow, and people will not be conscious of it. They will not say "We will not war against France because her prose is perfect," but because the prose of France is perfect, they will not hate the land. Intellectual criticism will bind Europe together in bonds far closer than those that can be forged by shopman or sentimentalist. It will give us the peace that springs from understanding.

Nor is this all. It is Criticism that, recognizing no position as final, and refusing to bind itself by the shallow shibboleths of any sect or school, creates that serene philosophic temper which loves truth for its own sake, and loves it not the less because it knows it to be unattainable. How little we have of this temper in England, and how much we need it! The English mind is always in a rage. The intellect of the race is wasted in the sordid and stupid quarrels of second-rate politicians or third-rate theologians. It was reserved for a man of science to show us the supreme example of that "sweet reasonableness" of which Arnold spoke so wisely, and alas! to so little effect. The author of the *Origin of Species* had, at any rate, the philosophic temper. If one contemplates the ordinary pulpits and platforms of England, one can but feel the contempt of Julian, or the indifference of Montaigne. We are dominated by the fanatic, whose worst vice is his sincerity. Anything approaching to the free play of the mind is practically unknown amongst us. People cry out against the sinner, yet it is not the sinful, but the stupid, who are our shame. There is no sin except stupidity.

Ernest. Ah! what an antinomian you are!

Gilbert. The artistic critic, like the mystic, is an antinomian always. To be good, according to the vulgar standard of goodness, is obviously quite easy. It merely requires a certain amount of sordid terror, a certain lack of imaginative thought, and a certain low passion for middle-class respectability. Æsthetics are higher than ethics. They belong to a more spiritual sphere. To discern the beauty of a thing is the finest point to which we can arrive. Even a colour-sense is more important, in the development of the individual, than a sense of right and wrong. Æsthetics, in fact, are to Ethics in the sphere of conscious civilization, what, in the sphere of the external world, sexual is to natural selection. Ethics, like natural selection, make existence possible. Æsthetics, like sexual selection, make life lovely and wonderful, fill it with new forms, and give it progress, and variety and change. And when we reach the true culture that is our aim, we attain to that perfection of which the saints have dreamed, the perfection of those to whom sin is impossible, not because they make the renunciations of the ascetic, but because they can do everything they wish without hurt to the soul, and can wish for nothing that can do the soul harm, the soul being an entity so divine that it is able to transform into elements of a richer experience, or a finer susceptibility, or a newer mode of thought, acts or passions that with the common would be commonplace, or with the uneducated ignoble, or with the shameful vile. Is this dangerous? Yes; it is dangerous—all ideas, as I told you, are so. But the night wearies, and the light flickers in the lamp. One more thing I cannot help saying to you. You have spoken against Criticism as being a sterile thing. The nineteenth century is a turning point in history simply on account of the work of two men, Darwin and Renan, the one the critic of the Book of Nature, the other the critic of the books of God. Not to recognize this is to miss the meaning of one of the most important eras in the progress of the world. Creation is always behind the age. It is Criticism that leads us. The Critical Spirit and the World-Spirit are one.

Ernest. And he who is in possession of this spirit or whom this spirit possesses, will, I suppose, do nothing?

Gilbert. Like the Persephone of whom Landor tells us, the sweet pensive Persephone around whose white feet the asphodel and amaranth are blooming, he will sit contented "in that deep, motionless, quiet which mortals pity, and which the gods enjoy." He will look out upon the world and know its secret. By contact with divine things, he will become divine. His will be the perfect life, and his only.

Ernest. You have told me many strange things tonight, Gilbert. You have told me that it is more difficult to talk about a thing than to do it, and that to do nothing at all is the most difficult thing in the world; you have told me that all Art is immoral, and all thought dangerous; that criticism is more creative than creation, and that the highest criticism is that which reveals in the work of Art what the artist had not put there; that it is exactly because a man cannot do a thing that he is the proper judge of it; and that the true critic is unfair, insincere, not rational. My friend, you are a dreamer.

Gilbert. Yes: I am a dreamer. For a dreamer is one who can only find his way by moonlight, and his punishment is that he sees the dawn before the rest of the world.

Ernest. His punishment?

Gilbert. And his reward. But see, it is dawn already. Draw back the curtains and open the windows wide. How cool the morning air is! Piccadilly lies at our feet like a long riband of silver. A faint purple mist hangs over the Park, and the shadows of the white houses are purple. It is too late to sleep. Let

us go down to Covent Garden and look at the roses. Come!
I am tired of thought.

THE TRUTH OF MASKS
A note on illusion

In many of the somewhat violent attacks that have recently
been made on that splendour of mounting which now charac-
terizes our Shakespearian revivals in England, it seems to have
been tacitly assumed by the critics that Shakespeare himself
was more or less indifferent to the costume of his actors, and
that, could he see Mrs. Langtry's production of *Antony and
Cleopatra*, he would probably say that the play, and the play
only, is the thing, and that everything else is leather and pru-
nella. While, as regards any historical accuracy in dress, Lord
Lytton, in an article in the *Nineteenth Century*, has laid it
down as a dogma of art that archæology is entirely out of place
in the presentation of any of Shakespeare's plays, and the
attempt to introduce it one of the stupidest pedantries of an
age of prigs.

Lord Lytton's position I shall examine later on; but, as regards the theory that Shakespeare did not busy himself much
about the costume-wardrobe of his theatre, anybody who cares
to study Shakespeare's method will see that there is absolutely no dramatist of the French, English, or Athenian stage
who relies so much for his illusionist effects on the dress of his
actors as Shakespeare does himself.

Knowing how the artistic temperament is always fascinated
by beauty of costume, he constantly introduces into his plays
masques and dances, purely for the sake of the pleasure which
they give the eye; and we have still his stage-directions for the
three great processions in *Henry the Eighth*, directions which
are characterized by the most extraordinary elaborateness of
detail down to the collars of S.S. and the pearls in Anne Bol-
eyn's hair. Indeed it would be quite easy for a modern manager to reproduce these pageants absolutely as Shakespeare had

them designed; and so accurate were they that one of the Court officials of the time, writing an account of the last performance of the play at the Globe Theatre to a friend, actually complains of their realistic character, notably of the production on the stage of the Knights of the Garter in the robes and insignia of the order, as being calculated to bring ridicule on the real ceremonies; much in the same spirit in which the French Government, some time ago, prohibited that delightful actor, M. Christian, from appearing in uniform, on the plea that it was prejudicial to the glory of the army that a colonel should be caricatured. And elsewhere the gorgeousness of apparel which distinguished the English stage under Shakespeare's influence was attacked by the contemporary critics, not as a rule, however, on the grounds of the democratic tendencies of realism, but usually on those moral grounds which are always the last refuge of people who have no sense of beauty.

The point, however, which I wish to emphasize is, not that Shakespeare appreciated the value of lovely costumes in adding picturesqueness to poetry, but that he saw how important costume is as a means of producing certain dramatic effects. Many of his plays, such as *Measure for Measure, Twelfth Night, The Two Gentlemen of Verona, All's Well that Ends Well, Cymbeline,* and others, depend for their illusion on the character of the various dresses worn by the hero or the heroine; the delightful scene in *Henry the Sixth,* on the modern miracles of healing by faith, loses all its point unless Gloster is in black and scarlet; and the *dénoûment* of the *Merry Wives of Windsor* hinges on the colour of Anne Page's gown. As for the uses Shakespeare makes of disguises the instance[s] are almost numberless. Posthumus hides his passion under a peasant's garb, and Edgar his pride beneath an idiot's rags; Portia wears the apparel of a lawyer, and Rosalind, is attired, in "all points as a man"; the cloak-bag of Pisanio changes Imogen to the youth Fidele; Jessica flees from her father's house in boy's dress, and Julia ties up her yellow hair in fantastic love-knots, and dons hose and doublet; Henry the Eighth woos his lady as a shepherd, and Romeo his as a pilgrim; Prince Hal and Poins appear first as footpads in buckram suits, and then in white aprons and leather jerkins as the waiters in a tavern: and as for

Falstaff, does he not come on as a highwayman, as an old woman, as Herne the Hunter, and as the clothes going to the laundry?

Nor are the examples of the employment of costume as a mode of intensifying dramatic situation less numerous. After slaughter of Duncan, Macbeth appears in his night-gown as if aroused from sleep; Timon ends in rags the play he had begun in splendour; Richard flatters the London citizens in a suit of mean and shabby armour, and, as soon as he has stepped in blood to the throne, marches through the streets in crown and George and Garter; the climax of the *Tempest* is reached when Prospero, throwing off his enchanter's robes, sends Ariel for his hat and rapier, and reveals himself as the great Italian Duke; the very Ghost in *Hamlet* changes his mystical apparel to produce different effects; and as for Juliet, a modern playwright would probably have lain her out in her shroud, and made the scene a scene of horror merely, but Shakespeare arrays her in rich and gorgeous raiment, whose loveliness makes the vault "a feasting presence full of light," turns the tomb into a bridal chamber, and gives the cue and motive for Romeo's speech of the triumph of Beauty over Death.

Even small details of dress, such as the colour of a major-domo's stockings, the pattern on a wife's handkerchief, the sleeve of a young soldier, and a fashionable woman's bonnets, become in Shakespeare's hands points of actual dramatic importance, and by some of them the action of the play in question is conditioned absolutely. Many other dramatists have availed themselves of costume as a method of expressing directly to the audience the character of a person on his entrance, though hardly so brilliantly as Shakespeare has done in the case of the dandy Parolles, whose dress, by the way, only an archæologist can understand; the fun of a master and servant exchanging coats in presence of the audience, of shipwrecked sailors squabbling over the division of a lot of fine clothes, and of a tinker dressed up like a duke while he is in his cups, may be regarded as part of that great career which costume has always played in comedy from the time of Aristophanes down to Mr. Gilbert; but nobody from the mere details of apparel and adornment has ever drawn such irony of contrast, such immediate and tragic effect, such pity and such pathos, as Shakespeare himself. Armed cap-à-pié, the dead King stalks on the battlements of Elsinore because all is not right with Denmark; Shylock's Jewish gaberdine is part of the stigma under which that wounded and embittered nature writhes; Arthur begging for his life can think of no better plea than the handkerchief he had given Hubert—

> Have you the heart? when your head did but ache,
> I knit my handkerchief about your brows,
> (The best I had, a princess wrought it me)
> And I did never ask it you again.

and Orlando's blood-stained napkin strikes the first sombre note in that exquisite woodland idyll, and shows us the depth of feeling that underlies Rosalind's fanciful wit and wilful jesting.

> Last night 'twas on my arm; I kissed it;
> I hope it be not gone to tell my lord
> That I kiss aught but he.

says Imogen, jesting on the loss of the bracelet which was already on its way to Rome to rob her of her husband's faith; the little Prince passing to the Tower plays with the dagger in his uncle's girdle; Duncan sends a ring to Lady Macbeth on the night of his own murder, and the ring of Portia turns the tragedy of the merchant into a wife's comedy. The great rebel York dies with paper crown on his head; Hamlet's black suit is a kind of colour-motive in the piece, like the mourning of the Chimène in the *Cid*; and the climax of Antony's speech is the production of Cæsar's cloak:—

>   I remember
> The first time ever Cæsar put it on.
> 'Twas on a summer's evening, in his tent,
> The day he overcame the Nervii:—
> Look, in this place ran Cassius' dagger through:
> See what a rent the envious Casca made:
> Through this the well-beloved Brutus stabbed. . . .
> Kind souls, what, weep you when you but behold
> Our Cæsar's vesture wounded?

The flowers which Ophelia carries with her in her madness are as pathetic as the violets that blossom on a grave; the effect of Lear's wandering on the heath is intensified beyond words by his fantastic attire; and when Cloten, stung by the taunt of that simile which his sister draws from her husband's raiment, arrays himself in that husband's very garb to work upon her the deed of shame, we feel that there is nothing in the whole of modern French realism, nothing even in *Thérèse Raquin*, that masterpiece of horror, which for terrible and tragic significance can compare with this strange scene in *Cymbeline*.

In the actual dialogue also some of the most vivid passages are those suggested by costume. Rosalind's

Dost thou think, though I am caparisoned like a man, I have a doublet and hose in my disposition?

Constance's

Grief fills the place up of my absent child,
Stuffs out his vacant garments with his form;

and the quick sharp cry of Elizabeth—

Ah! cut my lace asunder!

are only a few of the many examples one might quote. One of the finest effects I have ever seen on the stage was Salvini, in the last act of *Lear*, tearing the plume from Kent's cap and applying it to Cordelia's lips when he came to the line,

This feather stirs; she lives!

Mr. Booth, whose Lear had many noble qualities of passion, plucked, I remember, some fur from his archæologically-incorrect ermine for the same business; but Salvini's was the finer effect of the two, as well as the truer. And those who saw Mr. Irving in the last act of *Richard the Third* have not, I am sure, forgotten how much the agony and terror of his dream was intensified, by contrast, through the calm and quiet that preceded it, and the delivery of such lines as

> What, is my beaver easier than it was?
> And all my armour laid into my tent?
> Look that my staves be sound and not too heavy—

lines which had a double meaning for the audience, remembering the last words which Richard's mother called after him as he was marching to Bosworth:—

> Therefore take with thee my most grievous curse,
> Which in the day of battle tire thee more
> Than all the complete armour that thou wear'st.

As regards the resources which Shakespeare had at his disposal, it is to be remarked that, while he more than once complains of the smallness of the stage on which he has to produce big historical plays, and of the want of scenery which obliges him to cut out many effective open-air incidents, he always writes as a dramatist who had at his disposal a most elaborate theatrical wardrobe, and who could rely on the actors taking pains about their make-up. Even now it is difficult to produce such a play as the *Comedy of Errors*; and to the picturesque accident of Miss Ellen Terry's brother resembling herself we owe the opportunity of seeing *Twelfth Night* adequately performed. Indeed, to put any play of Shakespeare's on the stage, absolutely as he himself wished it to be done, requires the services of a good property-man, a clever wig-maker, a costumier with a sense of colour and a knowledge of textures, a master of the methods of making up, a fencing-master, a dancing-master, and an artist to personally direct the whole production. For he is most careful to tell us the dress and appearance of each character. "Racine abhorre la réalité," says Auguste Vacquerie somewhere; "il ne daigne pas s'occuper de son costume. Si l'on s'en rapportait aux indications du poète, Agamemnon serait vêtu d'un sceptre et Achille d'une épée." But with Shakespeare it is very different. He gives us directions about the costumes of Perdita, Florizel, Autolycus, the Witches of *Macbeth*, and the

413

apothecary in *Romeo and Juliet*, several elaborate descriptions
of his fat knight, and a detailed account of the extraordinary
garb in which Petruchio is to be married. Rosalind, he tells us,
is tall, and is to carry a spear and a little dagger; Celia is smaller,
and is to paint her face brown so as to look sunburnt. The children who play at fairies in Windsor Forest are to be dressed in
white and green—a compliment, by the way, to Queen Elizabeth, whose favourite colours they were—and in white, with
green garlands and gilded vizors, the angels are to come to
Katharine in Kimbolton. Bottom is in homespun, Lysander is
distinguished from Oberon by his wearing an Athenian dress,
and Launce has holes in his boots. The Duchess of Gloucester
stands in a white sheet with her husband in mourning beside
her. The motley of the Fool, the scarlet of the Cardinal, and
the French lilies broidered on the English coats, are all made
occasion for jest or taunt in the dialogue. We know the patterns
on the Dauphin's armour and the Pucelle's sword, the crest on
Warwick's helmet and the colour of Bardolph's nose. Portia has
golden hair, Phœbe is black-haired, Orlando has chestnut curls,
and Sir Andrew Aguecheek's hair hangs like flax on a distaff,
and won't curl at all. Some of the characters are stout, some
lean, some straight, some hunchbacked, some fair, some dark,
and some are to blacken their faces. Lear has a white beard,
Hamlet's father a grizzled, and Benedict is to shave his in the
course of the play. Indeed, on the subject of stage beards Shakespeare is quite elaborate; tells us of the many different colours
in use, and gives a hint to actors to always see that their own
are properly tied on. There is a dance of reapers in rye-straw
hats, and of rustics in hairy coats like satyrs; a masque of Ama-
zons, a masque of Russians, and a classical masque; several immortal scenes over a weaver in an ass's head, a riot over the
colour of a coat which it takes the Lord Mayor of London to
quell, and a scene between an infuriated husband and his wife's
milliner about the slashing of a sleeve.

As for the metaphors Shakespeare draws from dress, and the
aphorisms he makes on it, his hits at the costume of his age,
particularly at the ridiculous size of the ladies' bonnets, and the
many descriptions of the *mundus muliebris*, from the song of

Autolycus in the *Winter's Tale* down to the account of the Duchess of Milan's gown in *Much Ado About Nothing*, they are far too numerous to quote; though it may be worth while to remind people that the whole of the Philosophy of Clothes is to be found in Lear's scene with Edgar—a passage which has the advantage of brevity and style over the grotesque wisdom and somewhat mouthing metaphysics of *Sartor Resartus*. But I think that from what I have already said it is quite clear that Shakespeare was very much interested in costume. I do not mean in that shallow sense by which it has been concluded from his knowledge of deeds and daffodils that he was the Blackstone and Paxton of the Elizabethan age; but that he saw that costume could be made at once impressive of a certain effect on the audience and expressive of certain types of character, and is one of the essential factors of the means which a true illusionist has at his disposal. Indeed to him the deformed figure of Richard was of as much value as Juliet's loveliness; he sets the serge of the radical beside the silks of the lord, and sees the stage effects to be got from each: he has as much delight in Caliban as he has in Ariel, in rags as he has in cloth of gold, and recognizes the artistic beauty of ugliness.

The difficulty Ducis felt about translating *Othello* in consequence of the importance given to such a vulgar thing as a handkerchief, and his attempt to soften its grossness by making the Moor reiterate "Le bandeau! le bandeau!" may be taken as an example of the difference between *la tragédie philosophique* and the drama of real life; and the introduction for the first time of the word *mouchoir* at the Théâtre Français was an era in that romantic-realistic movement of which Hugo is the father and M. Zola the *enfant terrible*, just as the classicism of the earlier part of the century was emphasized by Talma's refusal to play Greek heroes any longer in a powdered periwig—one of the many instances, by the way, of that desire for archæological accuracy in dress which has distinguished the great actors of our age.

In criticising the importance given to money in *La Comédie Humaine*, Théophile Gautier says that Balzac may claim to have invented a new hero in fiction, *le héros métallique*. Of

Shakespeare it may be said that he was the first to see the dramatic value of doublets, and that a climax may depend on a crinoline.

The burning of the Globe Theatre—an event due, by the way, to the results of the passion for illusion that distinguished Shakespeare's stage-management—has unfortunately robbed us of many important documents; but in the inventory, still in existence, of the costume-wardrobe of a London theatre in Shakespeare's time, there are mentioned particular costumes for cardinals, shepherds, kings, clowns, friars, and fools; green coats for Robin Hood's men, and a green gown for Maid Marian; a white and gold doublet for Henry the Fifth, and a robe for Longshanks; besides surplices, copes, damask gowns, gowns of cloth of gold and of cloth of silver, taffeta gowns, calico gowns, velvet coats, satin coats, frieze coats, jerkins of yellow leather and black leather, red suits, grey suits, French Pierrot suits, a robe "for to goo invisibell," which seems inexpensive at 3*l.* 10*s.*, and four incomparable fardingales—all of which show a desire to give every character an appropriate dress. There are also entries of Spanish, Moorish and Danish costumes, of helmets, lances, painted shields, imperial crowns, and papal tiaras, as well as of costumes for Turkish Janissaries, Roman Senators, and all the gods and goddesses of Olympus, which evidence a good deal of archæological research on the part of the manager of the theatre. It is true that there is a mention of a bodice for Eve, but probably the *donnée* of the play was after the Fall.

Indeed, anybody who cares to examine the age of Shakespeare will see that archæology was one of its special characteristics. After that revival of the classical forms of architecture which was one of the notes of the Renaissance, and the printing at Venice and elsewhere of the masterpieces of Greek and Latin literature, had come naturally an interest in the ornamentation and costume of the antique world. Nor was it for the learning that they could acquire, but rather for the loveliness that they might create, that the artists studied these things. The curious objects that were being constantly brought to light by excavations were not left to moulder in a museum, for the contemplation of a callous curator, and the *ennui* of a policeman bored by the absence of crime. They were used as motives for the production of a new art, which was to be not beautiful merely, but also strange.

Infessura tells us that in 1485 some workmen digging on the Appian Way came across an old Roman sarcophagus inscribed with the name "Julia, daughter of Claudius." On opening the coffer they found within its marble womb the body of a beautiful girl of about fifteen years of age, preserved by the embalmer's skill from corruption and the decay of time. Her eyes were half open, her hair rippled round her in crisp curling gold, and from her lips and cheek the bloom of maidenhood had not yet departed. Borne back to the Capitol, she became at once the centre of a new cult, and from all parts of the city crowded pilgrims to worship at the wonderful shrine till the Pope fearing lest those who had found the secret of beauty in a Pagan tomb might forget what secrets Judæa's rough and rock-hewn sepulchre contained, had the body conveyed away by night, and in secret buried. Legend though it may be, yet the story is none the less valuable as showing us the attitude of the Renaissance towards the antique world. Archæology to them was not a mere science for the antiquarian; it was a means by which they could touch the dry dust of antiquity into the very breath and beauty of life, and fill with the new wine of romanticism forms that else had been old and outworn. From the pulpit of Niccola Pisano down to Mantegna's "Triumph of Cæsar," and the service Cellini designed for King Francis, the influence of this spirit can be traced; nor was it confined merely to the immobile arts—the arts of arrested movement—but its influence was to be seen also in the great Græco-Roman masques which were the constant amusement of the gay courts of the time, and in the public pomps and processions with which the citizens of big commercial towns were wont to greet the princes that chanced to visit them; pageants, by the way, which were considered so important that large prints were made of them and published—a fact which is a proof of the general interest at the time in matters of such kind.

And this use of archæology in shows, so far from being a bit of priggish pedantry, is in every way legitimate and beautiful. For the stage is not merely the meeting place of all the arts, but is also the return of art to life. Sometimes in an archæological novel the use of strange and obsolete terms seems to hide the reality beneath the learning, and I dare say that many of the readers of *Notre Dame de Paris* have been much puzzled over the meaning of such expressions as *la casaque à mahoitres, les voulgiers, le gallimard taché d'encre, les craaquiniers,* and the like; but with the stage how different it is! The ancient world wakes from its sleep, and history moves as a pageant before our eyes, without obliging us to have recourse to a dictionary or an encyclopædia for the perfection of our enjoyment. Indeed, there is not the slightest necessity that the public should know the authorities for the mounting of any piece. From such materials, for instance, as the disk of Theodosius, materials with which the majority of people are probably not very familiar, Mr. E. W. Godwin, one of the most artistic spirits of this century in England, created the marvellous loveliness of the first act of *Claudian,* and showed us the life of Byzantium in the fourth century, not by a dreary lecture and a set of grimy casts, not by a novel which requires a glossary to explain it, but by the visible presentation before us of all the glory of that great town. And while the costumes were true to the smallest points of colour and design, yet the details were not assigned that abnormal importance which they must necessarily be given in a piecemeal lecture, but were subordinated to the rules of lofty composition and the unity of artistic effect. Mr. Symonds, speaking of that great picture of Mantegna's, now in Hampton Court, says that the artist has converted an antiquarian motive into a theme for melodies of line. The same could have been said with equal justice of Mr. Godwin's scene. Only the foolish called it pedantry, only those who would neither look nor listen spoke of the passion of the play being killed by its paint. It was in reality a scene not merely perfect in its picturesqueness, but absolutely dramatic also, getting rid of any necessity for tedious descriptions, and showing us, by the colour and character of Claudian's dress, and the dress of his attendants, the whole nature and life of the man, from what school of philosophy he affected, down to what horses he backed on the turf.

And indeed archæology is only really delightful when transfused into some form of art. I have no desire to underrate the services of laborious scholars, but I feel that the use Keats made of Lemprière's Dictionary is of far more value to us than Professor Max Müller's treatment of the same mythology as a disease of language. Better *Endymion* than any theory, however sound, or, as in the present instance, unsound, of an epidemic among adjectives! And who does not feel that the chief glory of Piranesi's book on Vases is that it gave Keats the suggestion for his 'Ode on a Grecian Urn'? Art, and art only, can make archæology beautiful; and the theatric art can use it most directly and most vividly, for it can combine in one exquisite presentation the illusion of actual life with the wonder of the unreal world. But the sixteenth century was not merely the age of Vitruvius; it was the age of Vecellio also. Every nation seems suddenly to have become interested in the dress of its neighbours. Europe began to investigate its own clothes, and the amount of books published on national costumes is quite extraordinary. At the beginning of the century the *Nuremberg Chronicle*, with its two thousand illustrations, reached its fifth edition, and before the century was over seventeen editions were published of Munster's *Cosmography*. Besides these two books there were also the works of Michael Colyns, of Hans Weigel, of Amman, and of Vecellio himself, all of them well illustrated, some of the drawings in Vecellio being probably from the hand of Titian.

Nor was it merely from books and treatises that they acquired their knowledge. The development of the habit of foreign travel, the increased commercial intercourse between countries, and the frequency of diplomatic missions, gives every nation many opportunities of studying the various forms of contemporary dress. After the departure from England, for instance, of the ambassadors from the Czar, the Sultan and the Prince of Morocco, Henry the Eighth and his friends gave several masques in the strange attire of their visitors. Later on London saw, perhaps too often, the sombre splendour of the Spanish Court, and to Elizabeth came envoys from all lands, whose dress, Shakespeare tells us, had an important influence on English costume.

And the interest was not confined merely to classical dress, or the dress of foreign nations; there was also a good deal of research, amongst theatrical people especially, into the ancient costume of England itself: and when Shakespeare, in the pro-

419

logue to one of his plays, expresses his regret at being unable to produce helmets of the period, he is speaking as an Elizabethan manager and not merely as an Elizabethan poet. At Cambridge, for instance, during his day, a play of *Richard the Third* was performed, in which the actors were attired in real dresses of the time, procured from the great collection of historical costume in the Tower, which was always open to the inspection of managers, and sometimes placed at their disposal. And I cannot help thinking that this performance must have been far more artistic, as regards costume, than Garrick's mounting of Shakespeare's own play on the subject, in which he himself appeared in a nondescript fancy dress, and everybody else in the costume of the time of George the Third, Richmond especially being much admired in the uniform of a young guardsman.

For what is the use to the stage of that archæology which has so strangely terrified the critics, but that it, and it alone, can give us the architecture and apparel suitable to the time in which the action of the play passes? It enables us to see a Greek dressed like a Greek, and an Italian like an Italian; to enjoy the arcades of Venice and the balconies of Verona; and, if the play deals with any of the great eras in our country's history, to contemplate the age in its proper attire, and the king in his habit as he lived. And I wonder, by the way, what Lord Lytton would have said some time ago, at the Princess's Theatre, had the curtain risen on his father's Brutus reclining in a Queen Anne chair, attired in a flowing wig and a flowered dressing-gown, a costume which in the last century was considered peculiarly appropriate to an antique Roman! For in those halcyon days of the drama no archæology troubled the stage, or distressed the critics, and our inartistic grandfathers sat peaceably in a stifling atmosphere of anachronisms, and beheld with the calm complacency of the age of prose an Iachimo in powder and patches, a Lear in lace ruffles, and a Lady Macbeth in a large crinoline. I can understand archæology being attacked on the ground of its excessive realism, but to attack it as pedantic seems to be very much beside the mark. However, to attack it for any reason is foolish; one might just as well speak disrespectfully of the equator. For archæology, being a science, is neither good nor bad, but a fact simply. Its value depends entirely on how it is used, and only an artist can use it. We look to the archæologist for the materials, to the artist for the method.

In designing the scenery and costumes for any of Shakespeare's plays, the first thing the artist has to settle is the best date for the drama. This should be determined by the general spirit of the play, more than by any actual historical references which may occur in it. Most *Hamlets* I have seen were placed far too early. *Hamlet* is essentially a scholar of the Revival of Learning; and if the allusion to the recent invasion of England by the Danes puts it back to the ninth century, the use of foils brings it down much later. Once, however, that the date has been fixed, then the archæologist is to supply us with the facts which the artist is to convert into effects.

It has been said that the anachronisms in the plays themselves show us that Shakespeare was indifferent to historical accuracy, and a great deal of capital has been made out of Hector's indiscreet quotation from Aristotle. Upon the other hand, the anachronisms are really few in number, and not very important, and, had Shakespeare's attention been drawn to them by a brother artist, he would probably have corrected them. For, though they can hardly be called blemishes, they are certainly not the great beauties of his work; or, at least, if they are, their anachronistic charm cannot be emphasized unless the play is accurately mounted according to its proper date. In looking at Shakespeare's plays as a whole, however, what is really remarkable is their extraordinary fidelity as regards his personages and his plots. Many of his *dramatis personæ* are people who had actually existed, and some of them might have been seen in real life by a portion of his audience. Indeed the most violent attack that was made on Shakespeare in his time was for his supposed caricature of Lord Cobham. As for his plots, Shakespeare constantly draws them either from authentic history, or from the old ballads and traditions which served as history to the Elizabethan public, and which even now no scientific historian would dismiss as absolutely untrue. And not merely did he select fact instead of fancy as the basis of much of his imaginative work, but he always gives to each play the general character, the social atmosphere in a word, of the age in question. Stupidity he recognizes as being one of the permanent characteristics of all

European civilizations; so he sees no difference betwen a London mob of his own day and a Roman mob of Pagan days, between a silly watchman in Messina and a silly Justice of the Peace in Windsor. But when he deals with higher characters, with those exceptions of each age which are so fine that they become its types, he gives them absolutely the stamp and seal of their time. Virgilia is one of those Roman wives on whose tomb was written "Domi mansit, lanam fecit," as surely as Juliet is the romantic girl of the Renaissance. He is even true to the characteristics of race. Hamlet has all the imagination and irresolution of the Northern nations, and the Princess Katharine is as entirely French as the heroine of *Divorçons*. Harry the Fifth is a pure Englishman, and Othello a true Moor.

Again when Shakespeare treats of the history of England from the fourteenth to the sixteenth centuries, it is wonderful how careful he is to have his facts perfectly right—indeed he follows Holinshed with curious fidelity. The incessant wars between France and England are described with extraordinary accuracy down to the names of the besieged towns, the ports of landing and embarkation, the sites and dates of the battles, the title of the commanders on each side, and the lists of the killed and wounded. And as regards the Civil Wars of the Roses we have many elaborate genealogies of the seven sons of Edward the Third; the claims of the rival Houses of York and Lancaster to the throne are discussed at length; and if the English aristocracy will not read Shakespeare as a poet, they should certainly read him as a sort of early Peerage. There is hardly a single title in the Upper House, with the exception of course of the uninteresting titles assumed by the law lords, which does not appear in Shakespeare along with many details of family history, creditable and discreditable. Indeed if it be really necessary that the School Board children should know all about the Wars of the Roses, they could learn their lessons just as well out of Shakespeare as out of shilling primers, and learn them, I need not say, far more pleasurably. Even in Shakespeare's own day this use of his plays was recognized. "The historical plays teach history to those who cannot read it in the chronicles," says Heywood in a tract about the stage, and yet I am sure that sixteenth-century chronicles were much more delightful reading than nineteenth-century primers are.

Of course the æsthetic value of Shakespeare's plays does not, in the slightest degree, depend on their facts, but on the Truth, and Truth is independent of facts always, inventing or selecting them at pleasure. But still Shakespeare's use of facts is a most interesting part of his method of work, and shows us his attitude towards the stage, and his relations to the great art of illusion. Indeed he would have been very much surprised at anyone classing his plays with "fairy tales," as Lord Lytton does; for one of his aims was to create for England a national historical drama, which should deal with incidents with which the public was well acquainted, and with heroes that lived in the memory of a people. Patriotism, I need hardly say, is not a necessary quality of art; but it means, for the artist the substitution of a universal for an individual feeling, and for the public the presentation of a work of art in a most attractive and popular form. It is worth noticing that Shakespeare's first and last successes were both historical plays.

It may be asked what has this to do with Shakespeare's attitude towards costume. I answer that a dramatist who laid such stress on historical accuracy of fact would have welcomed historical accuracy of costume as a most important adjunct to his illusionist method. And I have no hesitation in saying that he did so. The reference to helmets of the period in the prologue to *Henry the Fifth* may be considered fanciful, though Shakespeare must have often seen

> The very casque
> That did affright the air at Agincourt,

where it still hangs in the dusky gloom of Westminster Abbey, along with the saddle of that "imp of fame," and the dinted shield with its torn blue velvet lining and its tarnished lilies of gold; but the use of military tabards in *Henry the Sixth* is a bit of pure archæology, as they were not worn in the sixteenth century; and the King's own tabard, I may mention, was still suspended over his tomb in St. George's Chapel, Windsor, in Shakespeare's day. For, up to the time of the unfortunate tri-

423

umph of the Philistines in 1645, the chapels and cathedrals of England were the great national museums of archæology, and in them was kept the armour and attire of the heroes of English history. A good deal was of course preserved in the Tower, and even in Elizabeth's day tourists were brought there to see such curious relics of the past as Charles Brandon's huge lance, which is still, I believe, the admiration of our country visitors; but the cathedrals and churches were, as a rule, selected as the most suitable shrines for reception of the historic antiquities. Canterbury can still show us the helm of the Black Prince. Westminster the robes of our kings, and in old St. Paul's the very banner that had waved on Bosworth field was hung up by Richmond himself.

In fact, everywhere that Shakespeare turned in London, he saw the apparel and appurtenances of past ages, and it is impossible to doubt that he made use of his opportunities. The employment of lance and shield, for instance, in actual warfare, which is so frequent in his plays, is drawn from archæology, and not from the military accoutrements of his day; and his general use of armour in battle was not a characteristic of his age, a time when it was rapidly disappearing before firearms. Again, the crest on Warwick's helmet, of which such a point is made in *Henry the Sixth*, is absolutely correct in a fifteenth-century play when crests were generally worn, but would not have been so in a play of Shakespeare's own time, when feathers and plumes had taken their place—a fashion which, as he tells us in *Henry the Eighth*, was borrowed from France. For the historical plays, then, we may be sure that archæology was employed, and as for the others I feel certain it was the case also. The appearance of Jupiter on his eagle, thunderbolt in hand, of Juno with her peacocks, and of Iris with her many-coloured bow; the Amazon masque and the masque of the Five Worthies, may all be regarded as archæological; and the vision which Posthumus sees in prison of Sicilius Leonatus—"an old man, attired like a warrior, leading an ancient matron"—is clearly so. Of the "Athenian dress" by which Lysander is distinguished from Oberon I have already spoken; but one of the most marked instances is in the case of the dress of Coriolanus, for which Shakespeare goes directly to Plutarch. That historian, in his Life of the great Roman, tells us of the oak-wreath with which Caius Marcius was crowned, and of the curious kind of dress in which, according to ancient fashion, he had to canvass his electors; and on both of these points he enters into long disquisitions, investigating the origin and meaning of the old customs. Shakespeare, in the spirit of the true artist, accepts the facts of the antiquarian and converts them into dramatic and picturesque effects: indeed the gown of humility, the "woolvish gown," as Shakespeare calls it, is the central note of the play. There are other cases I might quote, but this one is quite sufficient for my purpose; and it is evident from it at any rate that, in mounting a play in the accurate costume of the time, according to the best authorities, we are carrying out Shakespeare's own wishes and method.

Even if it were not so, there is no more reason that we should continue any imperfections which may be supposed to have characterized Shakespeare's stage-mounting than that we should have Juliet played by a young man, or give up the advantage of changeable scenery. A great work of dramatic art should not merely be made expressive of modern passion by means of the actor, but should be presented to us in the form most suitable to the modern spirit. Racine produced his Roman plays in Louis-Quatorze dress on a stage crowded with spectators; but we require different conditions for the enjoyment of his art. Perfect accuracy of detail, for the sake of perfect illusion, is necessary for us. What we have to see is that the details are not allowed to usurp the principal place. They must be subordinate always to the general motive of the play. But subordination in art does not mean disregard of truth; it means conversion of fact into effect, and assigning to each detail its proper relative value.

Les petits détails d'histoire et de vie domestique (says Hugo) doivent être scrupuleusement étudiés et reproduits par le poète, mais uniquement comme des moyens d'accroître la réalité de l'ensemble, et de faire pénétrer jusque dans les coins les plus obscurs de l'œuvre cette vie générale et puissante au milieu de laquelle les personnages sont plus vrais, et les catastrophes, par conséquent, plus poignantes. Tout doit être subordonné à ce but. L'Homme sur le premier plan, le reste au fond.

The Artist as Critic

The passage is interesting as coming from the first great French dramatist who employed archæology on the stage, and whose plays, though absolutely correct in detail, are known to all for their passion, not for their pedantry—for their life, not for their learning. It is true that he has made certain concessions in the case of the employment of curious or strange expressions. Ruy Blas talks of M. de Priego as "sujet du roi" instead of "noble du roi," and Angelo Malipieri speaks of "la croix rouge" instead of "la croix de gueules." But they are concessions made to the public, or rather to a section of it. "J'en offre ici toutes mes excuses aux spectateurs intelligents," he says in a note to one of the plays; "espérons qu'un jour un seigneur vénitien pourra dire tout bonnement sans péril son blason sur le théâtre. C'est un progrès qui viendra." And, though the description of the crest is not couched in accurate language, still the crest itself was accurately right. It may, of course, be said that the public do not notice these things; upon the other hand, it should be remembered that Art has no other aim but her own perfection, and proceeds simply by her own laws, and that the play which Hamlet describes as being caviare to the general is a play he highly praises. Besides, in England, at any rate, the public have undergone a transformation; there is far more appreciation of beauty now than there was a few years ago; and though they may not be familiar with the authorities and archæological data for what is shown to them, still they enjoy whatever loveliness they look at. And this is the important thing. Better to take pleasure in a rose than to put its root under a microscope. Archæological accuracy is merely a condition of illusionist stage effect; it is not its quality. And Lord Lytton's proposal that the dresses should merely be beautiful without being accurate is founded on a misapprehension of the nature of costume, and of its value on the stage. This value is twofold, picturesque and dramatic; the former depends on the colour of the dress, the latter on its design and character. But so interwoven are the two that, whenever in our own day historical accuracy has been disregarded, and the various dresses in a play taken from different ages, the result has been that the stage has been turned into that chaos of costume, that caricature of the centuries, the Fancy Dress Ball, to the entire ruin of all dramatic and picturesque effect. For the dresses of one age do not artistically harmonize with the dresses of another; and, as far as dramatic value goes, to confuse the costumes is to confuse the play. Costume is a growth, an evolution, and a most important, perhaps the most important, sign of the manners, customs, and mode of life of each century. The Puritan dislike of colour, adornment, and grace in apparel was part of the great revolt of the middle classes against Beauty in the seventeenth century. A historian who disregarded it would give us a most inaccurate picture of the time, and a dramatist who did not avail himself of it would miss a most vital element in producing an illusionist effect. The effeminacy of dress that characterized the reign of Richard the Second was a constant theme of contemporary authors. Shakespeare, writing two hundred years after, makes the King's fondness for gay apparel and foreign fashions a point in the play, from John of Gaunt's reproaches down to Richard's own speech in the third act on his disposition from the throne. And that Shakespeare examined Richard's tomb in Westminster Abbey seems to me certain from York's speech:—

> See, see, King Richard doth himself appear,
> As doth the blushing discontented sun
> From out the fiery portal of the east,
> When he perceives the envious clouds are bent
> To dim his glory.

For we can still discern on the King's robe his favourite badge —the sun issuing from a cloud. In fact, in every age the social conditions are so exemplified in costume, that to produce a sixteenth-century play in fourteenth-century attire, or *vice versâ*, would make the performance seem unreal because untrue. And, valuable as beauty of effect on the stage is, the highest beauty is not merely comparable with absolute accuracy of detail, but really dependent on it. To invent an entirely new costume is almost impossible except in burlesque or extravaganza, and as for combining the dress of different centuries into one, the experiment would be dangerous, and Shakespeare's opinion of the artistic value of such a medley may be gathered from his incessant satire of the Elizabethan dandies for imagining that they were well dressed because they got their doublets in Italy, their hats in Germany, and their hose in France. And it should be noted that the most lovely scenes that have been produced on our stage have been those that have been characterized by perfect accuracy, such as Mr. and Mrs. Bancroft's eighteenth-century revivals at the Haymarket, Mr. Irving's superb production of *Much Ado About Nothing*, and Mr. Barrett's *Claudian*. Besides, and this is perhaps the most complete answer to Lord Lytton's theory, it must be remembered that neither in costume nor in dialogue is beauty the dramatist's primary aim at all. The true dramatist aims first at what is characteristic, and no more desires that all his personages should be beautifully attired than he desires that they should all have beautiful natures or speak beautiful English. The true dramatist, in fact, shows us life under the conditions of art, not art in the form of life. The Greek dress was the loveliest dress the world has ever seen, and the English dress of the last century one of the most monstrous; yet we cannot costume a play by Sheridan as we would costume a play by Sophokles. For, as Polonius says in his excellent lecture, a lecture to which I am glad to have the opportunity of expressing my obligations, one of the first qualities of apparel is its expressiveness. And the affected style of dress in the last century was the natural characteristic of a society of affected manners and affected conversation—a characteristic which the realistic dramatist will highly value down to the smallest detail of accuracy, and the materials for which he can only get from archæology.

But it is not enough that a dress should be accurate; it must be also appropriate to the stature and appearance of the actor, and to his supposed condition, as well as to his necessary action in the play. In Mr. Hare's production of *As You Like It* at the St. James's Theatre, for instance, the whole point of Orlando's complaint that he is brought up like a peasant, and not like a gentleman, was spoiled by the gorgeousness of his dress, and the splendid apparel worn by the banished Duke and his friends was quite out of place. Mr. Lewis Wingfield's explanation that the sumptuary laws of the period necessitated their doing so, is, I am afraid, hardly sufficient. Outlaws, lurking in a forest and living by the chase, are not very likely to care much about ordinances of dress. They were probably attired like Robin Hood's men, to whom, indeed, they are compared in the course of the play. And that their dress was not that of wealthy noblemen may be seen by Orlando's words when he breaks in upon them. He mistakes them for robbers, and is amazed to find that they answer him in courteous and gentle terms. Lady Archibald Campbell's production, under Mr. E. W. Godwin's direction, of the same play in Coombe Wood was, as regards mounting, far more artistic. At least it seemed so to me. The Duke and his companions were dressed in serge tunics, leathern jerkins, high boots, and gauntlets, and wore bycocket hats and hoods. And as they were playing in a real forest, they found, I am sure, their dresses extremely convenient. To every character in the play was given a perfectly appropriate attire, and the brown and green of their costumes harmonized exquisitely with the ferns through which they wandered, the trees beneath which they lay, and the lovely English landscape that surrounded the Pastoral Players. The perfect naturalness of the scene was due to the absolute accuracy and appropriateness of everything that was worn. Nor could archæology have been put to a severer test, or come out of it more triumphantly. The whole production showed once for all that, unless a dress is archæologically correct, and artistically appropriate, it always looks unreal, unnatural, and theatrical in the sense of artificial.

Nor, again, is it enough that there should be accurate and appropriate costumes of beautiful colours; there must be also beauty of colour on the stage as a whole, and as long as the background is painted by one artist, and the foreground figures independently designed by another, there is the danger of a want of harmony in the scene as a picture. For each scene the colour-scheme should be settled as absolutely as for the decoration of a room, and the textures which it is proposed to use should be mixed and re-mixed in every possible combination, and what is discordant removed. Then, as regards the particular kinds of colours, the stage is often made too glaring, partly through the excessive use of hot, violent reds, and partly through the costumes looking too new. Shabbiness, which in modern life is merely the tendency of the lower orders towards tone, is not without its artistic value, and modern colours are often much improved by being a little faded. Blue also is too frequently used: it is not merely a dangerous colour to wear by gaslight, but it is really difficult in England to get a thoroughly good blue. The fine Chinese blue, which we all so much admire, takes two years to dye, and the English public will not wait so long for a colour. Peacock blue, of course, has been employed on the stage, notably at the Lyceum, with great advantage; but all attempts at a good light blue, or good dark blue, which I have seen have been failures. The value of black is hardly appreciated; it was used effectively by Mr. Irving in *Hamlet* as the central note of a composition, but as a tone-giving neutral its importance is not recognized. And this is curious, considering the general colour of the dress of a century in which, as Baudelaire says, "Nous célébrons tous quelque enterrement." The archæologist of the future will probably point to this age as a time when the beauty of black was understood; but I hardly think that, as regards stage-mounting or house decoration, it really is. Its decorative value is, of course, the same as that of white or gold; it can separate and harmonize colours. In modern plays the black frock coat of the hero becomes important in itself, and should be given a suitable background. But it rarely is. Indeed the only good background for a play in modern dress which I have ever seen was the dark grey and cream-white scene of the first act of the *Princesse Georges* in Mrs. Langtry's production. As a rule, the hero is smothered in *bric-à-brac* and palm trees, lost in the gilded abyss of Louis Quatorze furniture, or reduced to a mere midge in the midst of marqueterie; whereas the background should always be kept as a background, and colour subordinated to effect. This, of course, can only be done when there is one single mind directing the whole production. The facts of art are diverse, but the essence of artistic effect is unity. Monarchy, Anarchy, and Republicanism may contend for the government of nations; but a theatre should be in the power of a cultured despot. There may be division of labour, but there must be no division of mind. Whoever understands the costume of an age understands of necessity its architecture and its surroundings also, and it is easy to see from the chairs of a century whether it was a century of crinolines or not. In fact, in art there is no specialism, and a really artistic production should bear the impress of one master, and one master only, who not merely should design and arrange everything, but should have complete control over the way in which each dress is to be worn.

Mademoiselle Mars[,] in the first production of *Hernani*, absolutely refused to call her lover "*Mon Lion!*" unless she was allowed to wear a little fashionable *toque* then much in vogue on the Boulevards; and many young ladies on our own stage insist to the present day on wearing stiff starched petticoats under Greek dresses, to the entire ruin of all delicacy of line and fold; but these wicked things should not be allowed. And there should be far more dress rehearsals than there are now. Actors such as Mr. Forbes-Robertson, Mr. Conway, Mr. George Alexander, and others, not to mention older artists, can move with ease and elegance in the attire of any century; but there are not a few who seem dreadfully embarrassed about their hands if they have no side pockets, and who always wear their dresses as if they were costumes. Costumes, of course, they are to the designer; but dresses they should be to those that wear them. And it is time that a stop should be put to the idea, very prevalent on the stage, that the Greeks and Romans always went about bare-headed in the open air—a mistake the Elizabethan managers did not fall into, for they gave hoods as well as gowns to their Roman senators.

More dress rehearsals would also be of value in explaining to the actors that there is a form of gesture and movement that is not merely appropriate to each style of dress, but really conditioned by it. The extravagant use of the arms in the eighteenth century, for instance, was the necessary result of the large hoop, and the solemn dignity of Burleigh owed as much to his ruff as to his reason. Besides[,] until an actor is at home in his dress, he is not at home in his part.

Of the value of beautiful costume in creating an artistic temperament in the audience, and producing that joy in beauty for beauty's sake without which the great masterpieces of art can never be understood, I will not here speak; though it is worth while to notice how Shakespeare appreciated that side of the question in the production of his tragedies, acting them always by artificial light, and in a theatre hung with black; but what I

431

have tried to point out is that archæology is not a pedantic method, but a method of artistic illusion, and that costume is a means of displaying character without description, and of producing dramatic situations and dramatic effects. And I think it is a pity that so many critics should have set themselves to attack one of the most important movements on the modern stage before that movement has at all reached its proper perfection. That it will do so, however, I feel as certain as that we shall require from our dramatic critics in the future higher qualifications than that they can remember Macready or have seen Benjamin Webster: we shall require of them indeed, that they cultivate a sense of beauty. *Pour être plus difficile, la tâche n'en est que plus glorieuse.* And if they will not encourage, at least they must not oppose, a movement of which Shakespeare of all dramatists would have most approved, for it has the illusion of truth for its method, and the illusion of beauty for its result. Not that I agree with everything that I have said in this essay. There is much with which I entirely disagree. The essay simply represents an artistic standpoint, and in æsthetic criticism attitude is everything. For in art there is no such thing as a universal truth. A Truth in art is that whose contradictory is also true. And just as it is only in art-criticism, and through it, that we can apprehend the Platonic theory of ideas, so it is only in art-criticism, and through it, that we can realize Hegel's system of contraries. The truths of metaphysics are the truths of masks.

Phrases and Philosophies for the Use of the Young*

The first duty in life is to be as artificial as possible.

What the second duty is no one has as yet discovered.

Wickedness is a myth invented by good people to account for the curious attractiveness of others.

If the poor only had profiles there would be no difficulty in solving the problem of poverty.

Those who see any difference between soul and body have neither.

A really well-made buttonhole is the only link between Art and Nature.

Religions die when they are proved to be true. Science is the record of dead religions.

The well-bred contradict other people. The wise contradict themselves.

Nothing that actually occurs is of the smallest importance.

Dullness is the coming of age of seriousness.

In all unimportant matters, style, not sincerity, is the essential. In all important matters, style, not sincerity, is the essential.

If one tells the truth, one is sure, sooner or later, to be found out.

Pleasure is the only thing one should live for. Nothing ages like happiness.

* *Chameleon* I : 1 (December, 1894), 1–3.

433

It is only by not paying one's bills that one can hope to live in the memory of the commercial classes.

No crime is vulgar, but all vulgarity is crime. Vulgarity is the conduct of others.

Only the shallow know themselves.

Time is waste of money.

One should always be a little improbable.

There is a fatality about all good resolutions. They are invariably made too soon.

The only way to atone for being occasionally a little over-dressed is by being always absolutely over-educated.

To be premature is to be perfect.

Any preoccupation with ideas of what is right or wrong in conduct shows an arrested intellectual development.

Ambition is the last refuge of the failure.

A truth ceases to be true when more than one person believes in it.

In examinations the foolish ask questions that the wise cannot answer.

Greek dress was in its essence inartistic. Nothing should reveal the body but the body.

One should either be a work of art, or wear a work of art.

It is only the superficial qualities that last. Man's deeper nature is soon found out.

Industry is the root of all ugliness.

The ages live in history through their anachronisms.

It is only the gods who taste of death. Apollo has passed away, but Hyacinth, whom men say he slew, lives on. Nero and Narcissus are always with us.

The old believe everything: the middle-aged suspect everything: the young know everything.

The condition of perfection is idleness: the aim of perfection is youth.

Only the great masters of style ever succeed in being obscure.

There is something tragic about the enormous number of young men there are in England at the present moment who start life with perfect profiles, and end by adopting some useful profession.

To love oneself is the beginning of a life-long romance.

Oscar Wilde on the Witness Stand[*]

On the complaint of Wilde, the Marquess of Queensbury was charged with criminal libel on 2 March 1895. On the first day of the trial, 3 April, Wilde was cross-examined by Edward Carson about the issue of the *Chameleon* in which "Phrases and Philosophies for the Use of the Young" were published along with a story by another writer entitled, "The Priest and the Acolyte."

[Mr. Carson then read the following extract from "The Priest and the Acolyte."]:

Just before the consecration the priest took a tiny phial from the pocket of his cassock, blessed it, and poured the contents into the chalice.

When the time came for him to receive from the chalice, he raised it to his lips, but did not taste of it.

He administered the sacred wafer to the child, and then he took his hand; he turned towards him; but when he saw the light in the beautiful face he turned again to the crucifix with a low moan. For one instant his courage failed him; then he turned to the little fellow again, and held the chalice to his lips:

"The Blood of our Lord Jesus Christ, which was shed for thee, preserve thy body and soul unto everlasting life."

* From *The Trials of Oscar Wilde*, ed. H. Montgomery Hyde (London, Glasgow, Edinburgh, 1948).

Cross-examination continued—Do you approve of those words?—I think them disgusting, perfect twaddle.

I think you will admit that any one who would approve of such an article would pose as guilty of improper practices?—I do not think so in the person of another contributor to the magazine. It would show very bad literary taste. I strongly objected to the whole story. I took no steps to express disapproval of *The Chameleon* because I think it would have been beneath my dignity as a man of letters to associate myself with an Oxford undergraduate's productions. I am aware that the magazine may have been circulated among the undergraduates of Oxford. I do not believe that any book of work of art ever had any effect whatever on morality.

Am I right in saying that you do not consider the effect in creating morality or immorality?—Certainly, I do not.

So far as your works are concerned, you pose as not being concerned about morality or immorality?—I do not know whether you use the word "pose" in any particular sense.

It is a favourite word of your own?—Is it? I have no pose in this matter. In writing a play or a book, I am concerned entirely with literature—that is, with art. I aim not at doing good or evil, but in trying to make a thing that will have some quality of beauty.

Listen, sir. Here is one of the "Phrases and Philosophies for the Use of the Young" which you contributed: "Wickedness is a myth invented by good people to account for the curious attractiveness of others." You think that true?—I rarely think that anything I write is true.

Did you say "rarely"?—I said "rarely." I might have said "never"—not true in the actual sense of the word.

"Religions die when they are proved to be true." Is that true?—Yes; I hold that. It is a suggestion towards a philosophy of the absorption of religions by science, but it is too big a question to go into now.

Do you think that was a safe axiom to put forward for the philosophy of the young?—Most stimulating.

"If one tells the truth, one is sure, sooner or later, to be found out"?—That is a pleasing paradox, but I do not set very high store on it as an axiom.

Is it good for the young?—Anything is good that stimulates thought in whatever age.

Whether moral or immoral?—There is no such thing as morality or immorality in thought. There is immoral emotion.

"Pleasure is the only thing one should live for"?—I think that the realization of oneself is the prime aim of life, and to realize oneself through pleasure is finer than to do so through pain. I am, on that point, entirely on the side of the ancients—the Greeks. It is a pagan idea.

"A truth ceases to be true when more than one person believes in it"?—Perfectly. That would be my metaphysical definition of truth; something so personal that the same truth could never be appreciated by two minds.

"The condition of perfection is idleness: the aim of perfection is youth"?—Oh, yes; I think so. Half of it is true. The life of contemplation is the highest life, and so recognized by the philosopher.

"There is something tragic about the enormous number of young men there are in England at the present moment who start life with perfect profiles, and end by adopting some useful profession"?—I should think that the young have enough sense of humour.

You think that is humorous?—I think it is an amusing paradox, an amusing play on words.

What would anybody say would be the effect of "Phrases and Philosophies" taken in connexion with such an article as "The Priest and the Acolyte"?—Undoubtedly it was the idea that might be formed that made me object so strongly to the story. I saw at once that maxims that were perfectly nonsensical, paradoxical, or anything you like, might be read in conjunction with it.

After the criticisms that were passed on *Dorian Gray*, was it modified a good deal?—No. Additions were made. In one case it was pointed out to me—not in a newspaper or anything of that sort, but by the only critic of the century whose opinion I set high, Mr. Walter Pater—that a certain passage was liable to misconstruction, and I made an addition.

This is in your introduction to *Dorian Gray*: "There is no such thing as a moral or an immoral book. Books are well written, or badly written." That expresses your view?—My view on art, yes.

Then, I take it, that no matter how immoral a book may be, if it is well written, it is, in your opinion, a good book?—Yes, if it were well written so as to produce a sense of beauty, which is the highest sense of which a human being can be capable. If it were badly written, it would produce a sense of disgust.

Then a well-written book putting forward perverted moral views may be a good book?—No work of art ever puts forward views. Views belong to people who are not artists.

A perverted novel might be a good book?—I don't know what you mean by a "perverted" novel.

Then I will suggest *Dorian Gray* as open to the interpretation of being such a novel?—That could only be to brutes and illiterates. The views of Philistines on art are incalculably stupid.

An illiterate person reading *Dorian Gray* might consider it such a novel?—The views of illiterates on art are unaccountable. I am concerned only with my view of art. I don't care twopence what other people think of it.

The majority of persons would come under your definition of Philistines and illiterates?—I have found wonderful exceptions.

Do you think that the majority of people live up to the position you are giving us?—I am afraid they are not cultivated enough.

Not cultivated enough to draw the distinction between a good book and a bad book?—Certainly not.

The affection and love of the artist of *Dorian Gray* might lead an ordinary individual to believe that it might have a certain tendency?—I have no knowledge of the views of ordinary individuals.

You did not prevent the ordinary individual from buying your book?—I have never discouraged him.

Index

443

OSCAR WILDE was born in Dublin in 1854. He was educated at Trinity College, Dublin, and at Oxford. After publishing a book of poems in 1881, he made a year-long lecture tour of the United States in 1882. During the next eight years he became prominent as a critic and editor. In 1891 he published his novel, *The Picture of Dorian Gray*, his book of criticism, *Intentions*, and his argument for social reform, *The Soul of Man under Socialism*. Between 1892 and 1895 his plays dominated the London stage: *Lady Windermere's Fan* (1892), *A Woman of No Importance* (1893), *An Ideal Husband* and *The Importance of Being Earnest* (both 1895). His drama *Salome* was used by Richard Strauss as the libretto for his opera. After imprisonment from 1895 to 1897 for a sexual offense, Wilde published *The Ballad of Reading Gaol* under a pseudonym in 1898. He died in Paris in 1900.

RICHARD ELLMANN is a professor of English at Yale University, and from 1970 will be Goldsmiths' Professor of English Literature at Oxford. He is the author of *Yeats: The Man and the Masks* (1948) and *The Identity of Yeats* (1954). His biography *James Joyce* received the National Book Award. He edited *Giacomo Joyce* and Joyce's letters (volumes II and III), and translated *Selected Writings of Henri Michaux*. His most recent work is *Eminent Domain: Yeats among Wilde, Joyce, Pound, Eliot and Auden*.

VINTAGE POLITICAL SCIENCE
AND SOCIAL CRITICISM

A free catalogue of VINTAGE BOOKS *will be sent at your request. Write to* Vintage Books, 457 Madison Avenue, New York, New York 10022.